The linguistics of writing

The linguistics of writing
Arguments between language and literature

Edited by
Nigel Fabb, Derek Attridge, Alan Durant *and* Colin MacCabe

Methuen Inc., New York

Printed in Great Britain

Published in the United States of America
by Methuen Inc., 29 West 35 Street, New York, NY 10001

Library of Congress Cataloging in publication Data

The Linguistics of writing.

   Revised and edited version of an academic conference
held at the University of Strathclyde, July 1986.
   Includes indexes.
   1. Philosophy--Congresses. I. Fabb, Nigel.
II. University of Strathclyde.
P23.L524 1988   410   87-21997

ISBN 0-416-01841-6 *cased*

ISBN 0-416-01851-3 *paper*

Contents

Contents

Acknowledgements

These are the proceedings of a conference, 'The Linguistics of Writing', held at Strathclyde University, 4–6 July 1986. The conference was organised by the Programme in Literary Linguistics, a self-funded teaching and research programme which is part of the Department of English Studies at the University of Strathclyde. We thank Janet Fabb, Margaret Fabb, Margaret Philips and Rebecca Thomas for their help in the preparation of the manuscript. The Programme in Literary Linguistics supported the production of this book.

Nigel Fabb and Alan Durant

Introduction: The linguistics of writing: retrospect and prospect after twenty-five years

1 The theoretical issues and arguments which characterise recent debate about the relationship between the study of language and the study of literature have a history much longer than the last twenty-five years. Many of the most fundamental questions have antecedents across two millenia of philosophical enquiry. But the last twenty-five years appears distinct as a period in intellectual history because of a pressing concern in recent work – particularly in what has come to be called 'literary theory' – to transform and re-present such established questions in ways that can offer immediate leverage on the intellectual and political problems of 'Western', 'capitalist', or 'postmodern' present social formations. We can identify a particular moment of revaluation and redirection which cuts across the humanities and the social sciences in the late 1950s, a moment which for the inter-relationship of language and literature can be marked by the 'Conference on Style', held at Indiana in 1958, and published as *Style in Language* (1960).

2 As a collection of papers, *Style in Language* became an important back-bearing for research and pedagogy. But as a transitional event, it belonged to the intellectual past rather than the intellectual future. Surfacing behind its back were a whole range of initiatives, which were passed over with relatively marginal reference or interest at the conference itself. 1957 saw the publication of Chomsky's *Syntactic Structures*, Grice's essay 'Meaning', and Barthes's collected *Mythologies* – seminal works for generative linguistics, pragmatics and literary theory. Only slightly later, Kuhn's *The Structure of Scientific Revolutions* (1962) precipitated what has been called a crisis of rationality by showing that scientific activity is located in history and in the aims and practices of specific communities, thus hitting the wedge which would increasingly split apart linguistics and literary theory.

3 In linguistics, the quarter-century between *Style in Language* and now has arguably been dominated by two traditions: that of generative linguistics, with its modern connections with psycholinguistics and cognitive science; and by systemic linguistics, whose own connections are more with sociolinguistic study of the varieties in which languages exist and the communicative uses to which language is put. Across and between these two paradigms a diversity of activity takes place, in terms of precise research aims, method of enquiry and form of explanation; and during this period linguistics has become a more institutionalised discipline, in education and in medical and commercial applications.

In literary study during the same period, New Criticism has extensively been displaced by the intellectual and institutional influence of structuralism, with its concern to analyse the codes which underlie the organisation of texts. Gaining ground almost simultaneously, post-structuralism involves a range of developments out of structuralism which also stand in critical relation to it, including psychoanalytic, historiographic, Althusserian, reader-response and deconstructionist approaches, as well as a range of mixed or theory-synthesising forms.

Approaches to the study of texts other than literary texts have also acquired a new scale and seriousness: studies of the rhetorics of sound and sound-and-image in media studies; and investigations of journalism, advertising and other kinds of social discourse in cultural studies. Each of these specialisms has selectively developed, adapted and criticised concepts from linguistics and semiotics. Frequently, approaches from these fields have been linked in with analysis of the social circulation and power of texts developed in work on history and ideology, in traditions from Marx and the Frankfurt School, into modern cultural materialism.

4 The common element in these various developments is their pervasive concern with ideas of 'language'. Early in the century Saussure famously suggested that language might serve as the theoretical paradigm for all kinds of sign system, in a new anthropologically-inspired study of ourselves that would be known as 'semiology' or 'semiotics'. This formed the basis of many of structuralism's later claims to authority and method. Nevertheless, in much modern theoretical linguistics it has been rather the *differences* between human language and other signifying systems which have been stressed. This is both because of human language's apparently unique formal properties, and also in virtue of the specialised cognitive capacities human language seems to exploit as regards acquisition, production and processing. This revision to ideas of 'language' has led to a divergence between much modern linguistics and the broader semiotic and anthropological concern of linguistics of earlier periods.

During the same period, post-structuralism has also shifted in relation to this earlier view of language. Generally speaking, it has moved away from structuralism's earlier, respectful relation to linguistics. In a range of different kinds of critique, it has come instead to argue that it has gone beyond linguistics in its attention to forms of writing and other kinds of signification, by showing these to be radically unstable in that they allow for a multiplicity of finally indeterminate understandings which linguistics − except in institutionally marginalised forms − is unwilling to countenance.

Where does this leave the unifying impulse regarding the two fields of enquiry which prompted the *Style in Language* conference, and what are the implications for someone interested in questions of 'language' and 'writing' now? Developments in modern theoretical linguistics and in post-structuralism problematise once more the idea that the study of language and the study of forms of writing make up a relatively unified area of interest and enquiry. They appear to question any founding assumption that study of 'language' in abstract, theoretical terms is likely to offer crucial insights into the properties and circulation of the material kinds of writing in the world, through which our social being is constructed and mediated.

5 This book is an attempt to explore areas of agreement and dispute in this present situation. In the same way that *Style in Language* was produced as the result of a conference which brought together eminent practitioners in relevant fields, so too *The Linguistics of Writing: Arguments between Language and Literature* consists of proceedings from a conference. The range of fields from which practitioners were invited differs slightly from that of the 1958 conference, in reflection of an influential reorientation of the field marked most clearly by yet another conference and volume, Macksey and Donato's *The Structuralist Controversy: The Languages of Criticism and the Sciences of Man*. This conference, which took place in 1966 (proceedings published in 1970) in effect first introduced European structuralist and post-structuralist work into the United States. The 'Linguistics of Writing' conference itself was held in Glasgow in July 1986; the papers which make up this book were conceived, for that occasion, as attempts to assess directions taken and not taken across the range of approaches to analysing language and texts which have developed in these last decades. They have subsequently been revised for publication in book form, and are printed here in the conference ordering.

6 In inviting speakers and in publicising the conference, the organisers summarised its aims as follows.

The aims of this conference are to assess the achievements of the interdisciplinary study of literary language over the past quarter-century and to explore new directions for future work in this area. Taking as a benchmark the burgeoning of interest around 1960 in the use of linguistic techniques and models for literary analysis, the conference will examine the working out of that programme in the years that followed, and the major challenges which it faced including the impact of generative linguistics, the development of sophisticated political methodologies, and the post-structuralist critique of the dominant Western intellectual tradition. If 'The Conference on Style' held at Indiana University in 1958, recorded in the famous and influential *Style in Language* (1960), stands as a reflection of the activity and the promise of the years around 1960, the object of this conference – and the publication of its proceedings – is similarly to reflect the range and potential of the work being done in this area in the mid-1980s as well as measuring the distance we have travelled since 1958, and the new questions we have been called upon to answer. In particular, it is no longer possible to consider questions about language and literature without taking into account the social and political context in which all forms of discourse operate and within which the questions we are posing are themselves asked.

Speakers were free to interpret these aims according to their own interests and sense of priorities. The organising committee chose the route of minimal intervention in determining the content of papers; the intention was to arrange an *event* at which people with very different approaches to problems of language would relate to each other and to each others' intellectual concerns. The subtitle of this book – 'Arguments between language and literature' indicates that the conference laid out a space which was shared by and yet at the same time was outside the two professional fields of linguistics and literary theory, a space for dialogue where arguments and points of difficulty, as well as agreements and common aims, would be foregrounded.

7 The conference was to be a montage, not a synthesis. Participants who came expecting a definitive conclusion as to the 'state of the art', or a call to action, were disappointed. The first and last talks were respectively supertitled 'Closing Statement' and 'Opening Statement'; the reversal of the expected order suggested that 'The Linguistics of Writing' would mark a transition: it would refer back to Jakobson's pivotal 'Closing Statement' in *Style in Language*, but also, through the self-consciousness which the conference's own contradictions would promote, it would open new trajectories for future work.

In his speech welcoming participants at the beginning of the conference, Colin MacCabe predicted that four elements would animate the papers (as they do Strathclyde's *Programme in Literary Linguistics* which organised the conference, and whose instructional and research work the conference was intended to publicise). These four elements were stylistics, deconstruction, historical/social perspectives, and the emergence of English as a world language. He went on:

This extremely brief summary might suggest that the aim of the Programme and of the conference is to provide some totalising moment which would reconcile these four elements into a definitive theoretical model for the study of the relations between language and writing. Such a suggestion, with all its modernist confidence, would be totally inappropriate.

8 The conference was intended as a montage. In this it succeeded; it was the 'text' that the organisers wanted to present. But was it successful as a project? This would depend on how that text was interpreted in its context.

After the clear marking out of disciplinary divisions which characterised the second day of the conference, many participants voiced increasing dissatisfaction with their limited opportunities to contribute, and so an open discussion session was inserted before Colin MacCabe's talk. After this discussion period. MacCabe began his talk, but was interrupted by messages passed from the floor to the chair suggesting he should abandon his talk and re-open the conference to general discussion. Following a vote on this issue. MacCabe resumed his talk, after which the conference closed with a further period of discussion.

Given the connections between issues surrounding this disturbance to the planned conference programme and the concerns of the papers themselves, we now consider some of the ways in which discussants in the final session viewed the conference.

Two weeks before the conference, the possibility arose of televising the conference for later transmission on British television's Channel 4. Speakers were given a few days notice where possible, other participants found out when they arrived. The presence of a television camera and accompanying equipment undoubtedly altered the conference to some extent, perhaps foregrounding the event in itself instead of many of the arguments with which it was concerned. Some felt that this presence and influence was inappropriate; for many, also, the television lights were a source of physical discomfort.

Of the speakers who originally accepted invitations three had not come. Edward Said and Terry Eagleton withdrew well before the conference, and Fredric Jameson had to withdraw with a few days' notice. Some felt that the absence of these 'left' speakers resulted in a 'radical depoliticisation' of the conference, and the general lack of direct reference to politics was regretted. Fredric Jameson's paper has been included in this collection of papers from the conference in the place assigned to it in the original conference timetable.

Participants who were not in the position of being speakers were, it was said, not provided with sufficient opportunity to contribute; parallel sessions, or a longer conference, or fewer 'big name' speakers would in their view have remedied this. Given the advertised invocation of history and of 'sophisticated political methodologies', the absence of any explicit agenda-setting was disliked by a number of participants; again, it was argued that if fuller intervention by participants had been permitted, with the conference structured as debate and proposal, an agreed document of intent might have been drawn up. It was regretted that the conference programme had not been opened out to give a lower ratio of 'name' speakers to non-speaking participants. But consideration of practice, rather than ignorance about possible options, was responsible for the form of the conference. As Colin MacCabe put it, in reply to such complaints in the final discussion period:

When we sat down to think about this conference two years ago, one of the questions which was very clear to us was — and we would be nuts if it wasn't — that the discursive conditions of such a conference are extremely authoritarian. The question we had to answer was whether we thought that the advantages to be gained by getting the kind of contributions which we hoped we would get together into a short space of time was worth that particular structure. My judgement was then, and it is now, is that it was. There are of course various alternative models, including in particular a model in which you have main speakers and workshops. That's the standard model in which one attempts to arrange things so that participants at the conference can engage in more directly productive ways with what has been said. I should make it clear that I've got nothing in principle against such workshops. It was simply that in terms of the time, space and resources available to us that was not an option.

The narrowness of the range of speakers was criticised, specifically the fact that two-thirds were Anglo-American men. A similar narrowness of range was identified in the papers, whose combined concerns were felt to be too local to Britain, Europe, and North America. This criticism seems justified; while we do not think that any of the speakers could have been left out, there are areas which in retrospect could have been represented more fully. Changing forms of contact and innovation in post-colonial languages, and the emergence of English as a dominant international language (but in varieties which may conflict with regulated 'standard' forms) mean that broader international perspectives need to be combined with consideration of specific, local centres of language use.

9 Given many different ways in which the conference might be of interest, it would be inappropriate to argue a case through a series of 'main issues': to attempt to do so would be to impose one selective route where many others are possible. It may be helpful, nevertheless, to introduce a number of topics which are repeatedly raised and underlie much of the discussion in this volume. Five issues in particular are outlined in the rest of this introduction: the question of *writing* as a defining element of conference discussion of intellectual issues; the question of the *degree of idealisation* appropriate in the investigation of language; the question of *formalist and functionalist alternatives* in considering language structure; the question of the formation and definition of particular *intellectual specialisms*; finally, the question of the relation between forms of enquiry and their surrounding *social and historical circumstances* or contexts.

10 One purpose in settling on the phrase 'Linguistics of Writing' as a title for the conference was to attempt to distinguish its focus from a narrower concern with 'literature' and the stylistics of literature. Under one interpretation, 'writing' differs from 'literature' in not sharing the latter's sense of a selected corpus of 'writing' endowed with specific historical eminence or value.

Over the last twenty-five years there have been repeated assaults on the idea that literature can be usefully separated off from other kinds of written text. In the first place, it is difficult to identify any formal properties of literary language which do not also appear in non-literary language. Secondly, in much modernist literature 'literary language' achieves its effects by codeswitching between registers, including those of speech, and so embeds – and works largely by contrast with – varieties usually classified as non-literary language. Thirdly, it appears that both traditionally 'literary' and 'non-literary' kinds

of discourse share a common range of properties when considered pragmati-
cally, from the point of view of the kinds of communicative acts they perform.
The implication of such critiques is that concern for literary writing cannot
be easily disentangled from interest in 'writing' more generally: to contest,
as literary theory has frequently done, that a privileged literary canon should
provide the corpus of writing for study, appears to necessitate new kinds of
intellectual and educational interest in *all* kinds of written text, not just literary
ones: not the stylistics of literature but the stylistics of writing.

11 The term 'writing' broadens reference from concern with just 'literature';
but in doing so, it invites immediate contrast with 'speech'. Is speech excluded
by a focus on the linguistics of 'writing'?

This would certainly seem to be the case, if what is in question is simply the
traditional binary opposition of linguistic mediums: speech and writing. But,
even in the simplest view, there exist frequent hybrid or compound cases which
complicate the distinction. Some written texts (like the papers prepared for the
conference) are written, but with a view to being spoken; others are written
records of things which were originally spoken mainly spontaneously and without preparation – being planned, monitored and, if necessary, corrected at the
same time. Some texts (e.g. some of the chapters of this book) were originally
written to be spoken, then rewritten from the spoken version; and some texts
exist simultaneously in more than one medium (the chapters of this book were
enacted as 'live' speech from prepared scripts at the conference, but are now
stored in several forms: as written chapters; as recorded speech, with precise
details of tempo, intonation and accent accurately encoded on audio tape;
and as the soundtrack of videos, where sound is synchronised with rhetorics
of posture, facial expression and gesture in the image).

These complications to the binary classification might be insignificant, were
it not that historically and regionally available technologies of communication
serve to define and shape larger systems of social relations. In the history of
societies, the question of medium has been central to defining the different
social conditions of 'orality' and 'literacy'; and transition from oral cultures
to literate ones is widely thought to have consequences on fundamental
relationships to language, on the forms and functions of recorded history and
social knowledge, and possibly also on patterns of cognition. In these social
ramifications, it has generally been 'writing' which takes precedence,
establishing and regulating the forms of standardisation and power characteristic of literate cultures, particularly through the social value and authority
assigned to specific written texts and the prestige and social opportunity
associated with being literate.

Possibilities for transmitting and reproducing speech and writing in further
new and hybrid forms have greatly increased during the twentieth century.
Issues concerning technologies of communication have accordingly become
increasingly pressing, especially because of the overall shift they are producing

in very many parts of the world from literate societies to societies of 'secondary orality'. In such societies, the written medium is dislodged from many functions by communications which make use of transmitted and recorded speech, including film and television soundtrack, radios and telephones, and foreseen fifth-generation computers.

Questions concerning the roles of speech and writing in social developments of this kind provide something of the framework for the papers by Halliday and MacCabe in particular. What enables 'writing' to serve as a generic term in reference to the hybrid realisations of language encountered in modern communications, many of which involve forms of 'speech', is that in one sense made current by work in literary theory, 'writing' signals the defining properties of all forms of representation or text.

12 The new sense of 'writing' as characterising the properties of all forms of representation is particularly prevalent in post-structuralism. Texts in any medium, transmitted or recorded in any form, are signifying entities or practices which operate through a system of differential relations between sounds or letters — and in some degree are thus independent from the consciousness or authorship which appears to produce them (a problem examined in Banfield's paper). The opposition between speech and writing had once appeared to be an opposition between the spatially and temporally close bond of speaker and speech as against the cut umbilical cord separating writer and writing.

But literary theorists now argue that *all* texts are cut away from their origin, and so writing — emblematic of the dissociated text *par excellence* — can be generalised from a specific practice to a name for all texts; speech is thus one specific sub-type of writing. The impetus for this re-evaluation of writing has come especially from Derrida's critique of 'phonocentrism' (the fusing of the speaking voice and an imputed self-presence of consciousness which occurs when speech is considered primary over writing). Derrida contends that speech too has all the decentered and conventionalised, often alarming, properties of writing. Derrida's work — and Deconstruction which is largely derived from it — accordingly challenges the philosophical and linguistic tradition of taking speech as prior to writing, and demonstrates ways in which the freeplay of language in either medium displaces speakers from any central or proprietary position over meaning.

Culler in his paper argues that though linguistics owes more to writing than it thinks it does, nevertheless it is bound to a conceptualisation of language which places speech at its centre. Culler suggests that the 'deconstructive' properties of writing should instead be the centre of attention for a new linguistics of writing which would address also 'the forms of writing in speech'.

13 The issue of whether the discipline of linguistics can cope with these various senses of the term 'writing' proved to be one of the fissures dividing participants at the conference. Thus the phrase 'The linguistics of writing' has an oxymoronic edge to it, dividing those who study language and those who study literature. Under the influence of deconstruction, writing has come to stand for 'uncertain, unstable', opposed to the certainty and confidence of linguistic theory. 'Writing' has also come to stand for the material text, set in a historical and social context; thus it stands for 'concrete' as against the abstractness and idealisation of linguistics.

The first of these oppositions, concerning the stability of linguistics and writing, can be thought of in philosophy-of-science terms as a difference between realism about theories and anti-realism about theories. Realism about theories says that it is possible to have a provably true theory about the world (e.g. about language); anti-realism about theories denies this – theories may be useful, but truth is not a relevant notion. This debate is dramatised here in the debate between Kiparsky and Fish. Linguistic theory is characteristically realist about theories, and also realist about entities such as 'linguistic knowledge' or 'grammar' – which are considered to be cognitively instantiated. While 'sixties structuralism had a realist edge to it (realist about itself as a theory, though often anti-realist about the structures which it discovered), current literary theory tends to cruise in the anti-realist car driven by post-structuralism, and Derrida's insistence (as in his contribution here) on the need to deconstruct established formalisms. Some papers in this collection treat linguistics as a form of writing, with theoretical documents historically and socially constructed like any written text; thus Attridge emphasises the rhetoric and the historical boundedness of linguistics in Jakobson's 'Closing statement'. Because linguistics is writing, the argument runs, then it is just as unstable as writing, just as lacking in a grip on the real world. Whether theory can escape this decentredness of 'writing' (for Lodge, after Bakhtin, the 'dialogic') is an issue in Lodge's paper and discussion. From a different perspective, Hollander suggests that writing can become a kind of linguistics.

The second opposition of linguistics and writing also sees linguistics as unable to get a grip on the world, hamstrung by its idealisation and abstraction away from the specificities of time and physical and social space which characterise linguistic behaviour. All linguistic theories are theories about the regularities which characterise real data, and so every linguistic theory deals with idealised data – data which is collected in institutionally licensed ways (intuition, experiment, fieldwork) and viewed from a particular angle. Modern linguistics has been confident in permitting itself a large amount of idealisation. In this book idealisation is frequently questioned: does the idealisation which is assumed in the practice of much linguistics necessarily exclude the possibility of understanding language change (discussed in papers by Durant and Fabb, Halliday and Hasan)? Moreover, does the idealisation draw upon a sufficiently broad segment of linguistic behaviour, including both speech and writing, and linguistic situations where the participants are in control of different languages, dialects or registers, with such control being an index of power (discussed in the papers by Culler and Pratt)? If a linguistic theory accounts for just some sub-part of the linguistic data, is that sub-part interesting or trivial, and does that sub-account exclude other kinds of work on other parts of the data? Literary theory sometimes represents itself as a theory about everything, global and oceanic, seeing one principle as having overriding importance (for some, deconstruction is an overriding principle of this kind; Fish in his paper sees 'persuasion' as such an overriding principle). Thus it has little patience with the piecemeal approach of modern linguistics, some aspects of which (Chomsky's current work, for example) have 'modularity' (the opposite of 'globalism') as a guiding principle, a principle which is central to Kiparsky's paper.

14 The attack on idealisation is an attack on all modern linguistics. While agreeing to idealise, however, linguists differ on the degree or nature of idealisation, as manifested in the extent to which the grammar is directly related to linguistic behaviour. Functionalist linguistics is seen by some as a solution to the problem of idealisation and the relationship between theoretical constructs and the linguistic behaviour which they characterise. For functionalism (exemplified by the work of Halliday, Hasan or Leech) the structure of the grammar is determined by the use to which the grammar is put in actual behaviour. Formalist linguists (such as Chomsky, Halle and Kiparsky) take a different approach, much happier to idealise, treating grammar and use-of-grammar as distinct in principle. For formalists, linguistic structure (what people know when they know a language) is potentially arbitrary, determined by principles which might be language-specific and not derivable from any aspect of linguistic behaviour (what people produce when they use a language). For functionalists, linguistic structure is motivated by use, with the principles of the grammar shaped to linguistic behaviour. In practice, most linguists accept a mixture of formalist and functionalist explanations, but there is usually a clear tendency towards one pole. The difference between functionalist and formalist linguistics has been important in one part of the recent linguistics of writing, in stylistics; it has, for example, often been argued that a functionalist linguistics is more appropriate to stylistics' analysis of the linguistic structure of texts than a formalist linguistics because a functionalist grammar sees a direct correlation between use (e.g. an actual text) and structure, and moreover has a more extensive theory of how use and structure are related. Formalist linguistics is agnostic about the relation between structure and use; can it therefore be of any use in analysing the structures of a fragment of language behaviour, i.e. a text? Leech in his paper takes a strongly functionalist position, drawing on Jakobson's 'Closing statement'.

15 This apparent heterogeneity in approaches to questions of 'writing' – formalist, functionalist, deconstructionist, etc. – was cited by more than one participant as a major source of confusion. But terminological difficulties reflect differences over concepts, horizons and goals. 'Explication' and 'translation' may make possible interdisciplinary dialogue about writing which cuts across what are in effect these different languages; but this in itself cannot resolve more deep-seated issues regarding the formation of disciplines. Disciplines construct and define specific aims in representing and explaining the world; and they take different stances on what kind of intervention in the world might follow from them.

Understanding disciplines in terms of socially-constructed purposes and involvement opens the question of whether defining an object of enquiry in a particular way will determine the nature of the findings you will come up with, and so rule out findings of other kinds. Defining lines of interest and enquiry through directions of research, professional advancement and institutional support, fixes a centre of attention in certain problems or concerns; in doing so it inevitably marginalises others. The basis for such definition can range from ideals of rationality to notions of political appropriateness, strategy and pragmatism. Such approaches seek different kinds of authorisation for their descriptions and explanations of the world, and for action in it.

Repeatedly, there was discussion during the conference of the issue of centre and margins with respect to linguistics. One main line of argument (especially in discussion following papers by Léech, Halliday and Widdowson) was that important questions are closed off by an emphasis on 'communication' and on 'communication models' of language. Firstly, there is the question of language as success or failure: whether linguistics should and does presume that communication is generally successful, and consequently describe failures as machine-error or pathology; or whether it takes evidently successful communication as the unusual phenomenon (and so requiring remark and investigation). This topic was raised most directly by Antony Easthope in the discussion session following Halliday's paper. Underlying Easthope's critique of 'communication' approaches to language is a claim that these approaches rely on the notion of 'full subjects': self-possessed and autonomous human beings deemed to be free from social and historical determinations of being and activity. For post-structuralists, this view is untenable as a satisfactory basis for understanding language: the argument for this is that any such assumption marginalises the social production of signs and relations of signification (for example, the role of desire in determining social interaction, or different positions ascribed to men to women). To focus on communication, post-structuralists suggest, rather than developing a politics of discourse and pursuing socially specific analysis of signification, under-represents possibilities for intervention in language to challenge specific social relations. After Halliday's paper and others, discussion centred on the degree of social determination of language change, and on limits on scope and levels of political intervention in such processes. Similar difficulties beset taking any one 'language' as an object of study. It was questioned whether, in such frameworks of study, power relations which structure forms of linguistic interaction between unequal social groups, or between social groups in contact across different relations to use of a particular language (e.g. in situations of bilingualism or multilingualism) are adequately reflected in the concerns of linguistic theory. It was argued that concerns of this kind are never more than marginal to established forms of linguistic enquiry. But since many linguistic situations – possibly most, taking the world as a whole – involve multilingualism, and since all situations of language use involve contact and conflict between groups of participants across systems of social stratification, it was argued (by Pratt and MacCabe for example) that contact and conflict should be put more at the centre of linguistic enquiry, rather than modelling linguistics on a notionally homogeneous language community of ideal speaker-hearers.

But linguists disputed this representation of 'linguistics'. Firstly, it was suggested, linguistics involves a range of aspirations, methods and forms of argument which cannot be reduced to the 'ideal speaker-hearer' stereotype. Secondly, it was pointed out that not only is modern linguistics not structuralism, but that structuralism was systematically analysed, modified and in many respects abandoned, in linguistics of an earlier period: to identify structuralism and linguistics is therefore to invite confusion.

Speculations along these lines were about more than the foundations and findings of current linguistics; they were also about the future. How should alternative models, for example of a 'linguistics of contact', actually proceed? What would be the theoretical and practical basis of such studies?

16 Future possibilities depend not only on autonomous processes of theory formation; they will emerge as a result of pressures between theoretical work and the social circumstances and purposes of the institutions within which it develops. Precise connections between theory and such larger social relations cannot be predicted; but what is clear is that vigilance by people working in a discipline in relation to the Other of that discipline, to alternatives and critiques engendered in its margins, is imperative.

It is easier to reflect on connections between theory and social relations looking back than looking forward. In Derek Attridge's paper, those parts of Jakobson's work cited from the 'Style in Language' conference as influencing 'The Linguistics of Writing' are read historically in relation to broader social circumstances, especially the series of displacements which affect it from Moscow, to Prague and the United States. The apparent ease of reading off intellectual paradigms of the past in relation to social circumstances can lead to historical simplifications, however. The way these enter into accounts of intellectual work of earlier periods, presenting reduced and stereotypical versions convenient for later argument, is discussed in Raymond Williams's paper in relation to the avant-garde. Given such historical readings of theory, it becomes possible to speculate counterfactually, that the work would have been different – though in what precise ways it is not possible to determine –

if larger patterns of social circumstances had differed. As a consequence for the present, the chains of influence and authority might be different, too.

In Derrida's session, the theme of implications of travelling theory returns in more direct relation to the present period, in reference to the transplantation of modern deconstruction into intellectual life in the United States after development in a European setting. But it is not only movement between regions or countries which directs intellectual enquiry: money for research (in linguistics for example) may come tagged with particular research orientations required by sponsors, whether business, medical, or military.

It is, nevertheless, teaching, more than research, which fills the time of most modern academics. Assuming one important immediate context for most speakers and participants at the conference to be education, Durant and Fabb's paper relates forms of research to social context by recording the detail of a particular educational initiative, the Programme in Literary Linguistics at the University of Strathclyde, outlining proposals for specific kinds of action through course development.

Such connections between topics of academic interest over the last quarter century in the study of language and literature, and the circumstances of research in the present, leads back to the presentation of the conference. In particular, it is notworthy that economic changes affecting university departments provide a crucial reference for much of the present work the 'Linguistics of Writing' conference sought to investigate. In addition, the role of television in such events is new and provokes disagreement. On the one hand, it is possible to consider modern technologies of recording and transmission as an aspect of secondary oral societies which, though open to challenge on the basis of specific abuses or excesses, can no longer usefully be challenged through simple, principled opposition or rejection by specific social groups. Used appropriately, the argument runs, such technologies make possible broader access to intellectual concerns, and challenge kinds of stratification and élitism inherent in professionalisation of intellectual debate. Alternatively, (a view taken by some participants), televising the conference can appear symptomatic of developments in the 1980s seen under another light: the marginalisation of locally interactive situations by demands of larger audience constituencies and financial interests. As a focus for argument between readings of intellectual and academic life in the 1980s, the conference itself allowed issues in the changing circumstances of academic work to surface: does a conference in 1986 differ from one in 1958 partly by virtue of being able to stimulate broader discussion by relaying argument beyond the conferees able to participate at the time? Or is the appearance of such an event a sign of merger between intellectual life and forms of publicity and staged entertainment? On the evidence of views expressed at 'The Linguistics of Writing' conference, contemporary academic life exists somewhere between exclusive, professional high seriousness and the approach outlined by Stanley Fish to putting on lectures and symposia to promote a new department: 'It's like the old Judy Garland/Mickey Rooney movies, where any problem would be met by the suggestion, "let's put on a show in our father's barn" '.

17   In the famous opening words of his 'Closing statement' Roman Jakobson commented on the way that conferences can stimulate intellectual enquiry. It is therefore appropriate that, since he is repeatedly invoked throughout the proceedings which follow, we should call on Roman Jakobson to sign us off:

Fortunately, scholarly and political conferences have nothing in common. The success of a political convention depends on the general agreement of the majority or totality of its participants. The use of votes and vetoes, however, is alien to scholarly discussion where disagreement generally proves to be more productive than agreement. Disagreement discloses antinomies and tensions within the field discussed and calls for novel exploration.

Closing statement: linguistics and poetics in retrospect

In so far as these words call to mind a famous paper by Roman Jakobson, the gesture of opening with a 'closing statement' is an obvious one, perhaps even an inevitable one. The 'Linguistics of Writing' conference was planned to commemorate, to emulate, and to mark our distance from, an earlier conference, held at Indiana University in 1958 and published two years later in a volume edited by Thomas Sebeok under the title *Style in Language*.[1] That collection turned out to be one of the founding documents in English of what we can call 'literary linguistics', and one of the most memorable papers in it was Jakobson's 'Closing statement, from the viewpoint of linguistics', which he entitled 'Linguistics and poetics'. This paper has been reprinted, summarised, quoted from, and alluded to with remarkable frequency since its publication, and anyone who wishes to write or speak about the linguistic characterisation of poetic discourse is obliged to take account of it.

But if my own comments − which will pretend to none of the magisterial sweep and penetration of that earlier piece − also constitute some kind of 'closing statement', they will do so by registering, and setting up for debate, a sense of the completion or exhaustion of the long and fruitful enterprise for which Jakobson's 'Closing statement' can stand as an initiating moment. Such a point of exhaustion would also, of course, be a turning-point, and my retrospective look at Jakobson's achievement from our present vantage point is intended not as an act of interment or disavowal but as a preparation of the ground for a new 'linguistics of writing' − which will remain deeply indebted to Jakobson's work. In returning once more to that earlier 'Closing statement' I wish to consider some of the reasons for its immediate impact and lasting influence, and to ask to what extent its arguments and its aims have survived the mutations and revolutions in literary and linguistic thought that have marked the intervening decades.

That the essay in question achieved such a remarkable status points, I would contend, not only to its own intrinsic value but to a widely felt need in the 1950s for an authoritative statement about the special qualities of literary language. For some time literary studies, in Britain and America at least, had tended, in the name of critical sensitivity or empirical history, to dissolve the boundaries between literary and other uses of language; and though there were rumours that the story was rather different in places such as Russia and Czechoslovakia, full communication had been inhibited by barriers of language, culture, and politics.[2] At this historical moment Jakobson spoke with the immense prestige of one who had been centrally involved in those goings-on in Moscow and Prague, and he presented his argument *ex cathedra*, as though these were not matters for debate but truths he was laying before the expectant audience.[3] Jakobson confidently defines 'poetics' as what most of us would now call 'stylistics', and proceeds to claim for it an unparalleled importance in the literary domain:

Poetics deals primarily with the question, *What makes a verbal message a work of art?* Because the main subject of poetics is the *differentia specifica* of verbal art in relation to other arts and in relation to other kinds of verbal behavior, poetics is entitled to the leading place in literary studies. (p. 350)

And he has no hesitation in situating the flagship of literary studies in what he sees as its wider context: 'Since linguistics is the global science of verbal structure, poetics may be regarded as an integral part of linguistics' (p. 350). While this was a claim guaranteed to amuse or outrage most traditional literary critics and to disturb many theoretical linguists, it was a call to arms for the stripling discipline of stylistics.

Jakobson's thought is energised by an unquestioning faith in the power of positivistic thinking which must have been paticularly appealing in the late 1950s. He can declare ringingly: 'No manifesto, foisting a critic's own tastes and opinions on creative literature, may act as substitute for an objective scholarly analysis of verbal art' (p. 352), without evincing the slightest fear that his own analyses might be subject to his particular literary predilections or ideological biases. He thus offers an attractively democratic vision: no longer will literary analysis be the exclusive preserve of those who have mysteriously imbibed the capacity to make sensitive judgements. The insistence on complete explicitness, as in the then fledgling discipline of generative linguistics, will take away the mystique from literary criticism, and reveal the real and unchanging reasons why literary texts function as they do.

In facing the question of the *differentia specifica* of the language of literature, therefore, Jakobson is seeking clear definitions and distinctions which will, at the same time as offering a sharp focus, do justice to the evident lack of absoluteness in the relation between literary and nonliterary language. His solution, an extension of the proposals of Bühler and Mukařovský, is the famous map of linguistic functions, six in number, which characterise different kinds of linguistic event according to the different hierarchic relations of these functions. Poetry, in this scheme, is a use of language in which the poetic function dominates any of the others which might be present — the referential, the emotive, the conative, the phatic, and the metalingual. By this means, Jakobson appears to avoid many of the problems inherent in the notion of a norm against which a deviant poetic language is defined; any comparisons would have to be made five ways to encompass all the other possible functions of language. One of the recurrent problems of norm-and-deviation arguments − that whatever feature you come up with as the distinguishing mark of poetry turns out to exist in nonpoetic texts as well − appears to be solved: of course the poetic function occurs outside poetry, but it is only in poetry that it predominates over the others. The language of a poetic utterance. Jakobson asserts, is orientated, not toward the world it refers to, not towards the one who utters or the one who reads or hears, not toward the code or the channel of communication being utilised, but toward 'the message as such'.[4] Poetry is distinguished by its self-referentiality, which takes precedence over all the other operations performed by its language.[5]

How does the language of poetry achieve this state of self-referentiality? 'What', in Jakobson's words, 'is the empirical linguistic criterion of the poetic function?' (p. 358). Jakobson's pronouncement on this question is one of his most-quoted utterances: '*The poetic function projects the principle of equivalence from the axis of selection into the axis of combination*' (p. 358). It isn't surprising that this single sentence made a strong and continuing impact: it is impressively technical in its vocabulary, assured in its rhetoric, and free of any interference from the messy world of judgements, values, and power-relations; and it offers an objective and purely linguistic method of identifying what counts as poetry and what doesn't.[6] It provides just what was wanted − a key to the sealed chamber that had baffled literary thought for centuries.

It also dismisses as irrelevant several issues that have troubled accounts of literary language since Plato and Aristotle. The principle of projection has nothing to tell us about the difference between a good and a bad poem − just as the identification of the emotive function says nothing about the success or otherwise of any given expression of emotion and the referential function is in play whether the speaker is telling the truth or not.[7] It has no necessary relation to the author's intentions − if I wrote a text that was not a poem in terms of the projection principle, it would do no good to write *Poem* at the top of the page. And most significantly, perhaps, it excludes the *reader* from any role in the determination of what is or is not poetic language. Jakobson's stated position is clear: the reader is in the position of the 'addressee', the goal of the communicative channel, whose only requirement is that he or she is in a position to receive the message and has access to the code being used. It is therefore the message itself, which, by virtue of its in-herent properties − that is, in its adherence to the principle just enunciated − proclaims itself as poetic.[8] Those properties are empirical features of the text, available to objective analysis; and any reader, or body of readers, who in-sisted on the title 'poem' for a particular text which lacked these features would simply be wrong (unless the analysis of the text which claimed to show their absence were itself inadequate).[9]

There may, however, be a price to be paid for this assured singleness of purpose, and we need to scrutinise Jakobson's writing for any signs that what he has excluded remains a force to be reckoned with, even within his own argument. I am not proposing this from a position of superiority, as though I were capable of achieving a consistency unattained by Jakobson, but in the recognition that Jakobson's work necessarily looks different in the light of subsequent work, including that of the contributors to this book. My own text is therefore a product, both deliberately and inevitably, of the situation we found ourselves in in 1986.

The question I am posing in particular is whether Jakobson's exclusion of the reader, and the collectivity of which the reader belongs, is, or could ever be, successful; do his formulations manage to contain the determination of the literary *within* the text, and thus to achieve the cross-cultural and trans-historical universality he is seeking? We can begin with the familiar formula which encapsulates the proposed invariant of all poetic language: 'The set (*Einstellung*) toward the MESSAGE as such, focus on the message for its own sake, is the POETIC function of language' (p. 356). We may note, first of all, that in this definition Jakobson uses not a linguistic but a psychological terminology: the three words 'set', '*Einstellung*', and 'focus' all imply a mental attitude on the part of the reader – in spite of the fact that Jakobson's project is to define the 'poetic' in structural terms, not in terms of effect.[10] What one might have expected Jakobson to begin with is a specification of the exact linguistic and structural properties of poetry, that is, with the famous dictum about projection from one axis to the other; he could then have followed with the logically additional information that the effect of this property of poetic texts is to produce a set toward the message in the minds of its readers.

But the ordering of the argument as we have it indicates the force of the position Jakobson is attempting, but failing, to abandon: that the determination of what counts as poetry and what does not is ultimately in the hands of its readers, and any particular feature we might care to advance as the distinguishing characteristic of poetry can be tested only in the socio-cultural arena. A 'set toward the message' – assuming that we do not limit the word 'message' too narrowly – is a plausible definition of poetry precisely because it describes a cultural evaluation, a society's categorisation of certain texts as deserving a particular kind of attention and offering a particular kind of satisfaction. But a description of a defining structural property can never anticipate or exhaust a culture's behaviour (least of all when what is being attempted is a definition which takes account of cross-cultural variation). There are bound to be many other ways in which a set toward the message can be induced, such as a text's physical appearance or its categorisation within a particular institutional framework. There are also ceaseless historical changes at work, shifting the boundaries between the poetic and the nonpoetic, which Jakobson, in his grand synchronicity, ignores. What Jakobson is trying to establish is that a text's poetic status is an inherent property, which survives movement in time and space: thus he remarks 'A filibusterer may recite *Hiawatha* because it is long, yet poeticalness still remains the primary intent of this text itself' (p. 359).

This may help us to explain why the promise of a theory of linguistic functions which escapes the problems produced by norm-and-deviation approaches to poetic language is in fact never fulfilled. Jakobson makes it quite clear that the 'referential' function is to be thought of as the norm, the unmarked member of the set: 'Obviously we must agree with Sapir that, on the whole, "ideation reigns supreme in language ...", but this supremacy does not authorize linguistics to disregard the "secondary factors"' (353).[11] As Stanley Fish has shown, any notion of an 'ordinary language' against which a 'literary language' is defined, in terms of special features which it possesses (or lacks), impoverishes both terms in the distinction.[12] What such theories are designed to counter is the view that the difference between the 'literary' and the 'nonliterary' is produced historically by a particular culture, and Jakobson, were he genuinely to present his six functions in such a way as to privilege none of them, would be on the way to accepting such a view. (The general theory of markedness, so central to Jakobson's thinking, seems to me at times to run the risk of converting contingent hierarchies into universal ones, especially when what is at issue is not a physiologically determined feature but a socially constructed one.[13]) The relativity of the various functions, their determination by the uses to which they are put in specific contexts by speakers and hearers, writers and readers, cannot, for Jakobson, be allowed to threaten the founding distinction between the poetic and the nonpoetic, which must be protected as an essential, inherent, structural difference.

Let us return to the description of the defining feature of poetry: 'The set toward the message as such, focus on the message for its own sake, is the poetic function of language'. At first sight, this seems an odd use of the word *function,* which is usually equated with some effective activity, not a state. It can best be understood as a residue from an earlier stage in Jakobson's intellectual career, since the same word (in Czech) played a central part in the formulations of the Prague Linguistic Circle, of which Jakobson was of course a leading member; but we find a very different emphasis is given it by, for instance, Jan Mukařovský, whose arguments at other points come very close to Jakobson's. Any function, for Mukařovský, is a question of three factors: the object itself − in our case, the poem; the social consciousness − the cultural conventions in force; and the individual − the reader. Peter Steiner notes that 'The most common error in attributing a function to an object according to Mukařovský is to proceed from the object alone'.[14] The individual operates in terms of the social collectivity, which determines the function that is dominant in any object.

In the case of the other five functions which Jakobson enumerates, the social and psychological purpose of the particular kind of language is evident − it is serving to maintain a contact, express and convey an emotion, produce an effect upon a listener, check on the code, or, of course, communicate a cognitive content. But in the case of poetry there is a curious silence about its role in the socio-linguistic framework. We can no doubt deduce from Jakobson's comments a quite traditional aesthetic argument about the value and function of literature; we learn in the course of the description of the poetic function that it promotes 'the palpability of signs' (p. 356), that its employment in an election slogan 'reinforces its impressiveness and efficacy' (p. 357) and that it adds 'splendor' to Caesar's message, '*Veni, vidi, vici*' (p. 358); but in his definitions he seems to present poetry not only as self-referential but also as self-justifying. This avoidance of any appeal to the reader, and to the values or expectations he or she brings to the text, is part of a wider elision of the cultural determination of literature itself, in its many changing and differently interpreted forms, though the word 'function' remains like the ghost of these excluded possibilities.

We find a similar hesitation in the statement that is intended as an empirical description of the *differentia specifica* of verbal art, that which induces, automatically it would appear, a set toward the message: 'The poetic function projects the principle of equivalence from the axis of selection into the axis of combination'. Here we again have a rather odd use of the word *function*, as though it were some force acting within the poem, or operating upon it; and this sense is strengthened when Jakobson states that texts like advertising jingles 'make use of poetic function without, however, assigning to this function the coercing, determining role it carries in poetry' (p. 359). Mary Louise Pratt has pointed out that if the projection principle is operative in such texts but not to the extent that would make them poetry, 'some systematic way of measuring this lack in terms of the axes of selection and combination must be appended to the projection principle and must be testable against the available examples of versified laws, advertising jingles, and so on.'[15] In the absence of such a principle, we must suspect that in the final analysis the poetic function is determined not by the projection principle but some other principle, not necessarily intrinsic to the poem.[16]

Furthermore, the statement seems to be inverted: it asserts that the poetic function is active in *producing* a particular structural disposition, when one might expect Jakobson to say that it is produced by the disposition.[17] If this is not the case, what determines the domination of a message by the poetic — or any other — function? Again there is the lurking possibility that the classification of a text as a poem may in fact *precede* the special qualities it possesses, which then become a matter of reading strategies or socio-cultural categorisation and not empirical differences.

What is projected from the axis of selection — the associative or paradigmatic axis — to the axis of combination — the syntagmatic axis — is 'the principle of equivalence'; and Jakobson is at pains to explain, though he has not always been understood, that this does not mean merely 'the principle of similarity'.[18] Dissimilarity and antonymity are mentioned as well as similarity and synonymity, and the example he offers by way of immediate illustration is the equalisation of one syllable with another, one word-stress with another, one word-boundary with another, and so on. That is, in poetry, features of language which are usually merely the *carriers* of semantic content and have no importance in themselves and therefore no relations among themselves other than contiguity, gain that importance and enter into such relations. Any form of versification which uses syllables as a measure, for instance, has introduced a principle of equivalence along the sequence; so would a verse form which employs one sentence per line. Jakobson's account of all poetic features is in fact an extrapolation from his account of metrical form. (Indeed, as he himself once suggested, his whole intellectual career can be seen as growing out of his 'undergraduate attempt of 1911 to outline the formal properties of the earliest Russian iambs.'[19])

He has often been taken to mean that poetry is definable in terms of the additional patterning it introduces into language, the regular recurrence of similar items in the sequence.[20] Such a reading, though it is not strictly what Jakobson's theory states, is understandable, since it provides the kind of objective, empirical criterion that the argument appears to need. Patterns of similar items can be empirically identified, and perhaps some kind of cut-off point established at which the poetic function could be declared dominant over the others. Many of Jakobson's analyses of poems suggest that he did indeed believe that intricate patterning was a distinctive and discoverable feature of poems, and he certainly remained unconvinced by demonstrations that with an interpretative machinery as powerful as his, intricate patterns could be detected in virtually *any* stretch of language;[21] but in setting out the theory he avoids – and one can understand why – reducing poetry to a mechanically specifiable set of texts. The notion of 'equivalence', like the notions of 'set', and 'focus', is oriented toward the reader. The poetic function, in effect, *invites* the reader to treat as equivalent items in the sequence which would have simply been contiguous in nonpoetic language; thus the hypothetical verse-form made up of one sentence per line does not in itself make the sentences similar or dissimilar, but encourages the reader to treat them as having a relation of 'similarity or dissimilarity'. Jakobson's liking for Hopkins's word *parallelism* points in the same direction: items in parallel to one another invite an act of comparison, whereas items in a pattern imply no activity other than passive apprehension.[22]

Jakobson's insistence on the *semantic* aspect of his principle confirms the role of the reader, even though it is introduced with a flourish of positivism:

No doubt, verse is primarily a recurrent 'figure of sound'. Primarily, always, but never uniquely. Any attempts to confine such poetic conventions as meter, alliteration, or rhyme to the sound level are speculative reasonings without any empirical justification. The projection of the equational principle into the sequence has a much deeper and wider significance. Valéry's view of poetry as 'hesitation between the sound and the sense' is much more realistic and scientific than any bias of phonetic isolationism. (p. 367)

Thus in rhyme, the semantic relation between rhyme words is as important as the phonetic relation – and since the former relation is not itself marked, but can vary over the whole range of possibilities, the only applicable model is one that involves the reader, who takes the rhyme as an instruction to carry out a semantic comparison. Jakobson quotes Hopkins's definition of what the latter calls the two 'correlative experiences' involved in semantic equivalence: 'comparison for likeness' sake' and 'comparison for unlikeness' sake'; for Hopkins, too, the poetic function is posited upon the interpretative activity of the reader. Whether this process of comparison is a *necessary* and *universal* feature of the reading of poetry, as Jakobson wants it to be, becomes therefore an empirical question about traditions of reading in different periods and cultures; and it is Jakobson's generalising account itself that stands in danger of being accused of 'speculative reasonings without any empirical justification'.

A particularly interesting development of the argument occurs when Jakobson moves from the fusion of phonetic and semantic relations to the operation of semantic units themselves, which he does in order to bring the widely-observed phenomenon of poetic ambiguity within the compass of his explanation. 'In poetry not only the phonological sequence but in the same way any sequence of semantic units strives to build an equation' (p. 370). Again there is an odd displacement from the reader's interpretative activity to the language itself, as though the poem were struggling of its own accord towards its entelechy, but the argument indicates something of the real power of Jakobson's proposal. It seems to me very helpful to think of poetic discourse – at least that which characterises one identifiable type of poetry – as a discourse in which the reader is encouraged, by the text itself and by the cultural matrix within which it is presented, to derive 'meaning' (let us leave that word as vague as we can) from a number of linguistic features over and above the usual operations of lexis and syntax. The notion of ambiguity, while it appears to signify to Jakobson multiple meanings which any reader will perceive, could also suggest a range of potential meanings, not all of them available to any single reader, and it would then be possible to agree with Jakobson that 'ambiguity is an intrinsic, inalienable character of any self-focused message' (pp. 370–1), since the diversion of attention away from the semantic content to other features of the text is bound to complicate the simple transmission of meaning.[23] One might question whether the notion of 'projection' from one axis to another is necessary (apart from giving Jakobson's own sentence the very qualities of parallelism that it is referring to, making it an example as well as a definition of the poetic function); but the idea that poetic language often involves a number of additional possibilities in the inter-relations among linguistic and semantic elements, brought into play by a heightened sense of potential equivalences, is not one that can be easily dismissed.

That is not to say that it will do as the single explanation of poetic distinctiveness; we are only likely to accept it as that if we assume from the beginning that a single explanation is necessary, and we are probably less prone to that assumption today than we would have been in 1958. We might want, for instance, to insist that the other kind of poetic distinctiveness to which the discipline of stylistics has paid great attention − the contravention of linguistic rules − is equally important in focusing attention on the poetic message. But as one aspect of that complex set of procedures, historically-conditioned and always subject to historical change, which produces a special psychic and cultural space − or one had better say a number of such spaces − for certain texts we label 'poetic', the theory of multiple equivalences retains its value.

But how might we follow through the implication, suppressed in Jakobson, that readers are active in determining what is poetry and what is not? We would need some account of the role of ideology, of gender, of institutional practices, perhaps of the unconscious; and we would need to take account of our own position as culturally and ideologically situated readers. Upon these foundations we might attempt to build a theory of pleasure (which would need to be a fully historicised theory to do justice to the changing modes and functions of pleasure) in its relation to the phenomenon of poetry. The question would then arise: how does the operation of Jakobson's projection principle, in however complex a form, relate to the production of pleasure and to the value judgements associated with it? It must be something other than a simple correlation between the extent to which the principle of equivalence is exploited and the degree of pleasure produced by the poem; many a poem has been condemned as unpleasant or bad because of the excess of its parallelisms and repetitions.[24] It seems impossible at this point to avoid invoking some such notion as 'subtlety', 'judgment', or 'taste', and once we admit to this, we have to admit to the cultural production of the entire value-system within which poetry is appraised and authorised, since these terms represent systems that are neither individual nor universal. The more general issue that is touched on here is that the necessary idealisations and abstractions of 'theory' as understood in linguistics, especially since Saussure, appear to anyone who is engaged in 'theory' as understood currently within literary studies as simplifications of complex cultural and philosophical phenomena − since a great deal of recent literary theory has been devoted to showing the unworkability (and sometimes the unacknowledged political force) of such simplifications. This is one of the reasons why the work of the Bakhtin-Vološinov school has held much greater appeal to literary theorists in recent years than the work of Jakobson and the Russian Formalists.[25]

Jakobson clearly would not admit that his judgements were part of a culturally-produced value system. However, it is difficult to analyse poetry without making any explicit or implicit evaluative judgments; and Jakobson's 'empirical' studies of poems are perhaps not as far removed from the maligned activity of critics who 'foist their own tastes and opinions on creative literature' as he liked to think. Let us examine his description of the type of poetic analysis he championed in a paper roughly contemporary with the 'Closing statement':

Any unbiased, attentive, exhaustive, total description of the selection, distribution and interrelation of diverse morphological classes and syntactic constructions in a given poem surprises the examiner himself by unexpected, striking symmetries and anti-symmetries, balanced structures, efficient accumulation of equivalent forms and salient contrasts, finally by rigid restrictions in the repertory of morphological and syntactic constituents used in the poem, eliminations which, on the other hand, permit us to follow the masterly interplay of the actualized constituents.[26]

This is the extraordinary Jakobsonian rhetoric at full stretch: the analysis is presented as a demanding but essentially mechanical procedure, needing not taste or discrimination to achieve its purpose but patience, thoroughness, and accurate linguistic knowledge. Although, as Jonathan Culler has shown, the notion of exhaustiveness is a fiction, since the capacity to produce descriptive linguistic categories is infinite, and the analyst's choice of a very few to focus on must be guided by some initial decision about what is important and what is not,[27] the statement is impressive for its consistency with Jakobson's central argument about the poetic function as an objective property – except in one respect: it is shot through with a sense of admiration for the poets who are able to achieve such effects with language. Their work 'surprises' the examiner, its symmetries and antisymmetries are 'unexpected' and 'striking', its accumulations are 'efficient', and its interplay of constituents is 'masterly'. This response is understandable, and increases rather than diminishes one's respect for Jakobson as a reader of poetry, but it sits uneasily in a demonstration that poetry as such, good or bad, can be objectively defined. What would be the conclusion to be drawn from a poem whose symmetries did not surprise or impress? Would it be a bad poem or not a poem at all?

In fact, when we turn to Jakobson's analyses of particular poems we find that they are not simply demonstrations of the poetic function at work, but are clearly designed, like most traditional literary criticism, to persuade the reader of the magnitude of the poet's achievement. It is not just that the principle of equivalence allows poems to function differently from other kinds of language, it is that in the hands of great poets (or a productive oral tradition) the principle of equivalence is a resource which produces networks of association and contrast, interrelations of sound and sense, of remarkable unity, intricacy, and subtlety. (Jakobson's critical method, like any critical method, privileges certain kinds of writing – poetry over prose, the short poem over the long poem, the lyric over the narrative, the formally patterned over the freely varying, etc.; and Krystyna Pomorska, summarising Jakobson, can call the 'short lyric poem' 'poetry in its epitome' without any recognition that this valuation is produced by the theory rather than the other way round.[28]) The following are some of Jakobson's comments on individual poets and poems:

On Pushkin's lyric poetry (1936):

A masterful alternation of grammatical categories of person becomes a means of intense dramatization. There can hardly be an example of a more skillful poetic exploitation of morphological possibilities.[29]

On Yeats, 'The Sorrow of Love' (1977):

The exacting selection and arrangement of verbal symbols summoned in 'The Sorrow of Love' to build a harmonious system of rich semantic correlations [...] indeed warrant the poet's assertion: *And words obey my call.*[30]

e.e. cummings, 'love is more thicker than forget' (1979):

Close attention to 'love is more thicker' shows how sound correspondences acquire or enhance a semantic propinquity and how they act as kindred submorphemes upheld by a mysteriously complex and cohesive network of metrical, strophic, and compositional means.[31]

Similarly, Jakobson and Jones find in Shakespeare's Sonnet 129 an 'amazing external and internal structuration palpable to any responsive and unprejudiced reader' and refer to the 'cogent and mandatory unity of its thematic and compositional framework'.[32]

Even if he had excised all evaluative comments from his writing, however, the rhetorical function of Jakobson's minutely-detailed analyses is clear: it is not to show that the object before him is a poem, or, since we know it is a poem, that his definition of the poetic function holds good for one more example; it is to persuade by the amassing of detail that this verbal artefact has remarkable qualities of intricate structuration and cohesion – and that they enforce a particular interpretation, for in spite of the argument for the importance of poetic ambiguity, when it came to interpretation Jakobson had no doubt that poems possess fixed, timeless, and strictly limited meanings. (A secondary purpose of the exercise is to persuade the reader that only a Jakobsonian linguistic analysis can reveal these qualities, while of course claiming that they are there to be seen by any reader whose head isn't full of foolish literary prejudices.) The tools may be different, but the job is a time-honoured one: to persuade others to share one's preferences, and to show off one's skills as a critic.[33] Each analysis is an intervention in a cultural (and ultimately political) struggle, and the use of empirical vocabulary and the rhetoric of objectivity is, like the use by others of an impressionist vocabulary and the rhetoric of subjectivity, a strategy with its own advantages and disadvantages. But as I have tried to show, the rhetoric of objectivity, like all rhetorics, reveals itself as such in its language; to define is to attempt an act of exclusion, keeping out that which would threaten the logical form of the definition. Jakobson's definition of the poetic function attempts in the same gesture to protect both poetry and his own discourse from those forces which would render it impermanent, inconsistent with itself, and open to an infinity of future contexts, but it can succeed in doing neither. Both poems and academic papers, including this one, have their existence in a culture within which they are generated, fought over, prized or dismissed. One of the functions of poetry as a historically mobile cultural practice is to test and undermine existing norms (and one might say the same about conference presentations); Jakobson's attempt to fix, once and for all, the parameters of poetic language fails to take account of this function.

The critical assumptions in Jakobson's poetic analyses are, in fact, as traditional as his purposes: that the value of a poem inheres in its capacity to produce maximal unity from maximal diversity, and to fuse the realms of form and meaning. These assumptions, which he does not raise for questioning, can be traced to Romantic notions of organic form, and in the English tradition relate most closely to the critical practice and pronouncements of another lifelong seeker for universal keys, Samuel Taylor Coleridge,[34] though their pedigree goes back much further in Western culture. Jakobson's theory of poetic language, then, can be seen as belonging to, and participating in, a specific cultural history, which is also a social and political history, of which we too are a part.

Jakobson approaches the problem of poetic language not only with post-Romantic assumptions about literary form but also with a particular commitment to linguistic explanations – a prior commitment, if you like, to 'the message as such'. The diagram of the six fundamental factors in verbal communication, and the translation of this into the six functions of language is a masterly piece of theoretical rhetoric, with its implication that poetry's place is set out for it *in advance* by the necessary structure of the speech event; once the other five factors have had functions assigned to them, there remains only the 'message' to be taken care of, and only poetry is available to fill that slot. That the whole structure is only one of many possible ways of categorising speech events, that the sense of an exhaustive covering of the ground is only a convincingly-managed illusion, that the existence of an inherent property of poetic language remains to be demonstrated, are suspicions that fade in the bright sunlight of Jakobson's apodictic prose.

This feat of exclusion, echoed so often in linguistic and literary theory since then, is all the more striking when Jakobson's position in 1958 is compared with that of his earlier self and his former colleagues. It was Jakobson himself who, in Prague in 1928, produced with Jurij Tynjanov a manifesto which moves away from the Formalist isolation of the work of art from its context, at a time when Mukařovský was still arguing that literary analysis must stay within the boundaries of the work itself;[35] and the Prague Linguistic Circle, in which Jakobson played a leading part, was to develop a theoretical position 'emphasizing above all', as Peter Steiner puts it, 'the social context of the phenomena under study rather than the question of their invariants'.[36] But in the United States in the 1950s, after a World War and during a Cold War, Jakobson's work seems to be driven by the pursuit of the invariant, transcending the social and cultural differences which occur across space and time. He liked to look back on his career as an unwavering search for universals and essences; and all his detailed empirical investigations can be seen to be in the service of a totalising drive.[37] In his unquestioning dedication to a model of explanation based on Occam's razor – the best account is the one which subsumes the widest variety of phenomena under a single rule – he was scarcely an unbiased researcher (who is?), and the influence of this cast of thought on linguistic theory has been immense in this century.

We are left, then, with a sense of Jakobson's achievement as residing more in the questions his work provokes than in the confident maxims it proclaims. One of the questions is obviously whether the methods and the aims of objective analysis as understood by Jakobson are appropriate in the literary domain. Does a linguistics of writing – however broadly or narrowly we wish to define the latter word – require different objectives, different tools? And if the answer is yes, the further question remains: does linguistics proper, which has tended to see itself as concerned primarily with speech, have something to learn from this encounter with the written word and with literature? The work of Jacques Derrida would suggest that Jakobson's confident incorporation of literary studies into linguistics might be reversible, and that the particular problems which arise when we try to define, to categorise, to fix literary or philosophical writing might be characteristic of all uses of language. To close the chapter which Jakobson opened thirty years ago is by no means to reach the end of the story.

Notes

1   Thomas A. Sebeok (ed.), *Style in Language*, Cambridge, Mass., 1960. Page references to Jakobson's paper will be given in the text.

2   Nine years earlier, René Wellek and R. P. Warren had published their *Theory of Literature* (New York, 1949), with many intriguing references to Russian Formalism, and six years after that Victor Erlich's *Russian Formalism: History – Doctrine* (The Hague, 1955) provided the first full introduction for the English-speaking world.

3   The section of the paper outlining the six linguistic functions, including the description of the poetic function in terms of a 'set towards the message', was originally given as part of Jakobson's Presidential Address to the Annual Meeting of the Linguistic Society of America in 1956; it has been published as 'Metalanguage as a linguistic problem', in *The Framework of Language*, Michigan Studies in the Humanities No. 1, Ann Arbor, 1980, pp. 81–92.

4   Jakobson does not elaborate on the meaning of 'message' in this context. In particular, he appears to want it both to involve and to exclude semantic content; on the one hand, he makes it clear that he is not limiting the poetic function to a heightened attention to the sounds of the language, or more generally to the *signans*, but, on the other hand, to emphasise the existence in poetry of a set towards the meaning, the *signatum*, would leave the referential function – which he also calls the 'denotative' and 'cognitive' function (p. 353) – with a very limited role. Furthermore, such a separation of meaning and reference would contradict the coalescence of these two terms which was an increasingly important feature of Jakobson's thinking (see Linda R. Waugh, *Roman Jakobson's Science of Language*, Lisse, 1976, pp. 28–31). His position in the 1920s had been more clearly based on Husserlian phenomenology: poetry is characterised by a set towards 'expression', a term derived from Husserl in an attempt to name inherent as opposed to referential meaning; see Peter Steiner, *Russian*

Formalism: A Metapoetics, Ithaca, 1984, pp. 201–5. I discuss this tension within Jakobson's theory, which is most acute in the consideration of sound-symbolism, in 'Literature as imitation: Jakobson, Joyce, and the art of onomatopoeia', Ch. 5 of *Peculiar Language: Literature as Difference from the Renaissance to James Joyce*, Ithaca & London, 1988.

5 Although Jakobson avoids the word, this principle is of course derived from the notion of 'foregrounding', developed in Russian Formalism and of central importance in the discussions of the Prague School. In Mukařovský's account, for instance, 'the function of poetic language consists in the maximum of foregrounding of the utterance' – but this can be achieved in a number of ways, one of which must, in any given case, be dominant, 'Standard language and poetic language', in Paul L. Garvin (ed.), *A Prague School Reader on Esthetics, Literary Structure, and Style*, Washington DC, 1964, p. 19.

6 Saussure's associative relations, called by later writers 'paradigmatic' or 'systematic', become Jakobson's relations of similarity, operating on the axis of selection, and manifested in metaphor; Saussure's syntagmatic relations become – without any insistence on linearity – Jakobson's relations of contiguity, manifested in metonymy. See 'Two aspects of language and two types of aphasic disturbances', in Roman Jakobson & Morris Halle, *Fundamentals of Language*, The Hague, 1956.

7 Cf. Waugh's comment: 'Nor, as should be obvious, is the poetic function to be equated with "great" poetry; the poetic function may also occur in "doggerel"', 'The poetic function and the nature of language', in Jakobson, *Verbal Art, Verbal Sign, Verbal Time*, Oxford, 1985, p. 146.

8 See Waugh's summary: 'The "function" of a given message is, in Jakobson's terminology, an *intrinsic quality* of the message itself; thus, the focus upon the message is an inherent quality of a poem' ('The poetic function', *Verbal Art*, p. 148).

9 Another question, which, as Mary Louise Pratt and David Lodge have both emphasised, receives only a fudged answer from Jakobson, is: 'How does this definition of the poetic function bear upon prose literature?' (See Pratt, *Toward a Speech Act Theory of Literary Discourse*, Bloomington, 1977, pp. 34–5, and Lodge, *The Modes of Modern Writing: Metaphor, Metonymy, and the Typology of Modern Literature*. London, 1977, pp. 91–2.) The best Jakobson can do when he poses this question to himself is to categorise literary prose as a 'transitional linguistic area', existing somewhere between 'strictly poetic and strictly referential language' (p. 374): presumably in this case the two functions in question are nicely balanced. This marginalisation of the major component of the Western literary tradition indicates that something is amiss with the theory that necessitates it, and the notion that, say, Swift's *Gulliver's Travels* is different from Wordsworth's *Prelude* in that the fomer is halfway to being a referential text is plainly unsatisfactory.

10 This choice of words no doubt betrays the influence of Gestalt psychology and Husserl's phenomenology on the Prague school; see Peter Steiner's accounts in 'The conceptual basis of Prague Structuralism', in Ladislav Matejka (ed.), *Sound, Sign and Meaning*, Michigan Slavic Contributions, No. 6, Ann Arbor, 1978, pp. 353–6, and *Russian Formalism*, pp. 201–4, 208–10. A full study of Jakobson's debt to Husserl is Elmar Holenstein, *Roman Jakobson's Approach to Language: Phenomenological Structuralism*, Bloomington, Indiana, 1976.

11 Waugh, in summarising Jakobson's argument, has no hesitation in reinforcing this statement:

The referential function seems to be that function which is the unmarked one in the system of six. ... As evidence of the unmarked nature of the referential function, we may cite the fact that in many linguistic and philosophical studies of language, the referential function has been said to be the *only* function of language, or, if (some of) the other functions have been discerned, they have been declared to be 'deviant' or 'unusual' or needing special consideration. And even in our parlance about language, the referential function is spoken of as 'ordinary language'.

('The poetic function', *Verbal Art*, p. 144.)

12   Stanley Fish, 'How ordinary is ordinary language?', in *Is There a Text in This Class?*, Cambridge, Mass., 1980, pp. 97–111.

13   See, for instance, 'The concept of the mark', in Roman Jakobson & Krystyna Pomorska, *Dialogues*, Cambridge, 1980, pp. 93–8. Jakobson's comments indicate that, on the one hand, there was an early emphasis on the concept of markedness as a tool for examining cultural variety ('correlations encountered in the history of culture, such as life/death, liberty/oppression, sin/virtue, holidays/wordays, etc., can always be reduced to the relation α/notα; the relevant thing is to establish what constitutes the marked set for each period, group, people, and so on' – from a letter to Trubetzkoy in 1930); on the other, there is a tendency to equate the 'unmarked' with the 'natural', which gives rise to a number of problems always associated with the specification of that which is 'natural' in human behaviour as opposed to that which is 'non-natural'. I discuss these problems in *Peculiar Language*, especially Chs. 2 & 3.

14   'The conceptual basis of Prague Structuralism', p. 361.

15   Mary Louise Pratt, *Toward a Speech Act Theory*, p. 36; the whole chapter, entitled 'The "poetic language" fallacy', is a valuable discussion of these issues.

16   Samuel R. Levin, in his *Linguistic Structures in Poetry* (The Hague, 1962), while using a model very similar to Jakobson's, is rather more modest in his claims: 'We are not presuming, however, to give necessary or sufficient conditions for poetry; we are simply asserting that the exploitation of such equivalences seems to be manifest in most of those utterances or texts that we agree to call poems' (p. 30, n. 1). Levin in fact defines a much more precise and objectively identifiable feature in his notion of 'coupling' – the occurrence of items which are phonetically or semantically equivalent in equivalent positions in a syntactic or poetic structure. This might seem to move away from Jakobson's unacknowledged implication that what determines poetry is a reading strategy, but it is still a reading convention that chooses to make something of such linguistic phenomena, and the whole question of what might *count* as phonetic and semantic equivalence is not at all an objective matter. We are back with the historical question of what a culture makes of its texts (implicit in Levin's 'texts that we agree to call poems'); and Jakobson's discussion, in its vaguer account of the criteria involved, comes nearer to acknowledging this.

17   Earlier, Jakobson had offered the general statement: 'The verbal structure of a message depends primarily on the predominant function' (p. 353). The undecideability of this moment in the argument is dramatised in Waugh's description of poetic discourse as understood by Jakobson: 'The combination is built upon *and/or* produces equivalence and similarity relations between the combined elements' ('The poetic function', *Verbal Art*, p. 152; my emphasis).

18   Thus the Group μ paraphrase Jakobson's dictum as 'the projection of the principle of *similarity* from the paradigmatic axis onto the syntagmatic axis', *A General Rhetoric*, tr. Paul B. Burrell & Edgar M. Slotkin, Baltimore, 1981, p. 18 (my emphasis). They also write of a 'law of similarity', which they see as 'an imposition added to the sequence' (p. 11).

19   'My favorite topics', *Verbal Art*, p. 3.

20   Thus Jonathan Culler writes, after quoting Jakobson's dictum, 'In other words, the poetic use of language involves placing together in sequence items which are phonologically or grammatically related. Patterns formed by the repetition of similar items will be both more common and more noticeable in poetry than in other kinds of language', *Structuralist Poetics*, London, 1975, p. 56.

21   See Culler, *Structuralist Poetics*, Ch. 3. Jakobson's failure to be impressed is amusing:

A short time ago I was even asked the same question in print, by a lecturer at Oxford University, who had published a book, *Structuralist Poetics*, in which a chapter is devoted to my attempts at applying linguistics to poetics. The author made the experiment of taking a few lines out of one of my essays in order to interpret them from the point of view of poetics. The result was really extremely negative. I told him – I had a discussion with him in Oxford quite recently – that if it were a work of poetry, it would be an awfully bad poem. ('On poetic intentions and linguistic devices in poetry', *Verbal Art*, p. 70.)

That Jakobson should raise the issue of evaluation as a way out of this problem is not as surprising as might at first appear, as we shall see. He discusses the issue in Jakobson and Pomorska, *Dialogues*, but his defence is little more than an appeal to subjective impressions: 'The idea that it is possible to discover as many symmetrical properties as one wants is firmly contradicted by the concrete experience of analysis' (p. 118).

22   It is interesting to note that in discussing parallelism in music and painting, Jakobson is careful to qualify his position by a reference to the particular convention in force: 'In the musical art the correspondences of elements that are recognized, *in a given convention*, as mutually equivalent or in opposition to each other, constitute the principal, if not the only, semiotic value'; 'The laws of opposition and equivalence which govern the system of the spatial categories that are at work in a painting offer an eloquent example of similarities *imputed by the code of the school, in the epoch, of the nation*', 'A glance at the development of semiotics', in Jakobson, *The Framework of Language*, pp. 24, 25 (my emphases).

23   When Jakobson moves on to one of his favourite topics, sound-symbolism, a rather different claim emerges; if there were, as Jakobson believes there is, an 'undeniably objective' relation between a word's sound and its meaning which is reinforced in poetry (p. 372), then poetic language would be likely to narrow and constrain rather than complicate and generalise meaning.

24   Levin is very aware of this, acknowledging that 'it would be a mistake to conclude that the more couplings one finds or puts in a poem, the better is that poem'. But the only answer he has is in terms of 'the simultaneous action and interaction of all the other factors that operate in a poem' (*Linguistic Structures in Poetry*, p. 48), which sounds very much like a matter of traditional critical judgement and techniques of persuasion.

25   Tzvetan Todorov constructs a Bakhtinian model of the linguistic event to place side-by-side with Jakobson's, and quotes a passage from Medvedev attacking Jakobson's model for its static, simplified presentation of a changing, interacting complex; see *Mikhail Bakhtin: The Dialogical Principle*, tr. Wlad Godzich, Minneapolis, 1984, pp. 54–6.

26   'Poetry of grammar and grammar of poetry', first given as a paper in Russian in 1960, reprinted in *Verbal Art*, p. 42.

27   See *Structuralist Poetics*, pp. 56–8. Paul Kiparsky has suggested a limitation of the possible range of items in terms of the dictum: *the linguistic sames which are potentially relevant in poetry are just those which are potentially relevant in grammar* ('The role of linguistics in a theory of poetry', *Daedalus*, CII iii, Summer 1973, p. 235). While it is doubtless true that the perception of language is focused on those categorisations which are operative in normal linguistic structures, it is always open to a poet – or a culture – to produce a form of writing which makes use of other categorisations. The Renaissance placed the highest valuation on Latin and Greek verse organised in terms of the quantities of syllables, whereas these languages as they were spoken at this time did not possess quantitative distinctions of this kind (see Attridge, *Well-weighed Syllables: Elizabethan Verse in Classical Metres*, Cambridge, 1974). Kiparsky's careful use of 'potential' also leaves open a space for the determining role of cultural norms.

28   'Poetics of prose', *Verbal Art*, p. 171.

29   Quoted in 'Two poems by Puškin', *Verbal Art*, p. 47.

30   'Yeats' "Sorrow of Love" through the years', *Verbal Art*, p. 106.

31   *The Sound Shape of Language* (with Linda R. Waugh), Brighton, 1979, p. 228.

32   Roman Jakobson & Lawrence G. Jones, *Shakespeare's Verbal Art in 'Th' Expence of Spirit'*, The Hague, 1970, pp. 31, 32.

33   There is also an implication in Jakobson's phrasing that the *poet* is to be accorded admiration for the intricate work entailed in creating such an object, though this doesn't square very well with his insistence that his analyses make no assumptions about the consciousness with which any of these properties are imparted – see, for instance, 'Subliminal verbal patterning in poetry' and 'On poetic intentions and linguistic devices', both reprinted in *Verbal Art*. Commentators have often rewritten Jakobson's description of poetic language as though it referred to the act of composition; thus Terry Eagleton states, 'What happens in poetry ... is that we pay attention to "equivalences" in the process of *combining* words together as well as in selecting them: we string together words which are semantically or rhythmically or phonetically or in some other way equivalent', *Literary Theory: An Introduction*, Oxford, 1983, p. 99.

34   At times Jakobson's formulations come very close to Coleridge's; compare the former's statement – cited by Waugh as Jakobson's definition of a poem (*Verbal Art*, p. 148) – that a structure is 'not a mechanical agglomeration but a structural whole and the basic task is to reveal the inner ... laws of this system' with Coleridge's influential distinction (derived from A. W. Schlegel) between 'mechanical' and 'organic' form. Tzvetan Todorov has argued, in fact, that there is a chain of influence from Coleridge and the German Romantics via Poe, Baudelaire, and Mallarmé, whom Jakobson acknowledges as an important early source of ideas ('La poétique de Jakobson', in *Théories du symbole*, Paris, 1977, p. 340).

35   Jurij Tynjanov & Roman Jakobson, 'Problems in the study of literature and language', in Ladislav Matejka & Krystyna Pomorska (eds), *Readings in Russian Poetics: Formalist and Structuralist Views*, Cambridge, Mass., 1971, pp. 79–81. Other Jakobson texts from this period which show the same willingness to consider literature in its relation to the social and ideological environment are cited by Erlich (*Russian Formalism*, pp. 207–8, 257). See also Thomas G. Winner, 'Jan Mukařovský: the beginnings of structural and semiotic aesthetics', in Matejka (ed.), *Sound, Sign and Meaning*, p. 435.

36   'The conceptual basis of Prague Structuralism', p. 381, n. 48. See also Tony Bennett, *Formalism and Marxism*, (London, 1979) for a valuable discussion of the openness of Formalist arguments to a concern with the social determination of literature and literary value.

37   'The question of invariance in the midst of variation has been the dominant topic and methodological device underlying my diversified yet homogeneous research work', 'My favorite topics', *Verbal Art*, p. 3. Of course, to interpret a long and varied career as 'diversified yet homogeneous', given focus by a single quest, is itself an example of this motif in Jakobson's thought.

Language and the avant-garde

... As to the dialogue: I have rather broken with tradition in not making my characters catechists who sit asking foolish questions in order to elicit a smart reply. I have avoided the mathematically symmetrical construction of French dialogue and let people's brains work irregularly, as they do in actual life, where no topic of conversation is drained to the dregs, but one brain receives haphazard from the other a cog to engage with. Consequently my dialogue too wanders about, providing itself in the earlier scenes with material which is afterwards worked up, admitted, repeated, developed, and built up, like the theme in a musical composition.[1]

Again:

My souls (characters) are conglomerations from past and present stages of civilisation; they are excerpts from books and newspapers, scraps of humanity, pieces torn from festive garments which have become rags – just as the soul itself is a piece of patchwork.[2]

I take these descriptions of intention in writing from an unarguably modernist playwright who was moreover often seen, in the movements of the *avant-garde*, as a precedent: August Strindberg. Yet the descriptions occur in what is in effect his manifesto of naturalism, and this is my point in quoting them: as a challenge to certain tendencies in applied linguistics, and to forms of literary analysis seemingly derived from them, which have appropriated a selective version of modernism, and within this an internal and self-proving definition of the *avant-garde*, as a way of ratifying their own much narrower positions and procedures.

The most serious consequence of this appropriation is that what are actually polemical positions, some of them serious, on language and writing, can pass, however ironically, as historical descriptions of actual movements and formations: the summations *modernism* and *avant-garde* are, in most uses, obvious examples. For suppose we say, conventionally, that modernism begins in Baudelaire, or in the period of Baudelaire, and that the *avant-garde* begins around 1910, with the manifestos of the Futurists, we can still not say, of either supposed movement, that what we find in them is some specific and identifiable position about language, or about writing, of the kind offered by subsequent theoretical or pseudo-historical propositions.

Even at their most plausible — in a characteristic kind of definition by negative contrast, where the main stress is put on a common rejection of the representational character of language and thence of writing — there is not only an astonishing reduction of the diversity of actually antecedent writing practices and theories of language, but a quite falsely implied identification of actual modernist and *avant-garde* writing — with convenient slippages between the two loose terms — as based on attitudes to language which can be theoretically generalised, or at least made analogous, to what, borrowing the classifications, are themselves offered as modernist or *avant-garde* linguistic and critical positions and methodologies.

My challenge in quoting Strindberg, in his naturalist manifesto, is that he was evidently putting forward a version of character — as a 'conglomeration', an 'excerpt', 'pieces torn' and 'scraps' — which has been widely seen as characteristic of modernist writing and indeed of more general theory, together with a method of irregular writing, 'built up like the theme in a musical composition', also widely identified as 'modernist', which are yet quite unmistakably based on an affiliation to, even a desire to represent, actual social processes: 'I have ... let people's brains work irregularly, *as they do in actual life*'. One is even reminded of Ibsen's words, when he decided to abandon dramatic verse and cultivate 'the very much more difficult art of writing the genuine, plain language spoken in real life'.[3] 'My desire was to depict human beings and therefore I would not make them speak the language of the gods': Ibsen, who, if it is a question of movements, was so influential on Joyce.[4]

I am not of course saying that modernism was a naturalism, though dramatic naturalism was indeed one of its major early manifestations. But I am saying, certainly of modernism, and even, where I shall concentrate, of the *avant-garde*, that actual positions and practices are very much more diverse than their subsequent ideological presentations, and that we shall misunderstand and betray a century of remarkable experiments if we go on trying to flatten them to contemporary theoretical and quasi-theoretical positions.

For the present analysis I am accepting the conventional delineation of the *avant-garde* as a complex of movements from around 1910 to the late 1930s. In real practice there are no such convenient break-points. What is almost the only distinguishing feature, and even then incompletely, is less a matter of actual writing than of successive formations which challenged not only the art institutions but the institution of Art, or Literature, itself, typically in a broad programme which included, though in diverse forms, the overthrow and remaking of existing society. That certainly cuts it off from later formations which continued its technical practices, and its accompanying aggressiveness marks at least a change in tone from earlier formations which had pioneered some of its methods and which, in at least some cases, had comparably broad social and even political intentions. Within the irregularities and overlaps of any cultural history − its repeated co-presence of various forms of the emergent with forms of the residual and the dominant − that definition of period and type has a working usefulness.

Yet we cannot then jump to its farthest manifestations: to the phonetic poems and the automatic writing, and the body language of the Theatre of Cruelty. What we have, instead, to distinguish is a set of tendencies, in writing, which in this place and that had specific but in no way inevitable outcomes. Thus the movement of verbal composition towards what was seen as the condition of music has no predestined outcome in Dada. The movement of verbal composition towards the creation of what were seen as images has no predestined outcome in Imagist verses. Rather, in the diverse movements which are summarised as modernism or as the *avant-garde*, we have to look at radical differences of practice within what can be seen, too hastily, as a common orientation, and then relate both practices and orientation to certain uses and concepts of language and writing which historically and formally belong to neither.

The central issue may be that which was defined, ideologically, by Shklovsky, as 'the resurrection of the word'.[5] At the level of summary, this idea is often now used as a core definition of literary modernism, and is further associated with certain interpretations of the 'sign' in linguistics. Yet it was Shklovsky's colleague among the early Russian formalists, Eikhenbaum, who wrote that 'the basic slogan uniting the initial group was the emancipation of the word from the shackles of the philosophical and religious tendencies with which the symbolists were possessed'.[6] The local observation is just, yet it was precisely the Symbolists who had most clearly introduced the new emphasis on the intrinsic value of the poetic word. A word seen in this way was not a signal to something beyond it, but a signifier in its own material properties which, by its poetic use, embodied, rather than expressed or represented, a value. It is then true that this value, for the Symbolists, was of a particular kind: the poetic word as the ideoglyph of mystery or of myth. In some later tendencies of this sort, for example the Acmeists or the Yeats of the Dancer plays, this embodiment of the poetic word is refracted through existing literary or legendary material, a more specialised and often more exotic manifestation of the more general − and much older − use of classical myth and literature as a source of symbolic, self-valuable units of meaning. We can then go on to see the Formalist 'resurrection' or 'emancipation' of the word as a secularisation, a demystification, of the 'poetic word' of the Symbolists. What was being proposed instead was still a specific 'literary language', but now defined in terms of the word as empirical phonetic material. Yet it was then not simply the specific ideological freight of the Symbolist 'poetic word' that was being rejected, but, so far as possible, not only its ideological but any or all of its received semantic freight: the poetic word then being not simply a grammatical unit but available in what came to be called a 'transrational sound image'.

Moreover this was already a matter of practice. In the early years of the century, partially in Apollinaire and more directly in the poems which became known as *bruitiste*, verse composed as pure sound was being written in several European languages. The eventual outcome, along this very specialised line of development, was the phonetic poem, evident among some of the Futurists but more especially in Dadaism. In 1917, following a common earlier analogy, Hugo Ball wrote that 'the decision to let go of language in poetry, just like letting go of the object in painting, is imminent', and he had indeed just written his *Gadji Beri Bimba*. His own account of its public reading is instructive:

> I began in a slow and solemn way
> *gadji beri bimba glandridi launa lonni cadori ...*
> It was then that I realised that my voice, lacking other
> possibilities, was adopting the ancestral cadence of priestly
> laments, that style of chanting the mass in the
> catholic churches of East and West:
> *zimzim urallala zimzim urallala zimzim zanzibar*
> *zimzall zam.*[7]

Moreover it was done to drums and bells.

There is a sense in which the most extreme practitioners of these new theories of language and writing are markedly more acceptable than the contemporary makers of formulae. For what was being tested in practice, even where tested to destruction, was actually a major element of very old as well as very new kinds of verbal performance. The relapse to the rhythms of the mass in the middle of an outraging Dadaist spectacle is not only funny; it is, like the sudden locating appearance of Zanzibar, a reminder of how deeply constituted, socially, language always is, even when the decision has been made to abandon its identifiable semantic freight.

For of course the use of material sound and of rhythm, in both general communication and the many forms of drama, narrative, lyric, ritual and so on, is in no way a modernist discovery and is, moreover, never reducible, in another direction, to simplified accounts of meaning in language. From the Welsh *cynghanedd* to medieval alliterative verse it has been an element not only of practice but even of rules. In less ordered forms it has been virtually a constant component of many different kinds of oral composition and of writing, from dramatic blank verse to the nonsense-poem (that significantly popular nineteenth-century English form which certain phonetic poems much resemble). What is different, in some modernist and *avant-garde* theory and practice, is the attempt to rationalise it for specific ideological purposes of which the most common − though it has never been more than an element of these movements − is the deliberate exclusion or devaluing of all or any referential meaning.

We have already seen, in Hugo Ball, the false analogy with renunciation of the 'object' in painting. A true analogy would have been a decision by painters to give up paint. But we must go beyond these pleasantries to the substantial case which is at the root of so many of these diverse movements and indeed of some of their predecessors. This case is primarily historical, underlying the diverse formations and practices, but also underlying many of the developments in the study of language which, at an altogether later stage, are now used to interpret or recommend them. Yet the complexity of this history − indeed that which makes it history − is evident at once if we abstract and then offer to construe the substantial position from which so many of these initiatives were made. Indeed the difficulty of formulating it is, in a real sense, its history.

If I say, for example, as so many of these writers did, that language should be creative, as against its contemporary condition, I can be reasonably certain, given a sufficient diversity of audience, of being understood as saying at least seven different things: not only because of the manifold possibilities of 'creative' but because the 'contemporary condition' has been historically understood as at least one of the following: a state of active repression of human possibilities; a state of antiquated discourse and composition; a state in which language is dulled and exhausted by custom and habit or reduced to the merely prosaic; a state in which everyday, ordinary language makes literary composition difficult or impossible; a state in which a merely instrumental language blocks access to an underlying spiritual or unconscious reality; a state in which a merely social language obstructs the most profound individual expression. There are probably other variants and accompaniments, as there are certainly other slogans. But the extraordinary historical generalisation of what may − indeed I think must − still be grasped as the underlying position is too important to allow any intellectual retreat. What is being argued, in these diverse ways, leading to so many diverse formations and practices, has to be not summarised but explored.

It is only in one special outcome of this argument, in one part of modernism and a rather larger part of the *avant-garde*, that the difficulties and tensions are in effect collapsed. This is in the (themselves varied) attempts either to dispense with language altogether, as too hopelessly compromised and corrupted by this or that version of its condition, or, failing that, to do what Artaud proposed, 'substituting for the spoken language a different language of nature, whose expressive possibilities will be equated to verbal language'.[8] In straight terms this is vaudeville, but more practically we can see that a key element in both modernism and the *avant-garde* was a deliberate runningtogether, cross-fertilisation, even integration of what had been hitherto seen as different arts. Thus the aspiration to develop language towards the condition of music, or towards the immediacy and presence of visual imagery or performance could, if it failed (as it was bound to) in its original terms, be taken on into music or painting or performance art, or, significantly, into film of an *avant-garde* kind. These developments, however, go beyond the present argument. For though Apollinaire apostrophised 'man in search of a new language to which the grammarian of any tongue will have nothing to say',[9] and looked forward to the time when 'the phonograph and the cinema having become the only forms of "print" in use, poets will have a freedom unknown up till now',[10] he continued for his own part in his own written compositions. Even Artaud, much later in this development, continued to write, if only, as he claimed, for illiterates, years after he had conceived, in the Theatre of Cruelty, a kind of dramatic performance in which bodily presence and action, a dynamic of movement and image, would take decisive priority over what remained of dramatic language: an initiative which has been continued and even in some respects − ironically even in commercial cinema − generalised.

Thus we can return to the underlying history of direct positions in the practice of language, in relation to that almost neutral term, the 'contemporary condition'. 'Almost neutral', since for the Symbolists, for example, the so-called condition was not contemporary but permanent, though acute in the crises of their time. This is, incidentally, a way in which, with a certain effect of paradox, the Symbolists can be distinguished from one main sense of modernism. Their ways of writing verse were new, often radically so, but it was less among them than among their very different contemporaries, the Naturalists, that there came the familiar challenging rhetoric of the new, the *modern*, which required a new art: new bottles for this new wine, as Strindberg put it in his arguments for naturalism.[11] The idealist substratum of symbolism was the belief that the world transmitted by the senses − but then by all the senses and most profoundly in synaesthesia − should be understood as revealing a *spiritual* universe. The symbolist poem would then be an enabling form of such revelation, a mode of realised *correspondance* in Baudelaire's sense, in which the 'poetic word' becomes a verbal symbol, at once material in embodiment and metaphysical in its revelation of a spiritual but still sensual reality.

This concept was related, linguistically, to ideas of the 'inner form' of a word − indeed its internal creative capacity − as defined, for example, by Potebnia. It was often supported from the established idea of the distinctive 'inner forms' of languages, corresponding to the inner life of their speakers, as argued as early as Humboldt. This 'inner form' had then to be, as it were, discovered, released, embodied in the 'poetic word': and especially then by poets: the basis for speaking, as they did, of a 'literary language'. Within this whole concept these are already, one can say, distinguishable metaphysical and historical bearings: distinguishable but in practice ordinarily fused and confused. For the intention is metaphysical but the occasion can still be defined as the 'contemporary', or in that loose grand way the 'modern', crisis of life and society.

Characteristically, in the Symbolists, as clearly in Baudelaire and again in Apollinaire, this form of poetic revelation involved a fusion of present synaesthetic experience with the recovery of a nameable, tangible past which was yet 'beyond' or 'outside' time. And versions of this form of practice have continued to be important in many works which do not formally carry the specific marks of Symbolism as an identifiable historical movement. It is evident, for example, in the visionary and legendary Yeats and, in a different way, in Eliot, who is so often taken, in English, as the exemplary modernist poet but who in this respect, as in others, can be more precisely defined, in an idealist as well as a historical sense, as quintessentially Ancient and Modern.

And we have then only to go across from that whole tendency to the Futurists, with their wholesale rejection of any trace of the past, indeed, as Marinetti put it, with their campaigning 'modernolatry', to know the profound disjunctions which the usual summary of Modernism papers over. For now 'literary language', and indeed the whole institution and existing practice of literature, were the shackles which these heralds of the new time must break. Not an 'inner form' but the 'freedom' of words is what is now celebrated, for they are to be hurled in the shock of action or of play against a sclerotic literary or social order.

To be sure there still can be appeal to primeval energies against the decayed forms. This goes on into the Expressionists. It is a main theme of Brecht's *Baal*.

But there are also more specific changes in the handling of language, for example, Khlebnikov's use of his studies of the linguistic history of words to propose a form of release in the coming of new verbal forms, as in the famous poem the 'Incantation to Laughter', where the whole composition is a series of variations on the Russian word *smekh* = laughter. Mayakowsky's 'A Cloud in Trousers' in a broader way offers to break up, in a single operation, the habitual expectations, collocations and connections of both existing poems and existing perceptions. Significantly, it was from this Futurist practice that the early Formalists derived their concepts not only of the word as grammatical unit – the linguistic element of their arguments – but as a 'transrational sound image' – the literary element or potential. This can be connected – though not by direct influence – with the Bruitiste poems and with the phonetic poems of Dada, but it was to have much longer and wider though perhaps equally surprising effects.

For there is already an underlying dichotomy in this understanding of 'the word'. Whether as 'grammatical unit' or as 'transrational sound image' it can be projected in two quite different directions: on the one hand towards active composition, in which these units are arranged and combined, by conscious literary strategies or devices, into works; or, on the other hand, taking an ideological cue from 'transrational', into procedures much resembling traditional accounts of 'inspiration', in which the creative act occurs beyond the 'ordinary self' and more substantial, more original, energies are tapped.

It is interesting to reflect on the itinerary of this latter conception: from metaphysical notions of literal possession by gods or spirits in the moment of true utterance, through the conventional personifications of inspiring muses or great predecessors, ancestor poets, into the Romantic version of creative access to the new all-purpose personification of Nature, and finally – or is it finally? – to creative access to 'the unconscious'. Certainly we have to notice how commonly, in later modernism and in sectors of the *avant-garde*, both idealist notions of the Life Force (as in Bergson) and psychoanalytic notions of the Unconscious (as derived from Freud but perhaps more commonly from Jung) functioned in practice as modernised versions of these very old assumptions and processes.

The most relevant example, in *avant-garde* practice, is of course the 'automatic writing' of the Surrealists, which was based on one, or perhaps several, of the positions about language and its contemporary condition which we have identified. 'Everyday' and 'ordinary' language, or sometimes 'the language of a decadent bourgeois society', blocked true creative activity, or (for another different formulation was also employed) prevented us embodying – almost one can say 'representing' – the true process of thought. Thus Breton had said, in a still general way: 'words are likely to group themselves according to particular affinities, recreating the world in accordance with its old pattern at any moment'.[12] But this still broad position was sharpened to a more sweeping rejection: 'we pretend not to notice that ... the logical mechanism of the sentence appears more and more incapable of releasing the emotional shock in man which actually gives some true value to his life'.[13] And so to 'automatic writing': 'a pure psychic automatism by which one proposes to express, either verbally or in writing, or in any other way, the real functioning of thought: dictation by thought, in the absence of any control exercised by reason, and without any aesthetic or moral considerations'.[14] The terms of this rhetoric, confused and confusing as they ought to be seen, are now in many ways naturalised: that highly specific 'thought'/'reason' dichotomy, for example. Yet one can look back on 'automatic writing', for all the meagreness of its actual results, with a certain respect for its ambitions of practice, as distinguishable from its much looser though more suggestive ideological context. For language was being simultaneously identified with the blocking of 'true consciousness' and, to the extent that it could emancipate itself from its imprisoning everyday forms and, beyond that, from the received forms of 'literature', as itself the medium of the idealised 'pure consciousness'.

One way out of this contradiction was the move to surrealist film, but most writers stayed in the double position and then of course at once encountered the obvious and ominous question of 'communication'. Theoretically it might have been said that if psychic automatism could reach 'the real functioning of thought' it would be transparently, even universally, communicable, yet the means of psychic automatism were, in practice, if not alienating, at least distancing. Artaud could go on to say: 'The break between us and the world is well established. We speak not to be understood, but to our inner selves'.[15] Thus the purpose of writing (as we have since often heard) is not communication but illumination (a contrast which seems necessarily to modify the second term to self-illumination). There can be an emphasis – which indeed became a culture − on the experience itself, rather than on any of the forms of embodying or communicating it.

Automatic writing had been achieved, by the internal account, in somnambulist or trancelike states: drugs were one group of means to this state; several varieties of esoteric, mystical and transcendental philosophy another. Breton himself distinguished the poetic process as empirical; it did not 'presuppose an invisible universe beyond the network of the visible world'. Yet this older form of contrast − which would hold as a distinction, one way or the other, as late as the Symbolists − was now insignificant, within the ideological substitution of 'the unconscious' which could comfortably embrace 'reality' and 'hidden reality', 'experience' and 'dream', 'neurosis' and 'madness', 'psychic trace' and 'primal myth', in a dazzling shift of new and old concepts which could be selected as purpose served.

What came through, at its most serious, were unforeseen yet convincing or at least striking collocations, but this much more often in visual imagery than in language. The presumptive dismissal of 'everyday' content found a later rationalisation, for example in Adorno, in the idealisation of form as authentic − art-defining − image. But there was also a broad highway into the process rather than the product: the drug-experience as such; the esoteric and the occult as direct, but not artistic, practices; the support looked for in mystical philosophies becoming the new practice of the meditative and transcendental rather than the 'poetic' or 'creative' word.

That was one general way, later dividing, from the proposition of the transrational sound-image. Within Surrealist practice, for all the specificity of its forms, there was still construction through, if not from, the word. The other general way took construction in language more directly, but then again in diverse ways.

For the Expressionists, in writing, the emphasis was not on transcending contradictions − as in Breton's remark that 'Surrealism would have liked nothing better than to allow the mind to jump the barrier raised by contradictions such as action-dream, reason-madness, and sensation-representation'[16] but on raising them to a principle of form: sharply polarised states of mind, angrily polarised social positions, whose conflict was then the dynamic of truth. The discursive language which they identified in Naturalism − whether as reflection or discussion of a situation or problem, or as the social process which Strindberg had defined as the irregular engagement of minds or which Chekhov had realised in his writing of failures of communication, that negative group which yet, as a group, shared a social situation of which they needed to speak and which others should see and understand − all that kind of writing of speech was rejected, within the polar contradictions, for what is in effect the language of the cry, the exclamation.

In its early stages especially, the Expressionist word is indeed 'transrational', but for conflict rather than access. The idea of primeval energy in the cry is again evident, and in some later Expressionist work − in Toller and Brecht, for example – the cry is a consciously liberating, indeed revolutionary moment: the cry can become a shout or the still inarticulate cry a protest; that cry which fights to be heard above the news bulletins, the headlines, the false political speeches of a world in crisis; even the cry which can become a slogan, a fixed form, to shout as a means to collective action.

That direction in language sought, in its own terms, to intervene in the social process and to change reality by struggle. It is then at most a distant cousin of the 'transrational sound-image', though some relationship is there.

Yet this is one more case in which a specific and specialising development of actual writing practices cannot usefully be reduced to the general propositions about language which, in their own but different terms, were becoming influential. Thus we can see some relationship between certain versions of the 'poetic word' or the 'transrational sound-image' and certain modern linguistic definitions of the 'sign': indeed 'sign', as a term, with its available free associations to 'icon' or 'ideogram' or some visual representation, sometimes points us that way, and we can usefully recall Saussure's hesitations about it, since it can blur the necessary choice between 'sign' as *signifier*, a unit within an autonomous language system, and 'sign' in its very combination of 'signifier' and 'signified' as pointing both ways, to the language-system and to a reality which is not language.[16] But that is a question within the distinctive area of linguistics, and there is little point – indeed there is some obvious danger – in assimilating one or other version of the linguistic sign to the specific – and in fact diverse – concepts of the sound-image that were available to certain strategies in writing.

Thus, if we look back to the early Formalists, we find a failure to resolve this problem as it passes from linguistic definition to literary analysis or recommendation. To understand the word as empirical phonetic material is indeed a basis for a strategy of 'defamiliarisation' or 'estrangement', and it is true that exclusion of received or indeed any semantic content opens possibilities of semantic exploration as well as our old friends the phonetic poem or its upstart cousin, cross-cultural assonance: 'jung and easily freudened'.

Yet the Formalist position, as it came through into an influential tendency in literary theory, was a disastrous narrowing of the very facts to which it pointed. It became tied to rejections of what were called 'content' and 'representation', and even more damagingly of 'intention', which actually missed the point of active literary uses of the very quality that Volosinov called 'multiaccentual', an inherent semantic openness, corresponding to a still active social process, from which new meanings and possible meanings can be generated, at least in certain important classes of words and sentences.

Yet even that was still a linguistic proposition. The Formalists, though tying their linguistic position to certain kinds of literary practice – kinds heavily influenced by the practice of Futurism though most of their illustrative examples were from much earlier works and, of course, from folk-tales – limited the true potential of the position by a characteristic error. Under the spell of their own selected examples, of valued but highly specific uses, they forgot that every act of composition in writing, indeed every utterance, at once moves into specific processes which are no longer in that way open: which indeed, as acts, even in the most seemingly bizarre cases, necessarily have 'content' and 'intention' and which may, in any of many thousands of ways, even in these terms 'represent'. To retain the useful abstraction of basic linguistic material, which is properly the ground of linguistic analysis, in arguments which offer to deal with what is already and inevitably a wide range of practices, in which that material is for this and that purpose being used, has been to misdirect several generations of analysts and even, though fewer in number, some writers.

And perhaps, finally, there is more than a wide range of practices; perhaps, through the many complications, overlaps and uncertainties, there have been, through this period of active innovation and experiment, two fundamental directions which we can at least provisionally distinguish.

We can begin by noticing the two active senses of 'modern' in this context: 'modern' as a historical time, with its specific and then changing features; but 'modern' also as what Medvedev and Bakhtin, criticising it, called 'eternal contemporaneity', that apprehension of the 'moment' which overrides and excludes, practically and theoretically, the material realities of change, until all consciousness and practice are 'now'.

From the first sense, with its grasp of changes that were factually remaking society (a grasp that was of course variable, selecting this or that group of features, in this or that movement), a sense of the future, and then properly of an *avant-garde*, was extensively derived. From the second sense there was, and is, something else: a generalisation of the human condition, including generalisations of both art and language, and through them of consciousness. The 'modern', in this sense, is then either a set of conditions which allow this universal condition to be at last recognised, after the tied ideologies of earlier times, or else, as in the earliest movements, a set of circumstances in which the universal and true nature of life is especially threatened by a modernity which must be opposed or evaded: a modernism, as so often, against modernity: not an *avant* but an *arrière* garde: the literally reactionary tendency which should have culminated in Eliot.

Correspondingly there appear to be two basic contradictory attitudes towards language: that which, engaging with received forms and the possibilities of new practice, treats language as material in a social process; and that other which, as in several *avant-garde* movements, sees it as blocking or making difficulties for authentic consciousness: 'the need for expression ... born from the very impossibility of expression';[19] or what Artaud seems to mean when he writes: 'my thought abandons me at every step – from the simple fact of thought to the external fact of its materialisation in words'.[20]

Each of these positions is, we can say, a modernism, but we can then also say that while the first is modernist in both theory and practice, the latter is modernist in practice, but in its underlying theory, its finally intransigent idealism, at best a finding of new terms for the 'ineffable': even anti-theological, anti-metaphysical terms for that same 'ineffable', as they would of course now have to be.

The same basic contrast, within modernism, is evident in the forms of specification of 'the modern' itself: on the one hand those forms which engage with history and with specific social formations; on the other hand those which point to certain general features, approvingly or disapprovingly: features which then function in effect as 'background' to the foregrounded 'creative act'. Thus we are told, in an enumeration, of the facts of the city, of new technology, of changes in work and in class, of the weakening and collapse of traditional faiths, and so on, for the listing can be endless. Yet any or all of these probable features has to be seen as having influenced whole populations, whole social processes, whereas modernism and the *avant-garde*, in any of their forms, have never involved, as producers or as publics, more than minorities; often very small minorities. To be sure there is an internal way of meeting this objection: that while 'mass life' may flow this way or that, the significant movements are always those of minorities. That conceit has been heard from embattled innovators, where it is understandable, to privileged and even institutionalised groups, which when they are also attaching themselves to an *avant-garde* become absurd.

What matters, still, is not general features but specification. Certainly the city is relevant, and specifically the city as a metropolis. It is a very striking feature of many modernist and *avant-garde* movements that they were not only located in the great metropolitan centres but that so many of their members were immigrants into these centres, where in some new ways all were strangers. Language, in such situations, could appear as a new kind of fact: either simply as 'medium', aesthetic or instrumental, since its naturalised continuity with a persistent social settlement was unavailable; or, of course, as sytem: the distanced, even the alien fact. Moreover, these cities had become the capitals of imperialism. The old hegemony of capital over its provinces was extended over a new range of disparate, often wholly alien and exotic, cultures and languages. The evolutionary and family versions of language which were the basis of language studies in the period of formation of nation-states and confederacies were then replaced by studies of universal systems within which specificities were either, as in much literary practice, exotica, or were the local, momentary, and superficial features of more fundamental structures.

There was then both gain and loss: new possibilities of analysis beyond the naturalised forms; new kinds of false transfer of these analytic positions to practice and recommendations for practice. Within these specific conditions, various formations emerged: in political aspirations to a corresponding universality – the revolutionary groups; or in reactionary redoubts, preserving a literary language in either of its forms – a pure national language or a language of authenticity against the banalities or repressions of everyday language use.

But finally, and still much the most difficult to analyse, there were the formations of certain special innovations, and these most marked − to use shorthand for what would need to be a very complex socio-historical analysis − in three types of group: those who had come to the metropolis from colonised or capitalised regions; those who had come from what were already linguistic borderlands, where a dominant language coexisted with the practice or the memory of an older native language; and those who came as exiles − an increasingly important kind of formation − from rejecting or rejected political regimes. For in each of these cases, though in interestingly different ways, an old language had been marginalised or suppressed, or else simply left behind, and the now dominant language either interacted with its sub-ordinate for new language effects or was seen as, in new ways, both plastic and arbitrary: an alien but accessible system which had both power and potential yet was still not, as in most earlier formations, however experimental, the language or the possible language of a people but now the material of groups, agencies, fractions, specific works, its actual society a complex of writers and game-players, translators and signwriters, interpreters and makers of paradoxes, cross-cultural innovators and jokers. The actual social processes, that is to say, involved not only an Apollinaire, a Joyce, an Ionesco, a Beckett, but also, as Joyce recognised in Bloom, many thousands of extempore dealers and negotiators and persuaders: moreover not even, reliably, these as distinct and separate groups.

And indeed this was bound to be so, since the shift was occurring within accelerating general processes of mobility, dislocation and paranational communication which, over the decades, appeared to convert what had been an experience of small minorities to what, at certain levels, and especially in its most active sites and most notably in the United States, could be offered as a definition of modernity itself.

There was then a now familiar polarisation, of an ideological kind: between on the one hand the 'old, settled' language and its literary forms and on the other hand the 'new, dynamic' language and its necessarily new forms. Yet at each of these poles there is a necessary distinction. The cultural forms of the 'old, settled' language (always, in practice, never settled, however old) were indeed, at one level, the imposed forms of a dominant class and its discourse. But this was never the only level. Uses of a language of connection and of forms of intended communication remained an emphasis and an intention of other social groups, in both class and gender, whose specific existence had been blurred or contained within the imposed 'national' forms. Similarly, the cultural forms of the 'new, dynamic' language were never only experimental or liberating. Within the real historical dynamics they could be, and were, notably and deliberately manipulative and exploiting. The widespread adoption and dilution of *avant-garde* visual and linguistic modes by advertising and publicity agencies is only the most evident example; overtly commercial paranational art includes many more interesting, if less obvious, cases. There is then a practical linkage of a selective definition of modernity with the asymmetries of political and economic domination and subordination. This cannot be rendered back to isolated formal or technical levels.

Thus what we have really to investigate is not some single position of language in the *avant garde*, or language in modernism. On the contrary, we need to identify a range of distinct and in many cases actually opposed formations, as these have materialised in language. This requires us, obviously, to move beyond such conventional definitions as '*avant-garde* practice' or 'the modernist text'. Formal analysis can contribute to this, but only if it is firmly grounded in formational analysis.

Thus the 'multivocal' or 'polyphonic', even the 'dialogic', as features of texts, have to be referred to social practice if they are to be rigorously construed. For they can range from the innovatory inclusion of a diversity of voices and socio-linguistic relationships (as in that remarkable historical instance of English Renaissance popular drama, in an earlier period of dislocation and offered integration) to what is no more in effect, but also in intention, than the self-absorbed miming of others: a proliferation and false interaction of class and gender linguistic stereotypes from an indifferent and enclosing technical consciousness. The innovatory inclusion can be traced to its formation, but the isolated technique is more usually traceable to its agency, in direct or displaced domination. Similarly, the important inclusion, within a highly literate and culturally allusive context, of the active range and body of the everyday vernacular has to be distinguished not only formally but formationally from that rehearsal and miming of what is known in the relevant agencies as *Vox Pop*: that linguistic contrivance for political and commercial reach and control. The polar instances may be relatively easy to distinguish, but the complex range between them demands very precise analysis: some of it made more difficult by the facts of indeterminacy between 'literary texts' and 'general cultural discourse' which ironically, but then with very different intentions, elements in the *avant garde* had worked to bring about.

Moreover, and finally, the work can be done only if we begin moving beyond those received theoretical positions, in applied linguistics and derived forms of literary analysis, which have now to be seen as at many levels internal to these very processes; often, indeed, repeating, in what appear more formal ways, the operational manifesto phrases of specific *avant-garde* formations, though they offer to be independently explanatory of them and indeed of most other practices. Such positions are not collabnorators in the necessary work but in effect agents of its indefinite − its 'eternally contemporary' − postponement. On the other hand the history and practice of these same general movements, reviewed to disclose in some new ways the profound connections between formations and forms, remain sources of inspiration and of strength.

Notes

1 August Strindberg, Preface to *Lady Julie*, in *Five Plays*, Berkeley, 1981, p. 71.

2 *Ibid., p. 67.*

3 Henrik Ibsen, ed. W. Archer, *Collected Works*, London, 1906–8, VI, p. xiv.

4 *Ibid.*

5 V. B. Shklovsky, in Striedter & Sempel (eds), *Texte der Russischen Formalisten*, Munich, 1972, II, p. 13.

6 B. M. Eikhenbaum, 'La théorie de la "méthode formelle"', in *Théorie de la littérature* (ed. and tr. Tzvetan Todorov), Paris, 1965, p. 39.

7 Cit. M. Sanouillet, *Dada à Paris*, Paris, 1965, pp. 70 *et seq.*

8 A. Artaud, *The Theatre and its Double*, New York, 1958, p. 110.

9 G. Apollinaire, ed. M. Décaudin, *Oeuvres complètes*, Paris, 1965–66, III, p. 901.

10 G. Apollinaire, 'La Victoire', in *Calligrammes* (12th edn.), Paris, 1945.

11 Preface to *Lady Julie*, p. 64.

12 A. Breton, *Manifestes du surréalisme*; Coll. Idées, 23, Paris, 1963, p. 37.

13 A. Breton, *Point du jour*, Paris, 1934, p. 24.

14 *Manifestes du surréalisme*, p. 109.

15 A. Artaud, *Oeuvres complètes*, Paris, 1961, I, p. 269.

16 *Entretiens: 1913–1952*, Paris, 1952, p. 283.

17 Cf. R. Godel, *Les sources manuscrites du 'Cours de linguistique générale' de F. de Saussure*, Geneva, Paris, 1957, p. 192.

18 V. Volosinov, *Marxism and the Philosophy of Language*, New York, 1973.

19 G. Picon, *L'Usage de la lecture*, Paris, 1961, II, p. 191.

20 *Oeuvres complètes*, I, p. 20.

3 *Mary Louise Pratt*

Linguistic Utopias

We are in the process of creating a new civilization in which, for the first time, people everywhere are beginning to take part in the events that are shaping our common future. The realization of the dream of world-wide communication and the growing belief that men *can* plan for change are opening new potentialities for human relationships.
(Margaret Mead, 'One world, but which language?' *Redbook Magazine*, April 1966)

A language that works has been shaped by men and women, old people and little children, intelligent people and dunces, people with good memories and people with poor memories, those who pay attention to form and those who pay attention to sound, and people with all the diversity of interests present in their culture over generations. This very multiplicity of speakers creates the redundancy that makes a language flexible and intelligible to all different kinds of people who are its speakers at any time.
(ibid.)

On the fourth of July 1986, as this paper was in preparation, an enormous celebration was held in the United States to commemorate the centennial of the Statue of Liberty. 'It will include,' exulted the London *Times* (2 July 1986), '60,000 boats in New York Harbour, 3,100 dinners at $5,000 a plate, 22 of the world's tallest sailing ships on parade, 76 trombones in the all-American collegiate marching band, 300 Jazzercise ladies in leotards, 150 fiddlers, 200 dancing Elvis Presley look-alikes, and the largest fireworks display ever mounted.' At the time, one was tempted to undertake a neopoetic analysis of this event – as a Baudrillardian simulation re-enacting a lost form of patriotism, or as a next step in the elevation of high consumption and mass media to the status of official culture, or perhaps as the grandest ever projection of the principle of equivalence from the axis of selection into the axis of combination.

For my purposes here, however, it was more helpful to recall the original dedication of the Statue of Liberty a hundred years before. On that occasion, according to historian Leslie Allen (1985), a sizeable number of male dignitaries and two or three of their wives gathered round the base of the statue to perform the official dedication, while members of the New York City Women's Suffrage Association circled the island in a rented boat protesting the event. In a statement issued separately, the suffragists declared themselves amused that the statue of a woman should be raised to symbolise liberty in a country where women lacked even the most minimal political rights.

The imagined community

I would like to hold on to that picture of the statue surrounded by dignitaries surrounded by suffragists, as a parodic image of a kind of linguistics I propose to talk about here under the label 'linguistics of community'. This phrase is intended to underscore a utopian dimension shared by a good deal of modern linguistics, including what are sometimes called its 'critical' varieties. I use the term *community* here in the interesting sense suggested by Benedict Anderson in his book *Imagined Communities: Reflections on the Origin and Spread of Nationalism* (1983). Anderson observes that with the possible (but only possible) exception of 'primordial villages of face to face contact', human communities exist as imagined entities in which people 'will never know most of their fellow-members, meet them or even hear of them, yet in the minds of each lives the image of their communion'. 'Communities are distinguished', Anderson goes on to say, 'not by their falsity/genuineness, but by the style in which they are imagined. Javanese villagers have always known that they are connected to people they have never seen, but these ties were once imagined particularistically — as indefinitely stretchable nets of kinship and clientship. Until quite recently, the Javanese language had no word meaning the abstraction "society"' (p. 15).

What emerged 'quite recently', is of course the modern nation-state, an imagined community in whose origin and character Anderson is particularly interested. He proposes three features that characterise the 'style' in which the modern nation is imagined. First it is imagined as *limited* by 'finite, if elastic, boundaries'; second, it is imagined as *sovereign*; and third it is imagined as *community*, a 'deep, horizontal comradeship', a 'fraternity'. 'Ultimately', says Anderson, 'it is this fraternity [the genderedness of the term seems intended] that makes it possible over the past two centuries, for so many millions of people not so much to kill as willingly to die for such limited imaginings' (p. 16). As this image suggests, the nation-community is embodied metonymically in the finite, sovereign, fraternal person of the citizen-soldier.

Anderson believes that the European bourgeoisies are distinguished by their ability to 'achieve solidarity on an essentially imagined basis' (p. 74) on a scale far greater than previous élites. Literature and the linguistics of writing play a central role in his argument. Anderson maintains, as have others, that the main instrument that made bourgeois nationbuilding projects possible was print capitalism. The commercial circulation of books in the various print vernaculars, he argues, was what first created the invisible élite networks that would eventually constitute themselves and those they dominated as nations. (Estimates are that 180 million books were put into circulation in Europe between the years 1500 and 1600 alone). In the eighteenth century there flowered the novel and the newspaper, and two 'forms of imagining' which 'provided the technical means for 're-presenting' the kind of imagined community that is the nation' (p.30). Both these print forms present worlds in which multiple story lines are pursued discontinuously and simultaneously, connected only by their adjacency, and totalised in the imaginations of omniscient narrators or readers.

Now Anderson does not underscore this point, but the three characteristics he mentions, limitedness, sovereignty and community, make clear that the 'style of imagining' of modern nations is strongly utopian. I mean this in both the particularistic sense that they are imagined as islands, as discrete and sovereign social entities, and in the more general sense that the imagined version is an idealisation, embodying values like fraternity, equality or liberty, which the societies profess but, as the suffragists were pointing out, they have utterly failed to realise.

This prototype of the modern nation as imagined community is, I would like to suggest, mirrored in linguistics's imagined object of study, the speech community. Put another way, Anderson's limited, sovereign, horizontal brotherhood is the image in which the speech community often gets conceived in modern linguistics. Indeed, it makes sense to see a good deal of linguistic description, of both critical and 'uncritical' kinds, as engaged in producing this imagined utopian entity. Many commentators have pointed out how our modern linguistics of language, code, and competence posits a unified and homogeneous social world in which language exists as a shared patrimony – as a device, precisely, for imagining community. The prototype or unmarked case of language is generally taken in linguistics to be the speech of adult native speakers face to face (as in Saussure's diagram) in monolingual, even monodialectical situations – in short, the maximally homogeneous case linguistically and socially. This is the situation where the data are felt to be 'purest', where you can most clearly see the fundamentals of how language works, with minimal distortion, infelicity or 'noise'. Now one could certainly imagine a linguistic theory that assumed different things – that argued, for instance, that the best speech situation for linguistic research was one involving, for instance, a room full of people each of whom spoke two languages and understood a third, and held only one language in common with any of the others. A UN cocktail party, perhaps, or a trial in contemporary South Africa. Here, one might argue, is where you can most readily see how language works – it depends on what workings you *want* to see, or want to see first.

Behind Langue, behind Saussure's diagram, stands the image of the modern imagined community: discrete, sovereign, fraternal – a linguistic utopia. In the Chomskyan tradition a maximally homogeneous object of study is achieved in the construct of the ideal speaker whose competence the theory is to account for, while the 'deep, horizontal comradeship' Anderson talks about is embodied in the idea of competence as an innate, discrete resource all humans share. Though the ideal speaker is an abstraction, it (he) cannot in principle be characterised or even conceived in a socially neutral fashion. So, for instance, within formal grammar, national standard varieties do continue to function as standards, defining the problematics of phonology, negation or quantification, and so forth. The distance between langue and parole, competence and performance, is the distance between the homogeneity of the imagined community and the fractured reality of linguistic experience in modern stratified societies.

'Community' in discourse

Though more closely tied to social interaction, pragmatics and discourse theory likewise often produce language in the image of the imagined community. Work in pragmatics and inference assumes the existence of principles of co-operation and homogeneity corresponding to the 'deep, horizontal comradeship' Anderson talks about. In standard versions of speech act theory, the preparatory conditions for speech acts include conditions formulating shared understandings about who wants or needs to say what, and conditions that both speakers share the same competence in the single language in use. Research on interaction in conversation, classrooms, medical settings and so forth tends overwhelmingly to present exchanges in terms of single sets of shared rules and understandings, and the orderliness they produce. Disorders (like boatloads of suffragists) are almost automatically seen as failures or breakdowns not to be accounted for within the system. Models involving games and moves are often used to describe interaction. These preserve the sense of finite options, the presence of borders, rules shared among equal players. Despite whatever social differences might be at work, it is assumed that all participants are engaged in the same game and that the game is the same for all players.

Perhaps more importantly, in these games-models, only *legitimate* moves are named in the system, where 'legitimate' is defined from the point of view of the party in authority. Teacher-pupil language, for instance, tends to be described almost entirely from the teachers' point of view. According to one standard account, 'verbal interaction inside the classroom differs markedly from desultory conversation in that its main purpose is to instruct and inform' (Coulthard 1977, p. 101). The reference point here is obviously teaching, not pupiling (the term doesn't even exist) — indeed the pupils are not even conceptually present in that formulation, despite its mention of interaction. The standard Flanders taxonomy of classroom discourse posits seven discourse types for teachers, while for pupils there are only the two contentless categories, 'initiate' and 'respond' (see Coulthard 1977; Coulthard & Montgomery 1981).

Students are present, in other words, only as they are interpellated directly by teachers, and even then in a reduced and idealised fashion. Parodies, refusals, rebellions and so forth fall outside the account, and with them the struggles over disciplining that are such a fundamental part of the schooling process. ('Obviously,' we read in one account, 'there has to be some linguistic etiquette inside the classroom ... There are several ways in which teachers decide who will talk.' Coulthard & Montgomery 1981, pp. 9–10). Whatever students might be doing with each other, and however they might involve the teacher in those doings, remains invisible, despite being an important dimension of pupiling. Thus of the classroom exchange that follows, the most we are told is that it represents a normal instance of the standard 'teaching cycle':

T: Can you tell me why you eat all that food? Yes.
P: To keep you strong.
T: To keep you strong. Yes. To keep you strong. Why do you want to be strong?
P: Sir, muscles.
T: To make muscles. Yes. Well what you want to use – what would you want to do with your muscles?
P: Sir, use them.
(Coulthard & Montgomery 1981, p. 5)

Many questions could be asked about what the pupil is doing in this exchange, about what kind of pupiling is going on here. What is the social meaning of the minimalness of the responses in comparison with the questions? How is the pupil appropriating the teacher's language and distancing himself from it? How is his discourse gendered? How is he positioning himself in the pupil-based social order? The point here is not that standard descriptive approaches are altogether wrong, but that they are limited in ways they themselves do not acknowledge, ways the linguistics of community makes it difficult to acknowledge.

Sometimes the impulse to unify the social and linguistic world displaces other quite compelling social logics. There is an irony, for instance, in the thought of schoolrooms as stable, harmonious, smoothly-running discursive arenas in which teachers and pupils go on producing the same orderly cycles together day in and day out. For indeed, classrooms are supposed to be places where things change all the time, where pupils do and say different things from one day to the next because education and socialisation are going on. Seeing them as communities in the sense I am describing actually obscures those processes, or suggests they are not taking place. Child language, for instance, is commonly described in terms of its progression toward adult speech – which is to say it is analysed from the point of view of the adults raising the children. What would it look like if analysed as efforts by children to deal with the adults in charge over them, or as children's enactments of the gendered social category 'child', which they learn about from interacting with adults or watching TV shows about muppets? It is after all only through difference from children that adults know they are adults!

Medical and bureaucratic exchanges are examined by the linguistics of community along similar lines. Analyses tend to be conducted mainly in terms of whether the medical or bureaucratic objective is achieved, which is to say the analysis situates itself *within* those same structures of authority that govern the exchanges themselves. Such a stance limits possibilities of critical understanding − it cannot, for instance, readily distinguish co-operation from coercion, compliance or more complex responses, and indeed might see no need to make such distinctions. These limitations are exhibited by Aaron Cicourel's (1982) discussion of a case of a woman gynaecological patient who expresses continual scepticism about the diagnoses and treatment prescribed by her doctor, even while she submits to the treatment (a hysterectomy). This situation is defined by Cicourel as an abnormal one, since 'normally, the patient would follow the tacitly agreed upon aims of the conversation (submitting to a medical interview and examination), and would believe the speech acts expressed (the diagnosis and the action being offered by the physician)' (p. 72). Again, the social and verbal roles assigned to the patient here, submission and belief, are entirely reactive, and in fact nonverbal. Women familiar with the conversational genre known as the 'gynaecological horror story' will quickly question this norm on empirical grounds. Methodologically, Cicourel's characterisation simply presupposes established structures of medical authority, and therefore can neither examine nor question them.

And question them he does not. In fact Cicourel's analysis has the effect not only of legitimating the status quo but of actively delegitimating critique. The difficulty between the patient and the doctor is characterised as a clash between the woman's 'beliefs' and the 'factual knowledge' of the physician. The woman is seen as continually unable or unwilling to 'revise her beliefs' in the light of the information she is given by the doctor, a recalcitrance attributed to certain 'emotionally charged preoccupations' she has about the quality and reliability of medical care, and to certain 'experiences' she has undergone. Two non-interchangeable vocabularies thus construct the analysis: the doctor has *knowledge* in the form of *facts* and *information*; the patient has *beliefs* anchored in *emotion* and *experience*. On the one hand, one is led to ask why the doctor is nowhere assumed to have *beliefs* of his own that are in play; and on the other hand, one wonders why none of the woman's 'experiences' get to count as *knowledge* or *fact* (they include a period of working in a hospital and witnessing medical misconduct, caring for a husband dying of cancer in a military medical facility, seeing a television documentary on surgical fraud, and having been previously misdiagnosed for the same ailment by another gynaecologist).

The conclusion Cicourel offers is a generalisation to be applied, interestingly enough, to both medical patients and subjects in psychological experiments: scientists need to know that such people's 'schematised knowledge base' includes 'a set of metapropositions ... driven by emotional elements that can lead the patient or subject to deny or resist accepting contradictory facts, yet reveal an awareness of them; there is a general reluctance to revise beliefs in light of new evidence, while an active cognitive search continues for new information to support the metapropositions' (p. 72). Cicourel's analysis itself, made the subject/patient of a critical diagnosis, might well convince one of such a conclusion. At the same time it is obvious that despite the rigid intransigence of their metapropositions and emotional elements, people do change all the time.

'Community' as male

On the whole, as the example above might suggest, the linguistics of community has also been an androcentric project, reluctant to address language differentiations along gender lines. It has been an obstacle to understanding the social production of gender and the social reproduction of male dominance – surely one of the most urgent and viable critical projects now at hand. We all know speech activity is deeply, even ruthlessly, gendered. Practically any conversation or classroom exhibits radically different behaviour by and towards male and female participants. In formal grammar, however, gender is excluded along with all other social categories. In mainstream pragmatics, the mark of gender is present only implicitly in the lines drawn, for example, between which linguistic practices are seen as unmarked, felicitous, acceptable, co-operative, and so forth – what is in the system – and which are marked, deviant, infelicitous, or otherwise problematic for the system. Here for example, is a list of verbal practices which have been associated with women. They can be readily connected either to women's relative powerlessness or to their association with the domestic sphere:

1. Planting suggestions in the minds of other people so that they think they thought of it themselves.
2. Speaking to one person in such a way that another might hear and be affected in the desired fashion.
3. In academic writing, gradually building up evidence toward the main point rather than stating it at the beginning and then backing it up.
4. Storytelling as a way of communicating values (to children, for example).
5. Gossip as a means of supporting and surveilling each other, and as a form of power over men, who fear this secret network.
6. Talking often repetitively with one another for the purpose of maintaining a shared world (small talk).
7. Talking to subjects who don't know language at all (babies, animals, plants, TV sets, the walls).[1]

It is not my purpose to argue whether these practices in fact are used more by women than by men – quite likely they are not. What is of interest is the fact that they are associated with women, and that in mainstream pragmatics they often fall outside what is labelled normal, straightforward communication. Gossip, for example, is routinely referred to as violating conditions of relevance or the maxim of quantity or felicity conditions requiring that hearers need to know what speakers are telling them. Story-telling is nearly always considered pseudo-language of some kind, in which the rules governing normal communication are somehow suspended. Planting suggestions and other forms of manipulation violate speech-act theory's sincerity conditions. Talking to nonverbal entities, of course, violates pre-paratory conditions calling for shared competence.

The marginalisation of speech forms associated with women and women's spheres is symptomatic not simply of androcentrism in linguistics, but of an extraordinary, really pathologically narrow conception of what 'the normal system' or 'straightforward communication' is. Theories routinely exclude all forms of ludic activity, and other practices commonly associated with nur-turance, intimacy and socialisation. Even further off the scale, one assumes, would be the taboo practices of protest – demands, grievances, interruptions, refusals. The linguistic utopia, it seems, is not just any fraternity. As imagined by formal grammar and systematics, it seems often to be a fraternity of academics or bureaucrats, or perhaps talking machines speaking either the true–false discourse of science or the language of administrative rationale (see, for example, Bach & Harnish (1979) as discussed in Pratt (1986)).

One understands a particular reluctance to confront the issue of gender within the linguistics of *langue*. To include both the island full of dignitaries and the boatload of suffragists in the same picture is to introduce a deep cleavage indeed into the imagined community. It is to bring even the domi-nant class into a zone of profound internal incoherence and conflict that is almost unbearable to confront. It places the dignitaries at odds not just with the suffragists behind them, but with the wives at their sides, the statue before them, and indeed with themselves: why have they chosen to celebrate their ideal in an image not of themselves but of their subordinated other?

Subcommunity/Subutopia

Sociolinguists have often criticised the homogenising and normalising tenden-cies of formal grammar and discourse analysis and have placed the social variability of language at the centre of their agenda. In standard accounts, the language of a speech community is seen as divided into numerous different styles (Hymes 1974, for example) or registers (Halliday 1977, for example). This insistence on heterogeneity does not necessarily mean that the linguistics of community has been left behind, however. Styles, registers and varieties are typically treated not as lines which divide the community, but as shared property, a communal repertoire which belongs to all members and which all seek to use in appropriate and orderly ways. Here again one recognises the impulse to unify and harmonise the social world, the same impulse at work in the examples from discourse analysis discussed earlier.

Such is the momentum of the linguistics of community that when internal social division and hierarchy *are* studied, the linguist's choice is often to imagine separate speech communities with their own boundaries, sovereignty, fraternity and authenticity. To pick a well-known example, this is the angle from which William Labov (1972) represents American Black English. Indeed there is a real sense in which Labov's concept of Black English Vernacular (BEV) *created* a speech community along the utopian lines I have been referring to. Similarly, some early feminist work in linguistics sought to lay out an entity called 'women's language'. One could speak here of a 'linguistics of subcommunities', akin in many respects to ethnographic and sociological work on subcultures (for example, Hebdige 1979, Willis (1977). Considered as critical practice — as critical linguistics in the sense given by Roger Fowler and his associates (Fowler et al., 1979) — work of this type can be extraordinarily empowering. It indeed does challenge the normative force of standard grammar, insisting on heterogeneity, on the existence and legitimacy of lifeways other than those of dominant groups. In this way it participates directly, as has the work of many linguists working on the language of marginal and stigmatised groups, in the political and social enfranchisement of those groups.

What the 'subcommunity' approach does not do, however, is see the dominated and dominant *in their relations with each other* — this is the limitation imposed by the imaginings of community. The linguistics of community tends to construe social divisions rather the way nineteenth-century linguistics construed dialect differences, as products of pre-given obstacles to communication, like rivers and mountain ranges. Social difference is seen as constituted by distance and separation rather than by ongoing contact and structured relations in a shared social space. Language is seen as a nexus of social identity, but not as site of social struggle or a producer of social relations. As David Silverman and Brian Torode observe in *The Material Word* (1980), Labov's vindication of Black English Vernacular in effect suggests 'there is no problem here' or if there is a problem here, it has nothing to do with language (Silverman and Torode 1980, Chapter 8).

As one might expect within the linguistics of community, where Labov does encounter a problem is on the blurry frontier where dominated and dominant meet. He denounces the speech of a black middle-class speaker, asked by a white interviewer to give his views on the supernatural. The speaker 'fails' to speak in BEV, and instead produces the 'turgid, redundant, bombastic and empty' English of the American middle class. 'In the end', says Labov, 'we do not know what he is trying to say, and neither does he' (1972, p. 200). This reaction reveals rather startlingly the limits of a critical project grounded in an ideology of authenticity. Silverman and Torode try to surpass this limitation, reanalysing the exchange as an intervention on the part of the black speaker in the dominant, implicitly racist discourse introduced by the interviewer's questions. The interview itself is treated not as a one-sided display by the interviewee of the spontaneous speech patterns of his community, but as a concrete encounter between two subjects constituted within a hierarchical and conflictive web of social relations in which racism and race conflict are pervasive. This is not the kind of reading one can do from within a linguistics of community.

Interpretive community

There is an interesting parallel to be made here with literary criticism, where the concept of interpretive community has recently come to the foreground, a concept in many respects modelled on linguistics's speech community. Just as some linguists have dealt with language variation by simply reimagining the community as a set of autonomously-conceived subcommunities, so some reader-response critics deal with diversity of interpretation by positing separate interpretive communities (Fish, 1980). Interpretive differences simply indicate boundaries between these communities, again the way the Pyrenees divide Spanish from French (and Basque from both). The subcommunities themselves are again imagined like Anderson's nations – as sovereign, horizontal brotherhoods.

Again, the limitation of the approach is that the interpretive communities are not seen in their relations to and interaction with each other. It is symptomatic that the linguistics of subcommunities typically seeks its data from the private sphere, from domestic and leisure contexts where indeed ethnic groups, classes, age groups and so on seem most self-contained, their communication most homogeneous. Likewise for literature, interpretive communities are conceived on the whole as privatised entities, where reading is a form of leisure consumption, or at least a *sui generis* activity connected to nothing in particular outside itself (Pratt 1982).

In both the linguistic and literary conceptions of subcommunity, then, one readily discerns nostalgia for the lost totality of the larger community. In the literary case, diversity of interpretation is often spontaneously, though by no means necessarily, perceived as *lack* of consensus, a loss. And a loss there has certainly been, or rather a change. For if recognition of linguistic variability breaks up the imagined idea of homogeneous national languages, interpretive variability breaks up the idea of canonical national literatures held in common and forming the object of literary study. National literatures motivate what one might call a 'criticism of community', another long-standing utopian project whose task has been to secure a national patrimony or official culture. In the relativising reader response era, literary understanding gets reconstituted as a specialised, self-motivating professional activity or, as in the case of feminist and radical criticism, as an active disruption of the patrimony.

Reader response criticism and related anti-foundationalist developments register among other things a weakening of national literary projects, a process in turn linked, it seems, to a realignment of the university's own relation to the nation, nationalism, and the state.[2]

Indeed, the concept of the nation-community itself, as a cultural and political entity, is challenged by large-scale changes in the past thirty years. Economically and politically, we are told, the world order has become increasingly transnational, as nationally-based political structures continually find themselves challenged by transnational economic interests. The decolonisation struggles of the 1950s and 1960s produced new nations very different from the European model. Many were decidedly multilingual, and had no clear candidate for a national language or a national literary-artistic tradition. Some solved the problem by adopting European colonial languages whose relation to national identity would always be problematic. Within the borders of western nations, large-scale immigration, also since the 1960s, has produced new and dramatic linguistic and cultural diversity, making traditional nationalist imaginings problematic. One can scarcely be surprised that explicit connections between speech community and nation have disappeared from linguistic theorising, while the nostalgia for community, the impulse to unify the social world remain pervasive. Even as social theory flourishes, formal linguistics retreats ever farther into neuro-biologism and artificial intelligence, while sociolinguistics in many places seems methodologically and theoretically becalmed.

I have been discussing the linguistics of community so far as a utopian project that postulates unified, idealised social worlds. It will not be altogether surprising to find that it has dystopic versions as well, in which the unified social worlds are discovered, then denounced as claustrophobic and degraded. There have been, for instance, dystopic as well as utopian accounts of women's speech, the most conspicuous probably being Robin Lakoff's early *Language and Women's Place* (1975). Paul Willis's *Learning to Labour* (1977) might be seen as a dystopian account of pedagogical interaction. It is perhaps fruitful to think of Basil Bernstein's view of working-class language as a dystopian account within the linguistics of community. Working within the norms of the dominant class, Bernstein constructs working-class life as a linguistic dystopia whose internal character accounts for the social disenfranchisement of the working class (Bernstein 1971). A paradox results: Labov, because he is working within the linguistics of community, suggests Black English represents no problem; for Bernstein, because he is working within the linguistics of community, working class verbal culture represents nothing but a problem. As with most dystopian arguments, the solution that seems to follow from Bernstein's argument is the dissolution of the subcommunity, a move which completely transgresses the community ideal, and rightly enrages its adherents. (Literary criticism, incidentally, has its dystopia too: around the edifice of the utopian national canon spreads the behemoth of mass culture in an ever-expanding alien ooze ...)

Towards a linguistics of contact

I have been suggesting that the tendency to postulate social subgroups existing separately from each other gives rise to a linguistics that seek to capture identity, but not the relationality of social differentiation. It ignores the extent to which dominant and dominated groups are not comprehensible apart from each other, to which their speech practices are organised to enact their difference and their hierarchy. This is a point Noelle Bisseret Moreau has taken up (Moreau, 1984). Claiming that 'dissimilarities between language practices are meaningful only in the light of the [overall] social organization', Moreau argues that 'each class speaks itself according to the same hidden referent. This social referent is the dominant group ... because the social referent is the same for all classes, class language practices are *not* homogeneous, and this *non*-homogeneity is necessary for domination' (pp. 59–60). Here we have, I believe, a somewhat different style of imagining a speech community. In situations of domination, in Moreau's view, linguistic heterogeneity is *produced by* the homogeneity of the shared social referent (or dominant ideology). From this perspective, the codes, *langues* and competences postulated by the linguistics of community are embodiments of this shared social referent with respect to which all messages, paroles or performances situate themselves. (The same would be true for canonised literary texts.)

Moreau's view suggests a somewhat different linguistics. Dominated groups, in her view, are forced into what she calls a split subjectivity, because they are required simultaneously to identify with the dominant group and to dissociate themselves from it.[3] Their discourse consequently is both distinct from and permeated by that of the dominant group, as Moreau documents from interviews with women and working-class university students in Paris. Moreau is thus able to move out of an ideology of authenticity, and see social differentiation relationally. This move in turn makes possible a more effective critical stance in which the way language produces dominance can be addressed.

At the same time, Moreau's commitment to the concept of a unified, dominant social referent continues to tie her closely to the linguistics of community. In the end, her argument coincides with Bernstein's in seeing subordinated classes only in terms of their supposed lack of what the ruling class supposedly have – in Moreau's case, a unified subjectivity and a unified discourse to go with it. It is symptomatic that Moreau's analyses, like Labov's, rest on formal interviews in which the interview process itself is not examined. Interviewees' statements are treated as neutral self-representations, and no question is raised as to how the interview itself might be constraining interviewees to present themselves in terms of the discourse of unified subjectivity. The social solution that follows from Moreau's argument reasserts community: the dominated, she says, must find a distinct logic of their own in which to 'interpret their social condition' (p. 60), a way, that is, to unify their social world. As in the view of Jürgen Habermas, the only sure sign of a non-hierarchical society would be complete linguistic homogeneity (Habermas 1984).

Moreau's argument nevertheless offers an entry point for thinking about kinds of linguistics that might begin where the linguistics of community leaves off. Deconstruction has taught us a great deal about the need to decenter the centrifugal, homogenising tendencies of western thinking, not because they are false, but because they are limited in ways they themselves cannot acknowledge. Imagine, then, a linguistics that decentered community, that placed at its centre the operation of language *across* lines of social differentiation, a linguistics that focused on modes and zones of contact between dominant and dominated groups, between persons of different and multiple identities, speakers of different languages, that focused on how such speakers constitute each other relationally and in difference, how they enact differences in language. Let us call this enterprise a *linguistics of contact*, a term linked to Jakobson's notion of contact as a component of speech events, and to the phenomenon of contact languages, one of the best recognised challenges to the systematising linguistics of code. The term is not a satisfactory one, particularly because it attracts utopian overtones of its own, but let it suffice for the moment.

To give a highly contrastive example of how such a linguistics of contact might look at the world, let me illustrate it with the very loaded but pertinent case of South African apartheid. White westerners are encouraged to think of apartheid in terms of the segregation of whites and blacks. This is the way the western press predominantly portrays it, juxtaposing shots of Soweto or the so-called homelands with shots of white luxury suburbs. This is also the way apartheid asks to be understood, the way it represents itself to itself — as separation, apartness. Linguistically, it invokes a world where white speaks to white, in Afrikaans or English, and black speaks to black, in Zulu, Xhosa or one of many other languages.

The picture changes somewhat, however, if you think of apartheid as referring to particular forms of relatedness of whites and blacks, as a system in which they are not at all separate, but continually in each other's presence and contact, in workplaces, businesses, in dealings with the state, through religious organisations, surveillance procedures, through writing of many kinds. Such a perspective foregrounds different dimensions of the lived texture of apartheid society. It sees apartheid as activity, something people are doing, something enacted through practices in which difference and domination are ongoingly produced in conflict. When zones of contact are centered one can see, for example, the enormous significance of domestic labour in radical social stratification, of the fact that, in the case of South Africa, within nearly every white household there lives at least one black woman labourer, whose duties include maintenance and socialisation of white children. One can begin to enquire how through these interactions, through simultaneously intimate and ruthlessly exploitive relations, apartheid is acted out, reproduced, and opened to change. One can also ask how very differently apartheid is lived by children, women, and men.

Such might be the perspective of a linguistics of contact, a linguistics that placed at its centre the workings of language across rather than within lines of social differentiation, of class, race, gender, age. As my example suggests, it is as a critical project that I am discussing this linguistics here, that is, as a project intended to inform a critical scholarly praxis. In the case of what has come to be called 'critical linguistics' (Fowler et al., 1979), the project is to produce critical knowledge of the workings of domination and dehumanisation on the one hand, and of egalitarian and life-enhancing practices on the other. As Fredric Jameson has taught us (Jameson, 1981), the utopian has a place in such critical projects. At the same time, one would want to avoid, in the case of a linguistics of contact, a utopian impulse to joyfully display all humanity in tolerant and harmonious contact across all lines of difference, or a dystopian impulse to bemoan a world homogenised by western media or run only by misunderstanding and bad intentions.

I have been speaking of a linguistics of contact in hypothetical terms, but of course many readers will already know of linguists, ethnographers, sociologists and literary critics who are doing work of the kind I am describing. I would like to use my last few paragraphs to mention some examples of work in the areas of speech, writing, and literary study that is pertinent to a linguistics of contact. This enumeration is intended only to be illustrative, and not in the least programmatic. Not coincidentally, it is made up mainly of work in cultural and ethnographic studies rather than in mainstream linguistics. The examples come mostly from a zone of contact in which I have a personal scholarly interest, namely the frontiers of European colonialism, where the limitations of a linguistics of community are perhaps most striking.

In the case of writing, a linguistics of contact will be interested in the conditions under which literacy is taught, by whom, through what institutions, what texts, and in what language. One thinks here of the work of Elinor Ochs and Alessandro Durante (1981) on literacy teaching in New Guinea, for example. Second, where does writing come into play within relations of domination, or relations between states and citizens? How is it assimilated? Shirley Heath's (1983) work on oral processing of written texts in a small southern community touches on these issues, as does Homi Bhabha's (1985) study of oral renegotiating of biblical doctrine in nineteenth-century India.

A linguistics of contact will be deeply interested in processes of appropriation, penetration or co-optation of one group's language by another – and in how or whether to distinguish among those three kinds of contact. One pertinent example is the one mentioned earlier, of the black middle-class speaker seen by Labov as copying white English and by Silverman and Torode as appropriating and intervening in white English. These are the questions Silverman and Torode (1980) began sorting out through their concept of interruption.

In writing, Johannes Fabian (1985) has studied the use of Swahili terms in two European travel accounts about East Africa. He concludes that this appropriation mediated a contradiction for the European writers between the need to use given forms of discourse for a home audience, and the need to capture the immediacy and shock of the contact experience. How, one wonders, does this practice look from the point of view of the Swahili speakers? In a related vein, Vicente Rafael (1984) has examined the discursive dilemmas of Spanish religious authorities introducing Christianity into the Philippines. On the one hand, supplying Tagalog analogues for Christian terms like 'obligation' or 'sin' inevitably meant incorporating indigenous ideologies that conflicted with Christianity; on the other hand, simply introducing the Spanish terms into Tagalog texts as 'untranslatable' items meant that key concepts existed as floating signifiers to which Tagalog speakers could attribute their own meanings. Within and between languages, these kinds of interpenetrations and appropriations are so common that, contrary to Moreau's claim (Moreau, 1984), nobody's world will be found to be linguistically or subjectively homogeneous, not even that of dominant classes. When seen as a site of social reproduction and struggle, language cannot be imagined as unified.

As the examples I have outlined suggest, a linguistics of contact would take the much-debated slipperiness of signifiers for granted, and will be much concerned, as students of contact languages are, with the improvisational dimensions of meaning-making. (When told by a Glaswegian to be sure to take a 'woolly jumper' with me on a visit to Glasgow I did not need to determine what 'jumper' meant to my interlocutor in order to know (a) that it did not mean what it means in my own usage and (b) that I should come prepared for cool weather.)

Of equal significance to a linguistics of contact is the immensely widespread phenomenon of bilingualism, less as an attribute of a speaker than as a zone for working out social meanings and enacting social differences. In the American Southwest, an Anglo who addressed a native Spanish speaker in Spanish would almost invariably receive a reply in English — the minority language speaker uses the dominant language to reject the majority language speaker's attempt to unify the social world. A rather different dimension of bilingualism is discussed in Braj Kachru's work on the phenomenon of 'international English' which, he argues, is creating élites in other countries, who are then able to erect language barriers within their own societies and develop English-based social practices which enact and reproduce their privilege. Here the second language becomes the sole instrument creating new social stratification (Kachru, 1984).

To a linguistics of contact, the distinction between speech production and reception is likely to be of much greater importance than it is to the linguistics of community. For a linguistics of contact, it is of great interest that people can generally understand many more varieties of discourse or even languages than they can produce, or understand them better than they can produce them.

What Bernstein would call 'restricted code' speakers necessarily have extensive competences in 'elaborated codes', at least on the reception end, competences they develop in continual dealings with elaborated codes in workplaces, educational institutions, mass media, political or religious participation, dealings with the state and so forth. What is the nature of these competences, and how are they engaged in reproducing class relations? Likewise, white English speakers in the United States do acquire degrees of reception competence for Black English, a phenomenon one must take into account in order to understand the co-optation of Black culture in America, or the political possibility of a Jesse Jackson, or the limits on that political possibility.

How does one study the internal variability of reception, the fact, for instance, that women and men learn to listen differently, with women highly trained at second guessing, at looking for emotional subtexts that will divulge the unspoken need to be met, the desire to be fulfilled? I think here of Tanya Modleski's work on television soap operas (Modleski 1981).

Finally, there is obviously an agenda for literary criticism here. A main item on it is the range of phenomena now being studied under such rubrics as 'colonial discourse', and the 'discourse on the Other'. Another is what Ronald Carter (1986) and others refer to as contact literatures, literatures in European languages produced outside Europe and North America. How are post-colonial societies grappling with western literary and cultural legacies? A related phenomenon is the current emergence of transnational academic and literary cultures that can almost instantaneously bring García Márquez, or postmodernism, or the linguistics of writing, to the lips of people all over the planet. They have given rise to global academic and literary élites which, to return to Benedict Anderson's terms, probably need to be imagined in a style very different from the sovereign, horizontal brotherhood of community.[4]

Such developments create the need for critics trained in the reception of works not anchored in national categories. There are films like *The Kiss of the Spider Woman*, made by a Brazilian from a novel by an Argentine living in exile, using North American and Latin American actors, Spanish, English and Portuguese languages, filmed in Brazil and (I think) Mexico, intended for release abroad with special thoughts for the large Spanish-speaking and homosexual viewing publics in the United States, and for the crisis in Central America. Or, to take a more disturbing example, what about the South African film *The Gods Must Be Crazy* which became a box-office hit even at the height of anti-apartheid sentiment? How did this film succeed so brilliantly in packaging the politics of apartheid in such a way as to neutralise the critical faculties of virtually the entire American film public? What did it say that white westerners wanted to hear? How did it make white westerners into a unified category?

Even as national dignitaries gather around their statues, and speak across the airwaves in national languages to imagined national brother-hoods, texts are appearing in their very midst that should puzzle them.

For example, a book recently enjoyed immense success in the United States called *The Golden Gate*. It is a sentimental-comic novel about California written by Vikram Seth, an East Indian, Oxford-trained ex-economist who studied for several years in China. The novel is written in verse, inspired, according to the author, by Charles Johnston's English translation of Pushkin's *Eugene Onegin*. Is this a work of American literature? Could one find a clearer example of the transnationalisation of culture? Alongside Seth's verse novel, there has appeared a book called *Shallow Graves* ([Larsen and Nga, 1986), an autobiographical work by two women, an American journalist and a Vietnamese office worker, who met in Vietnam and renewed their relation in the United States. It too is written as a verse novel, in English, following a Vietnamese form called the *truyen*. Such new forms, new challenges to linguistic, cultural, and critical understanding, will continue to appear and to call upon our capacities as linguistics and critics. Such challenges can only be ignored or mystified by a linguistics of community whose view of language is anchored in a normative vision of a unified and homogeneous social world. It is hard to give up the enormous mental comfort of that vision. But it is worthwhile to give it up, in hopes of gaining a linguistics and a criticism whose engagement with the social world is not confined to the utopian.

Notes

1   For these examples and others, see Lakoff (1975), Harding (1975), Hiatt (1977), Key (1977), Thorne and Henley (1975). For more contemporary views on the subject, see Thorne *et al.* (1983); Steedman *et al.* (1985), Kramarae *et al.* (1984).

2   Hobsbawm's claim that 'schools and especially universities are the conscious champions of nationalism' (quoted in Anderson 1983) seems no longer to apply in the 1980s, some twenty-five years after it was made.

3   One is reminded here of W. E. B. Dubois's concept of 'double consciousness' developed in his classic *Souls of Black Folk*.

4   Given Anderson's comments on the novel, it is worth noting that the international academic élite has recently begun to appear as the subject of novels such as those of David Lodge and Marilyn French. It would be interesting to examine whether the academic novel represents an attempt to imagine this transnational formation as a community in Anderson's sense, or whether its emergence reflects a shift in the novel away from the community model.

References

Leslie Allen, *Liberty*, 1985.
Benedict Anderson, *Imagined Communities: Reflections on the Origin and Spread of Nationalism*, London, 1983.

Kent Bach & Robert M. Harnish, *Linguistic Communication and Speech Acts*, Cambridge, Massachusetts, 1980.

Basil Bernstein, *Class, Codes and Control*, London, 1971.

Homi Bhabha, 'Signs taken for wonders', *Critical Inquiry*, Vol. 12, No. 1, Special issue on "Race", Writing, and Difference', ed. Henry Louis Gates, Jr., Chicago, 1985, pp. 144–64.

Ronald Carter, 'A question of interpretation: An overview of some recent developments in stylistics', in Theo D'haen (ed.), *Linguistics and the Study of Literature*, Amsterdam, 1986, pp. 7–26.

Aaron Cicourel, 'Language and belief in a medical setting', in Heidi Byrnes (ed.), *Contemporary Perceptions of Language: Interdisciplinary Dimensions*, Georgetown University Round Table, Washington, 1982, pp. 48–78.

R. M. Coulthard, *In Introduction to Discourse Analysis*, London, 1977.

R. M. Coulthard & Martin Montgomery (eds), *Studies in Discourse Analysis*, London, 1981.

Johannes Fabian, *Language on the Road: Notes on Swahili in Two Nineteenth-Century Travelogues*, Hamburg, 1985.

Stanley Fish, *Is There a Text in this Class?*, Cambridge, Massachusetts, 1980.

Roger Fowler, Gunther Kress, Robert Hodges & Tony Trew, *Language and Control*, London, 1979.

H. Paul Grice, 'Logic and conversation', Peter Cole & Jerry Morgen (eds), *Syntax and Semantics, Volume 3: Speech Acts*, New York, 1975, pp. 41–58.

Jürgen Habermas, *The Theory of Communicative Action*, Vol. 1, trans. Thomas McCarthy, Boston, 1984.

M. A. K. Halliday, *Explorations in the Functions of Language*, New York, 1977.

—— & Ruqaiya Hasan, *Cohesion in English*, New York, 1976.

Susan Harding, 'Women and words in a Spanish village', in Rayna Reiter (ed.), *Toward an Anthropology of Women*, Monthly Review Press.

Shirley Heath, *Ways with Words*, Cambridge, 1983.

Dick Hebdige, *Subculture: The Meaning of Style*, London, 1979.

Mary P. Hiatt, *The Way Women Write*, New York, 1977.

Dell Hymes, *Foundations in Sociolinguistics: An Ethnographic Approach*, Philadelphia, 1974.

Fredric Jameson, *The Political Unconscious: Narrative as a Socially Symbolic Act*, New York, 1981.

Braj Kachru, 'The alchemy of English: Social and functional power of non-native varieties', in Kramarae *et al.*, 1984, pp. 176–93.

Mary Ritchie Key, *Male/Female Language*, New Jersey, 1977.

Cheris Kramarae, Muriel Schulz & William O'Barr (eds), *Language and Power*, Beverley Hills, 1984.

William Labov, *Language in the Inner City*, Philadelphia, 1972.

Robin Lakoff, *Language and Women's Place*, New York, 1975.

Wendy Wilder Larsen & Tran Thi Nga, *Shallow Graves*, New York, 1986.

Casey Miller & Kate Swift, *Words and Women*, New York, 1977.

Tanya Modleski, 'The art of being off-center: daytime television and women's work', *Tabloid*, 4, 1981, pp. 18–24.

Noelle Bisseret Moreau, 'Education, ideology and class/sex identity', in Kramarae *et al.*, 1984, pp. 43–61.

Elinor Ochs & Alessandro Durante, 'Literacy in a Samoan village', Lecture presented at Conference on Literacy and Language Use, 12–14 November, University of Southern California, Los Angeles.

Mary Louise Pratt, 'Interpretative strategies/strategic interpretations: Anglo-American reader-response criticism', *boundary 2*, Fall 1983, reprinted in Jonathan Arac (ed.), *Postmodernism and Politics*, Manchester, 1986, pp. 26–54.

——— 'Ideology and speech act theory', *Poetics Today*, Vol. 7:1, 1986, pp. 59–72.

Vicente Rafael, *Contracting Christianity: Conversion and Translation in Early Tagalog Colonial Society*, PhD Dissertation, Cornell University, Ithaca, New York, 1984.

Vikram Seth, *The Golden Gate*, New York, 1986.

David Silverman & Brian Torode, *The Material Word*, London, 1980.

Dale Spender, *Man Made Language*, London, 1985.

Carolyn Steedman, Cathy Urwin & Valerie Walkerdine (eds), *Language, Gender and Childhood*, History Workshop Series, London, 1985.

Michael Stubbs, *Discourse Analysis: The Sociolinguistic Analysis of Natural Language*, Oxford, 1983.

Barrie Thorne & Nancy Henley (eds), *Language and Sex: Difference and Dominance*, Rowley, Massachusetts, 1975.

Barrie Thorne, Cheris Kramarae & Nancy Henley (eds), *Language, Gender, and Society*, Rowley, Massachusetts, 1983.

Paul Willis, *Learning to Labour: How Working Class Kids Get Working Class Jobs*, Farnborough, 1977.

A biblical pattern poem

It is a commonplace of literary criticism that an essential prerequisite for a proper appreciation of a text is a good grasp of its form. In what follows I shall try to show that one of the best-known psalms has striking formal properties that appear not to have been previously noticed. It is my hope that in bringing out these features of the psalm I shall contribute something towards a better understanding of a poem about which so much has been written that it might seem that there is no longer anything new to be said.

Some years ago, John McCarthy and I discovered that Psalm 137, the one that in the King James translation of the Bible begins with the words 'By the rivers of Babylon', is composed in conformity with a rudimentary vowel-counting metre which is quite similar to that utilised in most of the major poetry of the different Romance languages. (For details see Halle and McCarthy (1981)) Typically in such metres the number of vowels per line is limited in accordance with some simple principle. To make the writing of such lines a bit more challenging in most of these traditions not all vowels are counted equally. For instance, in French verse the *e-muet* counts only if followed by a syllable beginning with a consonant, whereas all other vowels are counted without regard to what follows. As an example, consider the well-known lines of Verlaine:

Il pleure dans mon coeur
Comme il pleut sur la ville,
Quelle est cette langueur
Qui penètre mon coeur?

If we count the vowels that are actually pronounced in each line in standard literary French, we get five in the first line, six in the second, five in the third, and five or six in the fourth. From the point of view of its metre, each line has precisely six vowels. We can get the correct count if, in conformity with the rule stated in the preceding paragraph, we count the *e-muet* in the first line. On the other hand, in the second line neither of the *e-muets* counts: the one in *comme* is discounted because it is not followed by a syllable with consonantal onset, whereas that in *ville* is not counted because no syllable whatever follows it. As required by the rule above, in the third line the *e-muet* of *cette* is counted, but not that of *quelle*, whereas in the fourth line the *e-muet* in *penètre* is counted.

The Old Testament verse that we shall discuss here conforms to a metrical scheme much like that of French. Syllables following the last stressed vowel in a line are systematically excluded from the count, and certain other vowels are not counted in certain contexts. For people interested in Old Testament verse I have listed the latter:

The so-called secondary *ḥatĕpîm*:
>   *ʔaˤleh* 'I shall rise' rather than *ʔaˤăleh*

The shwa in 'doubly open' syllables VC_1 -- C_2V:
>   *binʔôt* 'in pastures' rather than *binĕˤôt*

The *patah* preceding syllable final gutturals:
>   *ʔĕlôh* rather than *ʔelôah*

In a paper written in the spring of 1985 (Halle, to appear) I believe to have shown that the vowel counting metre that I have just described was used in addition to Psalm 137 also in the four texts listed below:

Genesis 4, 23–24:   The Curse of Lemekh
Psalm 23:   'The Lord is my shepherd, I shall not want'
Psalm 54:   'Save me, O God, by thy name'
Psalm 114:   'When Israel went out of Egypt'

My guess is that there are metrical texts of this type yet to be discovered in the Bible, but their number is not large. I have investigated a fair number of additional Old Testament poems, but except for the five just mentioned, I have so far been unable to find any that are clearly composed in the vowel counting metre put forth above.[1] I do not consider this especially surprising since the texts included in the Bible were composed over a period which is significantly longer than that separating us from Chaucer.

The discovery that some text has metrical structure is, of course, far from uncommon. For example, when I was a graduate student our teacher Roman Jakobson taught us that the text below is an instance of Slavic epic verse.

rusi jestI veselije piti   Rus(sia) takes pleasure in drinking
ne možemU bezU togo žiti   we cannot live without it

This text is to be found in the Russian Primary Chronicle, of which the oldest extant manuscript dates from the fourteenth century, and has been transmitted to us without any indication that it might be metrical. These words were supposed to have been uttered in 989 AD by the Grand Duke St Vladimir of Kiev in his reply to a missionary who was attempting to convert him and his people to Islam. The missionary had informed Vladimir that Islam prohibited its adherents from using alcohol, whereupon the sainted duke responded with the words above.

Jakobson pointed out that Vladimir's reply was a perfect example of the metre of Slavic epic verse, where each line is ten syllables long, and the fourth and tenth syllables coincide with the end of a polysyllabic word.[2] At this point the objection might be raised that the metrical organisation that Jakobson found in the above is the result of pure chance and is therefore without real significance, and the same objection might be raised against my proposal concerning the metre of the Biblical texts listed earlier. There are standard statistical methods to estimate precisely the likelihood of a line conforming to a particular metre arising accidentally. Although to my knowledge no one has actually calculated the statistical probability of a line conforming to the Slavic epic metre or any other metre arising by accident we may safely assume that it is quite low. If the probability of a single metrical line arising by accident is small,

the probability of two such lines
arising by pure chance is lower still.

In fact, if the probability of one metrical line arising by chance is one in a hundred, that of two such lines is one in ten thousand, three such lines one in a million, etc. But though the probability is low, occasionally such line sequences will arise by accident.

I have set off the phrase above because without any conscious intention on my part, the phrase is composed of two consecutive iambic pentameter lines. We thus have experimental proof that a metrical couplet may arise by pure chance. In view of this it would seem that with regard to a short text like Vladimir's reply, reasonable individuals may well disagree, some siding with Jakobson, others remaining sceptical. With regard to longer passages, however, even passages only a few lines longer, the belief that these might have arisen by accident is no more warranted than the belief that to win the Irish Sweepstakes one needs only to buy a ticket.

The Old Testament texts that we are discussing here are, in fact, considerably longer than the couplets illustrated. Thus, the probability that they might have arisen by accident is vanishingly small. For instance, Psalm 23 is composed of nine couplets with the syllable count[3]

7–7   8–5   8–5   8–10(5)   7–5   7–5   8–5   8–5   8–5

If we apply the same syllable count to the King James translation of Pslam 23, we obtain the distribution

10–10   9–6   9–4   14–10(5)   5–4   9–7   8–5   9–6   10–2

Even the most cursory comparison of the number distribution shows that there is a pattern in the first but none in the second. Patterns are readily discerned also in the remaining three texts listed as shown by their syllable distributions:

Gen. 4. 23–24:   10–10   8–8   8–8
Psalm 54:   8–8–8–7–7–8–8   8–8–8–7–7–8–8–(8)
Psalm 114:   8–7–8–7   7–8–8–6   7–8–8–6   8–7–8–7

The Curse of Lemekh from Genesis thus consists of three couplets. Pslam 54 is composed of two identical stanzas if the last line of the second stanza is disregarded, for which there is some semantic support. Psalm 114 consists of four stanzas in the chiasmatic arrangement A−B−B−A.[4] It is totally improbable that patterns with this much structure could have arisen by accident.

Consider now Psalm 137, which I have reproduced with translation:

I	ſal-nĕhārôt bĕbābel	7	On rivers in Babylon
	šām yāšabnû gam-bakî(nû)	7	there we sat and also wept
	bĕzokrēnû ʔet-siyyôn	7	as we were recalling Zion.
	ſal-ſărābîm bĕtôkān	7	On poplar-trees in her midst
	tālînû kinnôrôtē(nû)	7	we hung up our violins.
II	kî šām šĕ ēlû(nû)	5	For there our own captors
	šôbênû dibrê-šîr	6	asked from us words of song
	wĕtôlālēnû śimhān	7	and those who mocked us, rejoicing:
	širû lānû miššîr siyyôn	8	'Sing us some of the songs of Zion'.
III	ʔêk nāšîr ʔet-šîrê-yahwēh	8	How are we to sing Yahweh's songs
	ʔal ſadmat nēkār	5	on an alien soil?
	ʔim-ʔeškāhēk yĕrûšālēm	8	If I forget thee, O Jerusalem,
	tiškah yĕmînî	5	let my right hand wither!
	tidbaq lĕšônî lĕhikkî	8	Let my own tongue stick to my palate
	ʔim-lō? ʔezkĕrḗ(kî)	5	should I not recall thee,
	ʔim-lō? ʔaſleh yĕrûšālēm	8	should I not raise thee, O Jerusalem,
	ſal rôʔš śimhátî	5	.on my head in gladness.
IV	zĕkôr yahwḗh libnê ĕdôm	8	Recall, Yahweh, to Edom's sons
	ʔet yĕmê yĕrûšālēm	7	their deeds on the days of Jersualem,
	hā ōmrîm ſārû ā(rû)	6	who said: 'Strip it all down:
	ſad hayĕsôd bāh	5	to its bare foundations.'
V	bat-bābel haššĕdûdāh	7	O daughter of plundered Babylon,
	ʔašrê šeyyĕšallem-lāk	7	happy he who pays you back
	gĕmûlēk šeggāmalt lā(nû)	7	the evil that you have done us!
	ʔašrê šeyyōhēz wĕnippēs	8	Happy he who seizes and dashes
	ſ ōlālayik ſel-hassā(laſ)	7	your infants against the rock!

The text reproduced above is that established in Halle and McCarthy (1981) and differs in a number of details from the Masoretic text of the Hebrew Bible. As the arguments for the emendations are given in the cited paper I shall not discuss any of our emendations except for that in the first line because of its somewhat special interest. In the Masoretic text the first line of the psalm reads

ſal nahărôt bābel   'on the rivers of Babylon'

rather than, as proposed

ſal nĕhārôt bĕbābel   'on rivers in Babylon'

This reading, which was first argued for in Freedman (1971), is supported by the following arguments: a) The extra syllable 'in' is required by the metre, for the first and last stanza of the psalm are made up of lines that contain seven — not six — syllables. b) The introduction of the preposition is supported by line 4

ʕal-ʕarābîm bĕtôkān 'on poplar-trees in her midst'

It establishes an exact parallelism between these two lines in their prepositions, as is quite common in biblical poetry. c) An accidental haplography in copying a sequence of three identical letters is quite likely. d) The line has been preserved in one of the finds in the Qumran caves and contains there the preposition *be*.

Returning to the psalm it is easy to see that as pointed out by Freedman the poem is composed of five stanzas. Moreover, one notices at once that the first and the last, and the second and the penultimate stanzas have the same number of lines. In addition, the lengths of the lines — where length is measured by counting vowels in accordance with the proposed algorithm — constitute an additional pattern: we have a stanza of five lines each seven syllables long adjacent to a stanza of four lines of increasing (respectively, decreasing) length. The stanza in the middle consists of four couplets in which an eight-syllable line is paired with a five-syllable line.[5]

It hardly needs saying that such regularities do not normally arise in a poem without being consciously put there by the poet. Equally obvious — and of special relevance from the point of view of the linguistics of writing — is the observation that the regularities just pointed out imply that the poem was composed in a written form, for the regularities cannot be apprehended just by listening to the text. The psalm therefore is the creation of a literate poet writing for a literate audience exploiting possibilities provided by the fact that his medium is simultaneously both phonetic and graphic. These observations immediately bring up the further question as to the purpose the poet might have pursued in giving this unusual form to his poem.

A possible answer suggests itself if we examine the distribution of metrical vowels in the lines of the poem. To this end we perform a graphic transformation on the poem and represent each metrical syllable by an x, as shown below. We represent the lines from right to left because that is the direction of Hebrew writing:

```
            X X X X X X X
            X X X X X X X
            X X X X X X X
            X X X X X X X
            X X X X X X X

                X X X X X
              X X X X X X
            X X X X X X X
          X X X X X X X X

          X X X X X X X X
                X X X X X
          X X X X X X X X
                X X X X X
          X X X X X X X X
                X X X X X
          X X X X X X X X
                X X X X X

          X X X X X X X X
          X X X X X X X
          X X X X X X
          X X X X X

          X X X X X X X
          X X X X X X X
          X X X X X X X
          X X X X X X X X
          X X X X X X X
```

If, in addition, the poem is 'laid on its side' with its first line on the right and its last line on the left, we obtain the graphic pattern

```
    X               X     X     X     X   X
  X X X X X       X X     X     X     X   X X       X X X X X
  X X X X X      X X X    X     X     X   X X X     X X X X X
  X X X X X    X X X X  X X X X X X X X  X X X X   X X X X X
  X X X X X    X X X X  X X X X X X X X  X X X X   X X X X X
  X X X X X    X X X X  X X X X X X X X  X X X X   X X X X X
  X X X X X    X X X X  X X X X X X X X  X X X X   X X X X X
  X X X X X    X X X X  X X X X X X X X  X X X X   X X X X X

      V           IV          III          II          I
```

With a modicum of imagination and some good will this pattern may be seen as a building consisting of two wings – stanzas I and V – and a central structure composed of a sloping roof – stanzas II and IV – and four columns in the middle – stanza III. The obvious further inference that this pattern invites is that it represents the temple in Jerusalem, whose destruction by the Babylonians in 586 BC is the central event commemorated in the poem.

If my suggestion is correct we have before us a pattern poem of great antiquity. Pattern poetry is 'verse which by varying the length of lines forms a picture' (Church (1946)). Though of considerable antiquity and obviously popular down through the ages, pattern poetry has had a very cool reception from critics. The sixteenth-century English critic Gabriel Harvey wrote: 'Simmias Rhodius (c300 BC) a folishe idle phantastical poett that first devised this riminge with other triflinge and childishe toys to make verse that shoulde in proportion represent the form and figure of an egg, an ape, a winge, and sutche ridiculous and mad gugaws and crockchetts, and of late foolishly revived by sum, otherwise not unlearned, as Pieriors, Scaliger, Crispin and the rest of that crue ..' (quoted by Church *op. cit.*). Harvey's opinion is shared by the early twentieth-century American critic W.S. Walsh, who apparently attempted to go Harvey one better in the following passage (Walsh (1906) pp. 270–f.): 'There is pity, or even forgiveness, for all forms of human folly, imbecility, errors and crime, yet the makers of [Emblematic, Figurative or Shaped Poems] strain the divinity of forgiveness to an almost diabolical tension ... Though one's better self may revolt at the grotesque horrors of the medieval hell, one feels that not even the theological mind has ever conceived a punishment severe enough to castigate these tresspassers on our patience ...'. Yet Walsh is forced to admit just a few short sentences further on in his text that 'in spite of the degradation of the offence, great names in the past, great names even in the immediate present, must be grouped among the offenders. Indeed, so highly was it thought of at one time that the very name of the reputed inventor has been preserved to us.'

Pattern poems, as noted above, were composed by Greek poets as early as the third century BC. Wojaczek (1969) has shown that these poems were creations of poets belonging to a special club or guild active on the island of Kos, the most famous among whom was Theocritus (*c*. 310–250 BC). It is therefore natural to inquire whether the idea of writing pattern poetry was borrowed by the psalmist from the Greeks, or vice versa. We know that both Greeks and Jews were deeply involved in the affairs of the Persian empire during the fifth and sixth centuries BC. Recall that the Persian emperor Darius (522–486 BC), who authorised the rebuilding of the temple in Jerusalem and thereby officially ended the Babylonian exile that is the subject of Psalm 137 was also responsible for sending to Greece the Persian invasion force that was defeated in the battle of Marathon (490 BC). The involvement of Jews and Greeks with Persia must inevitably have led to contacts between the two peoples especially since both were heavily involved in commerce. As Bickerman has written: 'It is a widely spread error ... that the Jews ... were immune to foreign contagion and, until the Macedonian conquest, separated from the Greek world. As a matter of fact, excavations have shown that in the fifth and fourth centuries BCE, Palestine belonged to the belt of an eclectic, Greco-Egyptian-Asiatic culture, which extended from the Nile Delta to Cilicia' (Bickerman (1949) p. 75). That these contacts might also have resulted in literary influences, of which the pattern poem that we have just examined is one bit of evidence, is most plausible.

It is, of course, next to impossible at this distance in time to establish definitive links between the author of Psalm 137 and Theocritus, Simmias and other Greek poets. The remarkable popularity of pattern poems among readers as well as writers of poetry is persuasively attested by the mere fact that the poems survived in various manuscript copies from the third century BC until the sixteenth century AD when they were reproduced in some of the earliest printed books and elicited almost immediate imitation by poets writing in English, French and other languages.[6] Given the popularity of pattern poetry it would be quite unsurprising if a Jewish poet had decided to compose verse in this form and produced a poem that was ultimately included in the Old Testament canon. If these speculations are near the mark, one might guess that Psalm 137 was composed between 300 and 200 BC.

When I first thought about these matters it occurred to me that since the earliest translators of the Old Testament into Greek were active only a century or two after these dates, they well might have known that Psalm 137 is a pattern poem and might therefore have attempted to imitate the pattern in their translation, much as I have done it here in the English translation. A check of the Greek text of Psalm 137 in the Septuagint translation, however, made it quite clear that this aspect of the poem was not captured in the translation. It is therefore unlikely that the fact that Psalm 137 is a pattern poem was known to the Septuagint translators.

Pattern poems have been a recognised, albeit minor genre of Greek poetry but are otherwise unknown in Hebrew.[7] I am therefore inclined to believe that the author of Psalm 137 imitated a Greek model. It must however be admitted that nothing that I have said here excludes the hypothesis that pattern poems were a Jewish invention and were borrowed by the Greeks: or that both Greeks and Jews got the idea from an Eastern (Persian, Assyrian or Babylonian) source. What seems to me implausible in view of the close contacts between the two people all through the ages is that pattern poetry was invented by Greek and Hebrew poets independently. But unless and until additional evidence is uncovered all this must remain in the realm of speculation.

What I hope to have established more solidly than mere speculation is that Psalm 137 is a pattern poem representing the temple in Jerusalem. And knowledge of this fact cannot but affect and enhance our understanding of Psalm 137, this shocking mixture of elegaic sorrow and barbaric vengeance.

Notes

This work was supported in part by the Center for Cognitive Science, MIT.

1 Since originally giving this lecture on 4 July 1986 I have discovered a further metrical text in the Bible: Amos 3.3–6 'Can two walk together'. I hope to publish this in the near future.
2 For an instructive discussion of this metre, see R. Jakobson's Ilchester lecture given at Oxford University in 1950 and reprinted in Jakobson (1966) pp. 414–63.
3 The numbers enclosed in parentheses represent the syllable count of an alternative reading which seems to me plausible, although it has no support in any of the known Biblical manuscript sources.
4 For details see Halle (to appear).
5 The penultimate line in the poem has eight rather than seven syllables. It has been suggested to me that this irregularity is not accidental, but that it is a reflex of the taboo against creating anything that is absolutely perfect.
6 A very interesting discussion of pattern poetry from which I have learned a great deal is found in Hollander (1975).
7 John Hollander has suggested to me that the Jewish prohibition against graven images might well have played a role here.

References

E. J. Bickerman, 'The historical foundations of postbiblical Judaism', in L. Finkelstein (ed.), *The Jews: Their History, Culture and Religion*, New York, 1949, pp. 70–114.
M. Church, 'The first English pattern poem', *Proceedings of the Modern Language Association* LXI, 1946, pp. 636–50.
D. N. Freedman, 'The structure of Psalm 137', in H. Goedicke (ed.), *Near Eastern Studies in Honor of E. F. Albright*, Baltimore, 1971.
M. Halle, 'Syllable counting meters and pattern poetry in the Old Testament', to appear in a volume honouring the memory of Halm Blanc.
M. Halle, & J. J. McCarthy, 'The metrical structure of Psalm 137', *Journal of Biblical Literature*, 1981, pp. 161–7.
J. Hollander, 'The poem in the eye', in *Vision and Resonance, Two Senses of Poetic Form*, New York, 1975, pp. 245–87.
R. Jakobson, *Selected Writings IV: Slavic Epic Studies*, The Hague, 1966.
W. S. Walsh, *Handybook of Literary Curiosities*, Philadelphia, 1906.
G. Wojaczek, *Daphnis: Untersuchungen zur griechischen Bukolik*, Meisenheim am Glan, 1969.

5 *Geoffrey Leech*

Stylistics and functionalism

In his admirable critique of Jakobson's 'Closing Statement' of the 1958 *Style in Language* Conference, Derek Attridge has already discussed the model of linguistic functions presented by Jakobson in that memorable paper. The sections in which Jakobson discussed the functions of language also, naturally enough, form the pretext (or pre-text) for this chapter, which is on the theme of stylistics and functionalism.

These two terms 'stylistics' and 'functionalism' I will define simplistically for the present purpose as follows: stylistics is the study of style (particularly in literary texts, and more particularly, with a view to explicating the relation between the form of the text and its potential for interpretation). Functionalism (in the study of language) is an approach which tries to explain language not only internally, in terms of its formal properties, but also externally, in terms of what language contributes to larger systems of which it is a part or sub-system. Whether we call these larger systems 'cultures', 'social systems', 'belief systems', etc. does not concern me. What is significant is that functionalist explanations look for relations between language and what is not language, whereas formalist explanations look for relations between the elements of linguistic text itself.

It is commonly assumed, as I have just assumed, that functionalism is defined by contrast with its opposite, formalism. It is strange, then, that Jakobson, who provides us with one of the best-known classifications of language functions, should also, in his analyses of literary texts, be the most successful and influential practitioner of formalism. The basis of this paradox lies in Jakobson's well-known definition of the poetic function as 'the set (*Einstellung*) towards the *message* itself, focus on the message for its own sake' (1960, p. 356). It will be remembered that Jakobson's typology of functions attributed a different function to each of the six components in an archetypal linguistic situation:

addresser	EMOTIVE		context	REFERENTIAL
addressee	CONATIVE		message	POETIC
contact	PHATIC		code	METALINGUAL

By thus relating language to its communicative setting, he was in a *general* way providing a linguistic model which is functionalist in the sense I have specified. But the poetic function was an exception — for he represented the poetic function as the special case where the linguistic artefact has no function beyond itself, where (as it were) language turns in on itself.

As Attridge points out, the notion of a 'set towards' one aspect of the communicative situation — a focus or *Einstellung* — has implications of a psychological or social nature. But, rather than pursue this, let me reveal something of my own 'focus', prejudice — call it what you like — by adopting the commonplace idea that a 'function' presupposes some kind of orientation towards a goal. For example, we use language conatively *in order to* influence the addressee in some way; our emotive use of language *serves to* express our opinions or attitudes; the phatic use of language is *a means to* establish or maintain contact with one's interlocutor. These expressions which imply goals, ends, or objectives, do not have to suggest that there is a conscious purpose or precisely definable intention — in fact, in many cases it would be misleading to make any such suggestion. But I see no difficulty in assuming, as a general postulate, that functionalism implies goal-orientation. Thus one may re-interpret Jakobson's poetic function as follows: whereas in relation to other functions, a message/text is seen as a means to an end, in relation to the poetic function, a message/text is regarded as an end in itself. It is 'autofunctional', or to use a technical term, *autotelic*.

Moreover, function involves value. Whereas in relation to other functions, messages/texts are evaluated in terms of their efficacy in attaining extrinsic goals, in relation to the poetic function, they are evaluated by criteria intrinsic to themselves.

There are two further points to make about this concept of function, if its importance for the study of poetic language is to be appreciated.

First, a given utterance or text *may* have, and in general *will* have, more than one function. Multifunctionalism is the norm. This point has been emphasised by Jakobson (1960), as it has been by Halliday (1970, 1973), and by others who have provided functional typologies of language. It has also been emphasised (and Jakobson himself is particularly insistent on this) that one function may be placed in a subordinate relation to another — such that, for example, an utterance which is dominantly conative — like an advertise-ment or a political slogan — may be secondarily poetic. Within this framework, poetry (or literature — there is no need to distinguish between these two terms here) is definable as that kind of text in which the poetic function is dominant over others. But the framework allows for texts which combine a dominant poetic function with subsidiary functions of another kind: for example, a love poem is not only poetic, but emotive/expressive; a didactic poem is not only poetic, but also conative. Jakobson's functional model therefore exonerates him from the worst consequences of what Mary Louise Pratt (1977) has called 'the poetic language fallacy' — the presumption of a linguistically-definable dichotomy between 'literary language' and 'ordinary, non-literary language'. The functional model, on the contrary, makes the quality of literariness depend on the evaluation or interpretation of the text by readers, by a social or linguistic community: 'poeticalness [says Jakobson] is ... a total re-evaluation of the discourse and all its components whatsoever' (1960 p.377).

My second point is that there is an important interconnection between function and meaning. This applies to an individual utterance if we adopt Grice's (1957) explication of non-natural meaning: meaning understood as the speaker's intention that the utterance should produce some effect on an audience by means of the *recognition of this intention*. What from the speaker's viewpoint is function or communicative intention becomes from the hearer's viewpoint significance, or interpretation. There is a parallel to be drawn here between Jakobson and a contemporary of his who came from a different intellectual tradition, and whose perspective on poetic language was so different – I. A. Richards. Richards's four kinds of meaning, enunciated in his *Practical Criticism* (1929) overlap strikingly with Jakobson's functions:

sense: what is said, the state of affairs represented
            [cf Jakobson's referential function]
feeling: attitude to what is said
            [cf Jakobson's emotive function]
tone: attitude towards the hearer
intention: the author's aim, the effect he is endeavouring to promote
            [tone and intention can be seen as subdivisions of Jakobson's
            conative function.]

Furthermore, like Jakobson, Richards stresses relations of dominance or subordination between the categories: 'now one, now another of the functions may become predominant' (1929, p.183). (Notice how easily Richards moves between the terminology of meaning and the terminology of function.) Richards's description of the address*er's* end of the process of communication is easily seen as a metaphor for the multifunctionality of language: 'Whether we know and intend it or not, we are all jugglers when we converse, keeping the billiard-balls in the air when we balance the cue on our nose'.[1] Despite Richards's assimilation of the poetic function to the emotive function, there is enough similarity between Jakobson's and Richards's schemes to suggest the value of a more general comparison between various schemes of linguistic functions. In view of the apparent lack of constraints on the various functions of language that one might dream up, there is a surprising and reassuring degree of similarity between the various schemes proposed. This table attempts to represent their common ground, although it must necessarily do so only roughly:

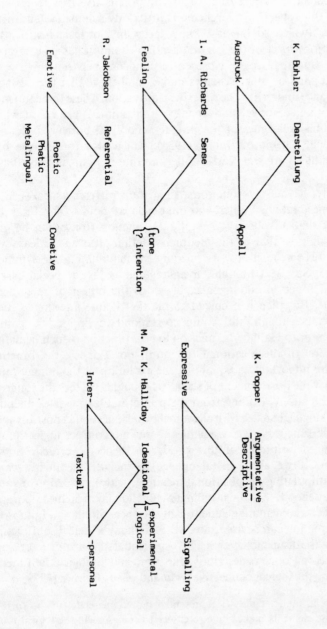

Figure I

I have been inclined to wonder whether Jakobson's scheme has any superiority over other schemes, in spite of its enduring popularity. It is tempting to suppose that the appeal of his scheme is in its tidy symmetry, and in the attractive idea (which so far as I know lacks any intrinsic justification) that every major aspect of the communication situation has its corresponding function. But at least the close correspondence between three of his functions and parts of other schemes makes me believe that there is some genuine substance underlying the superficial attraction. These three functions – the referential, emotive, and conative functions – are those which, together with his colleagues of the Prague School, he borrowed from the more traditional scheme of Bühler (1934), which also formed the basis for that of Bühler's student Karl Popper, and more indirectly for that of Halliday.

Very briefly, let me pick out some significant differences between the various schemes, taking Bühler and Jakobson as points of reference. I used to think that Jakobson's metalingual function (for which he gives only one example – that of the dictionary definition) was the least well-motivated of his six functions, useful only for maintaining the symmetry of the scheme. Surely, I thought, metalanguage is just a special case of the referential function of language, in which the object of reference is language itself. But then it occurred to me that if one interpreted meta-language broadly enough, this could correspond to Popper's argumentative function, or to Halliday's function logical function (which he defines as a subfunction of the ideational function). For Popper, the functions of language are important in explaining the evolution of the human mind, and particularly the development of scientific thought. He sees the functions as forming a hierarchy, leading from the primordial 'expressive function', which human language shares with all animal behaviour, to the most advanced 'argumentative function', which enables us to interconnect logically, and reflect on, our descriptions of the world, and hence to criticise and to evaluate them. If we allow metalanguage to include the meta*semantic* activity of manipulating propositional meaning, with its descriptive values of truth and falsehood, then the metalingual function takes on the importance assigned to the argumentative function by Popper. Similarly, Jakobson's metalingual function can be associated with Halliday's logical subfunction. Halliday draws the distinction between his experiential subfunction (corresponding, I suppose, to Popper's descriptive function) and his logical subfunction (exemplified by the logical connectives *and* and *or*) as follows (1979, p. 73):

In the experiential mode, reality is represented more concretely, in the form of constructs whose elements make some reference to *things* ... In the logical mode, reality is represented in more abstract terms, in the form of abstract relations which are independent of and make no reference to things.

Three further distinctive features of Halliday's scheme of functions deserve comment.

First, Halliday stresses that the functions of language are integrated within the grammar: that they are manifested in the organisation of the language in terms of system and structure. He thus achieves a kind of synthesis of function with form: functions determine not only how we use the language, but how the language itself is constructed.

Secondly, Halliday recognises that the emotive and conative functions cover the same ground – that the resources of language we use to express our own emotions and attitudes are to a large extent the same as those which we use to influence the emotions and attitudes of others. Hence he subsumes the addresser-oriented and addressee-oriented functions under the single heading of the 'interpersonal function'.

Third, having thus subtracted one term from Bühler's triad, he adds another term, and ends up with a new triad consisting of the ideational, interpersonal, and textual functions. The new term in the model – the textual function – is the area in which Halliday has probably contributed more than in any other, in explicating (under the inspiration of Prague School functionalism) such notions as theme and rheme and given and new. And yet one can argue that the textual function is not really a function of language in the strict sense of 'relating language to what is not language' at all: Halliday recognises its special status by calling it an 'enabling function' (1970, pp. 143, 165).

In the study of pragmatics (Leech 1983, p. 59), I have tried to reinterpret Halliday's three functions as a hierarchy of instrumentality. A linguistic event of communication can be described as constituting a transaction between addresser and addressee on three different planes: an interpersonal transaction (or discourse), an ideational transaction (or representation) and a textual transaction (or text) (see figure 2).

But these planes of instantiation are ordered in such a way that the discourse is enacted *by means of* the representation, and the representation is conveyed by means of the text. Each plane has the *function* of transmitting the plane or planes above it. Michael Short and I have explored the application of this kind of model to literature in our book *Style in Fiction* (1981). Thus a work of fiction can be considered as a text – as a linguistic object consisting simply of words in a particular order on the page; it can also be considered as a representation of a reality – or rather, in the case of a fiction, of a mock-reality. The text is the means of conveying that mock-reality to the reader, although in principle it might be conveyed by another means, such as a film, or strip cartoons. The discourse is the work of fiction in its fullest sense, as a transaction between the author and the reader, subsuming the various subdiscourses (e.g. the discourses of fictional characters) it may contain, including the authorial attitude to elements of the fiction and to the reader.

But before considering the implications of this model for stylistics, I would

Figure 2

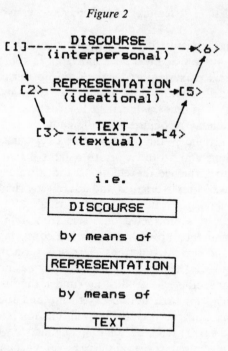

i.e.

DISCOURSE

by means of

REPRESENTATION

by means of

TEXT

like to say a little about its application more generally. A functional model of language is naturally to be associated with a functional model of language use, i.e. with a theory of rhetoric. Each of the planes, therefore, has its own principles of effective communication: there is an interpersonal rhetoric, an ideational rhetoric, and a textual rhetoric. We can take Grice's Cooperative Principle (Grice 1975) as the canonical example of ideational rhetoric, with its maxims of informativeness, of truthfulness, of relevance, and of clarity. The interpersonal rhetoric, concerning relations between the addresser and addressee, contains maxims of politeness, as well as second-order reflections on politeness or impoliteness, such as irony and banter. The textual rhetoric contains such maxims of well-behaved text as end-focus and end-weight — placing the information focus and the grammatically heavy elements towards the end of the information unit. It also contains maxims of economy of expression, and clarity of expression, operative, for example, in the choice between pronominalisation, ellipsis, and lexical repetition. The claim is not that speakers and writers invariably obey these maxims: indeed, it is essential to note that the maxims place conflicting claims upon the user. Rather, the claim is that by assuming that the goals of the addresser include reasonable adherence to these maxims, the addressee interprets infringements or floutings of them by making certain inferences, drawing certain conclusions, about what the addresser intends to communicate. Hence we explain a wide range of implicit or indirect meanings which arise in discourse interpretation. Here again we note that a functional orientation at the addresser's end leads to attribution of meaning at the address*ee's* end.

The addressee draws different kinds of conclusions. Consider a simple conversational example: a knock on the door is followed by *NOW what does he want?* On the textual plane, the fact that the emphasis falls on *now* means that end-focus has not been observed, and this in turn implies that the following part of the utterance is what the speaker takes as 'given'. This leads to the conclusion that on a previous occasion, a similar action (knocking at the door) was performed by the same person for a certain purpose. On the ideational plane, the fact that 'he' is mentioned without further specification implies that there is sufficient contextually shared knowledge to enable the addressee to understand which person is meant by the addresser; and so, on this basis, the addressee can draw a conclusion about the person's identity. On the interpersonal plane, both these 'lower level' inferences may contribute to an understanding of the speaker's motivation, which in this case is not, presumably, to elicit information (despite the interrogative form of the sentence), but to express annoyance; the utterance is a complaint or a grumble. In such conversational examples, a great deal depends on a shared context that speaker and hearer can take for granted, and since factors such as degree of shared knowledge may be unclear to both parties, there is considerable latitude for alternative interpretations and *mis*interpretations.

This is a different conception of multifunctionalism from Halliday's; but it leads me to declare support for Halliday's demonstration, in his study of Golding's *The Inheritors* (Halliday 1971) and elsewhere, that there is no discontinuity, in functional terms, between everyday communication and literature. The same methods and principles of interpretation apply to both. In particular, multiplicity and indeterminacy of meaning are characteristic of both literature and conversation; and in both literature and conversation, as readers or hearers, we have to engage our minds fully (in terms of background knowledge, intelligence, and imagination) to reconstruct the addresser's intention as well as we can.

We may now illustrate the three planes of rhetoric and interpretation by reference to literary examples. The textual plane can be illustrated by the varied meanings we can attach to the author's sequencing of elements, and to lexical repetition.

The sequencing of elements in fiction often assumes chronological ordering of events in the narrative; but it can also suggest 'psychological ordering', that is, the order in which impressions or elements of knowledge are apprehended by some fictional observer; or it can suggest what one may call 'rhetorical ordering' – i.e. the order in which the author intends impressions to be registered, for maximum effect, in the mind of the reader.

In this passage from Conrad's *The Secret Agent*, the psychological interpretation of sequencing seems to be dominant:

She saw there an object. That object was the gallows. She was afraid of the gallows.

The three sentences trace the step-by-step dawning of grim realisations in the mind of Mrs Verloc after her murder of her husband. In the following sentence from *Little Dorrit*, on the other hand, the dominant value of ordering appears to be that of rhetorical arrangement, so that the reader (having been temporarily taken in by Mrs Sparkler's seeming sincerity) may savour the step-by-step progression towards an ironic climax at the end of the sentence:

Mrs Sparkler, who was not unfeeling, had received them [the tidings of death] with a violent burst of grief, which had lasted twelve hours; after which she had arisen to see about her mourning, and to take every precaution that could ensure its being as becoming as Mrs Merdle's.

Lexical repetition, when it is a refusal to pronominalise, is at face value an offence against the maxim of economy of expression, and so acquires a stylistic significance of its own. Something of the multiple values attaching to repetition is suggested by the Conrad example. The repetitions of *object* and of *gallows* clearly have an emotively intensifying effect. But with *gallows* there is also an apparent offence against the maxim of end-focus, since the word's second occurrence is necessarily 'given', and should therefore be defocussed: '*She was aFRAID of the gallows*'. There is, however, a way in which we can motivate this apparent double infringement of textual maxims: we can suppose that *gallows* is used with two different meanings, and hence with two different emphases: a 'double-take' as in '*That object was the GALLOWS. She was afraid of the GALLOWS.*' The first 'gallows' is a visible object; the second 'gallows' is an institution, with all its associations of fear, shame, and death.

My next example illustrates the attribution of meaning through ideational and interpersonal rhetoric, and how this, like textual rhetoric, can manifest ambiguity:

Three years. Long in the aggregate, though short as they went by. And home was very dear to me, and Agnes too – but she was not mine – she was never to be mine. She might have been, but that was past!
(*David Copperfield*)

The question here is: to whom do we attribute the meanings expressed in the passage? Is it to the implied authorial consciousness of the mature David, looking back on his youth? Or is it to the young David, suffering the pangs of love, whose thoughts are here being reported in free indirect speech?

If it is the mature autobiographer's voice anticipating the future, then we find out later, when David does marry Agnes, that we have been conned. So retrospectively, to avoid imputing bad faith to the mature David (and by implication to Dickens), we should conclude that it *was* free indirect speech, reporting the fallible consciousness of the younger David. But perhaps the ambivalence is important at this stage in the story: it enables Dickens to avoid the opposite pitfalls of (a) letting us know too much too soon, and (b) being too blatantly guilty of misleading us.

These quotations illustrate functional stylistics as an explication of a literary work in which, not satisfied with a study of just the formal linguistic features, we seek an interpretation of linguistic features in terms of stylistic or rhetorical values. These values we attribute to the work in an attempt to explain *why* the author used this or that form of expression.

Returning to Jakobson, we have seen that in spite of his functional model of language in general, his definition of the poetic function required him to take a formalist approach to poetic language in particular. In Jakobson and Jones's (1970) analysis of Shakespeare's *Sonnet 129*, for example, there is an impressive and meticulous attention to the formal patterning of the text, but no explanation of how significances are to be read into such patterns (see Attridge's chapter, page 25). There is instead an unargued assumption that complexity of patterning is self-justifying; that virtuosity is its own reward. Criticisms of this formalistic approach have been many − see, for example, Fowler (1975).

From a functional point of view, the observation of formal structures, e.g. of parallelism, is merely the first step towards an exegesis of the text. Consider these syntactic parallelisms from Eliot's *Prufrock*:

After the novels, after the teacups, after the skirts that trail along the floor −

To have bitten off the matter with a smile,
To have squeezed the universe into a ball
To roll it towards some overwhelming question,
To say: 'I am Lazarus, come from the dead ...'

The significance lies not in the structural equivalences themselves:

the novels = the teacups = the skirts that trail along the floor

but in the fact that these equivalences challenge us to find some common factor of meaning linking apparently unconnected phenomena.

Hence the 'set towards the message', as a definition of the poetic or literary function of language, is too limiting, if the 'message' is understood simply as a text in a formal sense. But this does not mean we have to throw away Jakobson's definition entirely. Perhaps it should be reinterpreted in a truly functional sense, as the 'set towards the discourse' − the discourse being, as I have stated it, the literary work in its fullest sense: an interpersonal transaction between author and reader, including all three planes of discourse, representation, and text.

This redefinition corresponds to a view which has been expressed by Widdowson (and in somewhat similar terms by others) that a literary discourse is situationally autonomous, or autotelic. Widdowson says (1975, p.51):

... a piece of literary discourse is in suspense from the usual process of social interaction whereby senders address messages directly to receivers. The literary message does not arise in the normal course of social activity as do other messages, it arises from no previous situation and requires no response, it does not serve as a link between people or as a means of furthering the business of ordinary social life.

This discoursal autonomy, or autotelism, explains why when we appraise a discourse as a piece of literature, we discount the reality of its interactants. For the rhetoric of fiction, as Booth describes it (1961), the implied author and implied reader are more relevant to our understanding of a narrative than the real author or reader. Similarly, for a lyrical poem, the persona the poet presents (real or fictional) is more relevant than the poet's own biographical self.

This autotelism on the discourse plane corresponds with a parallel autotelism on the plane of representation. The domain of reference represented in a literary work need not correspond at all points with historical reality – it may, in fact be a fictional *mock*-reality. So whereas, for example, an autobiography is valued in part in relation to historical truthfulness, an autobiographical novel is not answerable to any such constraint.

Is there any parallel autotelic function on the third functional plane, that of the literary text as a formal object? I would argue that there is, and that it lies in the principle of iconicity which assumes, in literature, an importance far beyond that which it has in everyday language. A literary work, in its textual form, is what Epstein (1975) calls a 'self-reflexive artefact': its very physical substance imitates or enacts the meaning that it represents. I have already mentioned an example of this in textual sequencing: chronological sequencing mimics the order of events in a fiction; psychological sequencing mimics the order of impressions in the mind of some character or narrator. Thus sequencing, although it is recognised as such on the textual plane, can directly dramatise the ideational and interpersonal functions of the work. Whereas iconicity has only a minor role in everyday language use, in literature it comes into its own as an important communicative device.

The autotelic character of literature does not mean that the normal functions of language are suspended. It means, rather, that the other functions are subsumed under the autotelic function. In fact, these other functions are put to work more strenuously in literature, in that all interpersonal, ideational, and textual interpretations have to be extrapolated from the literary work itself: there can be no reliance on the specific contextual knowledge which is so important for conversational interpretation.

In view of what I have said about the diversity and ambivalence of functional interpretation, the autotelic quality of literature means that literature can become an experimental arena for possible discourses, possible experiential worlds, possible texts. Literature can be an 'adventure playground' within which the human communicative-interpretative faculty can be explored without the hindrance of real-life consequences.

One aspect of this exploration is that literary language can be superficially *dys*functional in striking ways, without adverse effects. Dysfunctional features, e.g. distortions of linguistic norm, obscurities, and ambiguities, challenge the reader to find new avenues of interpretation. Jakobson's definition of literary form in terms of patterns of equivalence ignores the important role of deviation from linguistic and other norms in literature: deviation being a negative characteristic of poetic language only so long as one confines oneself to form rather than function.

It seems clear that since the 1958 'Style in Language' conference linguistics and stylistics/poetics have moved from a predominantly formalist or structuralist climate of thought to a predominantly functionalist one. This trend has advanced alongside the development of such fields as pragmatics, text linguistics, discourse analysis, and social semiotics − where the emphasis has shifted away from language as a formal system towards language in use in society. But it may be felt, with some justice, that what we have gained by extending the frontiers of the subject in this way has entailed a sacrifice of rigour; functional stylistics still relies too heavily on selective and subjective judgement.

So, looking ahead rather than back, let us foresee an era in which the processes of interpretation are subjected to more careful study within the framework of 'descriptive rhetoric'. Grice's exploration of conversational implicature is one area where progress has been made in this direction, but there are many more areas (for example, in the study of iconicity) where knowledge is lacking, and where, to explain interpretations, we rely on impressions and guesswork. If progress leads us to overcome these weaknesses, we may look forward to a time when the combination of insight with rigour (which Jakobson admirably demonstrated within a formalist paradigm) will do justice both to literary works themselves as linguistic artefacts, and to the partly-shared, partly-variable processes of interpretation whereby readers find meaning in them.

Notes

1   The connection between Jakobson and Richards is worth exploring in the present context. Richards was the first contributor to that *Style in Language* volume to which Jakobson contributed his 'Closing Statement', and was the only contributor to that symposium older than Jakobson himself. Ten years later, in his late seventies, Richards became a belated but enthusiastic convert to the linguistic analysis of literature, on reading Jakobson and Jones (1970), which he reviewed in the *New York Review of Books*.

2   The distinction between 'discourse' and 'text' here corresponds to that of Widdowson (1975, p. 6).

References

W. Booth, *The Rhetoric of Fiction*, Chicago, 1961.

K. Bühler, *Sprachtheorie*, Jena, 1934.

L. Epstein, 'The self-reflexive artefact: the function of mimesis in an approach to a theory of value for literature', in R. Fowler (ed.), *Style and Structure in Literature: Essays in the New Stylistics*, Oxford, 1975, pp. 40−78.

R. Fowler, 'Language and the reader: Shakespeare's sonnet 73', in R. Fowler (ed.), *Style and Structure in Literature: Essays in the New Stylistics*, Oxford, 1975, pp. 79–122.

H. P. Grice, 'Meaning', *Philosophical Review*, 66, pp. 377–88. Reprinted in D. D. Steinberg & L. A. Jakobovits (eds), *Semantics: An Interdisciplinary Reader in Philosophy, Linguistics and Psychology*, Cambridge, 1971, pp. 53–9.

H. P. Grice, 'Logic and conversation', in P. Cole & J. L. Morgan (eds), *Syntax and Semantics*, Vol. 3: *Speech Acts*, New York, 1975, pp. 41–58.

M. A. K. Halliday, 'Clause types and structural functions', in J. Lyons (ed.), *New Horizons in Linguistics*, Harmondsworth, 1970, pp. 140–65.

M. A. K. Halliday, 'Linguistic function and literary style: an inquiry into William Golding's *The Inheritors*', in S. Chatman, *Literary Style: A Symposium*, Oxford, 1971, pp. 330–65.

M. A. K. Halliday, 'Modes of meaning and modes of expression: types of grammatical structure, and their determination by different semantic functions', in D. Allerton *et al.* (eds), *Function and Context in Linguistic Analysis*, Cambridge, 1979, pp. 57–79.

R. Jakobson, 'Closing statement: linguistics and poetics', in T. A. Sebeok (ed.), *Style in Language*, Cambridge, Massachusetts, 1960, pp. 350–77.

R. Jakobson & L. Jones, *Shakespeare's Verbal Art in 'Th' Expence of Spirit'*, The Hague, 1970.

G. N. Leech, *Principles of Pragmatics*, London, 1983.

G. N. Leech & M. H. Short, *Style in Fiction: A Linguistic Introduction to English Fictional Prose*, London, 1981.

K. R. Popper, *Objective Knowledge: An Evolutionary Approach*, Oxford, 1972.

M. L. Pratt, *Toward a Speech Act Theory of Literary Discourse*, Bloomington, 1977.

I. A. Richards, *Practical Criticism*, London, 1929.

H. G. Widdowson, *Stylistics and the Teaching of Literature*, London, 1975.

After Bakhtin

The widening fame and influence of Mikhail Bakhtin, whose name was scarcely known to Western scholars in 1958, is surely one of the salient features of the years since a famous conference held at Indiana University in 1958. In the minds of most, I suspect, the Indiana Conference on Style, or its proceedings which were published under the title *Style in Language* in 1960,[1] are chiefly associated with the name of Roman Jakobson, whose 'Closing Statement: Linguistics and Poetics', is, of all the items in that volume, certainly the most frequently reprinted and referred to. In fact, it was hardly representative of that conference, being based on a tradition of poetics and linguistics, deriving from the Russian Formalists and the Prague Linguistic Circle, little known to most of the other participants. The main aim of the Style in Language conference was to effect some *rapprochement* between the empirical-intuitive methods of the Anglo-American New Criticism, epitomised in the venerable presence of I. A. Richards, and the inductive, experimental methods of applied linguistics (exemplified by, for example, a statistical analysis of stylistic deviations in suicide notes – surely the psycholinguistic equivalent of dissecting cadavers in pathology labs).[2]

No, Jakobson's paper at that conference was not a closing statement, it was an opening statement. It opened many people's eyes to the existence of a structuralist poetics based on a Saussurean theory of language very different from what was known as 'structural linguistics' in Britain and America at that time; and it opened a phase in recent intellectual history in which European structuralism began to have a powerful impact on the humanities – at first in France, later in Britain and America – especially in linguistics and literary criticism. We are all familiar with the story, and with its sequel, when the Saussurean model of the linguistic sign, and the serene, deductive logic of the structuralist enterprise which it supported, began to be undermined or deconstructed by the critiques of the two Jacques, Lacan and Derrida. Thus was ushered in the era of post-structuralism, which we now inhabit, a noisy and crowded bazaar in which many different, competing voices are to be heard, peddling their wares. Most of them, however, feel obliged to take into account both the Formalist-Structuralist critique of the subjectivity of traditional literary criticism, *and* the deconstructionist uncovering of an unacknowledged subjectivity, a 'transcendental signified', at the heart of classical structuralism itself. The emphasis has shifted in recent years from the structuralist attempt to analyse discourses, including literary texts, in terms of the signifying systems of which they are manifestations, to the problem of reading, of interpretation. But this new hermeneutics is permeated by a fundamental scepticism about the possibility of recuperating a fixed or stable meaning from discourse. The nature of language is such, the deconstructionists tell us, that any text is bound to undermine its own claim to a determinate meaning.[3] The only control over the infinite proliferation of meanings, Stanley Fish tells us, is that exercised by an interpretive community, such as academic literary critics.[4] The effect of structuralism and post-structuralism on traditional literary studies might be compared to that of an earthquake followed by a tidal wave, for both undermined the idea, central to such studies, of the author as a substantial, historic entity, the unique and authenticating origin of the text, whose communicative intention, conscious or unconscious, intrinsic or extrinsic to the text itself, it was the business of the critic to elucidate. It was on this scene of crisis and contention in literary studies that Mikhail Bakhtin made his entrance – or his work did, for he was dead before many of us had heard of him.

We are 'after Bakhtin' in a special sense, for reasons that are well known. Although his first major work, *Problems of Dostoevsky's Art*, was published in Russia in 1929, it was hardly known inside or outside that country until it was reissued in a revised and much expanded form in 1963 under the title *Problems in Dostoevsky's Poetics*. In the intervening Stalinist years, Bakhtin was prevented from publishing under his own name. Towards the end of his life he was to some extent rehabilitated and allowed to publish, but much of his work, written over several decades, has only became available since his death in 1975. The drama of Bakhtin's life, the belatedness with which his extraordinarily original work has been received, has contributed to his appeal and perhaps encouraged the growth of a somewhat uncritical cult around his name, as Paul de Man warned in an article in *Poetics Today* in 1983.[5] It has also rendered his work assimilable by a number of different – and mutually opposed – critical ideologies. Bakhtin himself began writing in opposition to – or, as he would say, in dialogue with – the Russian Formalists, and was obliged to give his arguments a Marxist gloss by collaborating with or publishing under the names of his more conformist friends, Volosinov and Medvedev in the 1920s and 1930s. In consequence he has been eagerly enlisted by latterday Marxist critics who want to attack the alleged idealism of Saussurean linguistics and classical structuralism without succumbing to the nihilistic scepticism of deconstruction. There is some misrepresentation involved here. Bakhtin was no materialist, and his theories were not wholly incompatible with classical structuralism (let us not forget that Jakobson admired Bakhtin and personally helped to secure his rehabilitation). However,

Bakhtin's thought is so many-sided and fertile that he is inevitably open to colonisation by others.

I should admit my own interest. As a critic I have always been concerned with the construction of a poetics of fiction, and the development of a literary history of the novel grounded in such a poetics rather than in content or context. As a practising novelist I find the poststructuralist attack on the idea of the author and on the communicative function of language unappealing, to say the least. I have found the work of Bakhtin both useful and inspiring on all these counts, and like many other readers have been awestruck by the discovery that he was thinking his way, with the minimum of intellectual and material support, through the questions which preoccupy us, decades before we even thought of them. There is certainly a temptation to regard Bakhtin as some kind of prophet providentially sent to deliver us from our critical discontents, and his work as some kind of theoretical panacea. But the temptation must be resisted. There are problems, contradictions and loose ends in Bakhtin's thought, and grappling with them is part of being 'after Bakhtin'.

Bakhtin's thinking about language and literature is essentially binary, that is to say, he works with pairs of terms – monologic/dialogic, poetry/prose, canonical/carnivalesque, and so on. This habit of thought is of course characteristic of the whole structuralist tradition from Saussure onwards. One thinks of Saussure's *langue/parole*, Jakobson's metaphor/metonymy, Barthes's *lisible/scriptible*, and so on. However, there is a tendency for binary oppositions to become hierarchies, one term being privileged over the other. Sometimes this is a quite overt tactic, adopted for polemical purposes, as in the case of Barthes. But to the extent that a binary opposition becomes a hierarchy, its explanatory power in application to the totality of its subject matter is weakened. *S/Z* succeeds because it subverts its own hierarchy, by demonstrating how a *lisible* text can become *scriptible* in the hands of a clever critic. Jakobson frequently drew attention to the built-in bias of poetics and literary criticism towards metaphor rather than metonymy, a bias reflected in the relative neglect of realistic fiction by poetics and literary stylistics until recently. Bakhtin himself, one might say, began by questioning the privileging of *langue* over *parole* in Saussurean linguistics.

Saussure's linguistics is focussed on *langue*, on the abstract system of rules and differences that enables language to signify. Only the system is stable, repeatable and therefore describable in grammatical terms – the manifestations of the system being infinitely variable. Bakhtin in contrast called for a linguistics of *parole*, of language in *use*, recognising that this entailed taking into account the non-linguistic components of any speech act, and thus abandoning the hope of a scientifically-precise total description of language. In this respect he anticipated the interest of linguistics many decades later in what is sometimes called discourse analysis. To Saussure the word was a two-sided sign, signifier and signified. To Bakhtin it was a 'two-sided *act* ...

It is determined equally by whose word it is and for whom it is meant ... A word is territory *shared* by both addresser and addressee, by the speaker *and* his interlocutor.'[6]

'Every decoding is another encoding', another modern authority has asserted.[7] Bakhtin teaches us that this need not be a reason for denying the possibility of communicating meaning in discourse. To mean is precisely to take this condition, that every decoding is another encoding, into account when we speak. 'The word in living conversation is directly, blatantly, oriented towards a future answer word: it provokes an answer, anticipates it and structures itself in the answer's direction.'[8]

Here, however, at the very heart of Bakhtin's thinking about language, we encounter a puzzle or paradox, with which I shall concern myself in the rest of this paper. If language is innately dialogic, how can there be monologic discourse?[9] Bakhtin's literary theory, especially his theory of the novel, depends heavily on the distinction between monologic discourse on the one hand, and dialogic or (in an alternative formulation) polyphonic discourse on the other. The genres canonised by traditional poetics − tragedy, epic, lyric − are monologic: they employ a single style and express a single world-view. The discourse of the novel, in contrast, is an orchestration of diverse discourses culled from heterogeneous sources, oral and written, conveying different ideological positions which are put in play without ever being subjected to totalising judgment or interpretation. Originally Bakhtin attributed the discovery of this discursive polyphony to Dostoevsky. Later he came to think that it was inherent in the novel as a literary form, and he traced it back historically to the comic and satiric writing of the classical period that parodied and travestied the state-approved solemnities of tragedy and epic, and to the carnival tradition in popular culture that sustained an unofficial resistance to the monologic discourses of medieval christendom. (In passing it is important to note that Bakhtin did not believe that Christianity itself was essentially or originally a totalising, monologic ideology. In his view the New Testament is essentially dialogic, and, in such episodes as Christ's entry into Jerusalem on an ass and the crowning with thorns, distinctly carnivalesque. It was later commentators who tried to reduce the Socratic ambiguities and obliquities of Christ's teaching to a monologic system.)

Bakhtin's literary theory is attractive to me personally as both critic and novelist in putting the novel at the centre instead of at the margins of poetics, and approaching it via the typology of discourse rather than via the Aristotelian categories of plot and character, or the Romantic concept of 'style as the man'. If classical poetics privileged tragedy, modern poetics has tended to privilege the lyric poem, but, as Bakhtin himself pointed out, a stylistics which takes lyric poetry as the literary norm is quite inadequate to cope with the language of the novel.[10] That was the point I started from in my first work of criticism, called *Language of Fiction* (1966). That book was written in complete ignorance of Bakhtin (and, for that matter, of Russian Formalism and structuralism). But in omitting the definite article before the word *Language* in my title (it is, more often than not, restored in bibliographies) I was perhaps groping towards Bakhtin's perception that 'it makes no sense to describe "*the* language of the novel" because the very object of such a description, the novel's unitary language, does not exist.'[11] But in trying to bring a New-Critical attentiveness to verbal texture to bear on a number of nineteenth and twentieth-century novels, I still tended to select passages for analysis which were either authorial description or were focalised through characters with whom the implied author was in sympathy, and I never took a passage that consisted mainly of direct speech. In other words, I was looking almost unconsciously for the most direct linguistic expression of the implied author's attitudes, values and world view, and thus treating the novel by analogy with the lyric poem. But as Bakhtin reminds us, a novel is made up of more than one kind of language:

Herein lies the profound distinction between prose style and poetic style ... for the prose artist the world is full of other people's words, among which he must orient himself and whose speech characteristics he must be able to perceive with a very keen ear. He must introduce them into the plane of his own discourse, but in such a way that this plane is not destroyed. He works with a very rich verbal palette.[12]

As an example of what this means in practice, let me cite the opening passage of a short story by Katherine Mansfield, 'The Fly', which I discussed briefly in *Language of Fiction*, because it had been the subject of an interesting article in *Essays in Criticism* in 1962 by F. W. Bateson and B. Shahevitch, endeavouring to show (as I was) that 'close reading' was just as much 'in order for realistic fiction as for a poem', though the formal features to be analysed were different.[13]

'Y'are very snug in here', piped old Mr Woodifield, and he peered out of the great, green-leather armchair by his friend the boss's desk as a baby peers out of its pram. His talk was over; it was time for him to be off. But he did not want to go. Since he had retired, since his ... stroke, the wife and girls kept him boxed up in the house every day of the week except Tuesday. On Tuesday he was dressed and brushed and allowed to cut back to the City for the day. Though what he did there the wife and girls couldn't imagine. Made a nuisance of himself to his friends, they supposed ... Well, perhaps so. All the same, we cling to our last pleasures as the tree clings to its last leaves. So there sat old Woodifield, smoking a cigar and staring almost greedily at the boss, who rolled in his office chair, stout, rosy, five years older than he, and still going strong, still at the helm. It did one good to see him.[14]

This is not the place to attempt a detailed and exhaustive analysis of the passage. I wish merely to draw attention to the way in which the authorial narrator's discourse − most clearly identifiable, perhaps, in the similes, cast in the 'gnomic' present tense, '*as a baby peers out of its pram*' and '*as the tree clings to its leaves*' − is crossed by and intermingled with the discourses of the characters − Woodifield, whose repression of the idea of death, a repression that, in the person of the boss, proves to be the central theme of the story, is betrayed by the aposeopesis in the phrase '*since his ... stroke*', and Woodifield's womenfolk, whose impatient, patronising chatter is evoked in, '*Though what he did there the wife and girls couldn't imagine. Made a nuisance of himself to his friends, they supposed ...*' The familiarly possessive definite article here, '*the* wife and girls' suggests that Woodifield has heard or overheard their talk – that it is an indirect quote within an indirect quote. Or is it the narrator quoting the earlier occurrence of the same phrase in a sentence that is clearly Woodifield's indirect speech? The deixis of the passage is ambiguous and often undecidable. For instance: '*On Tuesday he was dressed and brushed and allowed to cut back to the City for the day.*' The passive constructions, *dressed and brushed*, recalling the ironic simile of the baby peering out of the pram, may encourage us to begin reading this sentence as authorial, but the idiomatic '*cut*' seems to belong to Woodifield's discourse, suggesting that he is well aware of the indignities of second childhood. The authorial narrator's '*Well, perhaps so*', seems disapproving of the women's dismissive attitude to Woodifield's weekly outing; and the rather poetic simile of the tree clinging to its leaves reproves the reader who may have taken the earlier simile of the baby in the pram as an invitation to patronise the old man. The reader, in short, instead of being told at the outset what the story is to be about, and whose story it is, and what position he should adopt towards the various characters in it, is listening, as it were, to a babble of different discourses, each with its own values, prejudices, ironies, and is obliged to construct and continuously revise his own hypothesis about the story's import.

To give Bateson and Shahevitch their due, they observed that 'This mixing of direct statement with indirect or concealed dialogue is used all through the story ... The result is that we have very little regular narrative. Instead, in a frame of thin lines of this quasi-narrative, which could almost be spoken by a chorus, we have the effect of drama.'[15] A very Bakhtinian remark, I think you will agree, the full implications of which the authors themselves did not perhaps appreciate. Certainly I did not when I first read it. To Bakhtin this fusion of author's discourse and characters' discourses through free indirect speech and what he called doubly-oriented speech was constitutive of the novel as a literary form. Characters, and the persona of the authorial narrator herself, are constituted not simply by their own linguistic registers or ideolects, but by the discourses they quote and allude to.

A corollary of Bakhtin's insight is that language which in itself is flat, banal, clichéd and generally automatised can become vividly expressive when mimicked, heightened, stylised, parodied and played off against other kinds of language in the polyphonic discourse of the novel. That is why a novelist, as Bakhtin says, must have a very keen ear for other people's words (not an essential qualification for the lyric poet) and why he cannot afford to cut himself off from low, vulgar, debased language; why nothing linguistic is alien to him, from theological treatises to the back of cornflakes packets, from the language of the barrack room to the language of, say, academic conferences.

Perhaps here, in relation to our own professional discourse, is the place to confront the question I posed earlier: if language is inherently dialogic, how can there be monologic discourse, on the postulated existence of which Bakhtin's literary theory depends? One answer might be that in writing, as distinct from oral speech, the physical absence of the addressee from the context of the speech act makes it possible for the addresser to ignore or suppress the dialogic dimension of language, and thus create the illusion of monologic discourse. It was after all in 'living conversation', not in writing, that Bakhtin said the work is 'directly, blatantly oriented towards a future answer word', in the passage I quoted earlier.

Consider the typical scholarly article or book in the fields of literary criticism and literary theory. Such discourses may take issue with the arguments and interpretations of other scholars (hence the ritual citation of other treatments of the subject at the outset) but they don't do so by directly engaging with these opponents in a dialogue. The professional scholar typically states his opinions as if they were facts, and avoids the pronouns 'I' and 'you', preferring the consensual terms 'we' and 'the reader', which bind together both addresser and addressee in a fiction of solidarity and agreement. The only literary critic I can think of who consistently employs an *I—you* form of address is D. H. Lawrence. This is interesting, because in *Women in Love*, Lawrence wrote what is probably the nearest thing to a Dostoevskean novel, in Bakhtin's terms, to be found in English Literature.[16] As critic, notably in *Studies in Classic American Literature*, he harangues, exhorts, questions and teases his readers somewhat in the style of Dostoevsky's Underground Man. More idiosyncratically still, he harangues, exhorts, questions and teases the writers he is discussing — Whitman, for instance:

'*And of these one and all I weave the song of myself —*'
Do you? Well then, it just shows you haven't *got* any self. It's a mush, not a woven thing. A hotch-potch, not a tissue. Your self.
Oh Walter, Walter, what have you done with it? What have you done with yourself? With your own individual self? For it sounds as if it had all leaked out of you, leaked out into the universe.[17]

The shock of encountering this style of critical discussion throws into relief the superficial monologism of most scholarly discourse.

I say 'superficial' because scholarly discourse is in fact saturated in the kind of dialogic rhetoric that Bakhtin named 'hidden polemic', when an utterance not only refers to a given topic, but engages with, or anticipates or seeks to discredit another actual or hypothetical speech act about the same topic. Our articles and monographs will make little sense to a reader who is outside the ongoing 'conversation' to which they belong, and who is unable to identify the echoes of, allusions to, sly digs at, flattering appeals to, other writers on the same subjects. But scholarly discourse aspires to the condition of monologue inasmuch as it tries to say the last word on a given subject, to affirm its mastery over all previous words on that subject.

In Bakhtin's perspective it is not possible to say 'the last word' about anything in the human sphere, whatever may be the case in the physical sciences, and he venerated Dostoevsky for founding his art of fiction upon this principle: at the end of Dostoevsky's novels, says Bakhtin, *'nothing* conclusive has yet taken place in the world, the ultimate word of the world and about the world has not yet been spoken, the world is open and free, everything is still in the future and always will be in the future.'[18] The pretence of literary and linguistic scholarship to say the last word about its subject therefore always entails a certain measure of self-deception or bad faith which manifests itself in various discursive symptoms. For instance it has been observed – I think it was in an article in *PMLA* some years ago – that the Prefaces and Forewords to academic books are always much milder and more tentative than the discourses they introduce: full of qualifications, disclaimers, professions of humility, effusive thanks to friends, colleagues and spouses – all propritiative and ingratiating gestures. It is as if the authors, rather dismayed by the monologic arrogance of the discourses they have produced, are seeking, at the last minute, a dialogue with their potential readers over the heads of these discourses.

From the same source comes the curious mixture of boredom, irritation and embarrassment with which one reads reviews of one's own books – I speak personally, but perhaps for others too. A review should be, in principle, a dialogic rejoinder to one's own discourse, but that discourse did not want or expect a rejoinder, it pretended to render all further discussion of the matter superfluous, to leave the reader in a state of dumb admiration. Hence, if your reviewer agrees with you, he seems to be stating the obvious, which is boring, or he agrees with you for the wrong reasons, which is embarrassing, and if he disagrees with you, it is because he has missed the point, or is airing a view of his own, which is irritating. He may, of course, have discovered some genuine flaw in your argument, which is most disconcerting of all, since it raises the awful prospect of having to try and revise or modify an argument that was not designed for revision and modification.

Some people, especially women, might say that I am describing or carica-turing a specifically male model of scholarly discourse, based on power and domination, and perhaps I am. I am not suggesting that academic critical discourse has to be like that, only that, by and large, it *is*. Even Bakhtin himself follows the model in the early chapters of his Dostoevsky book, where he is criticising other writers on Dostoevsky. In his theoretical work, however, he avoided the trap and managed to write a genuinely dialogic kind of criticism in which the key propositions are continuously open to self-questioning, modification and revision.

To define monologic discourse as a kind of illusion or fiction that is facilitated by writing rather than speaking does not entirely solve the problem raised by Bakhtin's privileging of dialogic discourse. What about the poetic genres classified by Bakhtin as monologic – lyric, epic, tragedy? Are they to be regarded as inherently less interesting and less valuable than the novel? It has to be admitted that the spectre of a critical dualism hovers over Bakhtin's work, and that it could easily encourage a limiting division of writers into sheep and goats such as the school of Leavis and *Scrutiny* encouraged in this country not long ago. There is a tendency in Bakhtin to assimilate everything that is progressive, life-enhancing, and liberating in writing to the concept of the novel. As Clark and Holquist observe, 'Bakhtin assigns the term "novel" to whatever form of expression within a given literary system reveals the limits of that system as inadequate, imposed or arbitrary. The canonical genres are then associated with whatever is fixed, rigid, authoritarian.'[19] The very notion of genre is defined by the repeatability of its rules and conventions. The novel, Bakhtin asserted, is an anti-generic genre: 'It is plasticity itself. It is a genre that is ever questing, ever examining itself and subjecting its established forms to review.'[20] This, of course, is absolutely true, and Bakhtin is not the only critic to have said it. But the question remains: must we therefore relegate the monologic genres to an inferior status?

In the evolution of the novel itself, Bakhtin saw a continual struggle between monologic and dialogic tendencies: between, on the one hand, a kind of prose fiction that was written in a single homogeneous style – Greek romance, Renaissance pastoral romance, the eighteenth-century novel of sentimental pathos (and, I would be inclined to add, the Gothic novel); on the other hand the kind of prose fiction that rejoiced in and exploited the multiplicity of languages and dialects in a given historical epoch – the Menippean satires of the classical world, the great works of Rabelais and Cervantes in the Renaissance, the English comic novel of the eighteenth century. Clark and Holquist call these two traditions the 'monoglot' and the 'heteroglot', and summarise Bakhtin's theory of the novel thus:

The two lines, heteroglot and monoglot, come together and merge at the beginning of the nineteenth century. Although the major representatives of the novel are from that point on mixed, features of the heteroglot line tend to dominate. Because the heteroglot line is more open to difference, it could more easily absorb the increasing tide of self-consciousness. In other words, the heteroglot novel was able to accommodate more of the self because it is more sensitive to otherness.[21]

This historicist, almost messianic view of the novel as a literary form helps to explain why it has dominated the modern era, and why the monoglot fiction of the past seems to the modern reader either quaint or tedious – why, for instance, we tend to prefer Nashe's heteroglot *The Unfortunate Traveller*, never reprinted in the seventeenth century, to the monoglot *Arcadia* of Sir Philip Sidney, immensely popular and frequently reprinted in the same period. But, the sceptical reader is likely to ask, what about the great writers who, either before or after the full flowering of the novel, chose to write in the medium of poetry – what about, to take a few names at random, Chaucer, Shakespeare, Milton, Keats, Browning, Eliot, Yeats?

Some of these writers can easily be accommodated in Bakhtin's literary-historical scheme by his concept of novelisation, that is, the infiltration and fertilisation of the canonic poetic genres by the heteroglot, carnivalesque discourse of the novel conceived in its broadest sense. Bakhtin never claimed that *verse* as a medium was necessarily monologic. One of his favourite sources of examples of dialogic discourse was Pushkin's verse novel, *Eugene Onegin*. I am not sure that he knew the work of Chaucer, but it would not be difficult to argue that the qualities in the *Canterbury Tales* which have made it seem, in comparison to most other Middle English texts, so startlingly modern and accessible to modern readers, are precisely those qualities which Bakhtin characterises as novelistic. Bakhtin did know Shakespeare, and apparently lectured on him, though I have not encountered any substantial discussion of Shakespeare in Bakhtin's published writings. However, it would not be difficult to construct a Bakhtinian reading of Shakespearean drama, which is manifestly polyphonic in comparison to classical or neoclassical drama, and to relate this to the evolution of Elizabethan theatre from the carnivalesque tradition of the mystery plays, with their parodic-travestying subplots and refusal of stylistic decorum. The history of nineteenth and twentieth-century poetry, especially the popularity of the dramatic monologue in this period, gives ample evidence of the novelisation of the lyric impulse as the novel became the dominant literary form. Browning and T. S. Eliot would be obvious examples. Indeed, *The Waste Land*, which originally bore the Bakhtinian epigraph, '*He do the police in different voices*', could be seen as the apotheosis of Bakhtin's poetic, since it is a work constructed wholly out of what Bakhtin called heteroglossia and polyglossia – fragments of speech and writing in different languages and different registers that interact and resonate without the restraints of narrative logic.

But still the nagging doubts persist: what about Milton, Keats, Yeats, and many other ostensibly monologic poets that they represent? If they are only redeemable through the loophole of novelisation, then the loophole would seem to be bigger than the boundary wall it punctuates. There is some evidence that Bakhtin himself was troubled by this built-in bias of his literary theory. In order to bring out the special qualities and formal characteristics of novelistic discourse, he perhaps exaggerated its difference from the poetic genres. Thus, in the essay, 'Discourse in the novel' probably written in 1934–35, we find him making a sharply defined distinction between the dialogism of prose and the polysemy of poetry:

... no matter how one understands the interrelationship of meanings in a poetic symbol ... this interrelationship is never of the dialogic sort; it is impossible ... to imagine a trope (say, a metaphor) being unfolded into two exchanges of a dialogue ... The polysemy of the poetic symbol presupposes the unity of a voice with which it is identical, and it presupposes that such a voice is completely alone within its own discourse. As soon as another's voice, another's accent, the possibility of another's point of view breaks through this play of the symbol, the poetic plane is destroyed and the symbol is translated on to the plane of prose.[22]

If this were so, one would have to say that a poem like Yeats's 'Among Schoolchildren' is a masterpiece of prose, since its primary symbols − swan, girl, scarecrow − are mediated through a wide spectrum of linguistic registers, from the homely to the hieratic, and the persona of the poet is present to us both as the sixty-year-old smiling public man seen by the nuns and their pupils, and the inner self racked by nostalgia, frustration and desire.

Can there, in fact, be such a thing as an *absolutely* monologic literary text? Bakhtin himself came to doubt it. In a remarkable passage, in an article written in 1959−61, and first published in 1976, quoted in Tzvetan Todorov's excellent monograph, *Mikhail Bakhtin: The Dialogic Principle*, Bakhtin says, or rather asks (for the passage is characteristically a dialogue with himself):

To what extent is a discourse purely single-voiced and without any objectal character, possible in literature? Can a discourse in which the author does not hear the author's voice, in which there is no one but the author and all of the author, can such a discourse become the raw material of a literary work? Isn't a certain degree of objectal character a necessary condition for any style? Doesn't the author always find himself *outside* of language in its capacity as the material of the literary work? Isn't every writer (even the purest lyric poet) always a 'playwright' insofar as he distributes all the discourses among alien voices, including that of the 'image of the author' (as well as the author's other *personae*)? It may be that every single-voiced and nonobjectal discourse is naive and inappropriate to authentic creation. The authentically creative voice can only be a *second* voice in the discourse. Only the second voice − *pure relation*, can remain nonobjectal to the end and cast no substantial and phenomenal shadow. The writer is a person who knows how to work language while remaining outside of it; he has the gift of indirect speech.[23]

Does this remarkable passage, which seems to collapse the distinction between dialogic and monologic discourse, render all Bakhtin's previous literary theory invalid? I think not. But it encourages us to apply the distinction in terms of dominance or 'set' rather than as two mutually exclusive categories − in the same way as one applies Jakobson's distinction between metaphor and metonymy, or Plato's distinction between diegesis and mimesis (from which Bakhtin's distinction ultimately derives). One could develop a typology of genres or modes of writing according to whether they exploit and celebrate the inherently dialogic nature of language in living speech, or suppress and limit it for specific literary effects. Performed with the kind of detachment and self-consciousness Bakhtin describes in the passage I have just read, monologism need not be naive or repressive. There is a prose monologism of the avant-garde. In the later fiction of Samuel Beckett, for instance, a post-modernist sense of solipsism, alienation and the absurd, is eloquently expressed by a monologic discourse that seems weirdly independent of any other source of speech, that proceeds by self-cancellation rather than interaction: 'a voice along with its own discourse', to use Bakhtin's phrase for the lyric poet. I am tempted to put some recent deconstructionist criticism in the same category. Beckett's Unnamable seems prophetic in this respect:

I seem to speak, it is not I, about me, it is not about me. These few general remarks to begin with. What am I to do, what shall I do, what shall I do in my situation, how proceed? By aporia pure and simple? Or by affirmations and negations invalidated as soon as uttered, sooner or later? Generally speaking. There must be other shifts. Otherwise it would be quite hopeless. But it is quite hopeless. I should mention before I go any further on, that I say aporia without knowing what it means.[24]

The concluding sentence of the passage from Bakhtin I just quoted seems to me particularly worth pondering: '*The writer is a person who knows how to work language while remaining outside of it; he has the gift of indirect speech.*' Bakhtin joins hands here with the speech act theorists who have defined literary discourse in terms of the peculiarity of its illocutionary force: a literary text is not a real speech act, but an imitation of a speech act. It is uttered and received at a second remove. Normal criteria of 'felicity' are therefore not always relevant.[25] Bakhtin's statement also engages with one of the most radical and controversial planks in poststructuralist literary theory, namely the disenfranchisement of the author. If we go back to Roland Barthes's seminal 1968 essay, 'The death of the author', we find him beginning thus:

In his story *Sarrasine* Balzac, describing a castrato disguised as a woman, writes the following sentence: '*This was woman herself, with her sudden fears, her irrational whims, her instinctive worries, her impetuous boldness, her fussings, and her delicious sensibility.*' Who is speaking thus? Is it the hero of the story bent on remaining ignorant of the castrato hidden beneath the woman? Is it Balzac the individual, furnished by his personal experience with a philosophy of Woman? Is it Balzac the author professing 'literary' ideas on femininity? Is it universal wisdom? Romantic psychology? We shall never know, for the good reason that writing is the destruction of every voice, of every point of origin. Writing is that neutral, composite, oblique space where our subject slips away, the negative where all identity is lost, starting with the very identity of the body writing.[26]

This is both very similar to Bakhtin and antithetical to him. Because the sentence from *Sarrasine* cannot with confidence be attributed to any single voice, Barthes argues that we must abandon the whole idea of writing having an origin. Bakhtin would say that this fusion of several different voices, by which the excitement of the focalising character is expressed and simultaneously ironised by the evocation of other, stereotyped social discourses about women – that this effect is constitutive of the novel as a literary form, and that it in no way prohibits us from inferring the existence of a creative mind that produces it by a kind of literary ventriloquism. In the late passage I quoted, he came to the realisation that this is true of all literary discourse, whether or not the surface structure of the text betrays the fact. Barthes says: because

the author does not coincide with the language of the text, he does not exist.
Bakhtin says, it is precisely because he does not so coincide that we must posit
his existence.

Notes

1   Thomas A. Sebeok (ed.), *Style in Language*, Cambridge, Massachusetts, 1960.
2   Charles E. Osgood, 'Some effects of motivation on style of encoding', in Sebeok
(ed.), *Style in Language*, pp. 293–306.
3   e.g., 'Deconstruction is not a dismantling of the structure of a text but a
demonstration that it has already dismantled itself', J. Hillis Miller, 'Stevens' rock
and criticism as cure, II' *The Georgia Review*, XXX, 2, 1976, p. 341.
4   Stanley Fish, *Is There A Text In This Class? The Authority of Interpretive
Communities*, Cambridge, Massachusetts, 1980.
5   Paul de Man, 'Dialogue and dialogism', *Poetics Today*, IV, 1983, pp. 99–107.
6   V. N. Volosinov (M. M. Bakhtin), *Marxism and the Philosophy of Language*,
trans. Ladislav Matejka & I. R. Titunik, New York, 1973, pp. 85–6.
7   Morris Zapp, in the present writer's novel, *Small World: An Academic
Romance*, London, 1984, pp. 25–6.
8   M. M. Bakhtin, *The Dialogic Imagination: Four Essays*, Michael Holquist (ed),
trans. Caryl Emerson & Michael Holquist, Austin and London, 1981, p. 280.
9   The question has, of course, been posed before. See, for instance, the interesting
exchange between Ken Hirschkop, 'A response to the forum on Mikhail Bakhtin', and
Gary Saul Morson, 'Dialogue, monologue, and the social: a reply to Ken Hirschkop',
in *Critical Inquiry*, XI, 1985, pp. 672–86. The most lucid and balanced discussion is
probably to be found in Tzvetan Todorov, *Mikhail Bakhtin: The Dialogic Principle*,
Manchester, 1984, pp. 66–8 & *passim*.
10   M. M. Bakhtin, *Problems of Dostoevsky's Poetics*, ed. & trans. Caryl
Emerson, Manchester, 1984, p. 200.
11   Bakhtin, *The Dialogic Imagination*, p. 416.
12   Bakhtin, *Problems of Dostoevsky's Poetics*, pp. 200–1.
13   F. W. Bateson & B. Shahevitch, 'Katherine Mansfield's *The Fly:* A critical
Exercise', *Essays in Criticism*, XII, 1982, pp. 39–53.
14   Katherine Mansfield, *The Collected Stories*, Harmondsworth, 1981, p. 412.
'The Fly' was first collected in Katherine Mansfield's *The Dove's Nest and other stories*,
1923.
15   Bateson & Shahevitch, 'Mansfield's *The Fly*', p. 49.
16   See the present writer's 'Lawrence, Dostoevsky, Bakhtin: D. H. Lawrence and
dialogic fiction,' *Renaissance and Modern Studies*, XXIX, 1985, pp. 16–32.
17   D. H. Lawrence, *Studies in Classic American Literature*, New York, 1964,
p. 165.
18   Bakhtin, *Problems of Dostoevsky's Poetics*, p. 166.
19   Katerina Clark & Michael Holquist, *Mikhail Bakhtin*, Cambridge, Massachusetts, 1984, p. 276.
20   Bakhtin, *The Dialogic Imagination*, p. 39.
21   Clark & Holquist, *Mikhail Bakhtin*, p. 293.

22   Bakhtin, *The Dialogic Imagination*, pp. 327–8.

23   M. M. Bakhtin, 'The problem of text in linguistics, philosophy, and the other human sciences: an essay of philosophical analysis', quoted by T. Todorov, *Mikhail Bakhtin*, p. 68.

24   Samuel Beckett, *Malone Dies, Molloy, The Unnamable*, London, 1959, p. 293.

25   See, for example, Richard Ohmann, 'Speech, action, and style', in Seymour Chatman (ed.), *Literary Style*, London & New York, 1971, pp. 241–59.

26   Roland Barthes, *Image–Music–Text*, trans. Stephen Heath, London, 1977, p. 142.

Directions from structuralism

The academic scene is fraught with mortality; the *-isms* of its trade have a way of dying a violent death. Take, for example, the *-isms* connected with the study of language: in this one field alone report of the demise of some *-ism* or other is always circulating. And yet, to speak thus is to give, perhaps, too decisive, too one-sided a picture. It may be that, like beauty, death too lies in the eye of the beholder. Perhaps the very phenomena some see as death violently perpetrated on an ageing conceptual system could be seen by others as simply a 'becoming' – an evolution, whose point of departure lay already within the system's earlier modes of being. But the latter view cuts out the drama, doing away with heroes; it denies the possibility of hero-worship. And, like death, hero-worship too is an essential ingredient of the academic scene: academics need to worship their heroes just as much as the religious need to worship their deities. So the cataclysmic view of change/becoming as violent death has a good deal to offer. Still if we are to make an announcement of death, then it is prudent that we should have at least some idea of the identity of the dying subject. One may exclaim: surely the identity of the dying subject in the study of language today is not so hidden that one would need to make this the central problematic of one's paper. Surely, it is a secret very well revealed that the dying subject is 'structuralism'. Does one need to say any more, once the name has been named?

I submit that one does, for at least two reasons. If structuralism is dying today, then this, its present death, is a 'second dying': could this second dying be just about as mythical as the 'second coming'? The question is at least worth exploring. Secondly, naming a name is not equal to saying what the name names: if what we are witness to now is 'post-structuralism', it is valid to ask what that structuralism is which this post-structuralism is 'post' to. Let me turn first to a regrettably potted history of the first death of structuralism, the first advent of post-structuralism, which was heralded by transformational-generativism. For there are a few ironic turns in this episode which somewhat discredit the dramaturgical account of how knowledge, if knowledge it is, progresses; the hero, the villain(s), the mortal combat to rescue the 'science of language' from the evils of structuralism – all, in this event, turned out to be figments of academic fantasy, which is not to say that nothing happened. But what happened was appreciably different from what either the *dramatis personae* or the not-impartial observers imagined was actually happening. The death-blow that Chomsky dealt against behaviourism (Chomsky 1959) was seen as annihilating the very basis of structuralism already said to be shaken to its roots by the advent of new 'trees' (Chomsky 1957). So it came about that the first dying of structuralism was proclaimed in the early sixties; and as happens in many 'primitive' communities, including the academic one, the name of the dead subject became taboo: to be called a structuralist was to be counted as dead. The living were the transformational-generativists, emerging victoriously from the valley of death bearing the talisman of competence, of intuition, of infallible rules, and of innateness, for all of which, let the good god be thanked.

But if structuralism is dying now, then either it is taking a long time dying or it was something else that died in the 'Chomskian revolution'. It is to be noted that Chomsky displayed considerable indifference to the not inconsiderable differences between that aggregate of principles and practices that went under the name of structuralism in America, and that other such aggregate which went by the same name (same? in what sense 'same'?) in Europe (Greimas 1974; Halliday 1974). Rather simplistically, the world of the study of language got divided into two neat halves – TG and the rest – pitted against each other. 'The rest' was, of course, defective: it was empiricist, data-oriented, behaviourist, incompetent to account for competence, for rule-governed creativity and much else, including the supreme gift of God to man in the shape of a universal grammar. For at least a decade, the Chomskian debate remained silent – or was it that it lacked all awareness? – about just those presuppositions regarding the nature of language which it shared with its adversary, the American structuralism. TG had arisen, not quite like some mythic race, out of divine fire, with no predecessors to its discredit, but from such distant ones that their voices could be heard down the corridor of time only by the chosen few. This too was necessary: Derrida (1974; 1978; 1982) has claimed that Western philosophy of language has been obsessed from time immemorial with the 'transcendental signified'; would it be equally valid to claim that Western academia has been just as much obsessed by an élitist notion of 'originality' which runs counter to the interpretation of human history as 'becoming'?

I do not apologise for this partial account of the first death of structuralism, for its partialness is quite intentional; it is relevant here only in that I perceive certain commonalities between this episode of the past(?) and that which is said to be unfolding now. As in the past, so in the present, at issue is the identity of structuralism; as in the past, so in the present, the 'post-ness' of post-structuralism is but an affix to structuralism, almost as if the very structure of the word iconically announced the impossibility of a clear break. I perceive, then, two central issues there, which are inter-related: first, the identity of structuralism is far from clear and obvious; secondly, whatever that identity, the cataclysmic, dramatic 'break' is less a break than revived variations on some hitherto forgotten or ignored theme(s). By the same token, it is difficult to arrive at the identity of what is 'called "post-structuralism" (but not, perhaps, with sufficient embarrassment over how empty the term is)' (Schmidt 1985, p. 166). The situation is then one rather nicely tangled, providing linguists, philosophers and literary critics with an open, never-ending possibility of cross-talk − or 'writing' if you prefer. But it could not have been otherwise; and this would have been obvious if Derrida were taken seriously, if the grammatological precepts had been applied with the recommended rigour to the signifier? signified? sign? whose writing is *structuralism*. It too would have all the qualities of indeterminacy that would prevent the easy assumption of unity and self-identity, often ascribed to any *-ism*, as if '*-ism*-ness' were guarantee of definite 'content'. If, as a linguistic sign, *structuralism* were to be regarded as subject to the same indeterminacies, if there were no definite signified always attached/attachable to this signifier, as Derrida has so brilliantly argued for signs in general, then what would it mean to say '... the structuralist invasion ...' (Derrida 1978, p. 3) or '... a structuralist reading, by its own activity, always presupposes ...' (Derrida 1978, p. 24). Is Derrida suggesting there is some 'invariant' structuralism or is he talking about any structuralist reading? If the latter, is there an implication that Derrida knows the full possibilities of 'structuralist reading(s)'? If so, I submit that there is no evidence to encourage this view. What does it mean to say '... modern structuralism has grown ...' (Derrida 1978, p. 27)? Is there an implication that there actually is a unified 'something' that could be called 'modern structuralism'? Even if we were to grant that Saussure is the first structuralist − a doubtful proposition on Derrida's own showing (1974); his voice echoes voices from the past − this does not preclude the possibility that in the manner of other, less momentous, sayings, Saussure's sayings too became at once same-and-different sayings in the discourse of others. *Structuralism* moved in so many directions, occurred in so many different textual environments, that it is no longer possible to talk about a structuralist reading, or modern structuralism.

The above comments are not meant to score a cute point: if anything they are offered as a sign of general puzzlement. Despite Rorty's stern warning about Derrida that 'he is not, to repeat, a philosopher of language' (Rorty 1982, p. 105), I have found Derrida's reflections on language fascinating − but this is not to say that the reading has not been mystifying. Part of the puzzlement arises from my perception that Salusinszky (1983) is not alone in believing 'that deconstruction, far from being structuralism's new ally, is that very movement which has undone structuralism'. Yet in many important respects, Derrida's positions appear to me to have been already voiced by precisely those scholars who would, by any definition, be regarded as structuralists − e.g. Saussure (1966), of course, but also Hjelmslev (1961), one of the few 'modern structuralists' to get some specific attention from Derrida. Take for example, the question of representation, a central concern of Derrida's from which arise critiques of the notions of signified, signifier, sign, concept, thought etc. Derrida is concerned that in the Saussurean model 'not only do the signifier and signified seem to unite, but also in this confusion, the signifier seems to erase itself or to become transparent, in order to allow the concept to present itself as what it is, referring to nothing other than its presence' (Derrida 1981, p. 22).

True that the text attributed to Saussure contains such statements as 'it [i.e. sound] is only the instrument of thought; by itself it has no existence', but what kind of a theory of 'differance' is it that fails to see the working of 'differance' in actual practice? Derrida remarks about the *Course* that 'Saussure's text, like any other is not homogeneous' (Derrida, 1981, p. 52); and, it certainly is true that the use of concept, thought, signified is not invariant. Some of this non-homogeneity is indicative of the fact that Saussure, like all of us, was not operating in a vacuum; other voices had discoursed, were discoursing on language. Even though one might ambitiously undertake to rebuild all previous knowledge purely from within, ways of saying that one has participated in as sayer/listener become one's ways of being. So Saussure's voice is not simply his voice; it is also the voice of pre-Saussures. On this, hopefully, there is no disagreement. However, some non-homogeneity seems to have been deliberate, using as point of departure the ways of saying prevalent in the general community. This, in the context of *Course*, was important, for the audience here did not consist of philosophers. Passages such as the following do not quite fit in with the facile picture Derrida presents (see quote above) of Saussure's view of the relationship between signified and signifier:

Without language, thought is a vague, uncharted nebula. There are no pre-existing ideas, and nothing is distinct before the appearance of language ... Phonic substance is neither more fixed nor more rigid than thought; it is not a mold into which thought must of necessity fit but a plastic substance divided in turn into distinct parts to furnish the signifiers needed by thought ... The characteristic role of language with respect to thought is not to create a material phonic means for expressing ideas but to serve as a link between thought and sound, under conditions that of necessity bring about the reciprocal delimitations of units ... Neither are thoughts given material form nor are sounds transformed into mental entities; the somewhat mysterious fact is rather that 'thought–sound' implies division, and that language works out its units while taking shape between two shapeless masses.
(Saussure 1966, p. 112)

This and other such passages, easily found throughout the *Course*, do not sound very much like the celebration of the 'transcendental signified' or a dangerous tendency toward logocentrism. If 'thought', 'concept' etc. are used, they are used at this early, pre-theoretical stage precisely where the term 'signified' will be used later, and this context does alter the value of 'thought', 'concept' in the *Course*.

It is useful to note here that Hjelmslev commenting on the above passage from Saussure had some critical remarks to make:

Saussure, in order to clarify the sign function, undertook the device of trying to consider expression and content each alone, without consideration of the sign function … But this pedagogical Gedankenexperiment, however excellently carried out, is actually meaningless, and Saussure himself must have found it so. In a science that avoids unnecessary postulates there is no basis for the assumption that content-substance (thought) or expression-substance (sound-chain) precede language in time or hierarchical order, or vice versa.
(Hjelmslev 1961, pp. 49–50)

Structuralism, then, denies the 'metaphysics of presence', at least some of the time if not all the time. To select only those parts of the writing to which could be ascribed a hankering for the real thing out there shows a bias; and establishing the reasons for this bias could conceivably provide a good project for deconstruction! It seems to me that neither Saussure nor Hjelmslev affirms the ultimate phenomenality of the signified; in particular, Hjelmslev was quite explicit on this issue. Compare then Peirce's notion of the sign, which Derrida approves of, with some of Hjelmslev's sayings. First Peirce via Derrida:

According to the 'phaneoroscopy' or 'phenomenology' of Peirce, *manifestation* itself does not reveal a presence, it makes a sign. One may read in the *Principles of Phenomenology* that 'the idea of manifestation is the idea of a sign'. There is thus no phenomenality reducing the sign or the representer so that the thing signified may be allowed to glow finally in the luminosity of its presence. The so-called 'thing-itself' is always already a *representamen* shielded from the simplicity of intuitive evidence. The *representamen* functions only by giving rise to an *interpretant* that itself becomes a sign and so on to infinity.
(Derrida 1974, p. 49)

On the next page of this text, the approved definition of the sign is quoted: '*Anything which determines something else (its interpretant) to refer to an object to which itself refers (its object) in the same way, this interpretant becoming in turn a sign, and so on ad infinitum* … If the series of successive interpretants comes to an end, the sign is thereby rendered imperfect, at least' (italics as in Derrida 1974, p. 50). Derrida goes on to comment, approvingly: 'From the moment that there is meaning there are nothing but signs. We *think only in signs*' (ibid.) ('*Think in*'? Surely not. *We think signs.*) How does all this compare with Hjelmsev's position? I neither have the time nor the ability to summarise Hjelmslev's already 'lean' statements. So a few quotations and comments will have to suffice.

Let us begin then with the fundamental Hjelmslevian point that in talking about signs, one is not talking about isolates/isolables, e.g. signifier *or* signified. 'The postulation of objects as something different from the terms of relationships is a superfluous axiom and consequently a metaphysical hypothesis from which linguistic sciences will have to be freed' (Hjelmslev

1961, p. 23). This general observation is pertinent to Hjelmslev's discussion of sign. Starting first with the 'vague conception bequeathed by tradition' according to which a sign 'is characterized first and foremost by being a sign *for* something else', Hjelmslev concludes from this popular notion that 'a "sign" is defined by a function. A "sign" functions, designates, denotes; a "sign" in contradistinction to a non-sign, is the bearer of a meaning' (Hjelmslev 1961, p. 43). Through an examination of what these meaning bearing entities are like (pp. 44–7), he proceeds to contrast the first view of the sign as 'an expression that points to a content outside the sign itself' with a second view in which 'the sign is an entity generated by the connexion between an expression and a content', attributing this latter view to 'in particular ... Saussure, and following him ... Weisgerber' (Hjelmslev 1961, p. 47; italics mine). This 'connexion' between 'expression' and 'content' is not one of apparent union, productive of confusion as Derrida would have us believe (see quote above). Rather, expression and content are functives productive of the sign function; Peirce's 'manifestation' or Halliday's 'realization' (Halliday 1979; also this volume) are then precisely that 'connexion' between the functives which is constitutive of the sign function. To quote Hjelmslev, again:

... a function [e.g. 'sign'] is inconceivable without its terminals [e.g. 'expression/ signifier' and 'content/signified'], and the terminals are only end points for the function and are thus inconceivable without it ... Thus there is ... solidarity between the sign function and its two functives, expression and content. There will never be a sign function without the simultaneous presence of both these functives ... The sign function is in itself a solidarity. Expression and content are solidary – they necessarily presuppose each other. An expression is expression only by virtue of being an expression of a content, and a content is content only by virtue of being a content of an expression. Therefore ... *there can be no content without an expression, or expressionless content; neither can there be an expression without a content, or content-less expression.* (Hjelmslev 1961, pp. 48–9; italics mine)

It seems to me that statements of this kind not only deny that the signified is 'always already' somewhere; they also deny that it makes any sense to say that the signifier is always already there (contra Easthope).[1] If I understand Hjelmslev right, in the domain of semiosis *nothing* is 'always already' there; the 'sensible' identity of *the* signifier is just as illusory as the 'intelligible' ideality or phenomenal presence of *the* signified. There is, in fact, no *the*-ness about any signifier except that which it acquires as a functive of the sign function; neither is there any *the*-ness about any signified, except in the same conditions as for signifier. The selection of nominals – signifier, signified – is perhaps a natural, i.e. non-innocent, use (for in semiosis the 'natural' is the 'non-innocent') of 'everyday language' which according to Derrida (1981, p. 19) 'is the language of Western metaphysics'. I personally prefer Whorf's formulation according to which, this is yet another example of 'objectification' (Whorf 1956, p. 139), a characteristic of Standard Average

European Languages — of their lexicogrammar; and Whorf would suggest that Western metaphysics arose out of the 'fashions of speaking' made possible by the structure of SAE. Curiously, to me this is more in keeping with Derrida's approach than Derrida's own comment, which assigns priority to metaphysics over language — or, shall we say, 'writing'? To return to Hjelmslev, because of his characterisation of signifier, signified and sign, we could never attribute to him locutions such as 'the sign *or* the representer' (Derrida 1974, p. 49) which is to Hjelmslev 'a vague conception [of the sign] bequeathed by tradition' (Hjelmslev 1961, p. 43); we could also be quite certain that he does not allow 'the thing signified' 'to glow in the luminosity of its presence' (Derrida 1974, p. 49). Like Peirce, he too sees the sign function extending into infinity. To appreciate this point, one must look into Hjelmslev's notions of content-substance, content-form, and his connotative semiotic. And once these concepts are examined carefully, Hjelmslev too can be seen to extend the sign-function into infinity. Relevant as this is, I shall move on to other questions.

Let me reiterate that Hjelmslev saw his own discussion of sign as an elaboration of Saussure's approach; and I believe, the nonhomogeneity of Saussure's text notwithstanding, Hjelmslev's reading of Saussure is less biased, less partial than Derrida's. Even so, I would not suggest that there are no differences between Saussure and Hjelmslev. It is certainly true that most linguists — particularly European ones — 'borrow most of their concepts' from Saussure (Derrida 1981, p. 23) but no one knows better than Derrida — that originator of 'grafting' — that the borrowing of concepts is quite unlike my borrowing of someone's copy of Grammatology. The discourses within which such 'borrowed' signs are embedded, within whose linearity (within whose syntagms) they have their existence, thus hinting at what they contrast with, what their paradigmatic provenance is — it is within the process of these discourses that the borrowed signs announce their nonidentity with the borrowed signs; thus borrowing a concept becomes 'a question rather of producing a new concept' (Derrida 1981, p. 26) — which is all a way of saying, for this 'new' concept is not to the 'old' concept, as a new pair of shoes is to the old. None of this should be news to anyone who has read in the Margins, played with 'differance', and wondered about 'trace'. The reason for talking about it is simply that it links, to my mind, once again with the question of the identity of structuralism. If Hjelmslev's structuralism is not-the-same-as Saussure's, and yet also the-same-as Saussure's, how could one talk about structuralism as such? Given that we cannot equate structuralism with Saussureanism, post-structuralism ought not to be synonymous with post-Saussureanism; and if what one is talking about is post-Saussureanism, then perhaps a more careful explication of Saussure's text — homogeneous or not — is required than I believe has been offered in Derrida's writing. If on the other hand, the debate is about structuralism, then we cannot stop simply with Saussure and Hjelmslev, Levi-Strauss and Jakobson: the discourses of structuralism are vast indeed and include much, much more than the few names singled out by fame. The differences amongst these structuralists are as important as are the non-differences. Even to imply that the identities across the many who count themselves as structuralist, truly constitute the essence of the signified connected with the signifier *structuralism* is a simplification not very different from that practised during the hey-day of the Chomskian revolution.

Hjelmslev favoured the use of the word *sign* as 'the unit consisting of content-form and expression-form and established by the solidarity ... called the sign function' (Hjelmslev 1961, p.58). This does mean that every sign is constituted by the solidary 'connexion' between signifier/expression and signified/content; the fact that this connexion is not governed either by any inherent quality of expression or of content – i.e. the arbitrariness that Saussure spoke of – is not a barrier to this postulate. On the contrary, their status as the functives of the sign function requires this to be the case. Peirce's 'manifestation' or Halliday's 'realization' cannot be the same as 'iconicity' or 'indexicality'. From the perspective of Saussure, Hjelmslev or Halliday, it makes no sense whatever to say as Easthope (op. cit.) does 'that human beings are always already situated within the signifier, and then only second-arily come into a position where they are able to line up the signifier and the signified'. Nor is there any reason why the view of sign presented by Saussure and elaborated by Hjelmslev should prevent 'an effective account of how language changes diachronically' (Easthope, op. cit.). On the contrary, the arbitrary connexion between the functives – signifier and signified – of the sign function is absolutely criterial for the very recognition and occurrence of any variation – diachronic *or* synchronic. If there was a problem with regard to variation in the Saussurean model – and there was – the root of it lies not in Saussure's conception of the nature of sign; it lies elsewhere, as would become evident if one drew upon the work of yet another scholar, Vilém Mathesius, who would be regarded as much a structuralist as Hjelmslev. There is though a curious fact about Mathesius: a founding member of Prague Linguistic Circle, Mathesius was 'already' a structuralist before the appearance of the *Course*. In particular his paper *On the potentiality of the phenomena of language*, on which I draw here to show how 'post-structuralism' already existed before concepts relevant to structuralism could be even 'borrowed' from Saussure, was delivered in 1911 and was published that same year in Czech.

Mathesius (1911) questioned some of the most important concepts which were to become fundamental to the Saussurean model of linguistics. Saussure, as is well-known, saw *'langue'* and *'parôle'* as interdependent: *langue* was both the 'instrument' and the 'product' of *parôle*. He maintained, however, that this 'interdependence does not prevent their being two *absolutely* distinct things' (Saussure 1966, p.18; my italics). Saussure has been greatly applauded for maintaining this sharp distinction (Culler 1975; 1976; Chomsky 1965 etc.), though there were those who doubted the validity as well as the usefulness of this distinction (Firth 1957; Jakobson 1985, Halliday 1970; 1973; 1978; Hasan 1984*a*, 1985 etc.). It is possible that the accolade grew with the mistaken interpretation of these terms as the rather pale precursors of the Chomskian distinction between 'competence' and 'performance'. Be it as it may, the sharpness of the boundary between *langue* and *parôle* is maintained while their interdependence is also recognised.

... what is language [*langue*]? It is not to be confused with human speech [*langage*], of which it is only a definite part though certainly an essential one. It is both a social product of the faculty of speech [*langage*] and a collection of necessary conventions that have been adopted by a social body to permit individuals to exercise that faculty ... speech [*langage*] is many-sided ... it belongs both to the individual and to society ... Language [*langue*], on the contrary, is a self-contained whole and a principle of classification.
(Saussure 1966, p. 9)

Langue is a 'social fact'; it is 'not complete in any speaker; it exists perfectly within a collectivity'; it 'is not a function of the speaker; it is a product that is *passively* assimilated by the individual' (p. 14). And this is to be contrasted with *parôle*, which is the 'executive side' of *langage*. 'Execution is always individual, and the individual is always its master' (p. 13). 'Speaking [*parôle*] ... is an individual act. It is wilful and intellectual' (p. 14). In the 'confused mass of heterogeneous and unrelated things' 'straddling several areas simultaneously – physical, physiological, and psychological' (p. 9) *langue* is an island of sanity, of order, of even certainty which would 'provide a fulcrum that satisfies the mind' (p. 9).

Language [*langue*], unlike speaking [*parôle*], is something we can study separately ... We can dispense with the other elements of speech [*langage*]; indeed, the science of language [*langue*] is possible only if the other elements are excluded ... Whereas speech [*langage*] is heterogeneous, language [*langue*] ... is homogeneous. It is a system of signs in which the only essential thing is the union of meanings and sound-images, and in which both parts of the sign are psychological.
(Saussure 1966, p. 15)

Although Saussure could not completely deny recognition to non-homogeneity in *langue*, the view of *langue* as a 'homogeneous' 'system of signs' was to dominate Saussure's thinking about the study of language. The study of variation in the Saussurean model poses a problem *not* because the sign is a function of its functives – signifier and signified; rather, the problem arises from Saussure's conception of the nature of that 'connexion' – its degree of determinacy. Although there are rare occasions when Saussure will recognise the possibility of indeterminacy as when he says: 'Among all the individuals that are linked together by speech [*langage*], some sort of average will be set up: all will reproduce – *not exactly, of course, but approximately* – the same signs united with the same concepts (p. 13; italics mine). However, in general,

Saussure glossed over the possibility of this indeterminacy: 'Language exists in the form of a sum of impressions deposited in the brain of each member of a community, *almost like a dictionary of which identical copies have been distributed to each individual* (see p. 13)' (Saussure 1966, p. 19; italics mine). It is probably on the basis of two such passages, the one quoted from above and the other on p. 13 where 'storehouse' is used as a metaphor for *langue*, that Chomsky (1965, 1974 etc.) has criticised Saussure for thinking of language as an inventory of signs; Saussure's talk of 'identical copies' understandably did not perturb Chomsky since he too, as some scholar has remarked wryly, believes that each infant is born with a copy of the Aspects of Syntax tucked away in the folds of its brain. Ironically, though, the problematic nature of Saussure's 'identical copies' is brought out all the more forcefully because the systematicity of *langue* is not only crucial to Saussure's concept of the sign, but also affirmed by him far more consistently than its 'inventory' aspect. About this, some more comments later. Here let me point out the conclusion that Saussure drew from the postulate of homogeneity: 'Taken as a whole, speech [*langage*] cannot be studied, *for it is not homogeneous* ... We must choose two routes that cannot be followed simultaneously; they must be followed separately' (Saussure 1966, p. 19; italics mine). These two separate routes, Saussure dubbed 'internal linguistics' – linguistics concerned with the 'homogeneous' system of *langue* – and 'external linguistics' – linguistics concerned with the 'heterogeneous' 'individual and momentary' 'combinations that depend on the will of the speaker', in short *parôle* where the individual is always the 'master'. Rather grudgingly, Saussure allowed that 'one might *if really necessary* apply the term linguistics to each of the two disciplines and speak of a linguistics of speaking [*parôle*]. *But that science must not be confused with linguistics proper, whose sole object is language* [*langue*] (Saussure 1966, pp. 19–20; italics mine).

The homogeneity of langue – that main attribute which makes 'internal linguistics' *the sole* object of linguistics – had far-reaching consequences; it bears a non-accidental relationship to such concepts as synchrony/diachrony, static/evolutionary and infects the *état de langue* with the same simplification by which the homogeneity of langue itself got 'established':

An absolute state is defined by the absence of changes, and *since language changes somewhat in spite of everything*, studying a language-state means in practice *disregarding changes of little importance* ... a concept of language-state can only be approximate. In static linguistics, as in all sciences, no course of reasoning is possible without the usual simplification of data.
(Saussure 1966, p. 102; italics mine)

Mathesius's 1911 article strikes against the assumption of homogeneity for the static, synchronic *état de langue*. 'By the term potentiality we mean ... instability at the given period'; it is not the same as 'dynamic changeability ... occurring in the course of time' (Mathesius 1964, p. 1). This 'instability at the given period' is sometimes called 'static oscillation', sometimes 'synchronic oscillation'. According to Mathesius, this phenomenon of 'static oscillation' concerns not only dialects but also 'language as the proper object of linguistic research' (p. 1). According to Mathesius

Language ... includes, *theoretically*, all the phenomena of language that occur in the concrete utterances of all individual speakers, belonging at the same time to the same broad language community ... *In reality*, of course, linguistics can never do justice to this fact, not only on account of the astonishing richness of language phenomena in general, but mainly in view of the fact that such a community ... witnesses the rise of new, even if transient, language phenomena day by day. For this reason ... linguistic analysis has almost invariably concentrated on [just] the main outlines of languages ... [since] such outlines usually prove to be more accessible to primitive methods of analysis.
(Mathesius 1964, p. 1).

But this concentration on 'the main outlines' using the available 'primitive methods' results in creating an illusion of 'simplicity', which is often naively regarded 'as an actual quality of the examined phenomena' (op. cit. p. 2) — i.e. language — rather than as the artefact of the artificial limitations 'almost invariably' imposed on the examination of language. Mathesius protests 'against mixing up the methodological simplification of language with its actual make-up' (p. 2), and recommends that linguists should examine more carefully the inherent instability — 'the potentiality of language phenomena' (p. 2) — to find out how this is 'actually manifested'. They should look into static/synchronic variation in the 'concrete' utterances of 'individual speakers within a community' as well as within the utterances of the same individual. The heterogeneity of *parôle* that Saussure was, perhaps just then in his lectures, setting aside as non-examinable constituted Mathesius' primary data. Here was 'post-structuralism' receiving ardent support from those who considered themselves 'structuralist' even before the arch-priest of structuralism, Ferdinand de Saussure, was recognised as 'the father' (Culler 1976) of modern structuralism. While Saussure was promising his audience that 'I shall deal only with linguistics of language [*langue*], and if I subsequently use materials belonging to speaking [*parôle*] to illustrate a point, I shall try never to erase the boundaries that separate the two domains' (Saussure 1966, p. 20), here was Mathesius claiming that an unnecessary simplification of language results by the simple affirmation *or* denial of absolute regularity: language is neither entirely homogeneous nor entirely heterogeneous; a recognition of both its systemic regularities *and* its variation is at once essential. Mathesius briefly reviews studies that indicate the presence of variation at the various levels of language: the phonic, the phonological, the lexicogrammatical and the semantic. The opinion although attributed to Kruszewski, I believe, would be shared by Mathesius that 'the basic feature of language' is 'the complexity and indefiniteness of its units' (Mathesius 1964, p. 27). It is in this inherent indeterminacy of language that the roots of its diachronic variation lie. 'The sentence, the word, the morphemic elements are indefinite as to their content. The sound, again, is indefinite physiologically ...' (op. cit. p.27). The acceptance of this inherent indeterminacy of the linguistic unit, however, does not seem to Mathesius any reason for suggesting, unlike Saussure, that in *parôle*, in his concrete utterances, the speaker is always the master. Mathesius, like Firth and Halliday later, would reject both the exaggerated regularity of a fictitiously homogeneous langue and the myth of complete 'free-will' for the individual speaker: human language is neither a prison-house nor utter freedom, with absolute autonomy and independence. Hence the term 'potentiality': the units of language permit a potential, within which a great deal of variation – 'oscillation' – is possible. Writing approximately half a century before Labov (1968) and Weinreich, Labov and Herzog (1968), Mathesius suggested that the study of the potentiality of the phenomena of language in synchrony would provide the best basis for the study of diachronic variation (see Mathesius 1964, especially last para.). This pre-Saussurean (?) post-structuralist, thus, questioned the very edifice of 'internal linguistics', based on a fictitious homogeneity which prevented 'an effective account of how language changes diachronically' (Easthope, op. cit.).

What is most ironic here is the fact that Saussure's concept of sign – which is today blamed for everything – was fully compatible with Mathesius' notion of potentiality. Selecting without bias from Saussure's nonhomogeneous text, I will attempt to show that Saussure denied the possibility of knowing *a* signifier/*a* signified in isolation. The signified is not a foot clad in an ill-fitting signifier-shoe, which slips (Eagleton 1983) to trip up the possibility of meaning. In the context of the Saussurean framework, it is mere obfuscation to talk of human beings as 'always already situated in the signifier' and 'only secondarily' coming to 'line up the signifier and the signified'. To me at least, such a formulation is tantamount to the claim that 'nothing' intervenes between the sensation of the hearing of some sound and the recognition of it as some signifier. Saussure's theory of sign neither affirms the presence of *a* signified nor of *a* signifier in isolation. If from the 'fictitious' point of view of an already given signifier, it is difficult to say how meanings get meant, the negation of the given-ness, in isolation, of either signifier or signified – and thus of the identity of the sign – does not make the question easier to answer. Nor do I believe that answers will be found simply by tracing the etymology of the sign *sign*. Carrying the sign *sign* back to Plato and beyond – as Derrida does – is an admirable proof of immersion in philosophical writing. Antiquity, however, is not a decisive court of appeal in disputes about the identity of a linguistic sign. There is no reason to assume identity of the sign *sign* across Plato and Saussure; and if there is any suggestion that Saussure's *sign* should have been the same as Plato's, what would such a suggestion be based on? Plato is not an obscure philosopher; if he had already solved the problem of the sign to Saussure's satisfaction, then Saussure would hardly be concerned with it, just as if Saussure had solved the problem of the sign to Derrida's satisfaction, Derrida would not have needed to write *Grammatologie*. Nor does the equation of Saussure's *signified* with *concept* in the sense of mental image appear justified to me. The image of image may conceivably be relevant where *signification* is the issue; however, Saussure's *signified* is not just *signification*; it concerns *value* as well: '... it is quite clear that initially the concept is nothing, that is only a value determined by its relations with other similar values, and that without them the signification would not exist ...' (Saussure 1966, p. 117).

... to consider a term simply as the union of a certain sound with a certain concept is grossly misleading. To define it in this way would isolate the term from its system; it would mean assuming that one can start from the terms and construct the system by adding them together when, on the contrary, it is from the interdependent whole that one must start and through analysis obtain its elements.
(Saussure 1966, p. 115)

Derrida's claim that Plato 'said basically the same thing' about sign though he had 'a more subtle, more critical and less complacent theory of image' (1974, p. 33) I note with interest, for it seems to me that whatever else Saussure's sign theory may be it certainly was not about 'image'. Saussure's *concept/idea* redefined as 'value determined by its relation to other similar values' certainly appears distant from Plato's 'ideal type'. The concept *concept* or *idea* undergoes a sea-change in Saussure's text, and it is in the light of this that I read the following:

The linguistic entity exists only through the associating of the signifier with the signified ... We constantly risk grasping only a part of the entity and thinking that we are embracing it in its totality ... A succession of sounds is linguistic only if it supports an idea. Considered independently, it is material for a physiological study, and nothing more than that. The same is true of the signified as soon as it is separated from its signifier ... Concepts ... become linguistic entities only when associated with sound images; in language, a concept is a quality of its phonic substance just as a particular slice of sound is a quality of the concept.
(Saussure 1966, pp. 102–3)

Assertions of this kind throw into question the very basis of a concept such as *homonymy* e.g. in *bear* (a kind of animal) and *bear* (tolerate) as much as they raise questions about the *synonymy* of *bear* and *tolerate*. In the case of homonymy, are we hearing the same signifier? In the case of synonymy, are we faced with the same signified? Neither signifier nor signified indicates the identity of the sign: 'The idea or phonic substance that a sign contains is of less importance than the other signs that surround it' (Saussure 1966, p. 120). The identity of signifiers, signifieds, and so of signs, is their relationship to signifiers, signifieds and signs.

The relations that Saussure postulated are well known – and again interdependent: the associative, paradigmatic, in absentia ones, and the linear, syntagmatic, in praesentia ones. Like all Saussure's pairs, these two are interdependent: a paradigm is a paradigm by virtue of its potential disposition in a syntagm, while a syntagm is a syntagm by virtue of combining members of more than one paradigm. What is notable though is the fact that the contradictions, the hesitations and the simplifications which appeared in Saussure's discussion of *langue* and *parôle* are reflected almost exactly in his discussion of the syntagmatic relation. 'In discourse, ... words acquire relations based on the linear nature of language because they are chained together' (Saussure 1966, p.123). What is this *'because'*? Are linearity and chaining two different phenomena? If so, how? '... the notion of syntagm applies not only to words but to groups of words, to complex units of all lengths and types (compounds, derivatives, phrases, whole sentences)' (p.124). But here another difficulty rears its head: we have already been told that one characterising feature of *parôle* is 'the combinations by which the speaker uses the language code for expressing his own thought' (p.14).

The sentence is the ideal type of syntagm. But it belongs to speaking [*parôle*], not language [*langue*] ... Does it not follow that syntagm belongs to speaking? I do not think so. Speaking is characterized by freedom of combinations; one must therefore ask whether or not all syntagms are equally free.' (p.124)

This line of enquiry leads Saussure to the conclusion that those syntagms are 'in' *langue* where improvisation, the exercise of free will by the speaker is impossible, as in 'fixed idiomatic expressions'; others where improvisation, exercise of free will is possible are 'in' *parôle*. '... But we must realise that in the syntagm there is no clear-cut boundary between the language [*langue*] fact, which is a sign of collective usage, and the fact that belongs to speaking [*parôle*] and depends on individual freedom' (p.125). This last passage calls to mind those others in which *langue* is invariant 'not exactly, of course, but approximately' (p.13) and where an *état de langue* too is declared invariant 'disregarding changes of little importance' (p.102). Derrida has said a good deal about how the metaphysics of presence fouled up Saussurean thinking; and the validity of some of these comments I have questioned. My reading of Saussure's theory of sign does not agree with Derrida's. Saussure's concept/signified has no existence outside the system of relations; the notion of 'differance' is not ruled out by it − rather, it is implied by the centrality of the associative and syntagmatic relations to the identity of the sign. To me it seems that Saussure's problem arises from two dogmas that are hardly ever absent from academic thought in the West: the purity of categories, and the affirmation of the individual's free will since Adam. Given that the connection between signifier and signified is arbitrary, Saussure must accept the role of communal practice i.e. conventionality. Conventionality and some measure of regularity of behaviour are two sides of the same coin. A language can be used by various members of the community only if there is some element of stability/invariance in it. Thus something *langue*-like − a social, collective fact – is undeniable. However the principle of the purity of categories does not permit acceptance of both invariance and variance: the variant, as Plato argued, cannot be studied. Further, Saussure appears to subscribe to the notion of the individual's 'free will' which is accommodated by his conception of *parôle*. Ideologically, the regularity of *parôle* cannot be maintained; theoretically, the existence of some regularity cannot *but* be invoked; and, again, ideologically order and chaos – homogeneity and heterogeneity – cannot be the characterising attributes of the very same phenomena.

All other problems in Saussure's framework are minor compared to this one. The purity of the categories of *langue* and *parôle* played havoc with Saussure's distinctions between associative and syntagmatic, between value and signification (Hasan 1985), between signifier and signified, thus threatening the entire edifice of his theory, while rendering his notion of *langue* so simplistic that no one who ever wished to enquire into what people *do* do with their language could ever adopt the model in its original form. But those who wished to find out what people *do* with their language, and how, were mostly those who got described as 'data-oriented'. And this is yet another structuralism. In pointing out directions from structuralism, I propose to conclude my contribution with an account of this 'data-oriented', 'behaviourist', 'taxonomist' structuralism. There is nothing like giving an academic a name and the rest follows. For lack of space, I shall refer only briefly to just two linguists: Firth and Halliday.

Firth rejected Saussure's *langue/parôle* dichotomy as well as his 'internal linguistics':

... we study language as part of the social process, and ... the systematics of phonetics and phonology, of grammatical categories or of semantics are ordered schematic constructs, ... a sort of scaffolding for the handling of events. The study of the social process and of single human beings is simultaneous and of equal validity.
(Firth 1957, p. 181)

The elements of the schematic construct 'have no ontological status ... being or existence. They are neither immanent nor transcendent, but just language turned back upon itself' (p. 181). The study of language as part of the social process meant looking at what Mathesius called 'concrete utterances'; thus, Firth's reputation in the Chomskian revolution as data-oriented. Firth also objected to any account of meaning as a relation in the mind between 'facts', 'things' and words: 'As we know so little about mind and as our study is essentially social I shall cease to respect the duality of mind and body, thought and word, and be satisfied with the whole man, thinking and acting as a whole, in association with his fellows' (Firth 1957, p. 19). For Firth meaning is not 'relations in a hidden mental process'; it is seen chiefly as

...situational relations in a context of situation and in that kind of language which disturbs the air and other people's ears, as modes of behaviour in relation to the other elements in the context of situation ... Meaning ... is to be regarded as a complex of contextual relations, and phonetics, grammar, lexicography and semantics each handles its own components of the complex in its appropriate context. (p. 19)

To remarks such as these can be attributed his fame as 'anti-mentalist', 'behaviourist' – a corrupting influence indeed in the age of the creativity of the innate rule-governed grammar. For Firth, the object of linguistics was to make statements of meaning. However, 'the statement of meaning cannot be achieved by one analysis, at one level, in one fell swoop' (p. 183). Human languages have *minor* and *major modes of meaning*: according to Firth phonetics and phonology are tools for making statements of meaning, just as much as the schematic construct called context of situation is a tool for the same purpose. The theory of context of situation, which Firth 'borrowed' from Malinowski (1923; 1935), was designed to describe 'language as part of the social process'. On the one hand Firth maintained that 'every time you speak, you create anew' (p. 142), on the other, he definitely did not allow Saussure's individual the same freedom, the same absolute mastery that the speaker enjoyed in the Saussurean framework, 'Once someone speaks to you, you are in a relatively determined context and you are not free to just say what you please' (p. 28). I should add that the notion of context with which Austin (1962), Searle (1969) or Derrida (1977) operate is somewhat different from that of Firth who thought of the term 'context of situation' as a technical term 'a suitable schematic construct to apply to language events ... a group of related categories at a different level from grammatical categories but rather of the same abstract nature' (p. 182). Just as with the notion of language Firth would accept both systemic regularity and the existence of variation, so also Firth's context of situation is concerned both with what is typical of various social processes as well as what is relevant to some specific instance of a given type of social process. It was the notion of language as system, the denial of any need to grant physical presence to the referent, the idea that human language could be described as relations of relations that unites Saussure, Hjelmslev and Firth. The idea of the homogeneity of *langue* so dear to Saussure was quite foreign to Firth who maintained that 'unity is the last concept that should be applied to language. Unity of language is the most fugitive of all unities whether it be historical, geographical, national or personal' (Firth 1957, p. 29). Denying 'unity', Firth, unlike Saussure, could also see language as systematic.

Halliday's framework, known now as the Systemic-Functional model, embraces the idea of system. For Halliday language is a 'resource for meaning' – it is a potential, not a constraining reproductive mechanism. The systemic quality of language does not imply reproducing the same linguistic units with the same sounds and the same meanings. The system is a resource for process. Anti-languages (Halliday 1976) show quite clearly that there are varieties in which speakers will not 'reproduce' even 'approximately', the same signifier united with the same signified. Despite this, Anti-languages stand in a systematic relation to the systems of non-antilanguages. Departure from system is as much a 'regard' to system as conformity with system; the unusual is unusual only by reference to the usual. When Halliday refuses to participate in the current dramatic lamentations about failures of communication, it may be useful to see this in its perspective. For Halliday, language has always been associated with the idea of the possibility of variation. But this variation is nonrandom in important respects: variations across social class, across generations, across professions – in short, across ideologies. Like Whorf, Wittgenstein (1958) and Bernstein (1981, MSS), Halliday believes that consciousness – and so ideology – is an artefact of processes of meaning. Ways of speaking are ways of meaning; and ways of meaning are ways of being, behaving and saying (Hasan 1984b; 1985; 1986). Failures of communication across ideologies do not have to be documented as a *notable* happening: 'contact' (cf. Pratt in this volume) is *not* necessarily 'convergence' – communication across ideologies, no doubt, takes place in the sense that some meanings do get exchanged but precisely because of the systemic variation – ideological-linguistic – it is very much open to question how the 'saying' and the 'hearing' calibrate. To accept the possibility of systematic variations of this kind is to be aware of the possibility of 'failures of communication' – a term used all too glibly, whose explication might throw the entire notion of the slipping signifier, 'the always already there' signifier into a vortex. The shock of the realisation of the possibility of the failure of communication is thus not a spectre that arises unexpected in such frameworks as it does where the predominant belief had been in *'une langue, une'* or in 'idealized' 'competence'. Variation is non-identity of meaning and wording; language is inherently variable. From this perspective, it is the successes in communication that need to be marvelled at, rather than failures (Halliday, below, p. 136); failures ought to occur more often!

The recognition of variation in Halliday's framework proceeds hand in hand with the affirmation of invariance. Using Malinowski (1923, 1935) and Firth, as his point of departure, Halliday has argued that the structure of language and its functionality are in a dialectic relation. Experience from the point of view of the sensing subject may be 'raw sensation', but experience of the world both outside us and inside us, if it is to be shared must be constructed through semiosis. As a mode of semiosis, human language 'performs' an *ideational* function: it permits the construction of sharable experience. In the structure of human language, we would find a specific part of the lexicogrammar which *realises/constructs* the ideational function. Sharing implies some social relation: the *social relations* too are *created/ altered/maintained* through language. This is the *interpersonal* function of language realised as a specific aspect of the organisation of the lexicogrammar. All sharing is situated – it is situated in the contexts of that community and is recognisable as some kind of social process within the terms of reference set by the community's culture. Discourse, talk, writing – managing its continuities and discontinuities is the *textual* function of language. This function of language too is *realised/constructed* by a particular aspect of the lexicogrammar of a language. The structure of language and the function of language are two sides of the same coin. These metafunctions of language are non-accidentally related to the 'schematic construct' called context of situation. If, arriving in the middle of an ongoing dialogue, we are, more often than not, able to say what is going on, how the interactants see each other, what social activity is at issue, this is not because there exists a mysterious telepathic bond between members of a community: it is because language constructs our world for us. The context is as much in language as it is outside language.

What such a theory says is that *speaking is wilful*: but the will that exercises control is not some divine freedom, not some self-enclosed intentionality, not the breath of God; it is the breath of others who matter in the life of the speaker. *Speaking is purposeful*: but the purpose is not autistic – it is fashioned by the community of purposes of those who surround us, whom we exploit or defend, whom we fight or protect. *Speaking is always a potential* – open and unlimited in its potentiality: but the actuality of speaking – and hearing – is always limited by who we are, how others see us, what rights we enjoy, what obligations we carry. If meanings get meant, if the potentiality of the sign is translated into 'an' actuality, this is because we are always already situated within a social context – a social context that we ourselves have brought about by our own sayings, our own interpretations. 'Language is the best show man puts on' (Whorf): it is freedom certainly, but let that freedom not blind us to the fact that it is also the most powerful weapon for social reproduction. And it is this potentiality of language that we can never ignore, for whilst we ignore it, it inexorably surrounds us. With a linguistics of this kind we do not need 'contact linguistics' (cf. Pratt, this volume); we only need to understand the meaning of 'contact' as a sign.

I have tried to show in this paper the variation, the potentiality, the synchronic oscillation, of the sign *structuralism*. I have not been able to always explicitly relate today's post-structuralist dictums, often dramatically displayed, with the approaches of others, but, hopefully, the reader can make such connections. If Schmidt (1985, p. 166) is right that *post-structuralism* is a term embarrassingly empty of content, it may be because there is too much content in the *structuralism* that it claims to supersede.

Notes

1   Editor's note: Antony Easthope raised a number of issues after M. A. K. Halliday's paper (this volume), particularly as these concerned what he termed 'the alternative tradition' in linguistics represented by the work of Bakhtin (Voloshinov) and Michel Pecheux. He suggested that communication models of language (citing those presented by Leech) presuppose 'that the signifier and signified are *always already* united in the sign'. He argued that the communication model should be challenged by an alternative argument: that human beings as speaking subjects are always already

situated within the signifier and then only secondarily come into a position where they are able to 'line up' signifier and signified. Easthope further proposed that language change would be better explained by the latter model ('the signifier acquires new signifieds: within every discourse it is aquiring a new signified') than by the communication model with its insistence on the already completed sign. This position is more fully developed by Antony Easthope in *Poetry as Discourse*, London, 1983.

References

J.L. Austin, *How to Do Things with Words*, Oxford, 1962.

Basil B. Bernstein, 'Codes, modalities and the process of reproduction', *Language and Society*, X, 1981, pp. 327–63.

Basil B. Bernstein, 'Elaborated and restricted codes; an over-view 1958–1985', in U. Ammon, K. Matthier, and N. Dittmar (eds.), *Sociolinguistics/Soziolinguistik*, Berlin, (MSS to appear in 1987).

Noam Chomsky, *Syntactic Structures*, The Hague, 1957.

Noam Chomsky, 'Review of B.F. Skinner, *Verbal Behaviour*', *Language*, XXXV, 1959, pp. 26–58.

Noam Chomsky, *Aspects of the Theory of Syntax*, Cambridge, Massachusetts, 1965.

Noam Chomsky, 'Noam Chomsky', in H. Parret (ed.), *Discussing Language*, The Hague, 1974.

J. Culler, *Saussure*, Glasgow, 1976.

J. Culler, *Structuralist Poetics*, Ithaca, 1975.

Jacques Derrida, *Of Grammatology*, translated G. Chakravorty Spivak, Baltimore, 1974.

Jacques Derrida, 'Limited Inc a b c ...', *Glyph* II, Baltimore, 1977.

Jacques Derrida, *Writing and Difference*, translated A. Bass, London, 1978.

Jacques Derrida, *Positions*, translated A. Bass, Chicago, 1981.

Jacques Derrida, *Margins of Philosophy*, translated A. Bass, Brighton, 1982.

T. Eagleton, *Literary Theory: An Introduction*, Oxford, 1983.

J.R. Firth, *Papers in Linguistics 1934–1951*, London, 1957.

A.J. Greimas, 'Algirdas J. Greimas', in H. Parret (ed.), *Discussing Language*, The Hague, 1974.

M.A.K. Halliday, 'Language structure and language function', in J. Lyons (ed.), *New Horizons in Linguistics*, Harmondsworth, 1970.

M.A.K. Halliday, *Explorations in the Functions of Language*, London, 1973.

M.A.K. Halliday, 'M.A.K. Halliday', in H. Parret (ed.), *Discussing Language*, The Hague, 1974.

M.A.K. Halliday, 'Anti-languages', *American Anthropologist*, LXXVIII, 1976, pp. 570–84.

M.A.K. Halliday, *Language as Social Semiotic*, London, 1978.

M.A.K. Halliday, 'Modes of meaning and modes of expression: types of grammatical structure, and their determination by different semantic functions', in D.J. Allerton, E. Carney & D. Holdcroft (eds.), *Functions and Context in Linguistic Analysis* Cambridge, 1979.

M.A.K. Halliday, & R. Hasan, *Language Context and Text: A Social Semiotic Perspective*, Geelong, Vic., 1985.

R. Hasan, 'What kind of resource is language?', *Australian Review of Applied Linguistics*, VII, 1984*a*, pp. 57–85.

R. Hasan, 'Ways of saying: ways of meaning', in R. P. Fawcett, M. A. K. Halliday, S. M. Lamb & A. Makkai (eds.), *The Semiotics of Culture and Language*, I, London, 1984*b*.

R. Hasan, *Linguistics, Language and Verbal Art*, Geelong, Vic., 1985.

R. Hasan, 'Meaning, context and text: fifty years after Malinowski', in J. D. Benson & W. S. Greaves (eds.), *Systemic Perspectives on Discourse*, I, New Jersey, 1985.

R. Hasan, 'The ontogenesis of ideology', in T. Threadgold, E. A. Crosz, G. Kress & M. A. K. Halliday (eds.), *Semiotics – Ideology – Language*, Sydney Association for Studies in Society and Culture, 1986.

L. Hjelmslev, *Prolegomena to a Theory of Language*, translated Francis J. Whitfield, Madison, 1961.

R. Jakobson, 'Sign and system of language: a reassessment of Saussure's doctrine', in K. Pomorska & S. Rudy (eds.), *Verbal Art, Verbal Sign, Verbal Time*, Oxford, 1985.

W. Labov, 'The reflection of social processes in linguistic structures', in J. A. Fishman (ed.), *Readings in the Sociology of Language*, The Hague, 1968.

B. Malinowski, *Coral Gardens and their Magic*, II, London, 1935.

B. Malinowski, 'The problem of meaning in primitive communities', Supplement to C. Ogden & I. A. Richards, *The Meaning of Meaning*.

V. Mathesius, 'On the potentiality of the phenomena of language', in J. Vachek (ed.), *A Prague School Reader in Linguistics*, Indiana, 1964.

Richard Rorty, *Consequences of Pragmatism*, Minnesota, 1982.

Imre Salusinzky, 'Intellectual War', *Times Literary Supplement*, 28 October 1983.

Ferdinand de Saussure, *Course in General Linguistics*, translated Wade Baskin, New York, 1966.

J. Schmidt, *Maurice Merleau-Ponty: Between Phenomenology and Structuralism*, London, 1985.

J. R. Searle, *Speech Acts*, Cambridge, 1969.

U. Weinreich, W. Labov & M. I. Herzog, 'Empirical foundations for a theory of language change', in W. P. Lehmann & Y. Malkiel (eds.), *Directions for Historical Linguistics: A Symposium*, Austin, 1968.

B. L. Whorf, 'The relation of habitual thought and behaviour to language' in J. B. Carroll (ed.), *Language, Thought and Reality*, Cambridge, Massachusetts, 1956.

L. Wittgenstein, *Philosophical Investigations* translated G. E. M. Anscombe, Oxford, 1958.

Dallying nicely with words

My subject concerns poetic linguistics. By that I don't mean to expand on either half of Roman Jakobson's chiastic title, 'Poetry of Grammar and Grammar of Poetry' so much as to suggest that particular bodies of poetic text seem implicitly to theorise about language, recasting categories of *langue, parole* and, certainly, *écriture* in terms of each other, and inventing fictional new ones. A poet's relation to his or her language is certainly not like that of a linguist, a philosopher or indeed even a humbler expositor. 'Good prose is like a window pane', said George Orwell, and we might add that only when it breaks are there concomitant refractions and opacities. But poetic language is as much mirror as window, and for poets, words are often like some agents in a larger fiction, not so much an epic or drama, but more a complex romance, of language. It has been pointed out over the last twenty-five years that the ways in which poetry revises other forms of discourse include troping them, and that this may involve figuration of structures and processes that linguistic study has classified and analysed. Donald Davie, in *Articulate Energy*, or Christine Brooke-Rose in *A Grammar of Metaphor*, stopped short of characterising poetic language as deploying fictional or notional syntax and accidence, but such scholars as Jay Keyser and Marie Borroff have gone further in suggesting that in both diction and the formation of fictional names and epithets an analogue of folk-etymology can be at work. But let me turn at once to an observation, at once poetical and theoretical, about the behaviour of poetic words.

At the opening of Act III of *Twelfth Night*, the two poetical characters, Viola and Feste, neither of whom speaks in *propria persona* for most of the play, exchange words and coins for the first time. After an introductory bout of word-play, turning on innocent locative and problematic instrumental uses of the preposition 'by', the Clown observes, with regard to the very rhetoric of their punning, 'A sentence is but a chev'ril glove to a good wit. How quickly the wrong side may be turned outward!' To which Viola replies, 'Nay, that's certain. They that dally nicely with words may quickly make them wanton.' This is a kind of meta-wit, and poetically intense, at that. Both 'dally' and 'wanton' – like the word 'sport' – have, in the late sixteenth century, erotic insides. Feste is coy in calling such an inside 'the wrong side', treating with kid gloves what should − had the technology been available, been more properly figured as a reversible coat. 'Wanton''s oldest general sense (wan + towen [= 'discipline' or 'train']) is of unruliness, although the OED distinguishes among a number of states of negatively valorised activity − unruly, frolicsome, capricious, self-indulgent, insolent, arbitrary, gratuitous, changeable, and, of course, erotically unsubdued (OED sense 7, 'luxuriant', seems to double in sense with 'erotic', at least in the examples cited). Viola asserts that playing with words (as opposed, perhaps, merely to using them) will cause them to lose control of themselves, and thereby perhaps, our control over them. But 'dally', primarily applied to discourse, has erotic overtones as well, and Viola's very words themselves imply that 'nice', precise, delicate wordplay will cause language to heat up erotically, if not (anachronistically) with the return of the repressed, then at least, figuratively, with an analogous turning of insides-out.

Feste picks this up immediately in his return, and the whole remainder of the exchange is instructive:

Viola. Nay, that's certain. They that dally nicely with words may quickly make them wanton.
Clown. I would therefore my sister had no name sir.
Viola. Why, man?
Clown. Why, sir, her name's a word, and to dally with that word might make my sister wanton. [+ *want one*?] But indeed, words are very rascals since bonds disgraced them.
Viola. Thy reason, man?
Clown. Troth, sir, I can yield you none without words, and words are grown so false I am loath to prove reason with them.

Words not only get out of hand, but their unruly activity eroticises what they signify. The bonds − sworn legal instruments, instead of one's word plainly and honourably given − put words into bondage. Such fetters improve neither the behaviour of language nor, certainly, its reputation. There is a final oblique reflection on words at the end of the scene. Viola gives Feste a coin, and he asks: 'Would not a pair of these have bred?', to which Viola replies 'Yes, being kept together and put to use'. 'Use' is itself used commonly in an erotic sense by Shakespeare (OED sense 3b), and two coins rubbing up against each other will breed, implies the clown, even as the sum of their two values will breed usuriously. And so with wanton words, at least in the fictional linguistics that momentarily surfaces in the two wordmongers' exchange of serious wit.

Another very different poet Friedrich Schlegel, wrote in his essay on incomprehensibility (*Über die Unverständlichkeit*) that 'words often understand themselves better than those who use them', and this personification by poetic thought of the elements of language typifies a kind of romance in which signifiers become agents, or even scenes.

I am not considering at the moment such issues as those of private or fictional dialects in which poets from Theocritus through Burns and Chatterton to Hugh MacDiarmid have written, nor, in the case of Spenser (whom Ben Jonson accused of having 'writ no language') the distribution of archaisms, coinages and unstable spellings in the interests of multiple readings that make it impractical to modernise the text of *The Faerie Queene*. Nor, indeed, shall I discuss here the metaphoric use of linguistic terminology in Hart Crane's poetry, for example. Rather, I want to consider some phenomena resulting from what I.A. Richards in *The Philosophy of Rhetoric* called 'the inter-inanimation of words',[1] one specifically erotic aspect of which Viola invoked. Released wantonness can be libertine in another way, and here again I quote Schlegel (*Critical Fragments*, no.65):

Poetry is republican speech: a speech which is its own law and an end unto itself, and in which all the parts [*Redeteile*] are free citizens and have the right to vote.[2]

The fictional morphology of Spenser's naming of persons and places is more to this point. It is not just the pre-Carrollian portmanteau words that I am thinking of, nor the Joycean play across languages, e.g. so that the Lady in *The Faerie Queene* Book V, in thrall to the tyrant Grantorto, is called Eirena, her name bringing together with ringing English irony the Celtic name of Ireland, or Erin, and the Greek *eirēnē*, or 'peace'. But the knight who is her champion is named Artegall, because of an Artagallo who in Geoffrey of Monmouth's chronicle was a half-brother of King Arthur, and his name gets implicitly etymologised as *Art + egal* or 'equal to Arthur', and as something like *l'art d'égalité*, or judgment of equity. But Artegall's name reacts erotically with that of his own lover, Britomart, a name from Virgil originally, but understood as a Martial Britoness (she fights battles disguised in armour as a knight). The first morpheme of 'Artegall' arouses the last three phonemes of 'Britomart''s final syllable, and they declare independence, in Schlegel's way, from the -mart morpheme, so that as James Nohrnberg has observed,[3] the eventual married condition of the bearers of the two names would produce a *Britomartegall* (even as another pair of lovers, in the same mythological region of the poem – Scudamor and Amoret – form a hypogrammatic *Scudamoret* at one point).

Spenser's visionary linguistics alone would be an instructive matter – typically, we would find it to be totally synchronic – but I should like to discuss some other kinds of fabulous grammars evoked at moments by poets' language. I shall skirt for the present the whole area of tone in poetry – whether in pursuit of what Robert Frost called 'the sentence sound', or, with Dwight Bolinger's *Intonation and Its Parts* in one hand and a number of samples of fine accentual-syllabic verse in the other, in a consideration of how the relations between voice and verse generate competingly powerful but virtual intonation patterns of their own at a new level, while still sharing the stage with the literally phonological ones. There might be a certain timeliness in this, as, at least in the United States, a whole new set of intonational phenomena seem to be arising, not in speech, but in the public performance of even minimal prose texts. Primarily in television news broadcasting, language has been overwhelmed by grimacing visage even as truth has by packaging; as a result of this, the ability to read aloud for sense — providing the discursive and prosaic basis of Frost's 'sentence sound' — seems almost to have become a disabling skill among younger persons employed to read aloud from the admittedly minimal syntax of the teleprompter. Idiolectal and random junctures, for example, occasioned by the inability to anticipate a line-break in the copy (something all radio people were trained to do) sound rather like illiterate attempts to read across enjambments, and every day one hears new entities being brought into being by inept performance. Thus, even on radio now, you get an announcement of a dance at 'the Martin Luther King # Junior High School' displacing the 'Jr' from its role in the dedicatee's name and changing the nature of the school. One might say that this was an exercise of poetic *technē* analogous to the deft articulation of enjambments by Milton, for example. But as Quintilian reminds us, every inadvertent trope is a solecism. I shall ask you to follow me into less dismal areas today.

I have been considering recently the *ad hoc* troping of schemes in poetry — how, for example, the ways in which such observations as those of the late W. K. Wimsatt about rhyme were indeed instances of something more general. Rhymes not only, by exploiting linkages between words, propound fictional ones between their referents (as in Latin verse, patterned juxtaposition of nouns and adjectives, irrelevant to syntax, plays a pseudo-attributive role). (These linkages, of course, may be antithetical as well as associative.) But in certain situations, the instrument of rhyming, and the sort of linkage it enforces, becomes allegorised as bondage — by Ben Jonson, for example, as fetters between words, and thereby, between lines, or by Milton, as fetters binding the poet to a Jonsonian neo-classicism (although Milton cleverly screens this by associating rhyme as an institution with medieval barbarism). And there are countless other tropes for rhyming that crafty verse enables, and true poetry often requires, the imagination to generate.

Two rhyming words (or phrases, or lines, or even larger syntactic units the words terminate and are synecdochic of), say a_1 and a_2, may be so deployed in a poem that they imply any one of a number of nonce theories of the effects of rhyme: e.g. a_2 is the echo of a_1; or a_1 and a_2 are in some kind of cause and effect relation, whether empirical or scholastic (i.e. a_2 is made up of a_1, or a_1 invented or formed a_2, or whatever); or a_1 is the soul, or the body, of a_2; or a_1 is a text and a_2 a commentary on it, or indeed, in a bi-testamentary relation, the fulfilment of it; or a_2 is a hidden or unacknowledged part of a_1 (or vice versa), and the rhyming occasion is a moment of analysis, or deconstruction, or revelation. So that rhyming enacts some local verbal magic *with* the words in question, but, beyond that, implies some general principle, some theory of rhyming, which is as powerfully figurative as the local trope whose epistemological grounding the theory would purport to explain.

Sometimes another scheme – itself tropically neutral until actually employed in poetry – will catalytically enable such an extension to occur. In George Herbert's 'Deniall', for example, each tightly-rhymed stanza ends in a four-syllabled, unrhymed, non-iambic line: 'And disorder' // 'Of alar[u]ms' // 'but no hearing' // 'Discontented', each touching on a question of the failure of language (in this case, in prayer). When, in the final stanza, a meta-prayer for the efficacy of the prayer envisions a fortuitous conclusion, rhyme, metre, broken scheme and broken hopes are repaired:

> O cheer and tune my heartless breast,
>   Defer no time;
> That so thy favours granting my request,
>   They and my mind may chime,
>   And mend my rhyme.

Even the muted chiming of the two whole phrases, 'Mind may chime / Mend my rhyme' is operative here, aside from how self-referential the 'chime-rhyme' pair is, and helps establish the fiction that rhyming is, far from being bondage, a kind of elemental discursive force, holding together the surface structures of utterance, their relations to the deep structures, and the whole rhetorical matrix within which utterance is framed. Interestingly enough, this fable of rhyming is established by the marked form of its abruptly revealed absence. But ultimately, the final line turns on three senses of the word 'rhyme': (a) the instance of rhyming two line termini, (b) rhym*ing*, or the process itself and (c) entire poem; it is through this last that the figuration of authenticity of discourse is finally accomplished.

A more egregious and original scheme, in Herbert's 'Paradise', again sees rhyme as elemental, but specifically functional. In this poem which meditates on what protective enclosure is, the rhymed triplets successively pare down the monosyllabic terminal word of the first line by a letter each time.[4] (The scheme is one of *aphaeresis* or *ablatio*, save that a phoneme, rather than a syllable, is removed.) Thus:

> I bless thee, Lord, because I GROW
> Among thy trees, which in a ROW
> To thee both fruit and order OW ...

It is as if each rhyming move revealed something crucial and implicit in the previous word. The fruit of this process is order itself – 'ROW' plucked from 'GROW', for instance, or, in the second tercet,

> What open force, or hidden CHARM
> Can blast my fruit, or bring me HARM
> While the inclosure is thine ARM?

There seems to be harm and danger hidden in the spell of charm, but hope lies in a refiguration of enclosure, not of words within words, or effects implicit in causes, but a figuration of a transcendent sort which wraps the word contained around the container (God's ARM, not a mere human limb whose power to enclose and thereby protect someone else is contingent upon its signifier's being itself 'inclosed' within HARM and, ultimately, CHARM.)

It is only in the last two tercets that the very process is finally and canonically troped. In the penultimate one, the prelapsarian work of gardening even in Paradise is invoked, the basic task being pruning of trees:

When thou dost greater judgments SPARE,
And with thy knife but prune and PARE,
Ev'n fruitful trees more fruitful ARE.

The analytic story tells us that in order to spare the coming fruit, one must pare down the present branches, that PARE is at the heart of the matter of SPARE, and that, ultimately, the ARE of 'fruitful are' will emerge. But the poem, and the allegorisation of the scheme, cannot end here, if only because the specific mode of reduction, of word-pruning, has not been addressed. Inevitably, then,

Such sharpness shows the sweetest FREND:
Such cuttings rather heal than REND:
And such beginnings touch their END.

In the revealed teleology, finally, the end of this kind of friendship, protection, enclosure — as well as the end of what could falsely be construed as rending, rather than closing up — is the end of ends itself; cutting back the extraneous front matter to disclose the final truth in the penultimate line leads to the final trope of regained paradise in, for Herbert's Christian vision, eternity, as well as in a termination of the poem, at once *le fin* and *le but*, termination and half-hidden objective.

Herbert is an exemplary allegorist of scheme and pattern, and one could go through *The Temple* and show a multitude of instances of this. (For example, the figuration of the scheme of *anadiplosis*, which Puttenham calls the 'redouble', in the poem called 'The Wreath', where it partakes of a dialectic of crooked-and-straight because of the governing emblem of weaving an utterance of praise, and reinforced by a strange chiasmic scheme of repetition of rhyming words.)

It is not only other schemes, but whole orders of scheme, that are susceptible, like rhyme, to reflexive troping and, even more, to the generation of *ad hoc* theorising about the scheme. And, as has been suggested, that very fragment of rhetorical theory may itself point back to some central figure of an entire poem. The orders of scheme I have in mind could range from whole verse forms (considered synchronically, of course, and without regard to their inevitable allusive dimension), anaphora, refrain, rhetorical question, stanzaic closure, to patterns like chiasm. None of these is naturally (by which I mean canonically) figurative: they all — again, like rhyming — enable troping to occur, but do not necessitate it. Neither are schemes naturally self-referential or reflexive: it is only the tropes of poets which make them so, and to which they return figuration. Chiasm, for instance, doesn't *mean* anything; but Robert Frost can, in a line which designates flowers at the rim of a forest pool and their reflections in it – 'These flowery waters and these watery flowers' – make the criss-cross pattern mean mirroring, as if it had existed all along only to conjoin an object and its representation. And reflection – representation – is somehow made bilateral, even as minds both reflect nature and, reflecting on it (in the punning senses established in the first line of the poem), are troped by it. But other chiasms in Marlowe, or Milton or Pope or Coleridge, say, will allegorise themselves and their workings in different ways.

As with the paranormal sequences of schemes, so with words and sublexical elements. Assonance and alliteration are most obviously like rhyme – and may, indeed, be variously figured as subcomponents of it – in this respect. But consider how an inferential pattern of linguistic analysis can serve as a scheme in a similar way, as in this beautiful stanza of Geoffrey Hill's (from *The Mystery of the Charity of Charles Péguy*):

Patience hardens to a pittance, courage
unflinchingly declines into sour rage,
the cobweb-banners, the shrill bugle-bands
and the bronze warriors resting on their wounds.

'Patience' hardening to 'a pittance' entails a parable about sound-change. In the fabulous linguistics of the quatrain in question, ablaut is not morphological but moral, the soft fruit of forbearance shrivelling into its own pit. In the second, appositive figure, 'courage/unflinchingly declines into sour rage', the implication is diachronic, as if sour rage were a suffixed, /au/-grade form, as it were, reflected in some latter-day satem language. But just as both instances denote a degenerative change occurring over time, the second has an overtone of the synchronic analysis of the 'patience' - 'pittance' ablaut, for the process exemplified is both declension and declination. There are other residues of the decay of courage into inane expressions of what is no longer there to express – 'the cobweb-banners, the shrill bugle-bands / and the bronze warriors resting on their wounds'. The great effectiveness of this last line depends upon the surprising substitution for the expected word ('spears'? 'shields'? 'laurels'?) the unpleasantly softening 'wounds'.

There is a blending of the morphological and the historical in the fictions about sound-change here. Certain poets' mythological grammars do indeed incline either toward the synchronic or the diachronic in their fables about interinanimated words. I have discussed elsewhere[5] how, in A.E. Housman's clause 'The chestnut casts its flambeaux', the Latin etymon of 'chestnut' (*castanea*) is redoubled in the presence of the delicate, unasserted pun on the verb "casts" (purely Germanic in origin), so that a hypogram, a notional *'castanea casta'* (the Latin *'casta'* = 'chaste' being likewise unrelated to *'castanea'*) is conjured up, and momentarily flowers in a sort of 'chaste-nut'.

This is a recognisably Miltonic kind of move, playing on English word and Latin etymon, flower and root, what meaning was then and is now, although there is no allegorising of the etymological process, as there is in *Paradise Lost*, no valorisation of the relation between past and present usage. It is as if Latin and English co-existed synchronously (as they did, for Housman, in his writing in prose). But I want here to continue with the matter of the latinate syntax which is so beautifully and tactfully engaged by the remainder of the sentence:

The chestnut casts its flambeaux, and the flowers
  Stream from the hawthorn on the wind away ...

Even before the hyperbaton of the second line is revealed, the 'flowers' seem momentarily to be the chestnut-blossoms, now no longer torch-like, on the ground. But after the enjambment, the flowers that should in normal syntax stream either away from the hawthorn, on the wind, or else on the wind, away from the hawthorn, now, more generally, stream away (a nonce verb modelled on the intransitive form of 'blow away'). Also, we encounter the sub-phrase 'the hawthorn on the wind', which is part of the picture. (An effect like this, with syntax like this, e.e. cummings would have had to underscore with violent bracketings of format.) This sort of thing happens in Latin poetry as normally as rhyming in later vernaculars. But Housman just makes it happen, without any built in reflexive, interpretive glossing. Two kinds of syntax are contrasted − the direct SVO of the chestnut's actively casting its flambeaux, marked by the fictional etymon seeming to connect subject and verb, and by the assonance of verb and object, as opposed to the hyperbatic, ambiguous rearrangement of the intransitive streaming away of the flowers. But Housman never actually does what Milton so often contrives in his local tropes on syntactic patterns, where there is always some larger moralization being pointed at.

Take, for example, a line from the middle of a passage in *Paradise Lost*, Book II, describing the activities of the fallen angels in their newly-organised, proleptically neoclassical civilization which might be called the culture of Pandemonium.

        Others more mild,
Retreated in a silent valley, sing
With notes angelical to many a harp
Their own heroic deeds and hapless fall
By doom of battle; and complain that fate
Free virtue should enthral to force or chance.
Their song was partial, but the harmony
(What could it less when spirits immortal sing?)
Suspended hell, and took with ravishment
The thronging audience. In discourse more sweet
(For eloquence the soul, song charms the sense),

Others apart sat on a hill retired,
In thoughts more elevate, and reasoned high
Of providence, foreknowledge, will and fate,
Fixed fate, free will, foreknowledge absolute,
And found no end, in wandering mazes lost.
                              (546–561)

I pass over the typical effect of the inversion discovered at the enjambment of 'that fate / Free virtue should enthral to force or chance', a typically neo-Virgilian device, to consider the pivotal line about the relation of philosophy and poetry: 'For eloquence the soul, song charms the sense'. Richard Bentley, the eighteenth-century classical scholar who edited Milton and emended everything of poetic interest that he could find, rewrote the line as 'Song charmes the Sense, but Eloquence the Soul' (objecting that 'the *Verb* ought of right to be in the first *Colon* of the Sentence').

For Bentley, the representation of the proposition in Milton's verse is nastily opaque, and for Bentley there is no problem in the platonising elevation of prose eloquence, or philosophy, more sweet (in the Renaissance musical sense of being well-tuned) than the music of poetry. But Milton knows that there *are* problems here: abstract and concrete, mediated and direct, absence and presence, all enter into the dialectic, and the syntax of the line becomes both instrumental and figurative in its behalf. If this were only a matter of *style* (as, less for Bentley than for the uncomprehending Ezra Pound), the high mode might have asserted itself in a more usual inversion: 'For eloquence the soul charms, song, the sense' would be perhaps a bit Popean in its rhythm and its even-handed balance. But for Milton, first things come first, and for him, syntactic order, as Donald Davie and Stanley Fish and others have demonstrated, is always to be read for its parabolic narrative, epistemological, historical and teleological.

What is the story of this line, then? The ellipsis of the verb 'charms' from the first clause is filled by the extension of its most direct normative position in the second one. But that position, immediately following its subject, 'song', awakens the Latin etymon lurking in 'charms' (*carmen*, 'song') and patent still in the modern senses of 'incantation' and 'spell'. Poetry, song, sings directly to sense, whereas eloquence, philosophy, charms the soul in another, higher way, in which the music of poetry is not literally there, just as the verb 'charms' – even in its extended sense of delighting, alluring, bewitching – is not literally 'there' in the clause describing the action of philosophising on the soul, and, finally, as soul is less literally present than sense. The charm of philosophy is less literally 'charm' in the prior sense of 'song', then, and the usual parable of linguistic diachrony in *Paradise Lost* is at work here as well. The primary sense of things is present (in both meanings of the adjective); the prior sense is absent, and must be secondarily derived. But presence somehow gets it all wrong, and it is this dialectic that the fictional linguistics of the poem is always assisting the rest of its sytem of figuration to undo.

Ultimately the fallen angels in Book II, whether composing epics or debating on their fiendish Areopagus, are getting it all wrong, in any case, and the issues of Fate and Freedom perplex them both. But in the course of dealing with the rhetorical activities of what are, after all, two different kinds of writing, Milton applies an *ad hoc* theory of syntax, based on a troping of SVO as an emblem of literalness, as opposed to the figurativeness of displacement.

The contention between current and obsolete, original lexical use that Milton is constantly staging is a reflection of Satan's dubious battle with God over the nature of authority. We might say, given the consequences of romantic theories of originality as self-origination (a domestication of Satan's view, in any case), that this is a dialectical struggle between two antithetical concepts of originality – that of prior, but absent source, and primary, present given. It is not that Milton always allegorises semantic change as a figure of the Fall itself (in the case of 'charms' there is no such mapping). But such an interpretation is paradigmatic for other figurations.

The peculiar effect by which English 'song' summons up the *carmen* in 'charms' is expanded in a fourfold way by G. M. Hopkins, whose morphophonemic fictions are far more complex than the rhythmic packing which frames them. At the opening of a poem called 'Binsey Poplars', Hopkins addresses the dear trees which

Quelled or quenched in leaves the leaping sun,
All felled, felled, are all felled,
    Of a fresh and following folded rank
      Not spared, not one ...

The word 'folded' follows the word 'following' and, ultimately, the reiterated 'felled', with most remarkable consequences. In the first place, it is as if there were some typical Germanic-strong-verb ablaut at work here, yielding (once, or formerly) 'folded' as a strange historical participle of 'felled'. Then there is the matter of 'folded' itself, lexically speaking: the rank is folded over in the sense that it is staggered, or wrapped onto itself (fold[1] < OE *faldan*). But the trees are also folded not in another sense of the same word, but homonymically, like sheep (fold[2] < OE *fald*), following each other in a linear flocking. The 'leaves' in the first of the quoted lines exerts some other pressure on 'folded', causing it momentarily to resonate with an echo of *'folium'* (even as there is a trace of another Latin false – but figuratively relevent – etymon, *'fello'* in 'felled': the chopping-down of the trees having been accomplished by fell, as well as felling, blows. All the other etyma here are Germanic, and the Latin false-roots only provide evocative shadowing. (Nevertheless, as the poem progresses, puns on a Latin etymon – as in an insistence on the *specere* of 'seeing' in the repeated word 'especial' and, particularly, in the identification 'self' and *'sylva'* in the insistence on how the 'strokes of havoc únselve / The sweet especial scene' become central.)

Etymology – not, as Curtius discussed it, as 'a mode of thought', but more specifically as a frame for trope − is foregrounded here, and the sequence 'felled-felled-felled-following-folded' engages both diachronic and synchronic fables of sound-shift. But Hopkins is perfectly capable of leaving words almost totally at linguistically referential ease: notice that 'rank', which is only faintly agitated by being rhymed later on with 'sank' and 'bank', is never called on to breed a punning overtone on its adjectival homonym, 'rank' = profuse, excessive, offensive (< OE *ranc*). And observe that the wonderful patterning of the first line engages no historical linguistics whatsover; its visionary morphology is all synchronic, and the momentary narratology of the alliterating '1' and where it goes, and the assonant pairs of /e/ and /iy/ and finally, the /n/ that underscores the appropriateness of 'quenched' for the 'sun' assumes that no word even meant anything else, nor had any other form.[6]

It is this sort of purely synchronic attention to words that characterises so much of what, following Dr Johnson, we might call 'representative versification', the purely associative analysis which legislates morphophonemes and symbolic values for them in the idiolect of a particular poem, and, often, of a single line.

Hopkins's interinanimated words are like Milton's in that they all have personal histories, and in that, as with modern psychologies, authentic inner states and essences are referred to stages in past lives. Poets like Spenser and Wallace Stevens tend to have more purely synchronic poetic grammars. Minor verse will seldom exhibit much of this fictive linguistic thought, seeking to attain a style without raising any disturbing questions about it. Words that work and play and breed and brood together will naturally take their phonological bodies very seriously indeed, even as their poets who dally nicely with them always do. The Duchess's advice to Alice, 'Take care of the sense and the sounds will take care of themselves', is as compromised by economic actuality as its prototype about pence and pounds got to be by the nineteenth century (it was coined, I believe, by William Lowndes around 1700). Taking care of the pence will keep your mind off the pounds you'll never have, and, for bad poetry, the situation is indeed analagous. Only the rich can offer such advice, and only someone whose word-hoard is sufficiently rich can afford to take what the Duchess has to say without danger.

But, as I have been suggesting, different word-hoards have different compartments and other interior arrangements, and elements of language are differently identified, sorted, classified and grouped in them. The few instances I have been examining exhibit particular fictional grammars − indeed, if viewed as being pathological ones they might be said to reveal acute situational morphophonemia and, in some cases, chronic synchrodiachronosis. These instances, too, have all been of pattern as parable, although the linguistic levels at which the parabolic patterning occurs can vary widely among different poets and texts. In their dallying with words, poets are like children playing with them, but for the highest stakes; they are like the proverbial straw-women to which Professor Pratt refers, in their gossip, their use of fictions for moral purposes (which Milton insisted, in *Areopagitica*, was necessary), their prosopopeia of plants and even abstractions; and ultimately, they are like strangers to their own languages, finding all sorts of uncanonical wrong sides to words, and making what might as well be mistakes, seeing what could only look like relations among words if you didn't really *know* them, and thereby knowing them, in some ways, even better.

Notes

1   I.A. Richards, *The Philosophy of Rhetoric*, New York, 1936, 47–66.

2   As translated by Peter Firchow in *Friedrich Schlegel's* Lucinde *and the Fragments*, Minneapolis, 1971, p.150.

3   See James Nohrnberg, *The Analogy of The Faerie Queene*, Princeton, 1976, p.607; also Patricia Parker, *Inescapable Romance*, Princeton, 1979, p.93. A.C. Hamilton's notes to his edition of the poem (London, 1977) are full of such observations.

4   See the discussion of this poem by Joseph H. Summers, *George Herbert: his Religion and Art*, Cambridge, Massachusetts, 1954, pp.138–9.

5   John Hollander, *Vision and Resonance* 2nd edition, New Haven, 1985, p.125.

6   Several considerations of this poem seem to miss this etymological troping; there is generally more interest in 'especial' as designating *haeccitas*, e.g. F.R. Leavis, 'Metaphysical Isolation', The Kenyon Critics, *Gerard Manley Hopkins*, New York, 1945, pp.121–3; Norman H. MacKenzie, *A Reader's Guide to Gerard Manley Hopkins*, Ithaca, 1981, pp.107–10; and Paul Mariani, *Commentary on the Complete Poems of Gerard Manley Hopkins*, Ithaca, 1970, pp.128–30.

Language and the order of nature

1 **Order out of language**

Out of the buzz and the hum in which mankind has been evolving – itself a kind of conversation, to our present way of thinking – has emerged what Rulon Wells once called the 'distinctively human semiotic': a special form of dialogue powered by a system we call language. With this we talk to each other; and in the process we construct the microcosmos in which each one of us lives, our little universes of doing and happening, and the people and the things that are involved therein.

And in the course of this semiotic activity, without really becoming aware of it we have also been construing the two macrocosmic orders of which we ourselves are a part: the social order, and the natural order. For most of human history, these deeper forms of dialogue have depended on substantially the same resource: ordinary, everyday, spontaneous, natural spoken language – with just some 'coefficient of weirdness' such as Malinowksi found in the more esoteric contexts of its use.[1]

All this dialogic construction is, by definition, interactive. At the micro level, we get to know our fellow-creatures by talking to them and listening to them; and they respond to us in the same natural language. At the macro level, the 'dialogue with nature', brilliantly scripted by Prigogine and Stengers in their book *Order Out of Chaos*,[2] is also interactive; but in another guise. When we want to exchange meanings with physical or biological nature we have to process information that is coded in very different ways, and that may need to go through two or three stages of translation before we can apprehend it.

We have always assumed that it *can* be translated; that the information coming in can in the last resort be represented and transmitted through the forms of our own natural languages. In fact, up until the last few millennia, no conceivable alternative could ever present itself; because language was beyond the range of our conscious reflection. It was simply part of ourselves – the label 'natural' language is entirely apt. Herbert Simon, in his *Sciences of the Artificial*, classified language among the artificial phenomena;[3] but he was wrong. Language is as much a product of evolution as we are ourselves; we did not manufacture it. It is an evolved system, not a designed system: not something separate from humanity, but an essential part of the condition of being human. These natural languages, then, sufficed to enable us to interpret both facets of our wider environment, the social order and the natural order; these were, after all, construed by generalising and abstracting from the micro-environments in which language had evolved all along.

It is just within the last hundred generations or so that some element of design has come into natural language; and just in certain cultural-historical contexts, those in which language has come to be written down. Writing has been an inherent part of the process. In these contexts the dialogue with nature has begun to take on new forms; we have learnt to measure, and to experiment; and to accompany these new semiotic modes, our languages have spawned various metalanguages – the languages of mathematics and of science. These are extensions of natural languages, not totally new creations; and they remain in touch. Even mathematics, the most 'meta-' of all the variants of natural language, is kept tied to it by an interpretative interface – a level one metalanguage which enables mathematical expressions to be rendered in English, or Chinese, or other forms of distinctively human semiotic.

2 Does language cope?

Now and again some part of the dialogue breaks down, and then it becomes news – like London Bridge; as long as it stays up it is not news, but when it falls down it will be. Yet what is really newsworthy about language is how rarely it does fall down. The demands that we make on the system are quite colossal; how is it that it so seldom gets overloaded?

As far as the social order is concerned, we can watch language at work construing this from a child's earliest infancy, because from the moment of birth language intercedes, mediating in the dialogue between an infant and its caregivers. This kind of language, which is language for loving and caring rather than for knowing and thinking, would seem to have no great demands being made on it, and only in pathological cases is it likely to break down. Since here language is not being required to refer, its success is judged other than referentially. But this least referential kind of discourse is in fact actively enrolled in constructing the social order. Predictably, since the social order is highly complex, the language that is creating it is also highly complex. Only, the two complexities are not related in a straightforward referential fashion. Language creates society; but it does so without ever referring to the processes and the structures which it is creating.[4]

This appears surprising only because we are obsessed with the referential properties of language. Yet language is 'not constrained by the need to refer':[5] even if a mother was aware of the features of the social order that her dialogue was bringing into being, her baby could scarcely be expected to understand them. She cannot talk to her child about social values, statuses and roles, decision-making hierarchies and the like. Yet all these are brought into being by her use of the grammar, as Hasan has convincingly demonstrated;[6] and this is why when people want to change the conditions of the dialogue, and the structures it is setting up, they do so by changing the grammar − thus illustrating how well the grammar is doing its job. The complaint is not that the language is not functioning properly, but that it is functioning all too well − it is the social order construed by it that is being objected to. But mostly the design for change is drawn up only at the surface of the language, rather than at the much less accessible, cryptotypic level of patterning by which the structures are really installed.

When we come to consider how language creates the *natural* order, we might expect matters to be different. This is an order of happenings, and things, and language is our primary means of reflecting on these. Here, presumably, the essential function of language is to refer − to make contact with what is 'out there'. But this too we shall have to call into question.

In this sphere there have been from time to time complaints of a different kind. It is often objected that language is letting us down; and this especially at certain times in history, when the pace of the dialogue is quickening and knowledge is accumulating very fast. At such times there arise proposals for improving language, making it a more effective tool for recording and extending our knowledge.

Thus the precursors and contemporaries of Newton set about remodelling language: first simply as shorthand, then as universal character (a script that would be the same for all languages, based on the logographic principle of Chinese), then as 'real character' (a new universal written language, with its own realisations in speech − the famous systems of Cave Beck, Dalgarno and John Wilkins), and finally conceived of as a calculus, a semiotic not so much for recording and transmitting knowledge as for creating it − a tool designed for thinking with, like the mathematical calculus newly invented by Leibnitz and by Newton himself. (This last was never realised; nor were any of the earlier systems that were realised ever used.)

Since 1900 the call has been heard again, heralded perhaps by de Broglie's famous observation that 'physics is in suspense because we do not have the words or the images that are essential to us'. We can follow this motif through Einstein, Bohr and Heisenberg, down to the present day as it becomes increasingly specific.[7] David Bohm devotes a whole chapter to language, in which he objects that 'language divides things into separate entities', and so distorts the reality of 'undivided wholeness in flowing movement'; and he proposes a new form of language called the 'rheomode', which gives the basic role to the verb rather than the noun.[8]

We shall return to these objections in a moment. But despite the shortcomings which the natural scientists of these two periods have found in the languages they had to work with, science has continued to progress – and to change direction fundamentally on both occasions. Languages have not given way beneath its weight, nor are there any very obvious signs of overload. By and large, the dialogue has worked. One thing that Bohm and his predecessors may have overlooked is that you do not need to keep engineering a language in order to change it; it will change anyway – because that is the only way it can persist.

3 Language as dynamic open system

Every language is constantly renewing itself, changing in resonance with changes in its environment. But this is not an incidental fact about language; it is a condition of its existence as a system – and without language as system there could be no dialogue at all.

The earliest linguists of India, Greece and China all recognized that languages change in their expression – in their phonetics and morphology. These effects have now been shown to be statistical:[9] variation sets in, from a variety of sources, internal and external; and this variation can either become stabilised, so that the system becomes inherently variable at that point, or a 'variable rule becomes categorical' and we say that sound change has taken place. The terminology ('variable rule', and so on) is unfortunate, since it leads people – or perhaps confirms their inclination – to look for hidden variables, so that all variable rules can be reduced to categorical status. But the data resist such interpretations; it is simply not the case that if we knew everything there was to know then we could predict every instance. In other words, variability in language is not a limitation of the observer; it is a feature of the system, and hence the statistically defined behaviour of the micro particles of language – for example the realisation of a particular vowel as a fronted or a backed variant – can induce the system to change.

Such expression variables are alternative realisations of some higher level constant (eg. 'the phoneme $/a/$'), which therefore constitutes the entry condition to that particular little system. To understand changes in the meaning potential of language we need to consider analogous statistical effects on the content plane.[10] Consider a grammatical system such as past/present/future primary tense in English, interpretable semantically as deictic reference to a linear scale of time (the traditional description was 'time relative to the moment of speaking'). In any instance of the context which serves as entry condition to that system – in grammatical terms, any instance of a finite clause – each term has an inherent probability of occurring. A speaker of English 'knows' these probabilities; having heard, by the age of five, say, about half a million instances he has a statistical profile of the lexicogrammar of the language. It is by the same token (more specifically, by the same set of tokens) that he knows the lexical probabilities: that *go* is more frequent than *grow* and *grow* is more frequent than *glow*. Now, grammar and lexis are simply the same phenomenon looked at from two different ends; but one difference between them is that the patterns we treat as grammatical are those which are buried much deeper below the level of people's consciousness, and so these patterns, and the probabilities associated with them, are much harder for people to become aware of – many people reject grammatical probabilities when they are told about them: they feel insulted, and take them as affronts to the freedom of the individual. Lexical patterns are nearer the surface of consciousness: hence lexical probabilities are quite readily recoverable, as a sense of 'this word is more frequent than that', and are therefore found easier to accept. (Logically, of course, there is no reason why being told that one is going to use *go* more frequently than *glow* should be any less threatening than being told one is going to use past more frequently than future; but these observations tend to provoke very different responses.)

Now, just as, when I listen to the weather report every morning, and I hear something like 'last night's minimum was six degrees, that's three degrees below average', I know that that instance has itself become part of, and so altered, the probability of the minimum temperature for that particular night in the year – so every instance of a primary tense in English discourse alters the relative probabilities of the terms that make up the primary tense system. Of course, to make these probabilities meaningful as a descriptive measure we have to sharpen the focus, by setting conditions: we are not usually interested in the average temperature at all times anywhere on the surface of the globe (though this is a relevant concept for certain purposes), but rather in the probable daily minimum on Sydney Harbour at the time of the winter solstice. There are various dimensions conditioning grammatical probabilities: we might specify the context of situation – for example the discourse of weather forecasting, which will considerably increase the weighting for future tense;[11] or we might specify a number of other concurrent grammatical features, such as whether the clause is declarative or interrogative. (There are also the transitional probabilities of the text as a stochastic process.) The more local the context, of course, the greater the moderating effect of a single instance.

Lemke has pointed out that many human systems, including all social-semiotic systems, are of a particular kind known as 'dynamic open systems'.[12] Dynamic open systems have the property that they are metastable: that is, they persist only through constant change; and this change takes place through interactive exchanges with their environment. In the course of such interaction, the system exports disorder; and in the process of exporting disorder, and so increasing the entropy of its environment, the system renews itself, gains information, imports or rather creates order and in this way continues to function. The system exists only because it is open. But it is now no longer itself; for such a system, the state of being is one of constant becoming. Language – natural language – is certainly a system of this general type.

Language (like other social semiotic systems) is a dynamic open system that achieves metastability through these statistical processes. Instances affect probabilities; from time to time probabilities thus rise to one or fall to zero, so that quantitative effects become qualitative and the system maintains itself by evolving, through a process of constant change.

In an ideal system, one having two states that are equiprobable, there is no redundancy. Once we depart from equiprobability, redundancy sets in. In all open systems the probabilities are skewed, so that the system carries redundancy. Lemke shows that a semiotic system is one that is characterised by redundancy *between (pairs of) its subsystems*: what he refers to as 'meta-redundancy'. To illustrate from the classic Hjelmslevian example of the traffic lights: the system has certain states, red, yellow and green. Since these are not equiprobable there is redundancy among them, at that level; but this simple redundancy is relevant only to the engineer who designs and instals them. There is then a *metaredundancy* between this system and the system of messages 'stop/go': this is the first order metaredundancy that defines the signifier and the signified. There is then a second order metaredundancy: this in turn 'metaredounds' with the system of behaviour of drivers approaching the signal: they stop, or else they drive on. And so on.

In other words: what the system 'says' (the wording: red/green), redounds with what it 'means' (the meaning: stop/go), which in turn redounds with what it does. But 'it' is a human system: it is people who drive the cars, people who construe the semantic opposition of stop/go, and people who switch on the lights, or at least programme the machine to do it for them. Traffic lights are in fact part of the social semiotic, even though I am using them here simply as an analogy for discourse that is 'worded' in the more usual sense – that is, in the form of lexicogrammar.

4 The emergence of metalanguages

Thus viewed as a social semiotic, language is a dynamic open system, probabilistic, and characterised by metaredundancy. These n-order metaredundancies define the levels, or strata, of the system: the relationship of metaredundancy is the general relationship whose manifestation in language we are accustomed to referring to as 'realisation'. Such a system is good for thinking with and good for doing with, these being the two complementary facets of all human semiosis.

When either of these facets comes under pressure, the system responds by creating special varieties of itself to meet the new demands. So in a period of rapid growth of science and technology new metalanguages appear. These new forms of language are both created by and also create the new forms of knowledge – since what we call knowledge is simply a higher level of meaning, still linked to the grammar by the chain of metaredundancies.

But it is at this point that the functioning of language starts to become problematic.

Let me refer again to David Bohm's *Wholeness and the Implicate Order*. Bohm is dissatisfied with the way language (as he sees it) fails to meet the demands of the new dialogue with nature, and he proposes the 'rheomode' – a form of language that would represent the flux of things, and construe experience as dynamic rather than static. His suggestions are simplistic and confined to a few variations in derivational morphology: for example, to get away from a 'language structure in which nouns are taken as basic, e.g. "this notion is relevant"' we reinstate the verb *to levate*, meaning 'the spontaneous and unrestricted act of lifting into attention any context whatsoever'; we then introduce the verb to *re-levate*, 'to life a certain context into attention again', whence *irrelevation, levation* and so on.[13] But the motive is clear: a new language is needed to encode a new view of reality.

There have been frequent assertions, throughout the history of quantum mechanics and the physics that derived from it, that it is impossible to talk about quantum ideas in language as it was received. The language of physics is under stress; and some of the more farfetched notions such as the 'many worlds' interpretation proposed by Everett and Wheeler – that there are as many alternative realities as there are quantum events – might be used to illustrate the incapacity of our natural language-based metalanguages to cope with these new semiotic demands. The metalanguages are too determinate, too rigid, too unable to accommodate complementarities. They cannot tell us 'that *all* is an unbroken and undivided whole movement, and that each 'thing' is abstracted only as a relatively invariant side or aspect of this movement'.[14]

Before examining these charges further, let us note an interesting paradox. When logicians and philosophers complain about language, their usual complaint is that it is too vague. When scientists find language letting them down, it is generally because it is too precise, too determinate. In part, no doubt, this reflects their two different ideologies. For the logician, if two things conflict they cannot both be true – so language should force them to reject the one or the other; and if language does not do this, then it is too loose, too vague. For the scientist, on the other hand, if two things are both true they cannot conflict – so the language should help them to accommodate both, and if it doesn't, it is too rigid, too determinate. (What I am labelling 'the logician', and 'the scientist' are of course two different ideologies – not the individual members of these two respected professions.)

But they are also probably talking about different languages. The logicians are thinking of non-technical natural language, from which their artificial languages, including mathematics, were first derived. The scientists are thinking of their own technical metalanguages that have been constructed on the basis of natural language: the various registers of physics, for example. And these scientific metalanguages are among the more designed varieties of human language – hence, like all designed systems, they do tend to be rigid and determinate. These are the very features which make such metalanguages unsuitable for just that purpose for which they were in fact designed: the dialogue with nature, for which it is essential to be able to mean in terms that are dynamic, non-compartmental and fluid – and above all, that do not foreclose.

The irony is, that that is exactly what natural language is like: dynamic, non-compartmental and fluid. But it has got smothered under the weight of the metalanguages that were built upon it.

5 Levels of consciousness in language

Let me begin this section with a quotation from Prigogine & Stengers' book *Order Out of Chaos* that I referred to at the outset:

[In quantum mechanics] there is an irreducible multiplicity of representation for a system, each connected with a determined [i.e. decided upon by the investigator] set of operators.

   This implies a departure from the classical notion of objectivity, since in the classical view the only 'objective' description is the complete description of *the system as it is*, independent of the choice of how it is observed ...

   The physicist has to choose his language, to choose the macroscopic experimental device. Bohr expressed this idea through the principle of complementarity ...

   The real lesson to be learned from the principle of complementarity, a lesson that can perhaps be transferred to other fields of knowledge, consists in emphasizing the wealth of reality, which overflows any single language, any single logical structure. Each language can express only part of reality.[15]

Here Prigogine & Stengers are of course talking about 'languages' in the sense of conceptual constructs; and they go on to say:

No single theoretical language articulating the variables to which a well-defined value can be attributed can exhaust the physical content of a system. Various possible languages and points of view about the system may be complementary. They all deal with the same reality, but it is impossible to reduce them to one single description.

It is my contention that natural language – not as it is dressed up in the form of a scientific metalanguage, but in its commonsense, everyday, spontaneous spoken form – does in fact 'represent reality' in terms of complementarities; and that these are complementary perspectives in precisely the sense in which Bohr was using the term.[16] Only, it does so non-referentially. Just as language construes the social order without referring to the system it is constructing, so likewise language construes the natural order – through the unconscious, cryptotypic patterns in the grammar, which create their own order of reality independently of whatever it is they may be being used to describe.

I shall illustrate the complementarities inherent in this 'de-automatised' sphere of the grammar in just a moment. But first we must recognise a problem. The features I am referring to in natural language are features of the 'cryptogrammar'; they function way below the usual level of consciousness. And the problem is, that when we start reflecting on them, bringing them up to our conscious attention, we destroy them. The act of reflecting on language transforms it into something alien, something different from itself – something determinate and closed. There are uses for closed, determinate metalanguages; but they can represent only one point of view about a system. The language of daily life, which shapes our unconscious understanding of ourselves and our environment, is a language of complementarities, a rheomode – a dynamic open system. The question is whether we can learn to use it to think with consciously. It may be impossible. I don't mean that it is impossible to *understand* the cryptogrammar of a natural language, but that its reality-generating power may be incompatible with explicit logical reasoning.

I have tried out a simple strategy for exploring the more unconscious features of the grammar. I selected a text – the headlines of a news broadcast, which I had taken down verbatim from the radio; I read it aloud to a group of students, and asked them to recall it. They gave me the motifs: death, disaster, violence and the like. I pressed them further: what was actually said? This time they gave me words: a list of the lexical items used, recalled with considerable accuracy although most of them had not figured in their first responses. Let me call the motifs level zero, and the lexical responses level one. I pressed them for a more specific account (still without reading the passage again), and they gave me the more exposed parts of the grammar: the word, group and phrase classes, the derivational morphology and so on. This exposed grammar we will call level two. I pressed them once more; and this time – since they were students of linguistics – they began to get to level three, the hidden grammar (the cryptotypes, in Whorf's terminology): the transitivity patterns, the grammatical metaphors and so on.

In our normal everyday concern with language we simpl. attend to the motifs. We are not concerned with wordings, and do not trouble even to remember them. We behave as if the metaredundancy – the realisation of meanings in lexicogrammar – is simply an automatic coding. If asked to reflect on the wording, we focus on the lexical end of the spectrum: the words, or rather the lexical items – since this is the edge that is nearest the domain of conscious attention. It takes much more effort to attend to the more strictly grammatical zone, especially to its more cryptotypic regions. And when we get there, we find ourselves back at the motifs again; but this time with a greatly heightened understanding, because now we can see why the text meant what it did, and we can appreciate the deeper ideological content of the discourse – the messages we had received without becoming aware of them.

The process of reflecting on natural language can be modelled in terms of these four levels of consciousness:

'meaning' (semantic level)

'wording' (lexicogrammatical level)

level 0: 'motifs'
{ level 1: 'words'
  level 2: 'phenotypes'
  level 3: 'cryptotypes'

where the spiral (cryptotypes as hidden motifs) in turn represents the dialectic of metaredundancy. Or, to put this in more familiar semiotic terms: the signified constructs the signifier (by 'realisation' – grammar in its automatised function), and the signifier constructs the signified (grammar, especially the cryptogrammar, in its de-automatised function). The problem of turning the cryptogrammar of a natural language into a metalanguage for reasoning with is that it has to become automatised – that is, the grammar has to be made to describe, instead of constructing reality by not describing, which is what it does best.

6 Everyday language as a theory of the natural order

I will try to enumerate some features of natural language, as embodied in our everyday informal discourse from earliest childhood, that constitute for us a theory of reality. They are features common to all languages, but in respect of which each language presents its own particular mix; I make one or two references to English, but in the main they are set out in general terms that could be applied to all.

– *Clausal structures*: the organisation of meanings in lexicogrammatical form (as 'wordings'). The gateway through which meanings are brought together and realised in ordinary grammar is the clause; and the clause nucleus is a happening (Process + Medium, in systemic terms). So natural languages represent reality as what happens, not as what exists; things are defined as contingencies of the flow.

– *Projection*: the general relation underlying what grammarians call 'direct and indirect speech'. The system of projection construes the whole of experience into two different kinds of event: semiotic events, and other events; the latter can then be transformed into semiotic events by processes of consciousness.

– *Expansion*: logical-semantic relationships between events. Two events provided they are of the same kind (as defined by projection) may be related to one another by one of a set of logical-semantic relations, such that the second one defines, extends, or in some way (such as time or cause) correlates with the first.

– *Transitivity*: *the theory of processes* (i). Natural languages construe experience out of different types of process; this plurality is universal, though the details of the system vary. English sets up 'outer' processes, those of the world perceived as external; 'inner' processes, those of (human-like) consciousness; and processes of attribution and representation. All are distinguished in the cryptogrammar.

- *Transitivity: the theory of processes* (ii). With regard to (at least) the 'outer' processes, natural languages incorporate two models: the transitive, which interprets 'mechanically', in terms of transmission, and the ergative, which interprets 'scientifically', in terms of causation. These two are complementary; the generalisations they make contradict each other, but every clause has to be interpreted as both.

- *Tense and aspect*: the theory of time. Similarly, natural languages embody two models of time: a theory of linear, irreversible time, out of past via present into future (tense), and a theory of simultaneity, with the opposition between being and becoming, or manifested and manifesting (aspect). Languages have very different mixtures (English strongly foregrounds linear time); but probably every language enacts both, and again the two are complementary in the defined sense.

In these and other features of their 'hidden' grammars, ordinary languages in their everyday, commonsense contexts embody highly sophisticated interpretations of the natural order, rich in complementarities and thoroughly rheomodal in ways much deeper than Bohm was able to conceive of. To be more accurate, we would have to say that it is these features *in a system of this dynamic open kind* that construe reality for us in this way. The system itself must be a metastable, multi-level ('metaredundant') system − that is, a human semiotic − with the further property (referred to by Leech in his paper) that it is 'metafunctional': it is committed to meaning more than one thing at once, so that every instance is at once both reflection and action − both interpreting the world and also changing it.

We have been reminded of 'the impossibility of recovering a fixed and stable meaning from discourse'. Of course this is impossible; it would be a very impoverished theory of discourse that expected it. But it is entirely possible − as we all do − to recover from discourse a meaning of another kind, meaning that is complex and indeterminate. The reason it is hard to make this process explicit is that we can do so only by talking about grammar; and to do this we have to construct a theory of grammar: a 'grammatics', let us call it. But this 'grammatics' is itself a designed system, another scientific metalanguage, with terms like 'subject' and 'agent' and 'conditional' − terms which become reified in their turn, so that we then come to think of the grammar itself (the real grammar) as feeble and crude because it doesn't match up to the categories we've invented for describing it. But of course it's the grammatics − the metalanguage − that is feeble and crude, not the grammar. To borrow Whorf's famous simile, the grammatics (grammar as metalanguage) is to the grammar (the language) as a bludgeon is to a rapier − except that a better analogy might be with the hand that wields the rapier. If the human mind can achieve this remarkable combination of incisive penetration and positive indeterminacy, then we can hardly deny these same properties to human language, since language is the very system by which they are developed, stored and powered.

7 The need for plurality of language

To quote Prigogine & Stengers again: 'Whatever we call reality, it is revealed to us only through active construction in which we participate'.[17] But, as they have already told us, 'the wealth of reality ... overflows any single language, any single logical structure. Each language can express only part of reality'.

I have suggested that our natural languages do possess the qualities needed for interpreting the world very much as our modern physicists see it. But from the time when our dialogue with nature became a conscious exercise in understanding, we have come to need more than one grammar — more than one version of language as a theory of experience. Rather, we have needed a continuum of grammars, from the rheomodal pole at one end to something more fixed and constructible at the other. For our active construction of reality we had to be able to adopt either a dynamic, 'in flux' perspective or a synoptic, 'in place' perspective — or some mixture of the two, with a complementarity between them.

So our language began to stretch, beginning — as far as the West is concerned — with the explosion of process nouns in scientific Greek from 550 BC onwards (e.g. kinesis 'movement', from kineo '(I) move'), and culminating (so far!) in the kind of semantic variation found in pairs such as:

experimental emphasis	we now start experimenting
becomes concentrated in	mainly in order to test
testing the generalizations	whether things happen regularly
and consequences derived	as we would expect if we were
from these theories	explaining in the right way
1-attic	1-doric

Let me label these two styles the 'attic' and the 'doric'. The attic mode is not of course confined to abstract scientific discourse; 2-attic is from a television magazine:

he also credits his former	he also believes that he
big size with much of his	succeeded in his career mainly
career success	because he used to be big
2-attic	2-doric

Represented in this new, 'attic' style, the world is a world of things, rather than one of happening; of product, rather than of process; of being rather than becoming. Whatever metaphor we use to label it with — and all these paired expressions capture some aspect of the difference — the emergence of the new attic forms of expression added a new dimension to human experience: where previously there had been one mode of interpretation, the dynamic, now there were two, the synoptic and the dynamic — or rather, two poles, with varying degrees of semantic space possible between them. There are now two ways of looking at one and the same set of phenomena.

The two are complementary, like wave and particle as complementary theories of light. Any aspect of reality can be interpreted either way; but, as with wave and particle, certain aspects will be better illuminated with the one perspective and others with the other. The doric style, that of everyday, commonsense discourse, is characterised by a high degree of grammatical intricacy — a choreographic type of complexity, as I have described it:[18] it highlights processes, and the interdependence of one process on another. The attic style, that of emergent languages of science, displays a high degree of lexical density; its complexity is crystalline, and it highlights structures, and the interrelationships of their parts — including, in a critical further development, *conceptual* structures, the taxonomies that helped to turn knowledge into science.

There was thus a bifurcation in the metaredundancy pattern, leading to the duality of styles that Rulon Wells spoke about at the conference whose aftermath we are celebrating here (he referred to them as 'nominal and verbal styles', but the distinction is really that of nominal and clausal).[19] Between the doric, or clausal, style and the attic, or nominal, style is a complementarity that itself complements the various first-order complementarities that we have already seen to be present within the doric system. But this second-order complementarity is of a somewhat different kind. The two perspectives are not on equal terms. The dynamic mode is prior; it comes first.

The dynamic mode is phylogenetically prior; it evolved first, along with the human species, whereas it is only in the last few millennia that the synoptic mode has come into being. It is also ontogenetically prior; it is what we learn as children — and carry with us throughout life. Whenever we are speaking casually and unselfconsciously, in typically human dialogic contexts, we go on exploiting the dynamic mode, which as we have seen embodies the deep experience of the species in cryptogrammatic form. The synoptic mode, on the other hand, embodies the more conscious reflection on the environment that is stored in scientific knowledge; historically it is derived from the dynamic by the processes of grammatical metaphor. Of course, once in existence it can enter daily life; there is nothing very abstruse or formal about *every previous visit had left me with a feeling of discomfort* ... Nevertheless it is a metaphoric derivative; the agnate *whenever I'd visited before I'd ended up feeling uncomfortable* ... is a prior form of semiosis. So how does the more synoptic mode, the attic style arise?

Thanks to the metaredundancy principle, it is possible to introduce variation at any one level of language without thereby disturbing the patterning at other levels of the system (that is, without catastrophic perturbations; the consequences are seen in continued gradual changes such as I described earlier). It is even possible to replace an entire level of the system in this way; and this is what happened with the development of writing. Writing provided a new mode of expression – which could 'realise' the pre-existing content patterns without disrupting them. At the same time, it provided a new interface, another kind of instantiation through which changes in the system could take place.

Writing evolved in the immediate context of the need for documentation and recording. But it opened the way to an alternative theory of reality.

8 The effects of writing

Conditions arise in history – essentially those of settlement – where experience has to be recorded: we need to store knowledge, and put it on file. So we invent a filing system for language, reducing it to writing. The effect of this is to anchor language to a shallower level of consciousness. For the first time, language comes to be made of constituents – sentences – instead of the dependency patterns – clause complexes – of the spoken mode. And with constituency comes a different form of the interpretation of experience.

It is important not to oversimlify the argument at this point. Both language itself, and the dimensions of experience that are given form by language, are extremely complex; and instead of hoping to gain in popularity ratings by pretending all is simple we do well to admit the complexity and try to accommodate it in our thinking. Let me take just three steps at this point.

Writing brings language to consciousness; and in the same process it changes its semiotic mode from the dynamic to the synoptic: from flow to stasis, from choreographic to crystalline, from syntactic intricacy to lexical density. Note that this is *not* saying that writing imposes organisation on language. On the contrary: there is every bit as much organisation in spoken language as there is in written, only it is organisation of a different kind. Written language is corpuscular and gains power by its density, whereas spoken language is wavelike and gains power by its intricacy. I am not, of course, talking about writing in the sense of orthography, contrasting with phonology as medium of expression; but about *written language* – the forms of discourse that arise as a result of this change of medium (by a complex historical process that is based partly on the nature of the medium itself and partly on its functions in society). Similarly in talking about spoken language I mean the forms of discourse which evolved over the long history of language in its spoken mode; the mode in which language itself evolved.

Writing puts language in chains; it freezes it, so that it becomes a *thing* to be reflected on. Hence it changes the ways that language is used for meaning with. Writing deprives language of the power to intuit, to make indefinitely many connections in different directions at once, to explore (by tolerating them) contradictions, to represent experience as fluid and indeterminate. It is therefore destructive of one fundamental human potential: to think on your toes, as we put it.

But, secondly, in destroying this potential it creates another one: that of structuring, categorising, disciplinising. It creates a new kind of knowledge: scientific knowledge; and a new way of learning, called education. Thus writing changed the social semiotic on two levels. Superficially, it created documentation – the filing of experience, the potential to 'look things up'. More fundamentally, it offered a new perspective on experience: the synoptic one, with its definitions, taxonomies and constructions. The world of written language is a nominalised world, with a high lexical density and packed grammatical metaphors. It is these features that enable discourse to become technical; as Martin has shown, technicality in language depends on, not writing as such, but the kind of organisation of meaning that writing brings with it.[20] Until information can be organised and packaged in this way – so that only the initiate understands it – knowledge cannot accumulate, since there is no way one discourse can start where other ones left off. When I can say

the random fluctuations in the spin components of one of the two particles

I am packaging the knowledge that has developed over a long series of preceding arguments and presenting it as 'to be taken for granted – now we can proceed to the next step'. If I cannot do this, but have to say every time that particles spin, that they spin in three dimensions, that a pair of particles can spin in association with one another, that each one of the pair fluctuates randomly as it is spinning, and so on, then it is clear that I will never get very far. I have to have an 'expert' grammar, the kind of grammar that is prepared to throw away experiential information, to take for granted the semantic relations by which the elements are related to one another, so that it can maximise textual information, the systematic development of the discourse as a causeway to further knowledge. That kind of grammar shuts the layman out.

It would take too long to demonstrate in detail how this written grammar works. Let me refer briefly to its two critical properties: nominalisation, and grammatical metaphor. Most instances involve a combination of the two. For example,

such an exercise had the potential for instrusions by the government into the legitimate privacy of non-government schools

Apart from *had*, the clause consists of two nominal groups: *such an exercise* and *the potential for instrusions by the government into the legitimate privacy of non-government schools*. The second of these displays one of the principal devices for creating nominal structures: nominal group *non-government schools* embedded inside prepositional phrase *of non-government schools* embedded inside nominal group *the legitimate privacy of non-government schools* embedded inside prepositional phrase *into the legitimate privacy of non-government schools*; another prepositional phrase *by the government*; the two both embedded in the nominal group *intrusions by (a) into (b)*, itself embedded inside the prepositional phrase *for intrusions ...*, embedded inside the nominal group *the potential for ...* And most of these embeddings involve grammatical metaphor: *potential*, nominal expression of modality 'be able to', perhaps even a caused modality 'make + be able to'; *instrusions*, nominal expression of process 'intrude'; *privacy*, nominal expression of quality 'private'; *legitimate*, adjectival expression of attitudinally qualified projection 'as they could reasonably expect to be', and so on. (That these are marked, metaphorical realisations in contrast to unmarked, 'congruent' ones is borne out in various ways: not only are the congruent forms developmentally prior – children typically learn to process grammatical metaphor only after the age of eight or nine – but also they are semantically explicit, so that the metaphorical ones can be derived from them but not the other way round. But note that the 'metaphor' is in the grammar; there is not necessarily any lexical shift.)

So to the third step. Writing and speaking, in this technical sense of written language and spoken language, are different grammars which therefore constitute different ways of knowing, such that any theory of knowledge, and of learning, must encompass both. Our understanding of the social and the natural order depends on both, and on the complementarity between the two as interpretations of experience. I sometimes ask teachers about this question: whether there are things in the curriculum they consider best learnt through talking and listening, and other things best learnt through reading and writing. They have seldom thought about this consciously; but their practice often reveals just such a complementarity – processes and process sequences, such as sets of instructions, and including logically-ordered sequences of ongoing argument, are presented and explored in speech, whereas structures, definitions, taxonomies and summaries of preceding arguments are handled through writing. Thus the complementarity of speech and writing creates a complementarity in our ways of knowing and of learning; once we are both speakers and writers we have an added dimension to our experience.

Having proclaimed the complementarity, however, I shall now take a fourth step – and end up by privileging speech. Again I stress that I am not talking about the channel; we can all learn to talk in written language, and a few people can manage the harder task of writing in spoken. I am talking about the varieties – spoken language and written language – that arose in association with these two channels. So by speech I mean the natural, unself-monitored discourse of natural dialogue: low in grammatical metaphor, low in lexical density, high in grammatical intricacy, high in rheomodal dynamic. This is language as it evolved as a dynamic open system; these are the features that keep it open, in the far-from-equilibrium state in which it enacts, and so construes, the semiotic parameters of our social, biological and physical levels of being. The frontiers of knowledge, in a post-quantum *nouvelle alliance*,[21] need a grammar of this kind to map them into the realm of 'that which can be meant'. But this mapping does not depend on reference, with the grammar being used in an automatised way to describe. If quantum ideas seem inexpressible, this may be because we have tried too hard to express them. They are almost certainly there already; what we must learn to do is to think grammatically – to recognise the ideological interpretant that is built into language itself.

9 Linguistics as metatheory

We have been saying that natural langauge is a theory of experience. But it is clear that language is also a *part* of human experience. Thus the system has to be able to include itself.

Lemke has pointed out that a social-semiotic system of this kind is not subject to the Gödelian restriction on self-reference.[22] Such a system can include itself in what it is describing – because it is a theory of praxis, of practices which operate irreversibly, ordered in time. Thus a grammar can also be, at the same time, a theory of grammar. I do not pretend to understand the argument at that point. But it is clear that, since we are interpreting language as it functions to create the natural and social order, and since it is itself part of that order, it must include itself in the description. And if we insist that linguists (*inter alios*!) should reflect on their own praxis as linguists, it is not just because such reflexivity is fashionable these days, but because we have learnt from quantum mechanics that the observer is an essential component in the total picture.

At the same time, as linguists we have learnt to be aware of the dangers of naïve scientism. We have heard at length – and with justice – of the superficial importation of Darwinian concepts into nineteenth-century historical comparatism; and there is a danger in the present situation too. Because we can see in post-quantum and far-from-equilibrium physics exactly the intellectual environment that is needed to make sense of language as we – independently – know it to be, we may all too easily latch on to these ideas and misinterpret them. And I am not claiming that, just by being aware of the danger, I have therefore avoided it myself.

Yet there are still two points to be made. One is that, for all its deflections and superficial applications where it did not fit, the Darwinian perspective was a fundamental one. Language has to be understood in a historico-evolutionary context, as part of evolutionary processes; the mistake is to apply these notions at places that are far too concrete and specific, instead of seeing them as the essential interpretative framework for our endeavours. And the same goes this time round, when all that comes from the sciences of nature resonates so sweetly with everything we as linguists have learnt to expect.

And secondly, it is not, in fact, the same scenario as before. History does not repeat itself – or only on the surface of things. This time, the communication is going both ways. We have become accustomed to accepting the privileged position of the natural sciences, which got their act together first: the nature of a scientific fact, notions of evidence and experimentation, and above all the relationship of the *instance* to the general principle – these were established first in physics, then in biology, and only a very late third in the social sciences.[23] So it was natural that physics should become the model for all the others.

Now, however, there are signs of a reversal. I quote David Bohm again: 'the speed of light is taken not as a possible speed of an object, but rather as the maximum speed of propagation of a signal'.[24] In the quantum world, events are explained not in terms of causality but in terms of communication, the exchange of information. This is what used to be called 'action at a distance'.[25] And from Prigogine & Stengers once more:[26]

A new type of order has appeared. We can speak of a new coherence, of a mechanism of 'communication' among molecules. But this type of communication can arise only in far-from-equilibrium conditions ...

What seems certain is that these far-from-equilibrium phenomena illustrate an essential and unexpected property of matter: physics may henceforth describe structures as adapted to outside conditions ... To use somewhat anthropomorphic language: in equilibrium matter is 'blind', but in far-from-equilibrium conditions it begins to be able to perceive, to 'take into account', in its way of functioning, differences in the external world ...

The analogy with social phenomena, even with history, is inescapable.

All this points us in a new direction. From now on, the human sciences have to assume at least an equal responsibility in establishing the foundations of knowledge. Their coat-tailing days are over. But if so, our practitioners will surely have to learn to behave responsibly, instead of squandering themselves in the wasteful struggle for originality in which everyone else must be deconstructed so that each can leave his (or her) mark. We have to learn to build on our predecessors and move forward, instead of constantly staying behind where they were in order to trample them underfoot.

More importantly, it means that we have to examine our basic concepts in the light of their more general relevance to the sciences of life and of nature. And as soon as we begin to do this, one thing stands out: that, among the human sciences, it is linguistics that finds itself inescapably in the front line. Partly because its object, language, is more accessible than those of sociology and psychology: more readily problematised, and seen to be opaque, than other forms of human behaviour. But more because, if we are to take seriously the notion that the universe is made of information, then we shall need a science of information – and the science of information is linguistics.

Why linguistics, rather than information science as at present constituted? Because natural language is the one non-designed human communication system, on the basis of which all other, artificial systems are conceived. It is presumably not a coincidence that, as technology has moved from the steam engine to the computer, so scientific explanations have moved from causality (limited by the speed of light) to communication (limited by the entropy barrier).[27] My colleague Brian McCusker observed that the universe was now 'one, whole, undivided and *conscious*', so that the science of sciences had to be psychology.[28] I think he should have said 'one, whole, undivided and *communicative*'. The source of interpretation of the universe as a communication system, in so far as this can be brought within the constraints of our understanding, has to be sought in grammar – the grammar of natural language, since that is where our understanding is born, and that is the means whereby we act and reflect on ourselves and our environment. If there is to be a science of sciences in the twenty-first century it will have to include linguistics – as at least a partner, and perhaps the leading partner, in the next round of man's dialogue with nature.

Notes

1 Bronislaw Malinowski, *Coral Gardens and their Magic* London, 1935. See the section entitled 'An ethnographic theory of the magical word'.

2 Ilya Prigogine & Isabelle Stengers, *Order Out of Chaos: Man's New Dialogue with Nature*, London, 1985. See especially pp. 41–4.

3 Herbert A. Simon, *The Sciences of the Artificial,* Cambridge, Massachusetts, 1969 (2nd ed., 1981). See p. 5, on language as 'strings of artifacts called symbols'.

4 Cf. Ruqaiya Hasan, 'The ontogenesis of ideology' in Terry Threadgold *et al.* (eds), *Semiotics – Ideology – Language*, Sydney Studies in Society and Culture, 3, Sydney, 1986, pp. 125–46. See especially example 6 on p. 134.

5 Quoted from David Butt, *The Relationship between Theme and Lexicogrammar in the Poetry of Wallace Stevens*, Macquarie University PhD thesis, 1984. Butt's forthcoming paper 'Randomness, order, and the latent patterning of text', develops this notion in ways that are central to the present discussion.

6 See Ruqaiya Hasan, 'Offers in the making: a systemic-functional approach' (forthcoming).

7 See Werner Heisenberg, *Physics and Philosophy: The Revolution in Modern Science*, New York, 1958. Especially Chapter X, 'Language and reality in modern physics'.

8 David Bohm, *Wholeness and the Implicate Order*, London, 1980 (Ark Paperbacks, 1983). See especially Chapter 2, 'The rheomode – an experiment with language and thought'.

9 See e.g. David Sankoff & S. Laberge, 'The linguistic marketplace and the statistical explanation of variability', in David Sankoff (ed.), *Linguistic Variation: Models and Methods*, New York, 1978. For the study of linguistic variation from this viewpoint, see Barbara M. Horvath, *Variation in Australian English: the Sociolects of*

Sydney, Cambridge Studies in Linguistics 45, Cambridge, 1985. Especially Chapter 5, 'Analytical methodology'.

10   Chris Nesbitt & Guenter Plum, 'Probabilities in a systemic grammar: the clause complex in English; in Robin P. Fawcett & David J. Young (eds), *New Developments in Systemic Linguistics, Vol. II: Theory and Application*, London, (in press).

11   Based on an analysis of weather reports in the *New York Times* and *Chicago Tribune*, May–June 1985. See M. A. K. Halliday & Christian M. I. M. Matthiessen, *Grammatical Metaphor in Text Generation* (forthcoming).

12   References throughout this paper are to J. L. Lemke's three articles 'Towards a model of the instructional process', 'The formal analysis of instruction' and 'Action, context and meaning', in J. L. Lemke, *Semiotics and Education*, Toronto Semiotic Circle: Monographs, Working Papers & Prepublications, Toronto, 1984.

13   *Wholeness and the Implicate Order*, pp. 34 ff.

14   *Ibid.*, p. 47.

15   *Order Out of Chaos*, p. 225.

16   Cf. John P. Briggs & F. David Peat, *Looking Glass Universe: the Emerging Science of Wholeness*, Glasgow, 1985, p. 54: 'Bohr approved of the uncertainty principle itself, believing it was an aspect of a deeper idea he called 'complementarity'. Complementarity meant the universe can never be described in a single, clear picture but must be apprehended through overlapping, complementary and sometimes paradoxical views. Bohr found echoes of this idea in classical Chinese philosophy and the theories of modern psychology.' He would have found them also in the grammar of natural languages.

17   *Order Out of Chaos*, p. 293.

18   M. A. K. Halliday, 'Spoken and written modes of meaning', in Rosalind Horowitz & Jay Samuels (eds), *Comprehending Oral and Written Language*, New York, 1986.

19   Rulon Wells, 'Nominal and verbal style', in Thomas A. Sebeok (ed.), *Style in Language*, New York & London, 1960, pp. 213–20.

20   See J. R. Martin, 'Intervening in the process of writing development', in Clare Painter & J. R. Martin (eds), *Writing to Mean: Teaching Genres Across the Curriculum*, Applied Linguistics Association of Australia, Occasional Paper 9, in press; also Peter Wignell, 'Organizing the phenomenal world', University of Sydney, Linguisitics Department Working Papers, in press.

21   The title of the original French version of Prigogine & Stengers's *Order Out of Chaos* was *La nouvelle alliance*.

22   *Semiotics and Education* see section 2.1 of 'Action, context and meaning', entitled 'Recursivity and praxis', pp. 71–3.

23   Culler identifies Durkheim, Freud and Saussure as those primarily responsible. See Jonathan Culler, *Saussure,* Glasgow, 1977.

24   *Wholeness and the Implicate Order*, p. 123.

25   John Gribbin, *In Search of Schrödinger's Cat: Quantum Physics and Reality*, London, 1985, p. 182.

26   *Order Out of Chaos*, p. 14.

27   *Ibid.*, p. 295.

28   Brian McCusker, 'Fundamental particles', in Robyn Williams (ed.), *The Best of The Science Show*, Melbourne, 1983, pp. 235–42 (quotation from p. 239).

Withholding the missing portion: power, meaning and persuasion in Freud's *The Wolf-Man*

Introduction

I was led to this paper by two moments in the proceedings of the 1958 Style In Language Conference; they are moments in which the topic of persuasion is allowed to surface and then is immediately suppressed. The first such moment coincides with the only substantive mention at the conference of Freud. Roger Brown is discussing the resistance of cognitive psychologists to psychoanalytic procedure in which, it is feared, 'anything can mean anything'.[1] Brown replies, in apparent defense of psychoanalysis, that one must take into account the fact that its results are often persuasive; and if they are persuasive it must be because the psychoanalytic evidence, while not falling obviously into the linear and logical forms with which we are familiar, is nevertheless speaking to the criteria by which we determine validity; presumably at a certain point the accumulation of evidence reaches a level which satisfies those criteria and at that point persuasion occurs. But if this is an argument that acknowledges persuasion, it also robs it of any independent force. In Brown's account persuasion is simply the name of a mechanism that is triggered when a level of statistical probability has been reached. A persuasion so defined has been thoroughly domesticated and is no longer a threat to the formal projects of linguistics and cognitive psychology.

The second moment at which the conference defends itself against the threat of persuasion occurs at the very end, after the last paper, in a discussion between the participants, a discussion one finds, if one finds it at all, in exceedingly small print. There, hidden from view lest it infect the entire volume, is a brief consideration of rhetoric. The topic is introduced by I. A. Richards who declares that the questions so often debated at the conference, the questions of value and meaning, are finally rhetorical; it is a matter he says, of the context of discourse and, as Isocrates observes, good discourse is discourse that works. The response is literally terror. C. E. Osgood protests that if the rhetorical view is accepted then even advertising can be thought of as good discourse, in fact as the best discourse; and W. K. Wimsatt adds that if rhetorical standards have any relevance at all, it is only with reference to productions like 'the speeches of Hitler during the last war'. Confronted with the choice of standing either with Hitler or with W.K. Wimsatt, Richards does the right thing, and in a supremely rhetorical moment withdraws from his defence of rhetoric. 'Mr Wimsatt and I', he says, 'are not in disagreement'.

I have two epigraphs for this essay. The first is from James Strachey's preface to his translation of Freud's *Introductory Lectures*. Freud, he says, was 'never rhetorical' and was entirely opposed to laying down his view in an authoritarian fashion.[2] The second is a report by the Wolf-Man of what he thought to himself shortly after he met Freud for the first time: this man is a Jewish swindler, he wants to use me from behind and shit on my head. This paper is dedicated to the proposition that the Wolf-Man got it right.

I

'I dreamt that it was night and that I was lying in my bed ... Suddenly the window opened of its own accord, and I was terrified to see that some white wolves were sitting on the big walnut tree in front of the window.' Thus begins Freud's account of the most famous dream in the literature of psychoanalysis, the centre-piece of his most famous case. Freud tells us that although the patient recalled the dream at a 'very early stage in the analysis', its 'interpretation was a task that dragged on over several years' without notable success.[3] The breakthrough, as it is reported, came in an instant and apparently without preparation. 'One day the patient began to continue with the interpretation of the dream. He thought that the part of the dream which said ... "suddenly the window opened of its own accord' was not completely explained' (p.179). Immediately and without explanation, the explanation came forth: 'it must mean: "my eyes suddenly opened." I was asleep ... and suddenly woke up, and as I woke up I saw something: the tree with the wolves.' It is important to note that the patient does not say, 'Now I remember', but rather, 'It *must* mean.' His is not an act of recollection, but of construction. The question I would ask − and it is a question that will take us far − is simply what is the content of 'must'? What compels him to this particular interpretation among all those he might have hit upon? To this Freud's answer is 'nothing,' at least nothing external to the patient's own efforts. For a long time, he tells us, his young charge 'remained ... entrenched behind an attitude of obliging apathy' (p. 157); he refused, that is, to 'take an independent share in the work'. Clearly Freud is here not only characterising his patient; he is also providing us with a scenario of the analysis in which both his and the patient's roles are carefully specified: the analyst waits patiently for the patient to begin to work on his own and suddenly 'one day' his patience is rewarded, when the patient declares, 'it must mean'.

There is, however, another scenario embedded in this same paragraph, and it is considerably less benign: the full sentence in which one finds the phrase 'independent share in the work' reads as follows: 'It required a long education to persuade and induce him to take an independent share in the work.' The sentence is obviously divided against itself, one half proclaiming an independence which in the other half is compromised when it is identified as the product of persuasion and force. That independence is further compromised when Freud reveals the method by which it has been 'induced'. At the moment when he saw that the patient's attachment to him had become strong enough to counterbalance his resistance, Freud announced that 'the treatment must be brought to an end at a particular fixed date, no matter how far it had advanced'. As it is delivered, the announcement would seem to indicate that Freud does not care whether or not 'advancement' will occur, but in fact it is a device for assuring advancement, and for assuring it in a form he will approve.[4] What Freud *says* is 'do as you like, it makes no difference to me'. What he *means* is, 'if you do not do as I like and do it at the time I specify, you will lose the satisfaction of pleasing me to whom I know you to be attached by the strongest of bonds because I forged them.' The coercion could not be more obvious and Freud does not shrink from naming it as an exercise of 'inexorable pressure'; yet in the very same sentence he contrives to detach the pressure from the result it produces: 'Under the inexorable pressure of the fixed limit [the patient's] resistance gave way, and now in a disproportionately short time, the analysis produced all the material which made it possible to clear up his inhibitions and remove his symptoms.' Here the analysis is presented as if it were independent of the constraints that father it, and at the end of the sentence the clearing up of inhibitions and the removal of symptoms appear as effects without a cause, natural phenomena that simply emerge in the course of their own time, the time, presumably, when the patient suddenly, and of his own accord, exclaims, 'It *must* mean'.

It is a remarkable sequence, and one that is repeated in a variety of ways in the paragraphs that follow. Always the pattern is the same: the claim of independence − for the analysis, for the patient's share, for the 'materials' − is made in the context of an account that powerfully subverts it, and then it is made again. Each claim is a disclaimer on the part of the analyst of the control he is everywhere exercising; and his effort to deny his effort extends to a denial that he is exerting any influence on himself: 'readers may ... rest assured that I myself am only reporting what I came upon as an independent experience, uninfluenced by my expectations.' Here there are two claims, one more audacious than the other: the first is that his mental processes function independently of his psychic history (a claim directly at odds with the thesis of this very case); the second is that a similar independence can be achieved by those readers who rest in the assurances he offers. In other words, he counsels submission to himself as a way of being free, and he presents this counsel in the context of an argument for his own disinterestedness. Put yourself in my hands, he says, because my hands are not mine, but merely the instruments of truth.

Of course this is exactly what an analyst says (not always explicitly) at the beginning of a treatment. In effect the reader is being put on the couch where he is given the same double message Freud gives to his patient: be independent, rely entirely on me. In rapid succession Freud issues a series of confusing and contradictory directions. First he tells us, you must 'eliminate' your 'pre-existing convictions' and consider only the evidence. But within a few sentences we learn that there will be no evidence to consider; 'Exhaustive verbatim reports', he declares, 'would ... be of no help at all', and, besides, such reports are not available anyway since 'the technique of the treatment makes it impossible to draw them up' (pp. 158–9). This leaves us at the mercy of what the analyst chooses to tell us, and it would seem that we are simply to exchange his 'pre-existing convictions' for our own. But no; in a dazzling reversal the reader's independence is reaffirmed when it is revealed that one of his pre-existing convictions will be retained: the conviction that psychoanalysis, as Freud practises it, is the true and only way. It is only for such readers, 'already ... convinced by their own clinical experiences' (p. 159), that Freud writes, and because they are convinced those readers will be proof against any attempt, on the part of Freud or anyone else, to convince them. The logic, to say the least, is suspect, but if one accepts it (and we are not given time to do anything else) one will also accept the amazing conclusion that this analysis is not published 'in order to produce conviction'.

The claim not to be producing conviction is of a piece with the other claims or disclaimers that fill the opening pages. Always they are disclaimers of influence and always their effect is to extend the influence they would disclaim. The inducing of independence undermines it; the denial of a strategy of conviction is itself a strategy of conviction. The text's overt assertions are continually in conflict with the actions it performs, as Freud proclaims the autonomy of a succession of children – the patient, the reader, the analysis – even as he contrives to control them.

The question that arises is one of motive. Why is Freud doing this? Is it a matter, simply, of a desire for personal power? The text suggests that he would reply in the negative and say that he was only defending the honour of psychoanalysis against what John Wisdom has identified as the oldest charge against it, the charge that it 'acts by suggestion', that what the analyst claims to uncover (in the archaeological sense of which Freud was so fond) he actually creates by verbal and rhetorical means.[5] Freud is vehement in his rejection of this accusation, declaring at one point that 'it is unjust to attribute the results of analysis to the physician's imagination' (p. 231) and confessing at another that he finds it 'impossible' even to argue with those who regard the findings of psychoanalysis as 'artefacts' (p. 195). These and similar statements would seem to suggest that his motives are not personal, but institutional; he speaks not for himself, but on behalf of the integrity of a discipline. But since the discipline is one of which he is quite literally the father, and his defense of its integrity involves him in the same contradiction that marks his relationship with the patient and the reader: no sooner has he insisted on the independence of psychoanalysis as a science than he feels compelled to specify, and to specify authoritatively, what the nature of that science is; and once he does that he is in the untenable position of insisting on the autonomy of something of which he is unable to let go. By rising to the institutional level Freud only reinscribes the dilemma inherent in his role as analyst and author. He cannot be both liberator and master at the same time; and in so far as that is the task he assigns himself he becomes the object of his own manipulation, demanding of himself, as he demands of the patient and the reader, that he be active and passive at the same time.

Freud's response to this double bind is to deny it by producing accounts of the analysis in which the actions he is unwilling to acknowledge are performed by others. The first such displacement occurs in the third paragraph of chapter I, when he weighs the virtues and defects of competing methodologies. The two possibilities are (1) analysing a childhood disorder when it first manifests itself in infancy, or (2) waiting until the patient is an 'intellectually mature adult' (p. 155). Since Freud is at this very moment engaged in the second practice it is not surprising that he decides in favour of it, but he must find a way to defend it against the objection (which he anticipates) that because of the passage of time what results will be the product of interpretation. He replies by asserting that interpretation will play an even greater part if the child is examined directly because 'too many words and thoughts have to be lent' to him. In contrast, when one analyses an adult, these 'limitations' do not obtain, although one must then 'take into account the distortion and refurbishing to which a patient's past is subjected when it is looked back upon' (p. 155). Once one begins to examine it, this is a curious contrast, since it is hard to tell the difference between 'lending words' and 'refurbishing'. What makes the contrast work is the fact that the sentence shifts the burden of 'refurbishing' on to the patient. It is a brilliant move which allows Freud to admit interpretation into the scene while identifying it as the work of another, leaving himself the (honourable) work of undoing its effects. In only a few brief sentences, he has managed to twice distance himself from the charge of suggestion, first by pushing it off onto the practitioners of a rival method, and second by making it into a property of the illness of which his now innocent labours are to be the cure.

The strategy then is to foreground an accusation and to defend against it by turning it back on those who would make it; attribute to others what they would attribute unto you; allow the accusation to surface, but keep pushing it away. In another place it is pushed away before it appears because it is presented as an accusation not against Freud but against his patients, including, presumably, this one. The accusers are his opponents, Jung and Adler, who reject the thesis of infantile neurosis, regarding it as an elaborate rationalisation that allows neurotics to avoid confronting their problems by projecting them onto a past for which they can then not be held responsible. 'The supporters of this view', says Freud, 'assume that the importance of childhood is only held up before our eyes in analysis on account of the inclination of neurotics for expressing their present interests in reminiscences and symbols from the remote past' (p. 192). In short, they deny the very reality of infantile neurosis.

To this Freud replies not directly, but by means of the vocabulary with which he repeatedly characterises these nay-sayers. He says of them that they unthinkingly reject what is new, cling obstinately to comfortable interpretations and turn their back on the unmistakable evidence brought forward by psychoanalysis. But these are also the terms in which he describes the behaviour of infantile neurotics like his patient, whose illness is thereby validated when evidence of it is discovered in the actions of those who would dispute it. In this way the thesis of infantile neurosis is at once defended against its detractors and made into a weapon with which to club them, as the conditions of being an infantile neurotic and of being an opponent of Freud turn out to be one and the same. It is a master stroke which accomplishes several things at once: whatever Freud's opponents might say about his handling of the present case is discredited in advance, because they are too much like its subject; and more importantly, Freud's reader is simultaneously introduced to the opinions of those opponents and innoculated against their effect; for as he is given what appears to be a choice, but is in fact an offer he can't refuse: you can either accept what I am about to tell you or you can look forward to being stigmatised as a resistant and recalcitrant infant; either cast your lot with me or with those bad children who are so sick that they do not even recognise their illness.

II

Those of you who know the text may already have realised that until this point I have been dealing only with the very brief first chapter and the opening paragraph of chapter II, some five pages out of a total of more than one hundred. And yet in a sense, most of the work of the case study has already been done, for although we have yet to hear a single detail either of the patient's history or of his therapy, we are already so much under Freud's influence that when the details finally do appear, they will fall into the places he has prepared for them. Although Freud will repeatedly urge us in the following pages to take up our 'independent share' in the work, that independence has long since been taken from us. The judgment he will soon solicit is a judgment he already controls, and as he begins his narration proper, he increases that control by dictating the terms by which his efforts (or as he would have it, non-efforts) will be judged. 'I am unable', he says, 'to give either a purely historical or a purely thematic account of my patient's story; I can write a history neither of the treatment nor of the illness, but I shall find myself obliged to combine the two methods of presentation' (p. 158). A 'purely historical' account would be a narrative account tracing out relationships of cause and effect; and by declaring that he is unable to provide it, Freud releases himself from the requirement that in his explanations one thing be shown to follow from another. A 'purely thematic' account would be one in which the coherence of events and details was a matter of their relationship to a single master theme; and by declaring that he is unable to provide it, Freud releases himself from the requirement that his explanations go together to form an unified whole. In effect he neutralises criticism of his conclusions before they are offered and is in the enviable position of being at once the architect and judge of his own performance.

The crowning (and typical) touch is the word 'obliged' ('I shall find myself obliged'), for it allows him to present himself as operating under the severest of constraints just at the moment when he is fashioning the constraints under which and within which both his patient and his reader will labour. What obliges him, it turns out, is the nature of the unconscious, which he tells us, is not a linear structure ruled by the law of contradiction, but a geological accumulation of forms that never completely disappear and live side by side in an uneasy and unpredictable vacillation:

That there should be an instantaneous and clear-cut displacement of one phase by the next was not in the nature of things or of our patient; on the contrary, the preservation of all that had gone before and the co-existence of the most different sorts of currents were characteristic of him. (p. 204)

This picture of the unconscious is offered as if it provided independent support of both his thesis and his procedure; but it *is* his thesis, and, it is indistinguishable from the argument it authorises. That is, the unconscious is not a concept but a rhetorical device, a place holder which can be given whatever shape the polemical moment requires.[6] If someone were to object to Freud's interpretation of a particular detail, he could point for confirmation to the nature of the unconscious, and if someone were to dispute the nature of the unconscious, he could point to the evidence of his interpretations; and all the while he could speak of himself as being 'obliged' by constraints that were at once independent *of* him and assured the independence *from* him of his patient and his reader. The rhetorical situation could not be more favourable. Freud can present himself as a disinterested researcher and at the same time work to extend his control until it finally includes everything, the details of the analysis, the behaviour of the patient and the performance of the reader; and he manages to do all of this before the story of the Wolf-Man has even begun to unfold.

I am aware that this is not the usual description of Freud's labours, which have recently been characterised by Peter Brooks as 'heroic',[7] a characterisation first offered by Freud in 1938 as he cast a final retrospective look at his most famous case.[8] In Brooks's reading the Wolf-Man is a 'radically modernist' text (p. 279) a 'structure of indeterminacy' (p. 275) and 'undecidability' which 'perilously destabilises belief in ... exhaustive accounts whose authority derives from the force of closure' (p. 277). Freud's heroism, according to Brooks, consists precisely in resisting closure, in forgoing the satisfaction of crafting a 'coherent, finished, enclosed, and authoritative narrative' (p. 277).

This is an attractive thesis, but it has absolutely nothing to do with the text we have been reading, although, as we shall see, Brooks has reasons, and apparently good ones, for thinking as he does. Meanwhile we can note that Freud's own characterisation of his narrative insists precisely on those qualities Brooks would deny to it: completeness, exhaustiveness, authority, and, above all, closure. The requirement that he expects his presentation to meet is forthrightly stated in a footnote as he begins to interpret the wolf dream: 'it is always a strict law of dream-interpretation that an explanation must be found for every detail' (p. 186). This is the vocabulary not of any 'post-modernist narrative' or 'structure of indeterminacy', but of a more traditional and familiar genre – one of which we know Freud to have been very fond – the classic story of detection; a genre in which an absolutely omniscient author distributes clues to a master meaning of which he is fully cognisant and toward which the reader moves uncertainly, but always under the direction of a guide who builds the structure of the narrative and the structure of understanding at the same time. There is, however, a large difference between Freud's detective story and other instances of the genre: in the novels of Conan Doyle or Agatha Christie author and reader are engaged in a contest in which they are armed with the same weapon, their ability to reason along lines of cause and effect. These are, however, precisely the lines that Freud has told us he will not pursue, and as a result the reader comes to his task with a double disability: not only must he look to Freud for the material on which his intelligence is to work; he must also be supplied with a way of making that material intelligible. And of course it will be Freud who supplies him, and who by supplying him will immeasurably increase the control he already exercises. Not only will he monitor the flow of information and point to the object that is to be understood; he will stipulate to the form in which the act of understanding will be allowed to occur.

That is the business of Chapter III, 'The seduction and its immediate consequences'. The seduction in question is (or appears to be) the seduction of the Wolf-Man by his sister. The occasion is a succession of dreams 'concerned with aggressive actions on the boy's part against his sister or against the governess' (p. 164). For a while, Freud reports, a firm interpretation of these dreams seemed unavailable; but then 'the explanation came at a single blow, when the patient suddenly called to mind the fact that when he was still very small … his sister had seduced him into sexual practices.' What happens next is a bit of sleight-of-hand: first of all, the patient's recollection is not the explanation, which therefore does not come at a single blow (at least not at the single blow to which the reader's attention is directed). Rather, the explanation emerges as the result of interpretive work done by Freud, but never seen by us; the 'single blow', in other words, occurs off stage and what we are presented with is its result, offered as if it were self-evident and self-generating. These dreams, Freud says, 'were meant to efface the memory of an event which later on seemed offensive to the patient's masculine self-esteem, and they reached this end by putting an imaginary and desirable converse in the place of the historical truth.' That is to say, the patient's masculine self-esteem was threatened by the fact that his sister, not he, was the aggressive seducer, and this threat is defended against in the dream material by reversing their respective positions. One critic has objected to this as one of Freud's 'apparently arbitrary inversions',[9] but it is far from arbitrary, for it is in effect a precise and concise direction to both the patient and the reader, providing them with a method for dealing with the material they will soon meet, and telling them in advance what will result when that method is applied: 'if you want to know what something – a dream, a piece of neurotic behaviour – means, simply reverse its apparent significance, and what you will find is an attempt to preserve masculine self-esteem against the threat of passivity and femininity.' – The real seduction in this chapter (which is accomplished at this moment and in a single blow) is the seduction not of the patient by his sister, but of both the patient and the reader by Freud who will now be able to produce interpretive conclusions in the confidence that they will be accepted as the conclusions of an inevitable and independent logic.

Moreover, in performing this act of seduction, Freud at once redoubles and reverses the behaviour he explains: if the patient defends against his passivity by 'weaving an imaginative composition' in which he is the aggressor, Freud defends against his own aggression by weaving an imaginative composition in which he is passive; and if it is the case, as Freud will later argue, that the patient is ambivalent and conflicted – at a level below consciousness he wants to be both passive and aggressive – it is no less the case with Freud who wants to be the father of everything that happens in the analysis and at the same time wants the analysis to unfold of its own accord. One is tempted then to say that the story Freud tells is doubled by the story of the telling or that his performance mirrors or enacts the content of the analysis. In fact it is the other way around; the content of the analysis mirrors or enacts the drama of the performance, a drama that is already playing itself out long before it has anything outside itself to be 'about', and playing itself out in the very terms that are here revealed supposedly for the first time, the terms of the preservation and concealing of masculine self-esteem and aggression. What Freud presents as mere preliminary material – his prospective discussion of evidence, conviction and independence – is finally the material that is being worked through even when the focus has ostensibly shifted elsewhere, to the patient and his infantile pre-history. The real story of the case is the story of persuasion and we will be able to read it only when we tear our eyes away from the supposedly deeper story of the boy who had a dream.

Both stories receive their fullest telling in chapter IV, which begins as this paper begins: 'I dreamt that it was night and I was lying in my bed.' Here finally is the centrepiece of the case, withheld from the reader for three chapters, and now presented as the chief object of interpretation. But of course, it appears as an already interpreted object, even before the first word has been said about it, since we know in advance that whatever configuration emerges need only be reversed for its 'true' meaning to be revealed; and lest we forget what we have been taught Freud reinforces the lesson with a pointed speculation. 'We must naturally expect', he says, 'to find that the dream material reproduces the unknown material of some previous scene in some distorted form, perhaps even distorted into its opposite' (p. 178). He then reports, as if it were uninfluenced by his expectations, the moment when the patient takes up his 'independent share in the work'. 'When in my dream the window suddenly opens of its own accord, it must mean "my eyes suddenly opened".' Indeed it must, given the interpretive directions he has received and it is hardly surprising to hear Freud's response: 'No objection could be made to this'. To be sure, there could be no objection to a meaning he has virtually commanded, and in what follows the pretence that the work is independent is abandoned. 'The point', he says, 'could be developed further', and he immediately proceeds to develop it, not bothering even to indicate whether the development issues from him or from his patient:

What then if the other factor emphasised by the dreamer were also distorted by means of a transposition or reversal? In that case instead of immobility (the wolves sat there motionless ...) the meaning would have to be: the most violent emotion. ... He suddenly woke up, and saw in front of him a scene of violent movement at which he looked with strained attention. (p. 179)

There remains only the final step of determining what the scene of violent motion was precisely, but before taking that step Freud pauses in a way that heightens its drama. 'I have now reached the point', he says,

at which I must abandon the support I have hitherto had from the course of the analysis. I am afraid it will also be the point at which the reader's belief will abandon me. (pp. 180–1)

Presumably it is because of gestures like this one that Brooks is moved to characterise Freud's text as open and non-authoritative; but I trust that *my* reader (or hearer) will immediately see this as the gesture of someone who is so confident in his authority that he can increase it by (apparently) questioning it. We can hardly take seriously the fear that he will be abandoned by the reader's belief, since that belief – our belief – rather than being independent of his will is by now the child of his will, accepting as evidence only what he certifies. Abandon him? To abandon him at this point would be to abandon the constraints and desires that make us, as readers, what we are. By raising the possibility Freud only tightens the bonds by which we are attached to him, and makes us all the more eager to receive the key revelation at his hands. I give it to you now:

What sprang into activity that night out of the chaos of the dreamer's unconscious memory traces was the picture of copulation between his parents, copulation in circumstances which were not entirely usual and were especially available for observation. (p. 181)

The credibility of this revelation is not a function of its probability – we have had many demonstrations of how improbable it is that any such event ever took place – but of its explanatory power. It satisfies the need Freud has created in us to understand, and by understanding to become his partner in the construction of the story. As at so many places in the text, what Freud presents here for our judgment is quite literally irresistible; for resistance would require an independence we have already surrendered. In return for that independence we are given the opportunity to nod in agreement – to say, 'It *must* mean' – as Freud, newly-constructed primal scene in hand, solves every puzzle the case has seemed to offer. In rapid order he accounts for the patient's fear of wolves, his fantasies of beating and being beaten, his simultaneous identification with and rejection of his father, his marked castration anxiety:

His anxiety was a repudiation of the wish for sexual satisfaction from his father ... The form taken by the anxiety, the fear of 'being eaten by the wolf', was only the ... transposition of the wish to be copulated with by his father ... His last sexual aim, the passive attitude towards his father, succumbed to repression, and fear of his father appeared in its place in the shape of the wolf phobia. And the driving force of this repression? ... It can only have been his narcissistic genital libido, which ... was fighting against a satisfaction whose attainment seemed to involve the renunciation of that organ. (pp. 189–90)

What we have here is a picture of someone who alternates between passive and aggressive behaviour, now assuming the dominant position of the male aggressor, now submitting in feminine fashion to forces that overwhelm him. This, we are told, is the secret content of the patient's behaviour, expressed indirectly in his symptoms and fantasies, and brought triumphantly by Freud to the light of day. But if it is a secret, the drama of its disclosing serves to deflect our attention from a secret deeper still, the secret that has (paradoxically) been on display since the opening paragraphs. Once more Freud contrives to keep this secret by publishing it, by discovering at the heart of the *patient's* fantasy the very conflicts that he himself has been acting out in his relationships with the patient, the analysis, the reader, and his critics. In all of these relationships he is driven by the obsessions he uncovers, by the continual need to control, to convince, and to seduce in endless vacillation with the equally powerful need to disclaim any trace of influence, and to present himself as the passive conduit of forces that exist independently of him. He simply cannot help himself, and even when his double story is fully told, he has recourse to a mechanism that opens it again, not, as Brooks would have it, in order to delay or defeat closure, but in order to *repeat* it, and thereby to be master again.

III

The mechanism is the announcement that he has omitted a detail from the reconstruction of the primal scene. 'Lastly', Freud tells us, the boy 'interrupted his parents' intercourse in a manner which will be discussed later' (p. 182). This is the missing portion of my title, and by calling attention to it, Freud produces a desire for its restoration, a desire he then periodically inflames by reminding us of the deficiency in our understanding and promising to supply it. 'I have hinted', he says in chapter V, 'that my description of the primal scene has remained incomplete because I have reserved for a later moment my account of the way in which the child interrupted his parents' intercourse. I must now add that this method of interruption is the same in every case' (p. 203). Again he leaves us without the crucial piece of information and by suggesting that it is even more valuable than we had thought — it is a key not only to this case, but to all cases — he intensifies our need for it. Moreover, in a manner entirely characteristic, he then shifts that need on to the patient who is described in the following chapter as 'longing for someone who should give him the last pieces of information that were still missing upon the riddle of sexual intercourse' (p. 213). The displacement is transparent: it is of course we who are longing for a piece of information to be given us by a father with whom we will then join. Once again the drama of Freud's rhetorical mastery is at once foregrounded and concealed when it appears, only thinly disguised, as an event in his patient's history.

This technique of open concealment reaches a virtuoso level of performance when, in a gesture of excessive candour, Freud reveals that there is a subject he has 'intentionally ... left to one side' (p. 214). He then introduces as a *new* topic of discussion a term that names the very behaviour he has been engaging in all the while, anal eroticism. Of course as he presents it, it is an aspect only of the patient's behaviour, easily discernible, says Freud, in his inability to evacuate spontaneously without the aid of enemas; his habit of 'making a mess in his bed', whenever he was forced to share a bedroom with a despised governess; his great fear of dysentery; his fierce piety which alternated with fantasies of Christ defecating; and above all his attitude toward money with which he was sometimes exceedingly liberal, and at other times miserly in the extreme. All of this Freud relates to the management of 'excretory pleasure', which he says plays 'an extraordinarily important part ... in building up sexual life and mental activity' (p. 215). Of course he offers this observation with no intention of including himself or his own 'mental activity' within its scope. It is an observation about *others*, evidence (if it is evidence at all) only of his perspicuity. 'At last,' he tells us, 'I recognised the importance of the intestinal trouble for my purposes', but as we shall see, he says this without any recognition whatsoever of what his real purposes are. His announced purpose is to find a way of overcoming the patient's resistance. For a long time, the analysis was blocked by the Wolf-Man's doubt. He remained sceptical of the efficacy of psychoanalysis and it seemed that there 'was no way of convincing him' (p. 218) until

I promised the patient a complete recovery of his intestinal activity, and by means of this promise made his incredulity manifest. I then had the satisfaction of seeing his doubt dwindle away, as in the course of the work his bowel began, like a hysterically affected organ, to 'join in the conversation', and in a few weeks time recovered its normal function. (p. 218)

One might describe this remarkable passage as an allegory of persuasion were it not so transparently literal. One persuades, in this account, by emptying the other of his 'preexisting convictions'. The patient's doubts, or to speak more affirmatively, his beliefs, are quite literally eliminated; the fragmentary portions that comprise his convictions pass out through his bowel and he is left an empty vessel, ready to be filled up with whatever new convictions the rhetorician brings forward. (It is no accident that the German word 'abklären' means both to explain and to defecate: one must be emptied out before he can be filled up.) The bowel that is said to 'join in the conversation' is in fact the medium of the analyst's ventriloquism; it speaks, but the words are his. So is the satisfaction, as Freud explicitly acknowledges ('I then had the satisfaction'); the managing of 'excretory pleasure', the mainspring of the patient's psychic life, is taken over by the analyst, who gives up nothing while forcing the other to give up everything. And even as Freud reveals and revels in his strategy, he conceals it, telling the story of persuasion to a reader who is himself that story's object, and who, no less than the patient, is falling totally under the control of the teller.

All of these stories come together at the moment when the missing portion is finally put into place. 'I have already hinted', says Freud (in fact he has already already hinted) 'that one portion of the primal scene has been kept back'. In the original German the sentence is continued in a relative clause whose literal translation is 'which I am now able to offer as a supplement'. Strachey makes the clause into an independent unit and renders it 'I am now in a position to produce this missing portion' (p. 222). It would seem that this is one of those departures from the text for which the translator has been so often taken to task; but in fact Strachey is here being more literal than Freud himself; rather than departing from the text, he eliminates its coyness and brings us closer to the nature of the act the prose performs, an act to which Strachey alerts us by the insistent physicality of the words 'position' and 'produce'. Just what that position and production are becomes dazzlingly clear when the secret is finally out in the open: 'The child ... interrupted his parents' intercourse by passing a stool'. We commit no fallacy of imitative form by pointing out what hardly needs pointing out, that Freud enacts precisely what he reports;[10] the position he is in is the squatting position of defecation and it is he who, at a crucial juncture and to dramatic effect, passes a stool that he has long held back. What is even more remarkable is that immediately after engaging in this behaviour, Freud produces (almost as another piece of stool) an analysis of it. In anal-erotic behaviour, he tells us, a person sacrifices or makes a gift of 'a portion of his own body which he is ready to part with, but only for the sake of someone he loves' (p. 223). That love, however, is a form of possession or mastery, for in this pregenital phase the 'contrast between "masculine" and "feminine" plays no part' and 'its place is taken by the contrast between "active" and "passive"'. 'What appears to us as masculine in the activities of this phase ... turns out to be an expression of an instinct for mastery' (*Introductory Lectures*, p. 327). In other words, one who is fixed in the anal phase experiences pleasure as control, a control he achieves by the calculated withholding and releasing of faeces. What the anal-erotic seeks is to capture and absorb the other by the stimulation and gratifying of desire; what he seeks, in short, is power, and he gains it at the moment when his excretions become the focus and even the content of the other's attention. However accurate this is as an account of anal-eroticism, it is a perfect account of the act of persuasion, which is, I would argue, the primal act for which the anal-erotic is only a metaphor. It is persuasion that Freud has been practising in this case on a massive scale, and the 'instinct for mastery', of which persuasion is the expression, finds its fulfilment here when the reader accepts from Freud that piece of deferred information which completes the structure of his own understanding. Once that acceptance has been made, the reader belongs to Freud as much as any lover belongs to the beloved. By giving up a portion of himself Freud is not diminished but enlarged, since what he gets back is the surrender of the reader's will which now becomes an extension of his own. The reader on his part receives a moment of pleasure — the pleasure of seeing the pieces of the puzzle finally fitting together — but Freud reserves to himself the much greater pleasure of total mastery. It is a pleasure that is intensely erotic, full of the 'sexual excitement' (p. 223) that is said to mark the *patient's* passing of a stool; it is a pleasure that is anal, phallic and even oral, affording the multiple satisfactions of domination, penetration and engulfment. It is, in a word, the pleasure of persuasion.

In what remains of his performance Freud savours that pleasure and adds to it by placing it in apparent jeopardy. It is late in chapter VIII when he declares 'I will make a final attempt at re-interpreting the ... finding of this analysis in accordance with the scheme of my opponents' (p. 243). One might characterise this as a demonstration of openness were it not so obviously a demonstration of control. Freud is seizing an occasion to perform a rhetorical feat whose value lies (to borrow a phrase from gymnastics) in its degree of difficulty. (This is an old rhetorical tradition that goes back at least as far as the exercises of Seneca.) First he imagines what Jung and Adler would say if they were presented with the materials he has now marshalled. He pictures them as 'bad' readers, readers who are unconvinced, and he rehearses their likely objections. No doubt they would regard the primal scene as the invention of a neurotic who was seeking to rationalise his 'flight from the world' (p. 243) and who was 'driven to embark on this long backward course either because he had come up against some task ... which he was too lazy to perform, or because he had every reason to be aware of his own inferiority and thought he could best protect himself ... by elaborating such contrivances as these' (p. 244). What Freud is staging here is a moment of scrupulosity, very much like some earlier moments when he presses interpretive suggestions on a resistant patient, and then points to the patient's resistance as a proof of the independence of the analysis. Here it is we who are (once more) in the position of the patient as Freud urges on us an interpretive direction and waits for us to reject it 'of our own accord'; but of course at this late stage, any rejection we might perform would be dictated not by an independent judgment, but by a judgment Freud has in large measure shaped. Even so, he is unwilling to run the risk (really no risk at all) that we might respond in some errant way, and accordingly he responds for us:

All this would be very nice, if only the unlucky wretch had not had a dream when he was no more than four years old, which signaled the beginning of his neurosis ... and the interpretation of which necessitates the assumption of this primal scene. All the alleviations which the theories of Jung and Adler seek to afford us come to grief, alas, upon such paltry but unimpeachable facts as these. (p. 244)

Everything happens so fast in this sequence that we may not notice that the 'unimpeachable fact' which anchors it is the *assumption* of the primal scene. In most arguments assumptions are what must be proven out, but in this argument the assumption is offered as proof; and what supports it is not any independent fact, but the polemical fact that without the assumption, the story Freud has so laboriously constructed falls apart. In effect Freud says to us, 'look, we've worked incredibly hard to put something together; are we now going to entertain doubts about the very assumption that enabled us to succeed?' The primal scene is important because it allows the story of its own discovery to unfold. In that story – the story, basically, of the analysis – the wolf dream comes first and initiates a search for its origin; that search then leads to the 'uncovering' of the primal scene, and although it is the last thing to be put in place, it immediately becomes the anchor and the explanation of everything that precedes it. What Freud is relying on here is not something newly or additionally persuasive, but on the fact that persuasion has occurred, and that having occurred, we will be unwilling and indeed unable to undo it.

    In short, the primal scene is a rhetorical object, and it is the definition of a rhetorical object that it is entirely constructed and stands without external support; it is, we are accustomed to say, removed from reality; but we could just as well say that it becomes reality, that in so far as it has been installed at the centre of a structure of conviction it acquires the status of that which goes without saying and that against which nothing can be said. It then becomes possible to argue both for and from it at the same time; or, rather, it becomes possible to not argue at all, but merely to point to something that now stands as irrefutable evidence of itself, as something perspicuous, autonomous, and independent, as something that need not be defended or even presented, as something *beyond rhetoric*. That is what Freud does here when the imagined objections to the primal scene are met simply by invoking it as a self-evident and in-disputable authority. One might say then that at the conclusion of the case history the primal scene emerges triumphant as both the end of the story and its self-authenticating origin; but what is really triumphant is not this particular scene, which after all might well have assumed a quite different shape if the analysis had taken the slightest of turns, but the discursive power of which and by which it has been constructed. The true content of the primal scene is the story of its making. At bottom the primal scene is the scene of persuasion.

IV

Now if at bottom the primal scene is the scene of persuasion, then the one thing you cannot do in relation to persuasion is get to the bottom of it; for as the bottom or bottom line, it underwrites everything, including whatever efforts one might make either to elude it or achieve distance on it. Being persuasive, assuming the stance of a rhetorician, is not something you can choose to avoid; it is not something you can choose at all; nor is it something you can know in the sense of watching or catching yourself in the act. This brings me finally to several questions many of you will have been asking. To what extent does Freud know what he is doing? Does he know that he is being rhetorical? On one level the answer is: 'of course', and for evidence we need go no further than the first of the *Introductory Lectures* which begins by Freud announcing to his audience that he is about to treat them as if they were neurotic patients (p. 15). Later in the same lecture, he declares that all arguments, even those whose claim it is to be rational and disinterested 'arise from affective sources' and moreover, it could hardly be otherwise since it is 'inherent in human nature' to identify what one likes with what one takes to be true (p. 23). It follows then that whether one speaks or listens, the meanings that result will always have their source in some affective disposition. And then, immediately after having made these points, Freud turns around to say,

We, however, Ladies and Gentleman, can claim that ... we have no tendentious aim in view. Our intention has been solely to give recognition to the facts as we found them in the course of painstaking researches. (pp. 23–4)

At the very least we would seem to have a disjunction between Freud's general account of human nature and the claims he makes for his own assertions. The general account says that all knowledge is ultimately rhetorical ('arises from affective sources'); the claim he makes for his own assertions is that they are not rhetorical, but true. But were we to fault him for that claim and accuse him of bad faith we would be committing a deep philosophical mistake, the mistake of thinking that our convictions can and *should* be shaken by the knowledge that they are unsupported by anything external to themselves. It is a mistake because an awareness that the foundations we rest on are mutable and variable does not, in a moment of particular judgment, make those foundations any less ours or make us any less theirs. Whenever we are asked to state what we take to be the case about this or that, we will always respond in the context of what seems to us at the time to be indisputably true, even if we know, as a general truth, that everything can be disputed.[11] *One who has learned the lesson of rhetoricity does not thereby escape the condition it names.* The fact that Freud lays bare the rhetorical basis of all convictions does not protect him from the appeal and power of his own. There is finally no contradiction here, only a lack of relationship between a truth one might know about discourse in general − that it is ungrounded − and the particular truths to which one is temporally committed and concerning which one can have no doubts. Once more we come round to the deep point that the case of the Wolf-Man allows us to make: the rhetorical and constructed nature of things does not compromise their reality, but constitutes it, and constitutes it in a form that is as invulnerable to challenge as it is unavailable to verification. Like his patient, Freud can only know what he knows within the rhetoric that possesses him and he cannot be criticised for clinging to that knowledge even when he himself could demonstrate that it is without an extra-discursive foundation. At times in this essay I have spoken as if Freud ought to have been aware that his argument had its sources in his deepest anxieties; but it should now be clear that this is an awareness he could not possibly achieve, since, by the arguments of psychoanalysis itself, every operation of the mind, including the operation we might want to call awareness, issues from those same anxieties. The thesis of psychoanalysis is that one can not get to the side of the unconscious; the thesis of this essay is that one cannot get to the side of rhetoric. These two theses are one and the same.

Notes

1   Thomas A. Sebeok (ed.), *Style in Language*, Cambridge, Massachusetts, 1960, p. 385.
2   S. Freud, *The Complete Introductory Lectures on Psychoanalysis*, translated and edited by James Strachey, New York, 1966, pp. 5−6.
3   Muriel Gardner (ed.), *The Wolf-Man By the Wolf-Man*, New York, 1971, p. 177.
4   Freud has been much criticised for this strategy. See on this point Patrick J. Mahony, *Cries of the Wolf Man*, New York, 1984, p. 34; and Robert J. Langs, 'Misalliance in the Wolf-man Case', in Mark Kanzer & Jules Glenn (eds), *Freud and His Patients*, New York and London, 1980, pp. 375−80.
5   J. O. Wisdom, 'Testing an Interpretation Within a Session', in Richard

Wollheim (ed.), *Freud: A Collection of Critical Essays*, Garden City, New York, 1974, p. 340. There is of course a huge literature focusing on the issues of evidence and testability. For representative positions see the essays by Boden, Salmon, Gylmour, Alexander, and Mischel in the same collection. H. J. Eysenck articulates the general complaint of hard-core verificationists: 'clinical work is often very productive of theories and hypotheses, but weak on proof and verification' (*The Uses and Abuses of Psychology*, London, 1959, p. 228). Defences typically take the form of arguing that verification is indeed available, albeit not always in the (impossibly strict) forms demanded by Freud's critics. Recently the debate has been given renewed life by the publication of Adolf Grünbaum's *The Foundations of Psychoanalysis: A Philosophical Critique*, Los Angeles & London, 1984. Although Grünbaum disagrees with Karl Popper's contention that psychoanalytic hypotheses are non-falsifiable and therefore unscientific, he argues that psychoanalytic evidence, derived as it is from the clinical practice of free-association, is unavoidably contaminated by 'extraneous' influences such as the analyst's selection biases, the patient's sense of what the analyst wants to hear, the untrustworthiness of memory, etc. For a recent review of the literature and the issues see Marshall Edelson, *Hypothesis and Evidence in Psychoanalysis*, Chicago, 1984. The scientific question becomes a moral one in the work of J. M. Masson who argues (in *The Assault On Truth*, New York, 1984) that Freud's rejection of the seduction theory in favour of fantasy was a turning away from the empirical reality of his patients' suffering, and was prompted by the general unwillingness of a patriarchal society to face the idea of sexual violence in the family. In short Freud ceased being a truth-seeker and became an apologist. Both Masson and the philosophical critics agree that psychoanalysis will have a serious claim on our attention only if its methods and conclusions rest on some objective foundation; but this is an assumption rejected by another group of analysts who see the 'truth' of psychoanalysis as a narrative truth and invoke a standard not of correspondence with empirical facts but of coherence within a discursive structure. See Donald P. Spence, *Narrative Truth and Historical Truth: Meaning and Interpretation in Psychoanalysis*, New York & London, 1982; and volume 1, nos. 3–4 of Joseph Rippen (ed.), *International Forum for Psychoanalysis*, 1984.

6   Cf. Ernest Gellner, *The Psychoanalytic Movement*, London, 1985, p. 48: 'The concept of the Unconscious is a means of devaluing all previous certainties ... It is not so much a hypothesis as a suspension of all other hypotheses.' In other words, as a concept the unconscious validates *anything*, and this 'suspension' of 'all guidelines' is both its content and the operation (any operation at all) it makes possible.

7   Peter Brooks, *Reading For the Plot*, New York, 1984, p. 277.

8   'Analysis Terminable and Interminable', in *The Complete Psychological Works of Sigmund Freud*, vol. 23, London, 1964, p. 217.

9   S. Viderman, *Le Celeste et le Sublunaire*, Paris, 1977, p. 287.

10   See on this point Mahony, op. cit., p. 90: 'In effect, the analyst and the patient were locked in a quid pro quo of anal retention and release extending from the clinical setting to the pages of the deferred expository narrative.

11   For an elaboration of this point see S. Fish, 'Consequences', in *Critical Inquiry*, vol. 11, no. 3, March 1985, 440–1 and *passim*.

Towards a linguistics of writing

Since so much language comes to us as writing, it seems obvious that we need to develop a linguistics of writing: a linguistics that would attend seriously to the structures, strategies, and effects of writing. To do this would challenge the assumptions, nay, imperatives of linguistic science, which designate writing as a way of recording speech, a sign of a sign, which is irrelevant to the nature of language in general. We have all no doubt read some of the more intemperate statements by which linguists or theorists of language set writing aside as a corruption of speech: writing is a mode of representation that can erroneously affect or infect conceptions of language, which ought to be based solely on the proper and natural form of language, speech, whose priority to writing is at once phylogenetic, ontogenetic, functional, and structural.[1] The use of linguistics as a model for the semiological analysis of cultural artefacts of all sorts has consisted, it would be argued, of applying to other domains, including the study of written texts, models based on the assumed primacy of speech. To produce a pertinent linguistics of writing, then, would not be simply to take account of the special effects of the written character and of any supplementary conventions it might involve or structures on which it might depend; one would need to challenge the governing assumptions and rethink the study of language *ab initio*, so as not to prejudge issues by relying on a model of language based on an idealised conception of speech.

There is, it seems to me, much truth to this view. However, to conceive of the development of a linguistics of writing in precisely this way, on the presumption that linguistics has in fact been based on speech, risks mistaking the situation in which one finds oneself and thus misjudging what is at issue. One can argue that linguists' commands to ignore writing and concentrate only on speech are provoked by a silent suspicion that what we have had all along is in some respects a linguistics of writing – namely, a linguistics which, despite its pretences to the contrary, focuses on units more easily identified in writing than in speech. There are various aspects of the dependence of modern linguistics on writing, which Roy Harris wittily sums up in *The Language-Makers*, a book that deserves wider attention than it has received, in suggesting that the 'real discovery procedure' of modern linguistics is 'Assume that standard orthography identifies all the relevant distinctions, until you are forced to assume otherwise.'[2] Let me swiftly mention three indications of this dependence:

(1) We know that Saussure, despite his denunciation of the 'dangers' of writing, which 'disguises' language and whose 'tyranny' leads to errors of pronunciation that are 'pathological', nevertheless has recourse to the example of writing to explain the notion of the relational identity of linguistic units: the written character proves the best example of the linguistic unit.

(2) The idea of an ambiguous sentence − *Flying planes can be dangerous* − seems to owe something to the model of writing: the idea of a sentence as a sequence of words stipulated outside any context and stripped of any intonation contours. For if one were working solely with speech, one would have no reason to treat *George bought the picture* (an answer to 'Who bought the picture?') as the same as *George bought the picture*? (an expression of astonishment at his choice). The differences between the physical signals and the import of those two sequences are arguably greater than between *George bought the picture* and *George bought the painting*; and the inclination to treat the former pair as variant articulations of a single ambiguous object and the latter pair as two quite distinct objects seems more easily explained as an effect of the apparent self-evidence of writing than of the various factors purported to determine the identification of linguistic units. Ambiguities, which linguistics sets out to account for, frequently seem to be ambiguities of a written sentence presented as an example in a paper on linguistics rather than ambiguities in utterances, where the differences in intonation patterns and import would prevent listeners from confusing what seem quite distinct sequences.

(3) Finally, transformational-generative grammar seems to make more sense as a linguistics of writing than as a linguistics of speech. Not only is phonological form assigned at a late stage of derivation by an 'interpretive' component, and is thus not central to the conception of a linguistic sequence, but a vast array of features of ordinary speech − hesitations, interruptions, false starts, changes of construction − are all relegated to 'performance' and set aside as irrelevant to an account of the language. What is relevant, linguistic competence, is an ability to produce an infinite set of complete, well-formed sentences, with none of the imperfections of actual speech. As Roy Harris asks,

suppose we strip away this superficial phonetic garb of the sentence, what lies beneath it? Something which must have all its words in place, their order determined, their grammatical relationships established, and their meanings assigned − but which simply lacks a phonetic embodiment: a string of words with the sound turned off. In short, a linguistic abstraction for which there is only one conceivable archetype so far in human history: the sentence of writing.[3]

I am arguing, then, that we are likely to go astray if we assume that the linguistics we have is a linguistics of speech and that the corrective to it would

be a linguistics that took writing seriously. Certain aspects of writing –
specifically writing as manifestation of an ideal, iterable linguistic object –
have determined the linguistics which presents itself as a linguistics of speech;
in relation to this linguistics, attention to the materiality of speech itself could
be quite disruptive. A linguistics which sought to address all the contours of
hesitation and of emphasis, the tones of voice that function as modal operators
to indicate degrees of assurance, aggressiveness, modesty, and so on, as well
as all the dialectal variations of speech that carry social information, would
be distinctly more complicated than one which sought above all to assign the
correct grammatical descriptions to sentences regarded as ideal objects. Such
a linguistics, attending to potentially signifying qualities of speech – speech
as gesture, shall we say – would in fact be confronting a certain textuality
of voice: potentially signifying differences not easily reducible to systems of
convention.

A particularly interesting evocation of these problems is Dennis Tedlock's
work on oral narrative, particularly *The Spoken Word and the Work of
Interpretation*, which argues that our logocentric or phonocentric linguistics
is inadequate to oral narration. The distinction by which linguistics separates
phonetics from phonology, defining phonetics as the realm of physical signals
only and assigning questions of how physical features are put to use by
language to the realm of phonology, leaves phonetics outside of linguistics,
and with it numerous physical features of vocal signals which may be crucial
to the effect of oral narratives. When the relevance of these phonetic features
to differences of meaning is demonstrated, they are let back into linguistics
in supplementary fashion, designated as 'paralinguistic features,' 'suprasegmentals,' etc. When they are recognised as signals to be deciphered, the
code and the domain of codes are extended a little further. But, as Tedlock
writes,

It is not just that the phenomena of contouring, timing, and amplitude have somehow
been overlooked and present a new domain for decipherment, but that they have always
resisted reduction to particulate units of the kind that can be ordered within a closed
code. The pitch contours of an audible sentence mark it with a *degree* of incompleteness
of finality; a range of possible lengths for an audible line or a silence occupies a
continuum, and so does the range of possible loudness or softness within a line. Such
phenomena have both obvious and subtle effects on the meaning of what the storyteller
says, but the possible *shades* of meaning are infinite, whereas the deciphering eye allows
no shadings.[4]

Continuous rather than discrete phenomena take us outside the principles of
phonology and outside a phonologically-based linguistics – a code of
discreteness – though one can seek to bring these phenomena within its
perspective by working to identify contrasts on which physically continuous
phenomena can be said to depend for their significance, their production of
shades of meaning.

To break out of this perspective one might, for instance, take the heuristic step of treating a story-teller's narrative initially as a purely acoustic signal to be measured rather than as a code to be deciphered, working with devices for physical measurement that reveal regularities and discontinuities – striking physical variations in the signal. A machine that records variations of pitch and amplitude on a moving scroll produces a transcription of the narrative, a kind of writing that could provide various clues and stimuli for a new linguistics of writing. As Tedlock notes, 'Aspects of the speaking voice that our mechanical transcription graphs so clearly – including vast amounts of silence, utterances that vary greatly in length and often correspond neither with breath groups nor with intonational contours, hypertrophied syllables, and other features we will leave aside for now – go under the heading of 'paralinguistic features.'[5] Silence, which looks very important in a mechanical transcription of a performance, is granted a tiny role by phonology: pause junctures are allowed as gaps that make a semantic difference, but they are boundaries without duration, present or absent rather than signifying by their length. The timing crucial to a successful comedian, for example, lies outside phonology, although the length of a pause may determine whether an utterance plays as a joke or falls flat.

Tedlock notes that 'pause junctures, intonational markers, stresses, and vowel quantities lie at the borders of proper phonology. Each one can be and often is treated as supersegmental rather than segmental, prosodic rather than phonemic ... The one problem all these features pose in common is that of temporality, and a given feature will be accepted phonologically to precisely the degree that a way may be found to reduce its temporality to instantaneity.' 'What is left out when the acoustical signal of the speaking voice is transformed ... by means of phonological reduction,' he continues, is the temporal dimension, as if a musical score had 'no indication of total performance time, no time signature, no marks of sustained tempo, no marks of changing tempo, no indications of differential time value among the notes, no rests, and no ties.'[6] A good deal is missing. What mechanical transcription of narrative performance on a moving scroll does is to mark through this special writing the temporal dimensions elided by a phonology attuned to alphabetic writing.

The question is whether to attempt to integrate such features with a linguistics of the sign by drawing up supplementary rules, subcodes, etc. or to reconsider the structure of the enterprise, to deny the demands of codification any claim to priority and finality, to place the supposedly borderline cases at the centre and to consider the extent to which the supposedly discrete elements of linguistic codes are caught up in – are special cases of – the movement of signals. This is the basic structural question for a linguistics of writing: whether to extend linguistics to problematical but important domains, adding on descriptions in supplementary fashion, or whether to recast the enterprise by seeking to place the marginal at the centre. 'Even phonology itself appears in a new light,' writes Tedlock,

once we have made ourselves at home on its threshold rather than in its very midst
... There are even cases where a phonemic distinction is important with respect to content
in some words and melts into a continuum in others; that is to say, one might construct
one set of evidence to support a phonemic discontinuity and another set of evidence
to support treating two sounds as an allophonic variation of purely phonetic (as opposed
to phonological) interest.[7]

In another instance he argues that 'the place occupied by the inversion of stress
and pitch in the full spectrum of Zuni speech suggests that the kinds of concerns
opened up by poetics and sociolinguistics do not lie outside or beyond or even
on the boundary of proper linguistics, but may open up a breach that
penetrates to the very core of linguistics.'[8] This may be the strategy for a
linguistics of writing to pursue; the project of reversal may be fruitful, even
if the end is difficult to envisage.

Let me emphasise, though, the relevance of this prospect to a linguistics
of writing. When discussions of language claim to focus on speech and set
aside writing as unimportant, what they in fact do is set aside certain features
of language or aspects of its functioning. If writing, which seems inescapably
to involve mediation, impersonality, distance, the need for interpretation and
the possiblity of misunderstanding, and physical features that may exceed or
escape codes, is treated as a mere technical device, then one can treat as if
it were the norm of language an ideal associated with speech, namely the
experience of hearing oneself speak, where hearing and understanding seem
to be inseparable, where the expression seems bound to the meaning it arises
to express, where signifier and signified seem immediately joined in a sign that
seems both given to perception and immediately intelligible. A linguistics of
writing, by contrast, would be one that gives a central place to those aspects
of language set aside by this model, whether they are associated with the written
character or with features of speech neglected by linguistic idealisation.

If Ferdinand de Saussure's conception of language as a system of signs
can be seen as the basis for this first linguistics, the second linguistics will
confront from the outset the problems that obsessed the 'other Saussure',
as he has been called, the Saussure of the anagrams. Saussure believed
that he had discovered anagrams of proper names in the writings of Latin
poets. He amassed an impressive collection of examples and hypotheses about
rules governing this patterning, but he left his speculations unpublished because
he could find no references to the practice in classical texts and the advice he
sought about the statistical probability of the anagrams he discovered was
inconclusive. He confronted a paradoxical situation, as he wryly observed:
if one finds few anagrams, then these can be dismissed as the results of chance;
if one finds many, then that suggests that they are all too easy to find, a
commonplace product of the repetition of twenty-six letters.[9] As he wrote in
a letter, 'I make no secret of the fact that I myself am perplexed – about
the most important point: that is, how should one judge the reality or
phantasmagoria of the whole question.'[10]

'Reality' versus 'phantasmagoria' is a version of a familiar problem: the dilemma about the signifying status of patterns indentifiable in linguistic material. What has sometimes been seen as Saussure's chimerical obsession is his encounter with the problem of the relationship between the materiality of language and its signifying effects, the possibility that language functions in ways that bypass conventional linguistic codes and sign relations. Anagrams are a special case of a more general phenomenon, whose importance in the functioning of language needs to be assessed. In Saussure's account of language as system, *la langue* consists of signs which are the product of contrasts between elements that have no reality other than their differential function. These basic units are entirely defined by their ability to differentiate higher-level units, signs: the phoneme /b/ is the intersection of the contrasts that differentiate bat from pat, cat, fat, etc. If, when looking at a text, one begins to attend not to signs but to other patterns formed by their constituents and aspects of the materiality of those constituents, then a different perspective opens: the possibility of other signifying processes working beneath or alongside the manifest signs of the text.

Saussure himself was inclined to consider the repetition of letters important only when they could be seen as a dispersal or concealment of known signs relevant to the text's explicit statement. He thus ensured, while identifying another level and mechanism of signification, that its textual energies reinforced meaning that was already present: anagrammatic repetition signified by reiterating key proper names. The idea of literary discourse as, to borrow a formulation from Derrida's discussion of Genet, 'the patient, stealthy, quasi-animal or vegetable, tireless, monumnetal, derisory transformation of one's name, a rebus, into a thing or name of a thing' lurks beyond the Saussurian horizon.[11] The project of looking at the constituents of signs for their role in anagrams establishes, though, two possibilities: (1) seeing discourse as motivated by a formal procedure tied to investments that might not be reflected in the text's apparent meaning, such as a proper name that did not overtly appear, and (2) finding patterns of repetition that are not easily resolvable into regular signs – as in 'kingfishers catch fire', 'proud as a peacock', or 'a fresh and following folded rank'. Once one begins to think of letters or of phonetic qualities as possible constituents of other patterns, one is approaching language in a new way.

From this perspective, language seems not so much a system of signs, each joining a signifier with its signified, as an infinite pattern of echoes and repetitions, where readers are confronted with a problem of determining which of numerous possible patterns to pursue, which to treat as endowed with significance. Signs are not simply given to perception: to perceive the signifier at all is to confer on some patterns and not on others the status of meaningful expressions. It has been fashionable recently to speak of the play of the signifier or of the production of signifieds by the signifier, but this is something of a misnomer, for the question is precisely which identifiable features of a linguistic sequence belong to the signifier and which do not: whether patterns or relations are of the order of the signifier.

Saussure's work on anagrams has often been misconstrued as suggesting that meaning is the creation of readers, who find in language patterns they wish to find. Joe Gargery in Dickens' *Great Expectations* seems the satirical model of such a reader. He is, he tells Pip, '"oncommon fond of reading."

"Are you, Joe?"

"Oncommon. Give me," said Joe, "a good book, or a good newspaper and sit me down afore a good fire, and I ask no better. Lord!" he continued, after rubbing his knees a little, "when you *do* come to a J and an O and says you, 'Here, at last, is a J-O, Joe', how interesting reading is!"'[12] Our judgment of readers so dedicated to finding anagrams of proper names may well agree with Pip's, who reports 'I derived from this last that Joe's education, like steam, was yet in its infancy.' But this example poses a genuine question, for the J's and the O's are undoubtedly there. What enables us to say that a text with a thick scattering of them, like a text with plethora of stop consonants, or nasals, or liquids, is not affected by this? It is not a matter of statistical probability: questions about patterns may be posed in probabilistic terms if one is interested above all in whether they are to be counted as deliberate or accidental, but once the connection between the workings of language and the unconscious is admitted, this becomes a matter of less urgency. It is easy to believe that many striking patterns are the result of what Lacan calls 'the insistence of the letter in the unconscious.'

Countering Roman Jakobson's discovery of myriad patterns of symmetries and asymmetries in poetic texts, Michael Riffaterre proposed a 'law of perceptibility' which would rule irrelevant patterns that the reader could not perceive; but this manifestly fails as a principle of relevance, for any pattern in dispute has been perceived by a least one reader, and we can scarcely accept a model of language that eliminates in advance the possibility of discovering hitherto unnoticed patterns. Not only are we unaware of most of the rules and regularities of our language, but we all have had the experience of seeing a text illuminated by patterns and echoes we had not previously noticed but which, once pointed out to us, seem thoroughly compelling. The problem highlighted by Saussure's pursuit of anagrams is the exclusion, by a linguistics of the sign and the code, of an array of potential patterns, about which it is difficult to determine whether they have meaning or signifying effects. Its problematic examples offer a glimpse of the possibility that what we call codes, discrete phenomena, and signs or sign systems are only special cases of an endless generalised iteration or patterning.

These cases present themselves under a double aspect. On the one hand, meaning seems to be produced by the reader, who pursues some leads and not others; but on the other hand, linguistic effects of various sorts may be produced by forces that do not seem to involve linguistic conventions at all, as in the sound patterning of advertising slogans or of poetry, which may do its work without a reader or listener explicitly becoming aware of it. Either way, the model of language as a system of signs seems under attack. The idea that prior linguistic conventions enable listeners or readers to identify signifiers and know their meaning seems to be undermined from both sides by the processes anagrams expose: there is patterning that seems to work without prior conventions or listeners' recognition, and there is patterning that seems willfully created by readers, who must determine what to count as a signifier.

This vision of language, which emerges as one follows Saussure's attempts to perceive key names anagrammatically dispersed in the text, tantalisingly confronts the idea that language is a system of signs by suggesting (1) that there are forces at work below the level of the sign, and (2) that signs are not phenomenally given, so that the decision to treat certain patterns and not others as signifying patterns is an imposition of convention or meaning, not a recognition of conventionally established signs. I shall return to this shortly.

A linguistics of writing can proceed by paying attention to the forms of writing in speech, to possible relations and patterns relegated to the margins of linguistics. Acts of relegation, often curious places where an ideology of language imposes itself willy-nilly, can make excellent points of departure for a new linguistics. One striking instance is a passage where Saussure, defending the arbitrary nature of the sign, rejects onomatopoeia.

Onomatopoeic words might be held to show that a choice of signifier is not always arbitrary. But such words are never organic elements of a linguistic system. Moreover, they are far fewer than is generally believed. Words such as *fouet* ['whip'] or *glas* ['knell'] may strike some ears as having a certain suggestive sonority. But to see that this is in no way intrinsic to the words themselves, it suffices to look at their Latin origins. *Fouet* comes from Latin *fagus* ('beech tree') and *glas* from Latin *classicum* ('trumpet call'). The suggestive quality of the modern pronunciation of these words is a fortuitous result of phonetic evolution.[13]

As Derrida notes in *Glas*, the recourse to etymology in discussing the 'intrinsic' character of a particular sign is strange in a theorist who imperiously distinguishes between synchronic facts and diachronic facts, but odder still is the exclusion of the 'fortuitous' by one who tells us that language is essentially fortuitous. In order to define the linguistic sign as *essentially* fortuitous – arbitrary – Saussure excludes fortuitous *motivation*.

These paradoxical moves, like the exclusion of writing, alert us to the possibility that what is being set aside in order to leave a pure linguistic sign or linguistic system may in fact be a significant aspect of language: fortuitous motivation might be a general mechanism of language. Even if one grants Saussure's argument that onomatopoeias are never pure, never solidly grounded in resemblance, one might nevertheless take an interest in the contamination of arbitrariness by motivation, whether this motivation is produced by the craftsmanship of poets, by the fortuitous effects of linguistic evolution, by the keen eye of readers looking for anagrams, by the errors of speakers, or by the mechanisms of the unconscious.

Although linguistic tradition and its assumptions about language that we have made our own doubtless incline us to concede Saussure's claim, that in a sense the structure of French or English is not affected by the potential suggestiveness of various signifiers, still, we could also wonder, with Derrida, whether the language one speaks or writes is not always exposed to the contamination of arbitrary signs by suggestions of imitative motivation, whether effects of motivation are not inseparable from – central to – the workings of language, whether it does not bring into the linguistic system itself questions about the subterranean dispersal of the proper name and trouble the framing gesture that seeks to separate an inside of the system from the outside of practice. 'What if', Derrida asks, 'this mimesis meant that the internal system of language does not exist, or that one never uses it, or at least that one only uses it by contaminating it, and that this contamination is inevitable and thus regular and 'normal', belongs to the system and its functioning, *en fasse partie*, that is to say, both is a part of it and also makes the system, which is the whole, part of a whole larger than itself.'[14]

The very sentence in which Saussure sets aside motivation displays effects of motivation in ways which suggest that discourse may be driven by precisely the sort of phenomena he wishes to exclude from language. '*Fouet* ['whip'] and *glas* ['knell'],' he writes, 'may *strike* [*peuvent frapper*] some ears as having a certain suggestive sonority.' *Fouet* and *glas* both strike the ear, perhaps, because whips and bells strike: the term for what words do as they make a noise seems generated by the examples, or the choice of examples is generated by what words are said to do to the ear. This sentence, working to remotivate and thus link together supposedly arbitrary signs, displays a principle by which discourse frequently operates and suggests that arbitrary signs of the linguistic system may be part of a larger discursive system in which effects of motivation, demotivation, and remotivation are always occurring. Relations between signifiers and or between signifiers and signifieds can always produce effects, whether conscious or unconscious, and this cannot be set aside as irrelevant to language.

The lessons for a linguistics of writing drawn from Saussure's anagrams and the other examples we have considered might come more easily from writing such as *Finnegans Wake*, which poses in particularly virulent fashion the problem of echoes, patterns, motivation, forcing readers to establish relations while foregrounding the dilemma of 'Reality or phantasmagoria?' that perplexed Saussure. Consider the beginning of one relatively self-contained sequence, 'The Mookse and the Gripes'.

The Mookse and the Gripes.
Gentes and laitymen, fullstoppers and semicolonials, hybreds and lubberds!
Eins within a space and a wearywide space it wast ere wohned a Mookse. The onesomeness wast alltolonely, archunsitslike, broady oval, and a Mookse he would a

walking go (My hood! cries Anthony Romeo), so one grandsumer evening, after a great morning and his good supper of gammon and spittish, having flabelled his eyes, pilleoled his nostrils, vaticanated his ears and palliumed his throats, he put on his impermeable, seized his impugnable, harped on his crown and stepped out of his immobile *De Rure Albo* (socolled becauld it was chalkfull of masterplasters and had borgeously letout gardens strown with cascadas, pintacostecas, horthoducts and currycombs) and set off from Ludstown *a spasso* to see how badness was badness in the weirdest of all pensible ways.[15]

Finnegans Wake makes explicit a vision of language as sequences of letters and syllables echoing others, in ways that sometimes but by no means always form codified signs. It exposes interpretation as an abusive assimilation of sequences to other sequences: 'borgeously' is 'gorgeously' and 'Borghese'; 'horthoducts' are no doubt orthodox horticultural aqueducts; more dubiously, perhaps, 'Mookse' is moose (by phonetic propinquity), fox ('The Fox and the Grapes' resembles this fable), mock turtle ('Gripes' means Gryphon, as in Lewis Carroll's 'The Mock Turtle and the Gryphon'), and moocow (for reasons I shall come to in a minute). Most of all, the *Wake* presents what we are inclined to call 'echoes', drawing on a problematical term whose virtue is its conflation of an automatic acoustic process with a willful mimetic one. 'Eins within a space and a wearywide space it wast ere wohned a Mookse' echoes the opening of *Portrait of the Artist*: 'Once upon a time and a very good time it was there was a moocow coming down along the road.' 'A Mookse he would a walking go' recalls 'Froggy would a wooing go'. *Ere wohned* is Samuel Butler's anagram of 'nowhere' *Erewhon*, as well as the German 'he lived'. The significative status of such echoes is far from certain, and much of the energy of literary criticism is devoted to motivating them and deriving semantic consequences. Their status and the effects they induce, including the interpretive operations set in motion by them, are what a linguistics of writing particularly should address. The scope of the problem becomes clearest when the examples are tenuous: does 'the weirdest of all pensible ways' echo 'the best of all possible worlds'? Is this 'reality or phantasmagoria', as Saussure would ask? The shared elements seem minimal and the case for Mookse as Candide does not seem otherwise compelling. I cannot hazard a rule that would stipulate a connection yet am reluctant to abandon the relation. This, I submit, is language.

As in the case of anagrams, readers are cast simultaneously in contradictory roles: compelled to choose what possible relations to pursue, what to treat as significant, they are creators of meaning; condemned to wrack their brains for obscure words and less obscure quotations, to consult dictionaries, glossaries, and commentaries, they are inadequate recipients of a wickedly complex construction they cannot hope to grasp. The key point is that these opposites go together: the texts such as *Finnegans Wake* that most encourage readerly activity also convince one that it is the text which echoes. Readers feel that there is meaning insistent in the text: to recognise that *hybreds and lubberds* can be 'high-bred' and 'low bred', that *archunsitslike* contains the Greek *archon*, 'ruler', which explains this sort of sitting lonely ('the onesome-ness wast alltolonely'), that *broady oval* may be explained as 'bloody awful', is certainly to feel one has elucidated the lines' meaning, but these are in fact only relations, echoes, whose compelling character needs to be explained by a linguistics of writing.

Such passages suggest, first, that the words of a work are rooted in other words, whose traces they bear in different ways. Though this is made obvious by portmanteau words ('tighteousness', 'famillionarily', 'chalkfull', 'borgeously') that explicitly allude to others, or by unintelligible sequences that need to be interpreted as transformations of other words ('Mookse', 'spittish'), this is also true, as Derek Attridge writes, of all linguistic sequences, which are composed of syllables from other sequences and refer obliquely to these sequences by their similarities and differences.[16] What the *Wake* enables us to conceive is that the practice of recognising, say, *space*, as the sign 'space' is only a special case of a more general process of relating sequences to other sequences: reading *broady oval* as 'bloody awful'. The close connection between these two processes comes out clearly in cases of languages in contact, which Mary Louis Pratt has suggested we might take as a normal case of language. An American listening to a Glaswegian is in much the same position as the reader of *Finnegans Wake*. In speech we are always recognising the echoes of sequences we have heard before in sequences that are physically distinct and interesting in their distinctness, but this impresses us more in writing, and especially in writing such as *Finnegans Wake* where we are alert for the interest of variations and unexpected combinations.

A linguistics of writing, exploiting this model, would seek to invert the usual relation between discrete, already codified signs and the material usually deemed irrelevant except as a means of manifestation. It would treat discrete signs as special cases of a generalised echoing, and explore whether a linguistics could be constructed on such a model, and how far it could go. Above all it would need to attend to what lies outside an ordinary linguistics but furnishes much matter for literary criticism: the tantalising prospect, that caused Saussure so much anguish in his work on anagrams, of perceiving patterns, hearing echoes, and yet being uncertain, in principle as well as in practice, about their status. The task of linguistics has been to divide the signifying from the non-signifying, excluding the latter from linguistics, but if this boundary region is central to language and its functioning – and texts like the *Wake* suggest that it is – then this geography must be revised, and the uncertainty of echoes, the problematic materiality of language which may or may not carry meaning and produce effects, must lie at the centre of our concerns. A linguistics of writing must address a textuality linked to the materiality of language, which necessarily gets misread when transformed into signs, as it must be by our semiotic drive. Such a linguistics can work on the materiality of the spoken word as well as the written – of the 'greeaat fish' that gets away from the fisherman; of all those forms or sequences which we who are not accomplished storytellers cannot rely on ourselves to produce before a lecture audience, because they do not belong to a discrete code.

Mary Louise Pratt, John Hollander and I could all be seen as posing the same question for a linguistics of writing: given a series of phenomena which are linguistic in a broad sense — involved with and produced by language — and which have been set aside or treated as marginal by mainstream linguistics, does one seek to *extend* linguistics to include them or should one not rather, on the assumption that there has been something at stake in the relegation of these phenomena to the periphery, take the step of attempting to reconceive the study of language with these phenomena at the centre?

Mary Louise Pratt proposed that instead of relying on the idealisations of 'the speech community' we take as norm communication among people who may not belong to the same speech communities or do so only partly. Such communication is widespread, and to take it as the norm might give us a quite different view of language. John Hollander, in sketching the visionary grammars, the linguistic pathology ('acute synchrodiachronesis' or 'morpho-phonemia') of poetic word-play, which is generally treated as ancillary to 'real' grammar, might be taken to propose that we treat other sorts of language use as special cases of this generalised allusiveness. I am suggesting much the same thing. It may not be possible to construct a linguistics on this basis — a linguistics that resembles the one we have now — but it seems a worthy experiment, from whose failure we could learn almost as much as from its success.

Notes

1   See John Lyons, 'Human Language', in R. A. Hinde (ed.), *Non-Verbal Communication*, Cambridge, 1972, pp. 49–85.

2   Roy Harris, *The Language-Makers*, Ithaca, 1980, p. 9.

3   *Ibid.*, p. 18.

4   Dennis Tedlock, *The Spoken Word and the Work of Interpretation*, Philadelphia, 1983, p. 9.

5   *Ibid.*, p. 202.

6   *Ibid.*, p. 204.

7   *Ibid.*, p. 214.

8   *Ibid.*, p. 191.

9   Jean Starobinski (ed.), *Words Upon Words*, New Haven, 1979, p. 99.

10   *Ibid.*, pp. 105–6.

11   Jacques Derrida, *Glas*, Paris, 1972, p. 11.

12   Charles Dickens, *Great Expectations*, chapter vii.

13   Ferdinand de Saussure, *Cours de linguistique générale*, Paris, 1973, pp. 101–2.

14   Derrida, *Glas*, p. 109.

15   James Joyce, *Finnegans Wake*, London, 1964, p. 152.

16   Derek Attridge, 'Unpacking the Portmanteau', in J. Culler (ed.), *On Puns: The Foundation of Letters*, Oxford, 1987.

12   *Paul Kiparsky*

On theory and interpretation

Why has the exciting programme of linguistic poetics drafted in Jakobson 1960 not lived up to its promise? A common answer is that a theory of literature of the sort Jakobson had in mind is impossible for fundamental philosophical reasons. On the diagnosis to be defended here, the fault lies rather in the inadequate theories of language and communication on which it relied: the programme itself is sound, and where it has been coupled with the right linguistics and pragmatics it has already brought interesting results.

Recall that, in Jakobson's view of things, literature is the province of two theoretical disciplines: *poetics* and *semiotics*. Poetics, a branch of linguistics, is concerned with those aspects of verbal art which are rooted in the specific organisation of language as a representational system, for example with metrics and with syntactic parallelism, traditionally called 'figures of language'. Semiotics deals with those aspects (such as metaphor and other 'figures of thought') which stem from the communicative function of language, and consequently recur in other sign systems which serve that function. But Jakobson and his supporters, as well as their critics, missed the full import of dividing the labour in this way, because they accepted the structuralist and semiotic doctrine about language and communication, according to which all sign systems can be analysed by the same fundamental techniques. Specifically, they subscribed to the following two propositions:

1. both language and other semiotic systems are definable by networks of similarity and contiguity relations;
2. interpreting an utterance is definable as a decoding process.

From the perspective of those assumptions, linguistics and semiotics seemed closely akin in methodology and subject matter, so that not much depended on how the explicanda were partitioned between them.

But both assumptions have meanwhile turned out to be false. The study of grammatical structure has shown that neither syntax nor phonology can be reduced to similarity and contiguity relations (Chomsky 1972), and the emerging study of pragmatics has shown that communication involves inference as well as encoding and decoding (Grice 1975, Sperber and Wilson

1986).[1] Linguistics and semiotics deal with questions of a very different sort and neither can simply adopt the theories or methods of the other. The distinction between the tasks of poetics and semiotics in the study of verbal art thereby becomes crucial.

I shall develop this point by contrasting two views of poetic form: an essentialist view derivable from Jakobson's conception with the modifications I have suggested, and the conventionalist view currently popular in literary theory.

On the essentialist view the distinction between 'figures of language' studied by poetics, such as alliteration, rhyme, parallelism, and metrical form, and 'figures of thought' studied by semiotics, such as metaphor and irony, is fundamental. Figures of language, and the regularities which may govern their distribution in a work or body of literature, are grounded in the human language faculty; this is why they always involve linguistic categories of the sort that play a role in the grammars of languages, and why the rules governing them obey principles that also apply to linguistic rules and representations. As for the interpretation of a literary work, including figures of thought and the determination of its significance in the larger sense, it is taken to be a product of the same inferential processes that function in communication at large, to resolve ambiguity through context, to assign utterances their speech act interpretations, to detect irony and metaphor.

The conventionalist strategy is to deny this distinction and to claim that all these things are the results of certain conventional ways of perceiving, which are sanctioned by the authority of interpretative communities. On that view, neither individual instances of figures of language, nor their patterning in a work or body of literature, are 'facts' about texts. Rather, they are, like metaphors or ironies, interpretations which readers impose upon those texts through context-bound assumptions which they bring to them.

These two positions lead to different conclusions about whether literature is amenable to theoretical study. The conventionalist position is associated with a global 'anti-theory' stance, while the essentialist position implies that literary theory is in principle possible, even though it does not by itself guarantee that the subject is tractable in terms of practical research. I shall argue that poetics is in fact a viable enterprise both in principle and in research practice. For semiotics I shall claim only that the arguments claimed to demonstrate its impossibility are invalid if the field is properly reconstrued.

Before proceeding to compare these two positions, I shall briefly show how the essentialist view as here outlined differs from Jakobson's, and meets the principal criticisms that have been raised against the latter. One objection to Jakobson's version has been that it seems to entail that (at least within a given 'code', and setting actual ambiguity aside) a literary work must have one and only true interpretation, presumably a false consequence.[2] It is in fact not so clear that it does follow from Jakobson's view, but we will assume so for the sake of argument. In any case, if Jakobson's programme is implemented with a more adequate semiotics, say along the lines of Sperber & Wilson (1986), it certainly does not lead to any such conclusion. On the contrary, because inferential processes, whether in casual communication or in their most complex manifestations in art and science, are characteristically open-ended, global and integrative (unlike decoding in the classical semiotic model), they should lead to multiple interpretations. In fact, iterability considerations of the sort discussed by Derrida guarantee that the interpretation of a literary work must be more indeterminate than the interpretation of dialogue. First, the interpretation of any piece of communication is a function of the assumptions that are brought to bear on it.[3] As the radius of communication expands, the amount of shared background assumptions is attenuated and the indeterminacy correspondingly grows. Literary works are the limiting case in that the radius can be arbitrarily large. Secondly, while the interpretation of dialogue is constrained by the principle that the speaker formulates his sentences in such a way that the first interpretation consistent with the principle of relevance that occurs to the addressee is the intended one,[4] the reading of literary works is not,[5] and they are consequently open to constant re-interpretation.

A second objection to Jakobson's approach, also raised against various kinds of stylistics by Fish (1980), is that it never succeeded in discovering the putative 'codes' relating the interpretation of a literary work to the formal patterning of linguistic elements in it. But this objection is likewise inapplicable to our version of the programme, for we do not suppose that interpretation is decoding and therefore expect no such code in the first place. Rather, we take interpreting a literary work to be analogous to other interpretive activities such as construing the import of a remark in dialogue and explaining a datum in science. We assume that in interpretive activities – as opposed to such decoding activities as understanding the linguistic meaning of a sentence or reading a thermometer – there is in general no invariant or rule-governed translation from 'facts' to 'interpretations', but a process of inference to the best explanation of the type familiar from the philosophy of science.

What then is 'interpreting a literary work'? What does this activity have in common with those other interpretive activities? One answer would be that they all involve integrating a piece of new information (the literary work, the piece of dialogue, the experimental datum) into some previously existing cognitive structure. If this process fails, both the new information and the old information are reconsidered until a coherent picture is found. This is exactly what a conventionalist such as Stanley Fish denies. He claims that new information can never fail to fit into an existing cognitive framework; for every 'fact' is the result of interpretation, and therefore interpretation can never be based on fact. He means this quite seriously, and enthusiastically endorses all its corollaries: that in science 'theories always work and they will always produce exactly the results they predict' (p. 68), that in literature 'no reading, however outlandish it might appear, is inherently an impossible one' (p. 348), and that in general a thinker prevails by force of rhetorical persuasion, not by force of evidence or argument (this volume).

Fish documents his characterisation of literary interpretation with an examination of the critical history of Blake's 'The Tyger'. Proposed readings of this poem are quite diverse, and the tiger of the poem has been understood in at least the following ways: (1) the tiger is evil, (2) he is holy, (3) he is both, (4) he is beyond good and evil, and even (5) he is the poem itself. Fish's denies the very possibility of choosing among these alternatives on the basis of the text itself and justifies his position as follows:

> The rhetoric of critical argument ... depends upon a distinction between interpretations on the one hand and the textual and contextual facts that will either support or disconfirm them on the other; but as the example of Blake's 'Tyger' shows, text, context, and interpretation all emerge together, as a consequence of a gesture (the declaration of belief) that is irreducibly interpretive. It follows, then, that when one interpretation wins out over another, it is not because the first has been shown to be in accordance with the facts but because it is from the perspective of its assumptions that the facts are now being specified. It is these assumptions, and not the facts they make possible, that are at stake in any critical dispute. (1980, p. 340)

In what sense does the text itself 'emerge' with the context and the interpretation, and how does each of the different interpretations 'bring with it a new set of obvious and indisputable facts'? This might be taken either literally or metaphorically. If 'emerging' and 'bringing with it' are taken to refer literally to the actual coming into existence and creation of something that previously did not exist, then the statement is clearly false. The text of 'The Tyger', or the various properties of it is that the critics appeal to in defending their interpretations (say the wording of a certain line) certainly existed before those interpretations were put forward, in fact they existed from the moment Blake wrote the poem. And taken metaphorically, it reduces to a triviality which does not support his conclusion. It is true enough that the significance, or even the very existence[6] of some property of a text might be *noticed* only because of a proposed interpretation, and that different interpretations account for different sets of facts. But that doesn't mean that the interpretations mysteriously *create* those facts. What they do is to call attention to the facts, and to give them a specific significance – but this is to say that the facts themselves do exist independently of their interpretation, so the argument collapses. I conclude that Fish has not shown that interpretations can bring any texts or any properties of texts into existence, much less that they are *all* brought into existence by interpretations.

By way of example, let us consider some patterns of argument typical of critical practice. In general, one reasons either from how well an interpretation of a work fits into some larger scheme of things (e.g. whether it says something interesting or otherwise worth saying, whether it is consistent with some larger work of which it is a part, and so on), or else from how much significance it reveals in the text and how it accounts for its wording. All of these considerations appear to be derivable from the principle of maximising relevance, proposed as a universal principle by Sperber and Wilson. Consider the third of the abovementioned interpretations of 'The Tyger', namely that the tiger embodies good and evil. We could support it on the grounds that it makes the poem fit best into the *Songs of Experience*. We would then note that in Blake's metaphysical idealism, Innocence/Experience and the other correlated oppositions are not simple oppositions of two qualities, as in (1):

$$(1) \quad A \quad B$$

but second-order oppositions between a state in which an opposition is suppressed or neutralised (Innocence), and a state in which that opposition is manifested (Experience), as in (2):

$$(2) \quad A \quad A:B$$

Many of the poems fall into pairs which show this asymmetrical dualism of what Blake called the two 'contrary states of the human soul'. The poem which corresponds to 'The Tyger' in the *Songs of Innocence* is 'The Lamb'. It is then significant that there is no tiger in 'The Lamb', but there is a lamb in 'The Tyger', in the characteristic parallel opposition: 'Did he who make the lamb make thee?'

We could further support the third reading on the grounds that it explains otherwise unmotivated facts of the text. Why a tiger, and not some other beast, say a lion, wolf or boar? Because the light and dark stripes of the tiger is emblematic of the contradiction inherent in Experience − compare the white lamb of Innocence. The allied contrast between light and dark ('burning bright in the forests of the night') parallels this 'fearful symmetry' of the tiger as embodiment of Experience.

Supporting a reading in this fashion is very much like marshalling evidence for a theory in some empirical field of inquiry. There too, 'facts' do not wear their interpretation on their sleeves, but neither are they created by the interpretation. However great a stake we, or 'the interpretive community', have in a certain interpretation, to be convincing it still has to make the facts fall into place better than the alternatives do.[7]

A related argument by Fish against the very possibility of 'theory' is that one cannot get outside context. This one is especially interesting because he admits that by the same argument linguistics as currently practised too is doomed to fail as well. Indeed, he thinks that 'the generative model'[8] long ago 'collapsed' 'under the weight of unassimilable data'[9] (1980, p. 363); its success 'has been largely political' (1986, p. 125). Actually, just the opposite is the case: generative grammar has gained its position as the dominant theory in the field of linguistics (in the sense that it is the one which most linguists try to develop, to apply, or to overthrow) in spite of the fact that generative theorists have never 'politically' dominated the institutions of the field.[10] So I propose to turn Fish's point around and cite the success of linguistics as an encouraging prospect for literary theory.

In its most general form, Fish's argument that context invalidates both generative linguistics and literary theory goes like this: theory depends on 'substituting for the parochial perspective of some local or partisan point of view the perspective of a general rationality to which the individual subordinates his contextually conditioned opinions and beliefs', but this cannot be done:

... this substitution of the general for the local has never been and will never be achieved ... because the primary data and formal laws necessary to its success will always be spied or picked out from within the contextual circumstances from which they are supposedly independent. ... facts and rules ... are themselves interpretive products ..,. already contaminated by the interested judgments they claim to transcend. ... This abstracting-away-from must of course begin begin with data ... The trick then is to think of sentences that would be heard in the same way by all competent speakers no matter what their educational experience, or class membership, or partisan affiliation, or special knowledge ... The trouble is that there are no such sentences. ... Rather than being distinct from circumstantial (and therefore variable) conditions, linguistic knowledge is unthinkable apart from these circumstances. Linguistic knowledge is contextual rather than abstract, local rather than general, dynamic rather than invariant; every rule is a rule of thumb; every competence grammar is a performance grammar in disguise. (1986, pp. 110–11)

There are quite a few confusions here. The data for grammatical theory are not interpretations of sentences, which depend on 'context' in Fish's sense, but rather judgments about their acceptability, which depend rather on the speaker's internalised grammatical system and on certain processing constraints. 'Customs, conventions, educational experience, class membership, partisan affiliation, or special knowledge' are not involved in the grammatical knowledge that underlies a speaker's fluent command of a language. Moreover, theoretical abstraction, either from context or from processing factors, does not depend on eliminating these things *from the data*: there is a coherent linguistics of sentence structure, just as there is a coherent mechanics of frictionless planes and perfect vacuums, regardless of whether contextless sentences, frictionless planes and perfect vacuums occur in nature. Idealisation in science does not depend on obtaining 'pure' data but on 'dividing nature at the joints' in the right way. But in any case, linguists have moved from merely abstracting away from context to the beginnings of a theory of context. The study of the organisation of discourse and dialogue, for example, is currently an active area of research.[11] Note finally that contrary to what Fish supposes, a theory in the sense under discussion need not be deterministic. There is absolutely no reason why we could not have precise theories of non-deterministic regularities.

I conclude that none of Fish's general arguments for the impossibility of a theory of literature can be maintained.

Turning now from semiotics to poetics, we move from the purely pro-grammatic plane to an area where we can point to some actual results. But here too, the conventionalist view is strongly espoused by many of the most influential contemporary theorists:

> ... line endings exist by virtue of perceptual strategies rather the other way around. Historically the strategy that we know as 'reading (or hearing) poetry' has included paying attention to the line as a unit, but it is precisely that attention which has made the line as a unit (either of print or of aural duration) available. ... In short, what is noticed is what has been made noticeable, not by a clear and undistorting glass, but by an interpretive strategy. (Fish 1980, pp. 165–6)

> The same argument can be repeated for the most basic phenomena: any repetition of the same sound or letter is a function of phonological or orthographic conventions and thus may be regarded as the result of interpretive strategies of particular communities. There is no rigorous way to distinguish fact from interpretation, so nothing can be deemed to be definitively *in* the text prior to interpretive conventions. (Culler 1982, p. 74)

> The way you apply a rule is not just a technical affair: it is bound up with wider interpretations of reality, with commitments and predilections which are not themselves reducible to conformity to a rule. The rule may be to trace parallelisms in the poem, but what is to count as a parallelism? If you disagree with what counts for me as a parallelism, you have not broken any rule: I can only settle the argument by appealing to the authority of the literary institution, saying: '*This* is what we mean by a parallelism.' If you ask why we should follow this particular rule in the first place, I can only once more appeal to the authority of the literary institution and say: 'This is the kind of thing we do.' To which you can always reply: 'Well, do something else.' An appeal to the rules which define competence will not allow me to counter this, and neither will an appeal to the text ... Structuralism may examine and appeal to existing practice; but what is its answer to those who say: Do something else? (Eagleton 1983, p. 126)

I shall argue instead that alliteration, parallelism etc. are *perceived*, and that they are governed by the same principles as govern language itself, in the following sense. A fluent speaker of a language has internalised a grammar which enables him/her to assign certain kinds of syntactic and phonological representations to its utterances. His/her faculty of language (shared with all humans and constitutive of universal grammar) also equips him/her with certain 'modes of perceiving', that is, with the ability to parse those represen-tations in characteristic ways and to recognise whether they are alike with respect to some structural analysis. By virtue of his/her internalised grammar and of his/her language faculty, a speaker is able to perceive a structural equivalence in all words with a certain syllable onset, in all sentences with a certain structural pattern, and so on. These equivalence classes are, *ex hypothesi*, just those which could be specified in a potential grammatical rule of the language – not necessarily for an actual rule of his/her particular language. The hypothesis then is, first, that figures of language are defined as repetitions over exactly those equivalence classes, and second, that conventions which regulate them are themselves constrained by the faculty of language. For example, because the category of syllable onset is defined in universal grammar, words with identical syllable onsets are recognised as an equivalence class (i.e. they alliterate) whether or not the grammar of the language happens to contain rules referring to syllable onsets, and therefore alliteration is universally available as an organising principle of verse.

The interest of this hypothesis is, first, that it predicts that there should be certain general properties of literary form, and secondly that it relates those properties to independently motivated principles of grammatical theory. Thus, it entails a 'universal poetics' analogous to and closely related to universal grammar. If this view is correct, it should for example be the case that children presented with metrical verse perceive its rhymes and rhythms, and learn the organising patterns, without the benefit of explicit instruction.

I will now briefly consider some specific consequences of this idea. Culler speaks of alliteration as a 'repetition of sounds', but in fact that is an incorrect view. As far as is known, there are no alliteration systems that work on the principle that some sound or phoneme has to be repeated. Alliteration of words always involves identity of some structurally-defined portion of their initial syllable, such as the syllable onset; this is why *in* and *out* (both with no onset) alliterate just as *pin* and *pout* alliterate, even though *in* and *out* have no sound in common. And for the same reason *pea* and *mow* are fully as good a slant-rhyme pair as *peat* and *moat*. The interesting fact is that alliteration and slant rhyme work this way wherever they are used as systematic conventions of versification. Why should this be so? Purely conventional constraints would not be expected to recur in identical form in every system. We conclude that the constraints are motivated in the way we parse phonological representations, in the way our language faculty organises words and syllables into their constituents and matches up parts of them. Supporting evidence comes from the fact that reduplication and other phonological and morphological rules across languages work in just that same way, quite independently of whether the language happens to make use in its poetry of alliteration or not.[12]

As for parallelism, there is again reason to believe that we recognise it in virtue of our inherent language faculty. Most languages allow the suppression of equivalent, not necessarily morphologically identical, material in syntactically parallel sentences, e.g. *I am a child and thou a lamb*, from *I am a child and thou art a lamb*. The parallelism which licenses the omission of the second verb must be defined at a quite specific level of syntactic representation. Sentences are not parallel because they have the same or similar meanings. Nor are they parallel because they have the same deep structure. For example, actives and passives are not parallel, so that we cannot suppress *was seen* in *John saw Fred and Bill was seen by Mary*. On the other hand, any two subjects or objects are parallel no matter how much they differ in their internal structure. Syntactic processes are thus *structure-dependent* in a specific sense.

The interesting observation is that versification systems that are built on strict syntactic parallelism exhibit the same kind of structure-dependence.[13] Further, language itself makes a distinction between two kinds of parallelism, *analogous* – including synonymous as a special case – and *antithetical*. Suppression of repeated verbs is characteristic of analogous parallelism (*John saw Mary and Bill Max*), but is avoided in antithesis (we hardly say *John saw Mary but Bill Max*). And exactly this distinction between analogous and antithetical parallelism, 'comparison for likeness' sake and comparison for unlikeness' sake',[14] plays a role in the structural organisation of the versification of a language like Finnish where the traditional poetry is built around syntactic parallelism as a constitutive device. The conclusion to be drawn from these observations is that syntactic theory not only supplies the means for specifying the relevant constraints on parallelism in verse, but the constraints themselves and the definition of parallel structure are already latent in the syntactic system even in languages which don't use it as a basis for versification.

An analogous answer could be given to Culler's objection to Jakobson (cited above, p. 21), namely that one can produce distributional categories *ad libitum*:

One might for example begin by studying the distribution of substantives and distinguish between those which were objects of verbs and those which were subjects, those which were objects of singular verbs and objects of plural verbs and then one might sub-divide each of these classes according to the tense of the verb and so on. This can produce an almost unlimited number of distributional classes and thus if one wished to discover a pattern of symmetry in that text one can always produce some class whose members will be appropriately arranged. (Culler 1975, p. 57)

But neither on Jakobson's view nor on mine can grammatical categories be multiplied *ad libitum*; they are in fact a fixed set to be established within the theory of grammar. There may be debates about what is the right set[15] but it is certainly not possible to pull them out of the air. If categories such as objects of plural verbs have no status in linguistic rules then an adequate linguistic theory must exclude them, committing us to the prediction that they will play no role in poetic form either.

Metrical systems are an important test case for us because they are relatively well studied in cross-linguistic perspective. Earlier studies found themselves somewhat at a loss in explaining why metrical organisation is the dominant feature of poetry in the languages of the world. Jakobson was forced to compromise his otherwise stringent principle of isomorphism at exactly this point:

Measure of sequences is a device that, outside of poetic function, finds no application in language. (1960, p. 28)

More recent study both of the prosodic organisation of language and of the way in which the prosodic patterns of language are organised to define metrical systems show that this assessment was far too pessimistic. The basic insight to come out of phonology in the study of suprasegmentals is that *language itself is metrically organised*.[16] By this we mean that language itself has the attributes which we associate with 'metrical' systems: (1) *Periodicity*: stress is deployed according to an alternating pattern. A variety of processes operating in phonological systems serve that demand, eliminating stress clashes and assigning subsidiary stresses to secure this fundamentally periodic alternating rhythm characteristic of languages. (2) *Constituency*: the alternating strong and weak beats are grouped together, either as weak-strong or strong-weak depending on the language. This means that *feet* are part of language. (3) *Maximal articulation*: not only are syllables grouped into feet, but also those feet themselves are grouped into larger constituents; in fact there is a phonological hierarchy according to which utterances are divided exhaustively into groups each of which consists of entities on the next lower level of the hierarchy. That is, utterances are fully articulated at several hierarchical levels of prosodic structure. (4) *Even distribution*: there is a tendency to arrange phonological phrases in balanced fashion. For example, heavy noun phrases will be moved to the end of a sentence more readily than light ones will.

Metrical systems in verse show the same four properties, and are defined by the same categories.[17] Verse is fundamentally made up out of lines with some recurrent internal articulation into cola or feet or both. Attentive investigation reveals periodicity even in cases where superficial descriptions have neglected it. The Romance hendecasyllable has often been described as having lines consisting of simply ten or eleven positions, but Piera (to appear) shows that the system is fundamentally iambic. In Sanskrit, where the indigenous descriptive tradition does not recognise feet, and the various metres at first blush look like hopelessly arbitrary arrangements of longs and shorts, decomposition into cola is crucial (Pollock 1977). It follows that, in particular, line boundaries are indeed, contrary to Fish, 'facts of nature', specifically of human nature.

To say that verse is organised on the same principles as language is to make a claim about natural form. It is not to deny that anyone can invent any arbitrary organisation for a verse and make that the basis for a metrical system. One could base a verse form on the succession of digits in the decimal expansion of π, and no doubt some one has. A more serious case are figure poems, such as the one Halle analyses in his chapter. There is reason to believe that figure poems are apprehended in a rather different way. In the first place the pattern is (as Halle himself pointed out) *visual*. That is, you can't 'hear' the temple in a recitation of Psalm 137. Secondly, there is an essential cryptographic element involved. The temple figure appears to have been hidden for over two thousand years; until this paper was written, perhaps the only two people that had known about it were the psalmist himself, and Morris Halle. And thirdly, such patterns appear as experimental or occasional devices but apparently never as conventional verse forms. For these reasons

I will suppose that figure poems are governed by constraints of their own and that they should not be accounted for by the same theory as metrical verse.

To summarise, I have argued that grasping a literary work draws on a combination of the perceptual processes by which one understands the sentences of one's language and the inferential processes by which one interprets their significance, neither being simply a matter of conventional interpretation under the authority of an interpretive institution. This of course assumes that the distinction between perception and interpretation significant. Stanley Fish, however, would consider even the perception of language itself, that is even the very act of hearing the *d* in *dog*, or perceiving the black mark 'd' on paper as a *d*, as an interpretive act. For Fish, then, *everything* is interpretation. I am reminded of a story that I learned from J.R. Ross.[18] After a lecture on cosmology William James was approached by a little old lady who claimed that the earth is actually supported on the back of a giant turtle. 'But what does the turtle stand on?', the great philosopher patiently asked. 'A good question!', replied the lady. 'But my theory has an answer: the giant turtle stands on the back of another, even bigger turtle.' 'But what does that second turtle stand on, then?', persisted James. And the lady retorted triumphantly: 'It's no use, Mr. James! It's turtles all the way down!' And for Stanley Fish it really is interpretation all the way down.

But there are general grounds for believing that language has a biological basis (Chomsky 1972), and specific evidence that recognising 'dog' as *dog* involves psychological mechanisms which are perceptual, like those that figure in recognizing a patch of red, and unlike those interpretive processes which figure in drawing an inference. Fodor (1983) argues that word recognition, sentence parsing, and detecting linguistic intonation and rhythm are all *reflexes* handled in the brain by what he calls input systems, which are separate from the central processing system that handles inferences. Input systems, including those which process language, seem to have the following properties: (1) implementation by localised neural systems dedicated to those functions,[19] (2) mandatory operation (a sentence must be heard as a sentence), (3) limited central access to the mental representations that input systems compute, (4) rapid operation, (5) operation independent from higher-level knowledge.[20] If everything is 'interpretation' we will still have to reconstruct the distinction between perception and inference within this all-encompassing category, and we will be back where we started without having gained from the detour.

I will conclude this defence of the essentialist position by mentioning a further corollary of the view that I have been defending: literature is universal. Eagleton's (1983) statement that literature itself is a 'recent historical invention' is false (unless perhaps you take at face value Roland Barthes's definition of literature as 'that which gets taught'). In the sense in which I have been using the term and in which I believe it should be the subject matter of poetic and semiotic enquiry, literature is neither recent nor a historical invention. In fact no human community lacks a literature. There is no tribe on earth so wretched that it does not express its memories and desires in stories and poems, and not the least of the merits of Jakobson's programme for the study of verbal art is that it points to an explanation of this remarkable fact.

Notes

1 '... the linguistic meaning of an uttered sentence falls short of encoding what the speaker means: it merely helps the audience infer what she means. The output of decoding is correctly treated by the audience as a piece of evidence about the communicator's intentions. In other words, a coding-decoding process is subservient to a Gricean inferential process.' (S&W, 27).

2 This is not uncontroversial. There are those who argue that a literary work really does have one and only one true interpretation (Hirsch 1967, 1976, Juhl 1980).

3 For example, I may make a remark to you merely intending that it should be relevant to you and thereby inviting you to reflect upon it. The inferences that you in fact end up drawing from it may be different from the ones that I had in mind. The fact that inference makes communication inherently indeterminate in this way is very fortunate; a fully determinate communication system would actually be dysfunctional.

4 Sperber and Wilson (1986, p. 166) elegantly derive this as a theorem from the principle of relevance itself. Their formulation of the latter is that 'every act of ostensive communication communicates the presumption of its own optimal relevance', meaning that it is (1) worth the addressee's while to process, and (2) the most relevant one the communicator could have used to communicate.

5 Perhaps as a consequence of the fact that the reader of a literary work is not strictly its addressee. The deduction mentioned in the preceding footnote would then correctly fail for the case of literature.

6 As in the case of the Biblical figure poem discovered by Halle, this volume.

7 In the discussion of this paper at the conference Fish suggested that the kinds of arguments I adduced for reading (3) of 'The Tyger' are still parochial in that they depend on some version of the romanticist doctrine of organic form. Should my arguments for reading (3) be persuasive to you, it would then only be because you agree with that doctrine and therefore already specify the text from its point of view. However, the arguments in question actually rest only on selecting interpretations which maximise the relevance of the text, and not on the entire apparatus of the doctrine of organic form. Reading (3) makes the wording of the poem and the poem's place in the *Song of Experience* relevant in certain ways in which they are not relevant on the other readings. The doctrine of organic form, as well as notions like unity and coherence which have been considered desiderata in aesthetics (as well as in rhetoric and science) since antiquity, contain a more general invariant core which assigns relevance of parts of a work in terms of their function in the whole. What would be parochial is rather the opposite principle that the text should be interpreted so as to make it maximally irrelevant. A reading based on that principle (a dadaist interpretation, perhaps) would be perfectly possible and might even be highly interesting, but it would nevertheless be a *misinterpretation*, analogous to the wilful misconstruction of a statement or an unwarranted inference from a datum. It is a consequence of the position

here adopted that that such interpretations, and works intended to be so interpreted, exist only parasitically, as negations of interpretations and works that do conform to the principle of relevance.

8 Which he confusedly characterises as claiming 'that linguistic behaviour could be reduced to a set of abstract formal rules with built-in recursive functions'. The goal of generative grammar is of course not to characterise linguistic behaviour but knowledge of language.

9 A curious allegation, from someone who thinks that any data can be assimilated to any theory. These unassimilable data were supposed to have been the basis of a 'disquieting and finally successful challenge' to the model by 'a group of Chomsky's best students' in the late sixties. As every linguist would agree, the generative semantics episode (which has to be what Fish is referring to here) was in fact a complete failure.

10 As Newmeyer (1986) documents in some detail.

11 See e.g. Carlson (1983) for an interesting new approach.

12 Thus you cannot argue that this behaviour of alliteration is parasitic on some actual phonological rules in the language; both are based on the same faculty of language which says that words, feet, syllables are constituted in a particular way. See Kiparsky (1987) for further discussion of reduplication and its relation to alliteration in cross-linguistic perspective.

13 See Kiparsky (1973), O'Connor (1980, 1982) for examples and discussion.

14 A phrase of G.M. Hopkins' quoted by Jakobson (1960 and elsewhere).

15 Some current work assumes that grammatical categories are defined by a system of cross-classifying features and that phrasal categories are projections of lexical categories according to a fixed schema ('X-theory'). See further Gazdar, Klein, Pullum & Sag (1985).

16 Liberman & Prince (1977), van der Hulst & Smith (1982), Prince (1983), Selkirk (1984).

17 Hayes (1987), and essays by Prince, Hayes, Kiparsky and others in Kiparsky (to appear).

18 It appears as the epigraph to Ross (1967).

19 This is why brain injuries can specifically damage language or some sub-system of language.

20 Recent psycholinguistic work seems to confirm Fodor's proposal, indicating that syntactic parsing operates independently of the subject's appreciation of semantic context or of real-world background (Ferreira and Clifton 1986). What contextual information does is apparently to reject interpretations after they are made available by the input mechanism rather than to direct the analysis itself. The corollary would be, for example, that syntactic parallelism, contrary to Eagleton, is 'encapsulated' and not bound up with commitments and predilections.

References

Lauri Carlson, *Dialogue Games*, Dordrecht, 1983.
Noam Chomsky, *Language and Mind, (Enlarged Edition)*, New York, 1972.
Noam Chomsky, *Rules and Representations*, New York, 1980.
Jonathan Culler, *Structuralist Poetics*, Ithaca, 1975.

Jonathan Culler, *On Deconstruction: Theory and Criticism after Structuralism*, Ithaca, 1982.

Terry Eagleton, *Literary Theory: an Introduction*, Minneapolis, 1983.

Fernanda Ferreira & Charles Clifton, 'The independence of syntactic processing', *Journal of Memory and Language*, 25, 1986, pp. 348–68.

Stanley Fish, *Is there a Text in This Class?*, Cambridge, Massachusetts, 1980.

Stanley Fish, 'Consequences', in W. J. T. Mitchell (ed.), *Against Theory*, Chicago, 1986.

Jerry A. Fodor, *The Modularity of Mind*, Cambridge, Massachusets, 1983.

Gerald Gazdar, Ewan Klein, Geoffrey Pullum & Ivan Sag, *Generalized Phrase Structure Grammar*, Cambridge, Massachusetts, 1985.

H. P. Grice, 'Logic and conversation', in P. Cole & J. Morgan (eds), *Syntax. and Pragmatics 3: Speech Acts*, New York, 1975.

Bruce Hayes, 'Metrics and phonological theory', in F. Newmeyer (ed.), *Cambridge Survey of Linguistics*, Cambridge, Massachusetts, 1987.

Bruce Hayes, 'The phonology of rhythm in English', *Linguistic Inquiry*, 15, 1984, pp. 33–74.

Bruce Hayes, 'The prosodic hierarchy in meter', in Paul Kiparsky & Gilbert Youmans (ed.), *Perspectives on Meter*, New York, to appear.

E. D. Hirsch, Jr., *Validity in Interpretation*, New Haven, 1967.

E. D. Hirsch, Jr., *The Aims of Interpretation*, Chicago, 1976.

Harry van der Hulst & Norval Smith, *The Structure of Phonological Representations, I–II*. Dordrecht, 1982.

Roman Jakobson, 'Linguistics and poetics', in *Style in Language*, Cambridge, Massachusetts, 1961.

P. D. Juhl, *Interpretation: an Essay in the Philosophy of Literary Criticism*, Princeton, 1980.

Ellen Kaisse & Pat Shaw (eds), *Phonology Yearbook*, Cambridge, 1985.

Paul Kiparsky, 'The grammar of poetry', in *A Tribute to Roman Jakobson 1896–1982*, Berlin, 1983.

Paul Kiparsky, 'The phonology of reduplication', (to appear).

Mark Liberman & Alan Prince, 'On stress and linguistic rhythm', *Linguistic Inquiry*, 8, 1977, pp. 249–336.

F. Newmeyer, 'Has there been a "Chomskyan Revolution" in linguistics?', *Language*, 62, 1986, pp. 1–18.

M. P. O'Connor, *Hebrew Verse Structure*, Winona Lake, 1980.

M. P. O'Connor, '"Unanswerable the Knack of Tongues": the linguistic study of verse', in Lise Menn & Lorraine Obler (eds), *Exceptional Language and Linguistics*, New York, 1982.

Carlos Piera, 'Spanish verse and the theory of meter', (to appear).

Sheldon Pollock, *Aspects of Versification in Sanskrit Lyric Poetry*, New Haven, 1977.

Alan Prince, 'Relating to the grid', *Linguistic Inquiry*, 14, 1983, pp. 19–100.

Alan Prince, 'Metrical forms', in Paul Kiparsky & Gilbert Youmans (eds), *Perspectives on Meter*, New York, (to appear).

John Robert Ross, *Constraints on Variables in Syntax*, PhD thesis, Massachusetts Institute Technology, 1967.

Elizabeth Selkirk, *Phonology and Syntax*, Cambridge, Massachusetts, 1984.

Dan Sperber & Deirdre Wilson, *Relevance*, Cambridge, Massachusetts, 1986.

Reading without interpretation: postmodernism and the video-text

It has often been said that every age is dominated by a privileged form, or genre, which seems by its structure the fittest to express its secret truths; or perhaps, if you prefer a more contemporary way of thinking about it, which seems to offer the richest symptom of what Sartre would have called the 'objective neurosis' of that particular time and place. Today, however, I think we would no longer look for such characteristic or symptomal objects in the world and the language of forms or genres. Capitalism, and the modern age, is a period in which, with the extinction of the sacred and the 'spiritual', the deep underlying materiality of all things has finally risen dripping and convulsive into the light of day; and it is clear that culture itself is one of those things whose fundamental materiality is now for us not merely evident, but quite inescapable. This has, however, been a historical lesson: it is because culture has *become* material that we are now in a position to understand that it always *was* material, or materialistic, in its structures and functions. We postcontemporary people have a word for that discovery − a word that has tended to displace the older language of genres and forms − and this is of course the word *medium*, and in particular its plural, media, a word which now conjoins three relatively distinct signals: that of an artistic mode or specific form of aesthetic production; that of a specific technology, generally organised around a central apparatus or machine; that, finally, of a social institution. These three areas of meaning do not define a medium, or the media, but designate the distinct dimensions that must be addressed in order for such a definition to be completed or constructed. It should be evident that most traditional and modern aesthetic concepts − largely, but not exclusively, designed for literary texts − do not require this simultaneous attention to the multiple dimensions of the material, the social, and the aesthetic.

It is because we have had to learn that culture is a matter of media today that we have finally begun to get it through our heads that culture was always that, and that the older forms or genres, or indeed the older spiritual exercises and meditations, thoughts and expressions, were also in their very different ways media products. The intervention of the machine, the mechanisation of culture, the mediation of culture by the consciousness industry, this is now everywhere the case, and perhaps it might be interesting to explore the possibility that it was always the case throughout human history, and within even the radical difference of older, precapitalist modes of production.

Nonetheless, what is paradoxical about this displacement of literary terminology by an emergent mediatic conceptuality is that it takes place at the very moment in which the philosophical priority of language itself and of the various linguistic philosophies has become dominant and wellnigh universal (something to which we will have occasion to return in the course of this discussion). Thus, the written text loses its privileged and exemplary status at the very moment when the available conceptualities for analysing the enormous variety of objects of study with which 'reality' present us (now all in their various ways designated as so many 'texts') have become almost exclusively linguistic in orientation. To analyse the media in linguistic or semiotic terms therefore may well appear to involve an imperialising enlargement of the domain of language to include non-verbal — visual or musical, bodily, spatial — phenomena; but it may equally well spell a critical and disruptive challenge to the very conceptual instruments which have been mobilised to complete this operation of assimilation.

As for the emergent priority of the media today, this is scarcely a new discovery. For some seventy years, the cleverest prophets have warned us regularly that the dominant art form of the twentieth century was not literature at all — nor even painting, or theatre, or the symphony — but rather the one new and historically unique art invented in the contemporary period, namely film, that is to say, the first distinctively mediatic art form. What is strange about this prognosis — whose unassailable validity has with time become a commonplace — is that it should have had so little practical effect. Indeed, literature, sometimes intelligently and opportunistically absorbing the techniques of film back into its own substance, remained throughout the modern period the ideologically dominant paradigm of the aesthetic, and continued to hold open a space in which the richest varieties of innovation were pursued. Film, however, whatever its deeper consonance with twentieth-century realities, entertained a merely fitful relationship to the modern in that sense, owing, no doubt, to the two distinct lives or identities through which, successively (like Virginia Woolf's Orlando), it was destined to pass: the first, the silent period, in which some lateral fusion of the mass-audience and the formal or modernist proved viable (in ways and resolutions we can no longer grasp, owing to our peculiar historical amnesia); the second, or sound period, then coming as the dominance of masscultural (and commercial) forms through which the medium must toil until again reinventing the forms of the modern in a new way in the great *auteurs* of the 1950s (Hitchcock, Bergman, Kurosawa, Fellini).

What this account suggests is that, however helpful the declaration of the priority of film over literature in jolting us out of print culture and/or logocentrism, it remained an essentially *modernist* formulation, locked in a set of cultural values and categories which are in full postmodernism demonstrably antiquated and 'historical'. That film has today become postmodernist, or at least that certain films have, is obvious enough; but so have some forms of literary production. The argument turned however on the priority of these forms, that is, their capacity to serve as some supreme and privileged, symptomatic, index of the *Zeitgeist*; to stand, using a more contemporary language, as the cultural *dominant* of a new social and economic conjuncture; to offer − now finally putting the most philosophically adequate face on the matter − as the richest allegorical and hermeneutic vehicles for some new description of the system itself. Film and literature no longer do that, although I will not belabour the largely circumstantial evidence of the increasing dependency of each on materials, forms, technology and even thematics borrowed from the other art or medium I have in mind as the most likely candidate for cultural hegemony today.

The identity of that candidate is, however, no secret: it is clearly video, in its twin manifestations as commercial television and as experimental video or 'video art'. This is not a proposition one proves; rather, one seeks, as I will in the remainder of this essay, to demonstrate the interest of presupposing it, and in particular the variety of new consequences that flow from assigning some new and more central priority to video processes.

One very significant feature of this presupposition must, however, be under-scored at the outset: for it logically involves the radical and virtually a priori differentiation of film theory from whatever is to be proposed in the nature of a theory or even a description of video itself. The very richness of film theory today makes this decision and this warning unavoidable. If the experience of the movie screen and its mesmerising images is distinct, and fundamentally different, from the experience of the television monitor − something that might be scientifically inferred by technical differences in their respective modes of encoding visual information, but which could also be phenomeno-logically argued − then the very maturity and sophistication of film con-ceptualities will necessarily obscure the originality of its cousin, whose specific features demand to be reconstructed afresh and empty-handed, without imported and extrapolated categories. A parable can indeed be adduced here to support this methodological decision: discussing the hesitation Central European Jewish writers faced between writing in German and writing in Yiddish, Kafka once observed that these languages were too close to each other for any satisfactory translation from one into the other to be possible. Something like this, then, is what one would want to affirm about the relation-ship of the language of film theory and that of the theory of video, if indeed anything like this last exists in the first place.

Doubts on that score have, however, frequently been raised: nowhere more dramatically than at an ambitious conference on the subject sponsored by *The Kitchen* in October 1980, at which a long line of dignitaries trooped to the podium only to complain that they couldn't understand why they had been invited, since they had no particular thoughts about television (which some of them admitted they watched) – many then adding, as in afterthought, that only one half-way viable concept 'produced' about television occurred to them, and that was Raymond Williams's idea of 'total flow'.[1]

Perhaps these two remarks go together more intimately than we imagine: the blockage of fresh thinking before this solid little window against which we strike our heads being perhaps not unrelated to precisely the 'total flow' we observe through it.

For it seems plausible that in a situation of total flow, the contents of the screen streaming before us all day long without interruption (or where the interruptions – called *commercials* – are less intermissions than they are fleeting opportunities to visit the bathroom or throw a sandwich together) what used to be called critical distance seems to have become obsolete. Turning the television set off has little in common either with the intermission of a play or an opera or with the grand finale of a feature film, when the lights slowly come back on and memory begins its mysterious work. If anything like critical distance is still possible in film, indeed, it is surely bound up with memory itself. But memory seems to play no role in television, commercial or otherwise (or, I am tempted to say, in postmodernism generally): nothing here haunts the mind or leaves its afterimages in the manner of the great moments of film (which do not necessarily happen, of course, in the 'great' films). A description of the structural exclusion of memory, then, and of 'critical distance', might well lead on into the impossible, namely a theory of video itself: how the thing blocks its own theorisation becoming a theory in its own right.

My experience, however, is that you can't manage to think about things simply by deciding to: and that the mind's deeper currents often need to be surprised by indirection, sometimes, indeed, by treachery and ruse, as when you steer away from a goal in order to reach it more directly, or look away from an object in order to register it more exactly. In that sense, thinking anything adequate about commercial television may well involve ignoring it and thinking about something else: in the instance, experimental video (or alternatively that new form or genre called MTV, which cannot be dealt with here). This is less a matter of mass versus élite culture than it is of controlled laboratory situations: what is so highly specialised as to seem aberrant and uncharacteristic in the word of daily life – hermetic poetry, for example – can often yield crucial information about the properties of an object of study (language, in that case), whose familiar everyday forms obscure it. Released from all conventional constraints, experimental video allows us to witness the full range of possibilities and potentialities of the medium in a way which illuminates its various more restricted uses, the latter being subsets and special cases of the former.

Even this approach to television via experimental video, however, needs to be estranged and displaced if the language of formal innovation and enlarged possibility leads us to expect a flowering and a multiplicity of new forms and visual languages: that exists, of course, and to a degree so bewildering in the short history of video art (sometimes dated from Nam June Paik's first experiments in 1963) that one is tempted to wonder whether any description or theory could ever encompass their variety. I have found it enlightening to come at this issue from a different direction, however, by raising the question of *boredom* as an aesthetic response and a phenomenological problem. In both the Freudian and the Marxist traditions (for the second, Lukacs, but also Sartre's discussion of 'stupidity' in his war diaries, 'boredom' is taken, not so much as an objective property of things and works, but rather as a response to the blockage of energies (whether those be grasped in terms of desire or of praxis). Boredom then becomes interesting as a reaction to situations of paralysis and also, no doubt, as defence mechanism or avoidance behaviour. Even taken in the narrower realm of cultural reception, boredom with a particular kind of work or style or content can always be used productively as a precious symptom of our own existential, ideological and cultural limits, an index of what has to be refused in the way of other people's cultural practices and their threat to our own rationalisations about the nature and value of art. Meanwhile, it is no great secret that in some of the most significant works of high modernism what is boring can often be very interesting indeed, and vice versa: a combination which the reading of any hundred sentences from a book by Raymond Roussel, say, will at once dramatise. We must therefore initially try to strip the concept of the boring (and its experience) of any axiological overtones, and bracket the whole question of aesthetic value. It is a paradox one can get used to: if, as has just been suggested, a boring text can also be good (or interesting, as we now put it), exciting texts, which incorporate diversion, distraction, temporal commodification, can also perhaps sometimes be 'bad' (or 'degraded', to use a Frankfurt School language).

Imagine in any event a face on your television screen accompanied by an incomprehensible and never-ending stream of keenings and mutterings: the face itself remains utterly without expression and, unchanging throughout the course of the 'work', comes to seem some icon or floating immobile timeless mask. It is an experience to which you might be willing to submit out of curiosity's sake for a few minutes. When, however, you begin to leaf through your programme in distraction, only to discover that this particular video-text is twenty-one minutes long, than panic overcomes the mind and almost anything else seems preferable. But twenty-one minutes is not terribly long in other contexts (the immobility of the adept or religious mystic might offer some point of reference), and the nature of this particular form of aesthetic boredom becomes an interesting problem, particularly when we recall the difference between the viewing situation of this video text and analogous experiences in experimental film (we can always shut the first one off, without sitting politely through a social and an institutional ritual). As I have already suggested, however, we must avoid the easy conclusion that this tape or text is simply bad; one wants immediately to add, to forestall misconceptions, that there are many, many diverting and captivating video-texts of all kinds – but then one would also want to avoid the conclusion that those are simply better (or 'good' in the axiological sense).

There then emerges a second possibility, a second explanatory temptation, which involves authorial intention. We may then conclude that the video-maker's choice was a deliberate and a conscious one, and that therefore the twenty-one minutes of this tape are to be interpreted as provocation, as a calculated assault on the viewer, if not an act of outright aggressivity. In that case, our response was the right one: boredom and panic are appropriate reactions and a recognition of the meaning of that particular aesthetic act. Apart from the well-known aporias involved in concepts of literary intent and intention, the thematics of such aggressivity (aesthetic, class, gender, or whatever) are virtually impossible to re-establish on the basis of the isolated tape itself.

Perhaps, however, the problems of the motives of the individual subject can be elided by attention to the other type of mediation involved, namely technology and the machine itself. We are told, for instance, that in the early days of photography, or rather, of the Daguerrotype, subjects were obliged to sit in absolute immobility for periods of time which, although not long as the crow flies, could nonetheless be characterised as being *relatively* intolerable. One imagines the uncontrollable twitching of the facial muscles, for example, or the overwhelming urge to scratch or to laugh. The first photographers therefore devised something on the order of the electric chair, in which the heads of their portrait subjects, from the lowliest and most banal generals all the way to Lincoln himself, were clamped in place and immobilised from the back for the obligatory five or ten minutes of the exposure. Roussel, whom I've already mentioned, is something like a literary equivalent of this process, whose unimaginably detailed and minute description of objects – an absolutely in-finite process without principle or thematic interest of any kind – forces the reader to work laboriously through one sentence after another, world without end. But it may now be appropriate to re-identify Roussel's peculiar experiments as a kind of anticipation of postmodernism within the older modernist period; at any rate, it seems at least arguable that aberrations and excesses which were marginal or subordinate in the modernist period become on the contrary dominant in the systemic restructuration that can be observed in what we now call postmodernism. It is at any rate clear that experimental video, whether we date it from the work of the ancestor Paik in the early 1960s or from the very floodtide of this new art which sets it in the mid 1970s, is rigorously coterminous with postmodernism itself as a historical period.

The machine on both sides, then: the machine as subject and as object, alike and indifferently: the machine of the photographic apparatus peering across like a gun barrel at the subject whose body is clamped into its mechanical correlative in some apparatus of registration/reception. The helpless spectators of video time are then as immobilised and mechanically integrated and neutralised as the older photographic subjects, who became, for a time, part of the technology of the medium. The living room, to be sure (or even the relaxed informality of the video museum), seems an unlikely place for this assimilation of human subjects to the technological: yet an attention is demanded by the total flow of the video text in time which is scarcely relaxed at all, and rather different from the comfortable scanning of the movie screen, let alone of the cigar-smoking detachment of the Brechtian theatre-goer. Interesting analyses (mostly from a Lacanian perspective) have been offered in recent film theory of the relationship between the mediation of the filmic machine and the construction of the viewer's subjectivity – at once depersonalised, and yet still powerfully motivated to re-establish the false homogeneities of the ego and of representation. I have the feeling that mechanical depersonalisation (or decentering of the subject) goes even further in the new medium, where the auteurs themselves are dissolved along with the spectator (a point to which I will return shortly in another context).

Yet since video is a temporal art, the most paradoxical effects of this technological appropriation of subjectivity are observable in the experience of time itself. We all know, but always forget, that the fictive scenes and conversations on the movie screen radically foreshorten reality as the clock ticks, and are never – owing to the now codified mysteries of the various techniques of film narrative – coterminous with the putative length of such moments in real life, or in 'real time': something a filmmaker can always uncomfortably remind us of by returning occasionally to real time in this or that episode, which then threatens to project the same intolerable discomfort we have ascribed to certain videotapes. Is it possible, then, that 'fiction' is what is in question here and that it consists essentially in the construction of just such fictive and foreshortened temporalities (whether of film or reading) which are then substituted for a real time we are thereby enabled momentarily to forget? The question of fiction and the fictive would thereby find itself radically dissociated from questions of narrative and storytelling as such (although it would retain a key role and function in the practice of certain forms of narration): many of the confusions of the so-called representation debate (often assimilated to a debate about realism) are dispelled by just such an analytic distinction between fiction-effects and their fictional temporalities, and narrative structures in general.

At any rate, in that case what one would want to affirm is that experimental video is *not* fictive in this sense, does not project fictive time, does not work with fiction or fictions (although it may well work with narrative structures). This initial distinction then makes other distinctions possible, as well as interesting new problems. Film, for example, would clearly seem to approach this status of the non-fictive in its documentary form; but I suspect for various reasons that most documentary film (and documentary video) still projects a kind of residual fictionality – a kind of documentary constructed time – at the very heart of its aesthetic ideology and its sequential rhythms and effects. Meanwhile, alongside the non-fictional processes of experimental video, at least one form of video clearly does aspire to fictionality of a filmic type, and that is commercial television, whose specificities, whether one deplores or celebrates them, are also perhaps best approached by way of a description of experimental video. To characterise television series, dramas and the like, in other words, in terms of the imitation, by this medium, of other arts and media (most notably filmic narrative), probably dooms one to miss the most interesting feature of their production situation: namely, how, out of the rigorously non-fictive languages of video, commercial television manages to produce the simulacrum of fictive time.

As for temporality itself, it was for the modern movement conceived at best as an experience and at worst as a theme, even though the reality glimpsed by the first moderns of the nineteenth century (and designated by the word *ennui*) is surely already this temporality of boredom we have identified in the video process, the ticking away of real time, minute by minute, the dread underlying irrevocable reality of the meter running. Yet the involvement of the machine in all this allows us now perhaps to escape phenomenology and the rhetoric of consciousness and experience, and to confront this seemingly subjective temporality in a new and materialist way, and in a way which constitutes a new kind of materialism as well, one not of matter but of machinery: as though, rephrasing our initial discussion of the retroactive effect of new genres, the emergence of the machine itself (so central to Marx's organisation of *Capital*) deconcealed in some unexpected way the produced materiality of human life and time. Indeed, alongside the various phenomenological accounts of temporality, and the philosophies and ideologies of time, we have also come to possess a whole range of historical studies of the social construction of time itself, of which the most influential no doubt remains E. P. Thompson's classic essay[2] on the effects of the introduction of the chronometer into the workplace. Real time in that sense is objective time, that is to say, the time of objects, and a time subject to the measurements to which objects are subject; measurable time becomes a reality on account of the emergence of measurement itself, that is to say, rationalisation and reification in the closely related senses of Weber and Lukács; clock time presupposes a peculiar spatial machine, that is to say, it is the time of a machine, or better still, the time of the machine itself. I have tried to suggest that video is unique – and in that sense historically privileged or symptomatic – because it is the only art or medium in which this ultimate seam between space and time is the very locus of the form; and also because its machinery uniquely dominates and de-personalises subject and object alike, transforming the former into a quasi-material registering apparatus for the machine time of the latter and of the video image or 'total flow'. If we are willing to entertain the hypothesis that capitalism can be periodised by the quantum leaps or technological mutations by which it responds to its deepest systemic crises, then it may become a little clearer why and how video — so closely related to the dominant computer and information technology of the late or third stage of capitalism — has a powerful claim for being the art form of late capitalism *par excellence*.

These propositions allow us to return to the concept of total flow itself and to grasp its relationship to the analysis of commercial (or fictive) television in a new way. Material or machine time punctuates the flow of commercial television by way of the cycles of hour and half-hour programming, shadowed as by a ghostly afterimage, by the shorter rhythms of the commercials themselves. I have suggested that these regular and periodic breaks are very unlike the types of closure to be found in the other arts and even in film, yet they allow the simulation of such closures and thereby the production of a kind of imaginary fictive time. The simulacrum of the fictive seizes on such material punctuation much as a dream seizes on external bodily stimuli, in order to draw it back into itself and to convert it into the appearance of beginnings and endings, or in other words, the illusion of an illusion, the second-degree simulation of what is already itself, in other art forms, some first-degree illusory fictiveness or temporality. But only a dialectical perspective, which posits presences and absences, appearances and realities or essences, can reveal these constitutive processes: for a one-dimensional or positivistic semiotics, for example, which can only deal in the sheer presences and existent data of segments of commercial and experimental video alike, these two related yet dialectically distinct forms are reduced to cuts and lengths of an identical material, to which identical instruments of analysis are then 'applied'. Commercial television is not an autonomous object of study; it can only be grasped for what it is by positioning it dialectically over against that other signifying system which we have called experimental video or video art.[3]

The hypothesis, however, of some greater materiality of video as a medium suggests that its analogies are perhaps better sought for in other places than the obvious cross-referencing of commercial television, or of fiction or even documentary film. We need indeed to explore the possibility that the most suggestive precursor of the new form may be found in animation or the animated cartoon, whose materialistic (and paradoxically non-fictive) specificity is at least two-fold: involving on the one hand a constitutive match or fit between a musical language and a visual one (two fully elaborated systems which are no longer subordinate to one another as in fiction film), and on the other, the palpably produced character of animation's images, which in their ceaseless metamorphosis now obey the 'textual' laws of writing and drawing, rather than the 'realistic' ones of verisimilitude, the force of gravity, etc. Animation constituted the first great school to teach the reading of material signifiers (rather than the narrative apprenticeship of objects of representation — characters, actions, and the like). Yet in animation, as later in experimental video, the Lacanian overtones of this language of 'material signifiers' is inescapably completed by the omnipresent force of human praxis itself;

suggesting thereby an active materialism, of production, rather than a static or mechanical materialism of matter or materiality itself as some inert support.

'Total flow', finally, involves some significant methodological consequences for the analysis of experimental video, and in particular for the constitution of the object or unity of study such a medium presents. It is of course no accident that today, in full postmodernism, the older language of the 'work' – the work of art, the masterwork – has everywhere largely been displaced by the rather different language of the 'text', of texts and textuality – a language from which the achievement of organic or monumental forms is strategically excluded. Everything can now be a text in that sense (daily life, the body, political representations), while objects that were formerly 'works' can now be reread as immense ensembles or systems of texts of various kinds, superimposed on each other by way of the various intertextualities, successions of fragments, or yet again sheer process (henceforth called textual production or textualisation). The autonomous work of art thereby – along with the old autonomous subject or ego – seems to have vanished, to have been volatilised.

Nowhere is this more materially demonstrable than with the 'texts' of experimental video – a situation which, however, now confronts the analyst with some new and unusual problems, problems characteristic in one way or another of all the postmodernisms, but even more acutely here. If the old modernising and monumental forms – the Book of the World, the 'magic mountains' of the architectural modernisms, the central mythic opera cycle of a Bayreuth, the Museum itself as the centre of all the possibilities of painting – if such totalising ensembles are no longer the fundamental organising frames for analysis and interpretation; if, in other words, there are no more masterpieces, no more great books (and if even the concept of good books has become problematical) – if we find ourselves confronted henceforth with 'texts', that is, with the ephemeral, with disposable works that wish to fold back immediately into the accumulating detritus of historical time – then it becomes difficult and even contradictory to organise an analysis and an interpretation around any single one of these fragments in flight. To select – even as an 'example' – a single video text, and to discuss it in isolation, is fatally to regenerate the illusion of the masterpiece or the canonical text, and to reify the experience of total flow from which it was momentarily extracted. Video viewing indeed involves immersion in the total flow of the thing itself, preferably a kind of random succession of three or four hours of tapes at regular intervals: indeed, video is in this sense (and owing to the commercialisation of public television and cable) an urban phenomenon, demanding video banks or museums in your neighbourhood which can thus be visited with something of the institutional habits and relaxed informality with which we used to visit the theatre of the opera-house (or even the movie-palace). What is quite out of the question is to look at a single 'video work' all by itself: in that sense, one would want to say, there are no video masterpieces, there can never be a video canon, even an auteur theory of video (where signatures are still evidently present) becomes very problematical indeed. The 'interesting' text now has to stand out of an undifferentiated and random flow of other texts. Something like a Heisenberg principle of video analysis thereby emerges: analysts and readers are shackled to the examination of specific and individual texts, one after the other; or if you prefer, they are condemned to a kind of linear *Darstellung* in which they have to talk about individual texts one at a time. But this very form of perception and of criticism at once interferes with the reality of the thing perceived and intercepts it in mid-light stream, distorting all the findings beyond recognition. The discussion, the indispensible preliminary selection and isolation, of a single 'text' then automatically trans-forms it back into a 'work', turns the anonymous videomaker[4] back into a named artist or 'auteur', opens the way for the return of all those features of an older modernist aesthetic which it was in the revolutionary nature of the newer medium to have precisely effaced and dispelled.

In spite of these qualifications and reservations, it does not seem possible to go further in this exploration of the possibilities of video without inter-rogating a concrete text: which will be a twenty-nine minute 'work' called *AlienNATION*, produced at the School of the Art Institute of Chicago by Edward Rankus, John Manning, and Barbara Latham in 1979. For the reader this will evidently remain an imaginary text; but the reader need not 'imagine' that the spectator is in an altogether different situation. To describe, after-wards, this stream of images of all kinds is necessarily to violate the perpetual present of the image, and to reorganise the few fragments that remain in the memory according to schemes which probably reveal more about the reading mind than the text itself: do we try to turn it back into a story of some kind? (A very interesting book by Jacques Leenhardt and Pierre Józsa, *Lire la lecture*, Paris: *Le Sycamore*, 1982, shows this process at work even in the reading of 'plotless novels' − the reader's memory creates 'protagonists' out of whole cloth, violates the reading experience in order to reassemble it into recognisable scenes and narrative sequences, and so forth.) Or at some more critically sophisticated level, do we at least try to sort the material out into thematic blocks and rhythms, and to repunctuate it with beginnings and endings, with graphs of rising and falling emotivity, climaxes, dead passages, transitions, recapitulations, and the like? No doubt; only the reconstruction of these overall formal movements turns out differently every time we watch the tape. For one thing, twenty-nine minutes in video is much longer than the equivalent temporal segment of any feature film; nor is it excessive to speak of a genuine and a very acute *contradiction* between the virtually drug-like experience of the present of the image in the videotape, and any kind of textual memory into which the successive presents might be inserted (even the return and recognition of older images is as it were seized on the run, laterally, and virtually too late for it to do us any good). If the contrast here with the memory-structures of Hollywood-type fiction films is stark and obvious, one has the feeling − more difficult to document or to argue − that the gap between this temporal experience and that of *experimental* film is no less great. These op-art tricks and elaborate visual montages in particular recall the filmic classics of yesteryear, such as *Ballet mechanique*; but I have the impression that, above and beyond the difference in our institutional situation (art movie theatre for the latter, television monitor either at home or in a video museum for the former), these experiences are very different ones, and in particular that the blocks of material in film are larger and more grossly and tangibly perceptible (even when they pass by rapidly), determining a more leisurely sense of combinations than can be the case with these attenuated visual data on the television screen.

One is therefore reduced to enumerating a few of these video materials, which are not themes (since for the most part they are material quotations from a quasi-commercial storehouse somewhere), but which certainly have none of the density of Bazinian *mise en scene* either, since even the segments which are not lifted from already existing sequences, but which have obviously been filmed explicitly for use in this tape, have a kind of shabbiness of low-grade colour stock which marks them somehow as 'fictional' and staged, as opposed to the manifest reality of the other images-in-the-world, the image-objects. There is therefore a sense in which the word *collage* could still obtain for this juxtaposition of what one is tempted to call 'natural' materials (the newly or directly filmed sequences) and artificial ones (the pre-cooked image materials which have been 'mixed' by the machine itself). What would be misleading is the ontological hierarchy of the older painterly collage: here the 'natural' is worse and more degraded than the artificial, while this last no longer connotes the secure daily life of a new humanly constructed society (as in the objects of cubism) but rather the noise and jumbled signals, the unimaginable informational garbage, of the new media society.

First, a little existential joke about a 'spot' of time, which is excised from a temporal 'culture' that looks a little like a crêpe; then experimental mice, voice-overed by various pseudo-scientific reports and therapeutic programmes (how to deal with stress, beauty-care, hypnosis for weight loss, etc.); then SF footage (including monster-music and camp dialogue), mostly drawn from a Japanese film, *Godzilla vs. Monster Zero* (1966). At this point the rush of image materials becomes too dense to enumerate: optical effects, children's blocks and erector sets, reproductions of classical paintings, as well as mannequins, advertising images, computer printouts, textbook illustrations of all kinds, cartoon figures rising and falling, including a wonderful Magritte hat slowly sinking into Lake Michigan; sheet lightning; a woman lying down and possibly under hypnosis (unless, as in a Robbe-Grillet novel, this is merely the photograph of a woman lying down and possibly under hypnosis); ultramodern hotel or office building lobbies with escalators rising in all directions and at various angles; shots of a street corner with sparse traffic, a child on a big wheel and a few pedestrians carrying groceries; a haunting closeup of detritus and children's blocks on the lakeshore (in one of which the Magritte hat reappears, in real life: poised on stick in the sand); Beethoven sonatas, Holst's Planets, disco music, funeral parlour organs, outer-space sound effects, the *Lawrence of Arabia* theme accompanying the arrival of flying saucers over the Chicago skyline; a grotesque sequence as well in which friable orange oblongs (that resemble hostess twinkies) are dissected with scalpels, squeezed by vices, and shattered by fists; a leaky container of milk; disco dancers in their habitat; shots of alien planets; closeups of various kinds of brushstrokes; ads for 1950s kitchens; and many more. Sometimes these seem to be combined in longer sequences, as when the sheet lightning is overcharged with a whole series of opticals, advertisements, cartoon figures, movie music and unrelated radio dialogue; sometimes, as in the transition from a relatively pensive and mysterious art-musical accompaniment to the stridence of mass-cultural music and beat, the principle of variation seems obvious and crudely heavy-handed; sometimes the accelerated flow of mixed images strikes one as modelling a certain unified temporal urgency, the tempo of delirium, let's say, or of direct experimental assault on the viewer-subject; while the whole is randomly punctuated with formal signals – the 'Prepare to disconnect' which is presumably designed to warn the viewer of impending closure; and the final shot of the beach, which borrows a more recognisably filmic connotative language – dispersal of an object world into fragments, but also the touching of a kind of limit or ultimate edge (as in the closing sequence of Fellini's *Dolce vita*). It is all, no doubt, an elaborate visual joke or hoax (if you were expecting something more 'serious'): a student's training exercise, if you like; while such is the tempo of the history of experimental video that insiders or connoisseurs are capable of watching this 1979 'text' with a certain nostalgia, and remembering that people did that kind of thing in those days, but are now busy doing something else.

The most interesting questions posed by a video text of this kind – and I hope it will be clear that the text *works*, whatever its value or its meaning: it can be seen again and again (at least partly on account of its informational overload, which the viewer will never be able to master) – remain questions of value and of interpretation, provided it is understood that it may be the absence of any possible response to those questions which is the historically interesting matter. But our attempt to tell or summarise this text makes it clear that even before we reach the interpretative question – 'what does it mean?' or to use its petty bourgeois version, 'what is it supposed to represent?' – we have to confront the preliminary matter of form and of reading. It is not evident that a spectator will ever reach a moment of knowledge and of saturated memory from which a formal reading of this text in time slowly disengages itself: beginnings and thematic emergences, combinations and developments, resistances and struggles for dominance, partial resolutions, forms of closure leading on to one or another full stop. Could one establish such an overall chart of the work's formal time, even in a very crude and general way, our description would necessarily remain as empty and as abstract as the terminology of musical form, whose problems today, in aleatory and post-twelve-tone music, are analogous, even though the mathematical dimensions of sound and of musical notation enable what look like more tangible solutions. My sense is, however, that even the few formal markers we have been able to isolate − the lakeshore, the building blocks, the 'sense of an ending' − are deceptive; they are now no longer features or elements of a form, but signs and traces of older forms. We must remember that those older forms are still included within the bits and pieces, the bricolated material, of this text: Beethoven's sonata is but one component of this *bricolage*, like a broken pipe retrieved and inserted in a sculpture, or a torn piece of newspaper pasted onto a canvas. Yet within the musical segment of the older Beethoven work, 'form' in the traditional sense persists and can be named − the 'falling cadence', say, or the 'reappearance of the first theme'. The same can be said of the film clips of the Japanese monster movie: they include quotations of the SF form itself: 'discovery', 'menace', 'attempted flight', and so forth (here the available formal terminology − in analogy to the musical nomenclature − would probably be restricted to Aristotle or to Propp and his successors, virtually the only sources of a neutral language of the movement of narrative form). The question that suggests itself is then whether the formal properties within these quoted segments and pieces is anywhere transferred to the video-text itself, to the *bricolage* of which they are parts and components. But this is a question that must first be raised on the micro-level of individual episodes and moments. As for the larger formal properties of the text considered as a 'work' and as temporal organisation, the lakeshore image suggests that the strong form of an older temporal or musical closure is here present merely as a formal residue: whatever in Fellini's ending still bore the traces of a mythic residue − the sea as some primordial element, as the place at which the human and the social confront the otherness of nature − is here already long since effaced and forgotten. That content has disappeared, leaving but a faint aftertrace of its original formal connotation, that is to say, of its syntactical function as closure. At this most attenuated point in the sign system, the signifier has become little more than a dim memory of a former sign, and indeed, of the formal function of that now extinct sign.

The language of connotation which began to impose itself in the preceding paragraph would seem to impose a re-examination of the central elaboration of this concept, which we owe to Roland Barthes, who elaborated it, following Hjelmslev, in his *Mythologies*, only in his later 'textual' work to repudiate its implicit differentiation of first- and second-degree languages (denotation and connotation): something that must have come to strike him as a replication of the old divisions between aesthetic and social, artistic free-play and historical referentiality, which reflections like *Le Plaisir du texte* were concerned to evade or escape. No matter that the earlier theory (still enormously influential in media studies) ingeniously reversed the priorities of this opposition: assigning authenticity (and thereby aesthetic value) to the denotative value of the photographic image, and a guilty social or ideological functionality to its more 'artificial' prolongation in advertising texts which take the original denotative text as their own new content, pressing already existent images into the service of some heightened play of degraded thoughts and commercial messages. Whatever the stakes and implications of this debate, it seems clear that Barthes's earlier, classical conception of how connotation functions can be suggestive for us here only on condition it is appropriately complicated, perhaps beyond all recognition. For the situation here is rather the inverse of the advertising one: there 'purer' and somehow more material signs were appropriated and readapted in order to serve as vehicles for a whole range of ideological signals. Here, on the contrary, the ideological signals are already deeply embedded in the primary texts, which are already profoundly cultural and ideological: the Beethoven music already includes the connotator of 'classical music' in general, the SF film already includes multiple political messages and anxieties (an American Cold War form readapted to Japanese anti-nuclear politics, and both then folding into the new cultural connotator of 'camp'). But connotation is here, in a cultural sphere whose 'products' have functions which largely transcend the narrowly commercial ones of advertising images (while no doubt still including some of those and surely replicated their structures in other ways), a polysemic process in which a number of 'messages' coexist: thus, the alternation of Beethoven and disco no doubt emits a class message, high versus popular or mass culture, privilege and education versus more popular and bodily forms of diversion, but it also continues to vehiculate the older content of some tragic gravity, the formal time-sense of the sonata form itself, the 'high seriousness' of the most rigorous bourgeois aesthetic in its grappling with time, contradiction and death; as opposed to the relentless temporal distraction of the big city commercial music of the postmodern age, that fills time and space implacably to the point where the older 'tragic' questions seem irrelevant. All of these connotations are in play simultaneously: to the degree to which they appear easily reducible to some of the binary oppositions just mentioned (high and low culture), we are in the presence of a kind of 'theme', which might at the outside limit be the occasion for an interpretive act, and allow us to suggest that the videotext is 'about' this particular opposition. We will return to such interpretive possibilities or options later on.

What must be excluded, however, is anything like a process of demystification at work in this particular video text: all of its materials are 'degraded' in that sense, Beethoven no less than disco. And although, as we will shortly make clear, there is a very complex interaction at work here between various levels and components of the text, or various languages (image versus sound, music versus dialogue), the political use of one of these levels against another (as in Godard), the attempt somehow to purify the image by setting it off against the written or spoken, is here no longer on the agenda, if it is even still conceivable. This is something that can be clarified, I believe, if we think of the various quoted elements and components, the broken pieces of a whole range of primary texts in the contemporary cultural sphere, as so many *logos*, that is to say, as a new form of advertising language which is structurally and historically a good deal more advanced and complicated than any of the advertising images with which Barthes's earlier theories had to deal. A logo is something like the synthesis of an advertising image and a brand-name: better still, it is a brand-name which has been transformed into an image, a sign or emblem which carries the memory of a whole tradition of earlier advertisements within itself in a wellnigh intertextual way. Such logos can be visual or auditory and musical (as in the Pepsi 'theme'): an enlargement which allows us to include the materials of the sound track under this category, along with the more immediately identifiable logo-segments of the office-escalators, the fashion mannequins, the psychological counselling clips, the street corner, the lakefront, *Monster Zero*, and so forth. 'Logo' then signifies the transformation of each of these fragments into a kind of sign in its own right; yet it is not yet clear what such new signs might be signs of, since no product seems identifiable, nor even the range of generic products strictly designated by the logo in its original sense, as the badge of a diversified multinational corporation. Still, the term 'generic' is itself suggestive, if we conceive of its literary implications a little more broadly than the older more static tables of 'genres' or fixed kinds. The generic cultural consumption projected by these fragments is more dynamic and demands some association with narrative (itself now grasped in the wider sense of a type of textual consumption): in that sense, the scientific experiments are narratives fully as much as *Lawrence of Arabia*; the vision of while white-collar workers and bureaucrats mounting flights of escalators is no less a narrative vision than the SF film clips (or horror music); even the still photograph of sheet lightning suggests a multiple set of narrative frames (Ansel Adams, or the terror of the great storm, or the 'logo' of the Remington-type Western landscape, or the eighteenth-century sublime, or the answer of God to the rainmaking ceremony, or the beginning of the end of the world).

The matter grows more complicted, however, when we realise that none of these elements or new cultural signs or 'logos' exists in isolation: but that the video text itself is at virtually all moments a process of ceaseless apparently random interaction between them. This is clearly the structure which demands description and analysis, but it is a relationship between signs for which we have only the most approximate theoretical models. It is indeed a matter of apprehending a constant stream or 'total flow' of multiple materials, each of which can be seen as something like a shorthand signal for a distinct type of narrative or a specific narrative process. But our immediate questions will be synchronic rather than diachronic: how do these various narrative signals or logos intersect each other? Is one to imagine a mental compartmentalisation in which each is received in isolation, or does the mind somehow establish connections of some kind, and in that case, how can we describe those connections? How are these materials wired into one another, if at all?

Or do we merely confront a simultaneity of distinct streams of elements
which the senses grasp all together like a kaleidoscope? The measure of our
conceptual weakness here is that we are tempted to begin with the most
unsatisfactory methodological decision − the Cartesian point of departure
− in which we begin by reducing the phenomenon to its simplest form, namely
the interaction of two such elements or signals (whereas dialectical thinking
asks us to begin with the most complex form, of which the simpler ones are
considered derivatives).

Even in the case of two elements, however, suggestive theoretical models
are few enough. The oldest one is of course the logical model of *subject* and
predicate, which, divested of its propositional logo − with its statement-
sentences and truth claims − has in recent times been rewritten as a relationship
between a *topic* and a *comment*. Literary theory has for the most part been
obliged to confront this structure only in the analysis of metaphor, for which
I. A. Richards's distinction between a *tenor* and a *vehicle* seems suggestive.
The semiotics of Peirce, however, which seeks insistently to grasp the process
of interpretation − or semiosis − in time, usefully rewrites all of these
distinctions in terms of an initial sign in relationship to which a second sign
stands as an *interpretant*. Contemporary narrative theory, finally, with its
operative distinction between the fable (the anecdote, the raw materials of the
basic story) and the *mise en scene* itself, the way in which those materials are
told or staged: in other words their *focalisation*.

What must be retained from all of these formulations is the way in which
they pose two signs of equal nature and value, only to observe that in their
moment of intersection, a new hierarchy is at once established in which one
sign becomes something like the material on which the other one works; or
in which the first sign establishes a content and a centre to which the second
is annexed for auxiliary and subordinate functions (the priorities of the
hierarchical relationship seem reversible in such descriptions). But the terminology and nomenclature of the traditional models do not seem to register what
surely becomes a fundamental property of the stream of signs in our video
text, namely that they change places; that no single sign ever retains priority
as a topic of the operation; that the situation in which one sign functions as
the interpretant of another is more than provisional: it is subject to change
without notice, and in the ceaselessly rotating momentum with which we have
to do here our two signs occupy each other's positions in a bewildering and
wellnigh permanent exchange. This is something like Benjaminian 'distraction'
raised to a new and historically original power: indeed, I am tempted to suggest
that the formulation gives us at least one apt characterisation of some properly
postmodernist temporality, whose consequences now remain to be drawn.

For we have not yet sufficiently described the nature of the process whereby,
even allowing for the perpetual displacements we have insisted on, one such
element − or sign, or logo − somehow 'comments' on the other, or serves
as its 'interpretant'. The content of that process, however, was already implicit

in the account of the logo itself, which was described as the signal or shorthand for a certain kind of narrative. The microscopic atomic or isotopic exchange under study here can therefore be nothing less than the capture of one narrative signal by another, the rewriting of one form of narrativisation in terms of another, momentarily more powerful one, the ceaseless renarrativisation of already existent narrative elements by each other. Thus, to begin with the most obvious examples, there does not seem much doubt that images like the fashion model or mannequin sequences are strongly and crudely rewritten when they intersect with the force field of the SF movie and its various logos (visual, musical, verbal), at such moments, the familiar human world of advertising and fashion becomes 'estranged' (a concept to which we will return) and the contemporary department store becomes as peculiar and as chilling as any of the institutions of an alien society on a distant planet. In much the same way, something happens to the photograph of the recumbent woman subject when it is surcharged with the profile of sheet lightning: *sub specie aeternitatis*, perhaps? culture versus nature? At any event the two signs cannot fail to enter into a relationship with each other in which the generic signals of one begin to predominate (it is, for example, somewhat more difficult to imagine how the image of the woman under hypnosis could begin to draw the lightning stroke into its thematic orbit). Finally, it seems evident that as the image of the mice and the associated texts of behaviourist experiments and psychological and vocational counselling intersect, the combination yields predictable messages about the hidden programming and conditioning mechanisms of bureaucratic society. Yet these three forms of influence or renarrativisation – the generic estrangement, the opposition of nature and culture, the pop-psychological or 'existential' culture critique – are only a few of the provisional effects in a much more complex repertoire of interactions which it would be tedious, if not impossible, to attempt to tabulate (others might, however, include the high and low cultural opposition described earlier; and even the more diachronic alternation between the shabby and 'natural' directly filmed street scenes and the flow of stereotypical media materials into which they are inserted).

Questions of priority or unequal influence can now be raised in a new way, which need not be limited to the evidently central matter of the relative priority of sound and image. The psychologists distinguish between auditory and visual forms of recognition: the former being apparently more instantaneous and working by means of fully formed auditory or musical *Gestalts*; while the latter is subject to an incremental exploration which may in fact never crystallise into something appropriately 'recognisable'. We recognise a tune all at once, in other words; while flying saucers which ought to allow us to identify the generic class of a film clip may remain the object of some vague geometric gaze which never bothers to slot them into their obvious cultural and connotational position. In that case, it is clear how auditory logos would tend to dominate and to rewrite visual ones, rather than the other way round (one would have liked to imagine some reciprocal 'estrangement' of the SF music by the photographs of mannequins, for example, in which the former is turned back into late-twentieth century cultural junk of the same substance as these last).

Above and beyond this simplest case of the relative influence of signs from distinct senses and distinct media, there persists the more general problem of the relative weight of the various generic sytems themselves in our culture: is SF *a priori* more powerful than the genre we call advertising, or the discourse that offers images of bureaucratic society (the rat race, the office, the routine), or the computer print-out, or that unnamed 'genre' of visuals we have called *op art* effects (which probably connote a good deal more than the new technology of graphics)? Godard's work seems to me to turn on this question or at least to pose it explicitly in various local ways; some political video art − such as that of Martha Rosler − also plays with these unequal influences of cultural languages to make its effects and to problematise familiar cultural priorities. The video text under consideration here, however, does not allow us to formulate such issues as problems, since its very formal logic − what we have called the ceaselessly rotating momentum of its provisional constellations of signs − depends on effacing them: a proposition and a hypothesis that will lead us on into those matters of interpretation and aesthetic value which we have postponed until this point.

The interpretive question − 'what is the text or work *about*?' − generally encourages a thematic answer, as indeed in the obliging title of the present tape, *AlienNATION*. There it is and now we know: the alienation of a whole nation, or perhaps, a new kind of nation organised around alienation itself. The concept of alienation had rigour when specifically used to articulate the various concrete privations of working-class life (as in Marx's Early Manuscripts); and it also had a specific function when at a specific historical moment (the Khrushchev opening) radicals in the East (Poland, Yugoslavia) and the West (Sartre) believed it could inaugurate a new tradition in Marxist thinking and practice. It surely does not amount to much, however, as a general designation for (bourgeois) spiritual malaise: but this is not the reason for the discontent one feels when, in the midst of splendid postmodernist performances like Laurie Anderson's USA, the repetition of the word 'alienation' (as it were, whispered in passing to the public) made it difficult to avoid the conclusion that this was indeed what that also was supposed to be 'about'. Two virtually identical responses then follow: so that's what it was supposed to mean; so that's all it was supposed to mean. The problem is twofold: 'alienation' is first of all, not merely a *modernist* concept but also a modernist *experience* (something I cannot argue further here, except to say that 'psychic fragmentation' is a better word for what ails us today, if we need a word for it). But it is the problem's second ramification which is the decisive one: whatever such a meaning and its adequacy (qua meaning), one has the deeper feeling that 'texts' like *USA* or *AlienNATION* ought not to have any 'meaning' at all, in that thematic sense. This is something everyone is free to verify, by self-observation and a little closer attention to precisely those moments in which we briefly feel that disillusionment I have described experiencing at the thematically explicit moments in *USA*. In effect, the points at which one can feel something similar during the Rankus-Manning-Latham videotape have already been enumerated in another context: they are very precisely those points at which the intersection of sign and interpretant seems to produce a fleeting message: high versus low culture; in the modern world we're all programmed like laboratory mice; nature versus culture; and so forth. The wisdom of the vernacular tells us that these 'themes' are corny, as corny as 'alienation' itself (but not old-fashioned enough to be camp). Yet it would be a mistake to simplify this interesting situation and to reduce it to a question of the nature and quality, the intellectual substance, of the themes themselves: indeed, our preceding analysis has the makings of a much better explanation of such lapses.

We have tried to show, indeed, that what characterises this particular video process (or 'experimental' total flow) is a ceaseless rotation of elements such that they change place at every moment, with the result that no single element can occupy the position of 'interpretant' (or that of primary sign) for any length of time; but must be dislodged in turn in the following instant (the filmic terminology of 'frames' and 'shots' does not seem appropriate for this kind of succession), falling to the subordinate position in its turn, where it will then be 'interpreted' or narrativised by a radically different kind of logo or image-content altogether. If this is an accurate account of the process, however, then it follows logically that anything which arrests or interrupts it will be sensed as an aesthetic flaw. The thematic moments we have complained about above are then just such moments of interruption, of a kind of blockage in this process: at such points, a provisional 'narrativisation' – the provisional dominance of one sign or logo over another, which it interprets and rewrites according to its own narrative logic – quickly spreads out over the sequence like a burn spot on the film, at that point 'held' long enough to generate and emit a thematic message quite inconsistent with the textual logic of the thing itself. Such moments involve a peculiar form of reification, which we might characterise equally well as a *thematisation*: a term of Paul DeMan who used it for example to characterise the misreading of Derrida as a 'philosopher', whose 'philosophical system' was somehow 'about' writing. Thematisation is then the moment in which an element, a component, of a text is promoted to the status of official theme, at which point it becomes a candidate for that even higher honour, the work's 'meaning'. But such thematic reification is not necessarily a function of the philosophical or intellectual quality of the 'theme' itself: whatever the philosophical interest and viability of the notion of the alienation of contemporary bureaucratic life, its emergence here as a 'theme' is registered as a flaw for what was essentially formal reasons. The proposition might be argued the other way around, by identifying another possible lapse in our text as the excessive dependence on the 'estrangement-effects' of the Japanese SF film clips (repeated viewings, however, make it clear that they were not so frequent as one remembered): if so, we have here to do with a thematisation of a narrative or generic type, rather than a degradation via pop philosophy and stereotypical doxa.

We can now draw some unexpected consequences from this analysis, consequences which bear not only on the vexed question of interpretation in postmodernism, but also on another matter, that of aesthetic value, which had been provisionally tabled at the outset of this discussion. If interpretation is understood, in the thematic way, as the disengagement of a fundamental theme or 'meaning', then it seems to me clear that the postmodernist text − of which we have taken the videotape in question to be a privileged exemplar − is from that perspective defined as a structure or sign-flow which resists meaning, whose fundamental inner logic is the exclusion of the emergence of themes as such in that sense, and which therefore systematically sets out to shortcircuit traditional interpretive temptations (something Susan Sontag prophetically intuited at the very dawn of what was not yet called the postmodern age). New criteria of aesthetic value then unexpectedly emerge from this proposition: whatever a good, let alone a great, videotext might be, it will be bad or flawed whenever such interpretation proves possible, whenever the text slackly opens up just such places and areas of thematisation itself.

Thematic interpretation, however − the search for the 'meaning' of the work − is not the only conceivable hermeneutic operation to which texts, including this one, can be subjected; and I want to describe two other interpretive options before concluding. The first returns us to the question of the referent in an unexpected fashion, by way of that other set of component materials to which we have so far paid less attention than to the quoted inscribed and recorded spools of canned cultural junk which are here inter-woven: those − characterised as 'natural' materials − were the segments of directly-shot footage, which, above and beyond the lakeshore sequence, essentially fell into three groups. The urban streetcrossing, to begin with, a kind of degraded space, which − distant poor cousin in that to the astonishing concluding sequence of Antonioni's *Eclipse* − begins faintly to project the abstraction of an empty stage, a place of the Event, a bounded space in which something may happen and before which one waits in formal expectation. In *Eclipse*, of course, when the event fails to materialise and the lovers neither one appear at the rendezvous, place − now forgotten − slowly finds itself degraded back into space again, the reified space of the modern city, quantified and measurable, in which land and earth are parcelled out into so many commodities and lots for sale. Here also nothing happens; only the very sense of the possibility of something happening and of the faint emergence of the very category of the Event itself is unusual in this particular tape (the menaced events and anxieties of the SF clips are merely 'images' of events, or if you prefer, spectacle-events without any temporality of their own).

The second sequence is that of the perforated milk carton, a sequence which perpetuates and confirms the peculiar logic of the first one, since here we have in some sense the pure event itself, about which there's no point crying, the irrevocable. The finger must give up stopping the breach, the milk must pour out across the table and over the edge, with all the visual fascination of this starkly white substance. If this quite wonderful image seems to me to revert even distantly to a more properly filmic status, my own aberrant and strictly personal association of it with a famous scene in *The Manchurian Candidate* is no doubt also partially responsible.

As for the third segment, the wackiest and most pointless, I have already described the absurdity of a laboratory experiment conducted with hardware store tools on orange objects of indeterminate size, which prove to have something of the consistency of a hostess twinkie. What is scandalous and vaguely disturbing about this homemade bit of dada is its apparent lack of motivation: one tries, without any great satisfaction, to see it as Ernie Kovaks parody of the laboratory animal sequence, and in any case nothing else in the tape echoes this particular mode or zaniness of 'voice'. All three groups of images, but in particular this autopsy of a hostess twinkie, reminds one vaguely of a strand of organic material which has been woven in among an inorganic texture, like the whale blubber in Joseph Beuys's sculpture.

Nonetheless, a first approach suggested itself to me on the level of unconscious anxiety, where the hole in the milk carton – following the assassination scene in the film I've referred to, where the victim is surprised at a midnight snack in front of the open refrigerator door – is now explicitly read as a bullet hole. I have meanwhile neglected to supply another clue, namely the computer-generated 'x' that moves across the empty street crossing like the sights of a long-range rifle. It remained for an astute listener to an earlier version of this chapter to make the connection and point out the henceforth obvious and unassailable: for the American media public the combination of the two elements – milk and hostess twinkie – is too peculiar to be unmotivated. In fact, on 27 November 1978 (the year immediately before the production of this particular videotape), the San Francisco city supervisor Harvey Milk was shot to death by a former supervisor, who entered the unforgettable plea of not-guilty by reason of insanity, owing to the excessive consumption of hostess twinkies.

Here, then, at last the referent itself is disclosed: the brute fact, the historical event, the real toad in this particular imaginary garden. To track such reference down is surely to perform an act of interpretation or hermeneutic disclosure, of a very different kind than that previously discussed: if *AlienNATION* is 'about' this, then such an expression can only have a sense quite distinct from its use in the proposition that the text was 'about' alienation itself.

The problem of reference has been singularly displaced and stigmatised in the hegemony of the various poststructuralist discourses which characterises the current moment (and along with it, anything that smacks of 'reality', 'representation', 'realism' and the like − even the word 'history' has an *r* in it): only Lacan has shamelessly continued to talk about 'the Real' (defined however as an absence). The respectable philosophical solutions to the problem of an external real world independent of consciousness are all traditional ones, which means that however logically satisfying they may be (and none of them are really very satisfactory from a logical standpoint), they are not suitable candidates for participation in contemporary polemics: the hegemony of theories of textuality and textualisation means, among other things, that your entry ticket to the public sphere in which these matters are debated is an agreement, tacit or otherwise, with the basic presuppositions of a general problem-field, something traditional positions on these matters refuses in advance. My own feeling has been that historicism offers a peculiarly unexpected escape from this vicious circle or double bind.

To raise the issue, for example, of the fate of the 'referent' in contemporary culture and thought is not the same thing as to assert some older theory of reference or to repudiate all the newer theoretical problems in advance: on the contrary such problems are retained and endorsed, with the proviso that they are not only interesting problems in their own right, but also, at the same time, symptoms of a historical transformation.

In the immediate instance that concerns us here, I have argued for the presence and existence of what seems to me a palpable 'referent' − namely death and historical fact, which are ultimately not textualisable and tear through the tissues of textual elaboration, of combination and free play ('the Real,' Lacan tells us, 'is what resists symbolization absolutely'). I would want to add at once that this is no particularly triumphant philosophical victory for some putative realism or other over the various textualising world-views. For the assertion of a buried referent − as in the present example − is a two-way street whose antithetical directions might emblematically be named 'repression' and *Aufhebung* (or 'sublation'): the picture has no way of telling us whether we are looking at a rising or a setting sun. Does our discovery document the persistence and stubborn all-informing gravitational charge of reference, or on the contrary the tendencial historical process whereby reference is systematically processed, dismantled, textualised, and volatilised, leaving little more than some indigestible remnant?

However this ambiguity is handled, there remains the matter of the structural logic of the tape itself, of which this particular directly filmed 'sequence' is only a single strand among many, and a particularly minor one at that (although its properties attract a certain attention). Even if its referential value could be satisfactorily demonstrated, the logic of rotating conjunction and disjunction that has been described above clearly works to dissolve such a 'value', which cannot be tolerated any more than the emergence of individual themes. Nor is it clear how an axiological system could be developed in the name of which we might then affirm that these strange sequences are somehow better than the random and aimless 'irresponsibility' of the collages of media stereotypes.

Were one to propose some final way of 'interpreting' such a tape — an interpretation which would seek to foreground the process of production itself, rather than its putative messages, meanings or content — then some distant consonance might be invoked between the fantasies and anxieties aroused by the idea of assassination and the global system of media and reproductive technology: the structural analogy between the two seemingly unrelated spheres is secured in the collective unconscious by notions of conspiracy while the historical juncture between the two was burned into historical memory by the Kennedy assassination itself, which can no longer be separated from its media coverage. The problem posed by such interpretation in terms of autoreferentiality is not its plausibility: one would want to defend the proposition that the deepest 'subject' of all video art, and even of all postmodernism, is very precisely reproductive technology itself. The methodological difficulty lies rather in the way in which such a global 'meaning' — even of some new type and status than the older interpretive meanings we have touched on above — once again dissolves the individual text into an even more disastrous indistinction than the total-flow/individual-work antinomy evoked above: if all video-texts simply designate the process of production/reproduction, then presumably they all turn out to be 'the same' in a peculiarly unhelpful way.

I will not try to solve any of these problems, but will rather restage the approaches and perspectives of the historicism I have called for by way of a kind of myth I have found useful in characterising the nature of contemporary (postmodernist) cultural production and also in positioning its various theoretical projections.

Once upon a time — at the dawn of capitalism and middle-class society — there emerged something called the sign which seemed to entertain unproblematical relations with its referent. This initial heyday of the sign — the moment of literal or referential language or of the unproblematic claims of so-called scientific discourse — came into being because of the corrosive dissolution of older forms of magical language by a force which I will call that of reification, a force whose logic is one of ruthless separation and disjunction, of specialisation and rationalisation, of a Taylorising division of labour in all realms. Unfortunately that force — which brought traditional reference into being — continued unremittingly, being the very logic of capital itself. Thus this first moment of decoding or of realism cannot long endure; by a dialectical reversal it then itself in turn becomes the object of the corrosive force of reification, which enters the realm of language to disjoin the sign from the referent. Such a disjunction does not completely abolish the referent, or the objective world, or reality, which still continues to entertain a feeble existence on the horizon like a shrunken star or red dwarf. But its great distance from the sign now allows the latter to enter into a moment of autonomy, of a relatively free-floating Utopian existence, as over against its former objects. This autonomy of culture, this semi-autonomy of language, is the moment of modernism, and of a realm of the aesthetic which redoubles the world without being altogether of it, thereby winning a certain negative or critical power, but also a certain otherworldly futility. Yet the force of reification, which was responsible for this new moment, does not stop there either: in another stage, heightened, a kind of reversal of quantity into quality, reification penetrates the sign itself, and disjoins the signifier from the signified. Now reference and reality disappear altogether, and even meaning – the signified – is problematised: instead we are left with that pure and random play of signifiers which we call postmodernism, and which no longer produces monumental works of the modernist type, but ceaselessly reshuffles the fragments of preexistent texts, the building blocks of older cultural and social production, in some new and heightened bricolage: metabooks which cannibalise other books, metatexts which collate bits of other texts.

Such is the logic of postmodernism in general which I have tried to illustrate in its strongest and most original and authentic form in the new art of experimental video.

Notes

1   Readers of collections like E. Ann Kaplan, *Regarding Television*, American Film Institute Monograph No. 2, Maryland, 1983 and John Hanhardt, *Video Culture: A Critical Investigation*, NY, 1986 may find such assertions astonishing. A frequent theme of these articles remains, however, the absence, tardiness, repression, or impossibility of video theory proper.

2   'Time, Work-discipline, and Industrial Capitalism', *Past and Present*, No. 38, 1967.

3   This is a point I have tried to argue more generally about the relationship between the study of 'high literature' (or rather, high modernism) and that of mass culture, in 'Reification and Utopia in Mass Culture', *Social Text* no. 1, 1977, (reprinted in *The Politics of the Simulacrum*, London, forthcoming).

4   I mean here essentially the *good* anonymity of handicraft work of the medieval kind, as opposed to the supreme demiurgic subjectivity or 'genius' of the modern Master.

New courses in the linguistics of writing

1 The intellectual context

The frame of reference of this volume reflects a theory-revolution in the humanities which took place in the 1960s and 1970s. From the point of view of literary study in particular, though, there is a surprising thing about this revolution: that the way in which it has been carried through into new forms of instruction seems to have been far more as courses about the theoretical developments themselves than as new modes of study implied by them.

If this is true, then it is also disappointing, especially with respect to education in the medium of English. During the period in which these theoretical developments have taken place, English has consolidated its role as principal second-language in the world: it exists in many places as a 'national' and native language; elsewhere, it exists as an 'official' language, 'associate' language or second language; everywhere, it exists as a foreign language. This is not merely a fact about scale of use: it of course affects the range of varieties in which English exists; and growing out of very different kinds of social experience, these changing varieties have given rise to new forms of literary and cultural expression.[1] At the same time, significant changes have taken place in education in Britain. In particular, there has been a major reduction in the teaching of formal, grammatical analysis of language, and also major alterations in the way history and religion are taught. Combined with changes in the social and ethnic composition of the population, these educational shifts problematise any assumption made in teaching that students are already familiar with a system of terms and concepts for analysing language, or with a shared field of cultural or historical reference. A theoretical revolution in the study of language and literature which doesn't have a good deal to say about changes of this sort, by way of concrete response and proposal, is simply out of touch with the societies and cultures it claims to be talking about.

In this chapter, we discuss the question of developing new kinds of curriculum for language and literary studies in the light of these changing circumstances. As a way into doing this, we describe one limited initiative currently in progress, the postgraduate courses organised at the University of Strathclyde by the Programme in Literary Linguistics.

The chapter is divided into three sections. In Section One, we explore the intellectual context for new courses. Why should there be new courses at all? How do courses in the Programme in Literary Linguistics relate to existing disciplines concerned with related, overlapping concerns: linguistics, literary studies, and established forms of 'stylistics'? In Section Two, we focus on four distinctive features of the Programme. Then, in Section Three, mindful that our initiatives have been limited in scope by time and resources, we speculate about possibilities for more substantial developments on the lines we are following.

1.1 Why study literature at all?

Studying literature involves a commitment to analysing history and forms of culture. Analysing a culture of which you are yourself a part is one way of intervening in that culture, helping it stay the same or change. In literary study, our interventions in the field of culture are achieved by reading and commenting on a particular corpus of works which we characterise as 'literary'. Why this particular corpus? The answer usually is: that works in such a corpus offer special insights into the nature and possibilities of human expression.

But what does it mean: 'offering special insights into the nature and possibilities of human expression'? We might isolate two main, opposing views. On view treats literary texts as *objects* which are themselves of value; the other treats literary texts as *tools* by which to study what value is.

1.1.1 Familiarisation: the 'touchstones' argument
The first view we often associate with Matthew Arnold. Literary study, in this view, serves the classical-humanist purpose of supporting forms of cultural hegemony: it draws attention to exemplary traditions of excellence through cultural criticism and acts of 'revaluation'. This approach reached its first real efflorescence in Arnold's view of 'touchstones', linked to his belief that the study of literature could revitalise a society embattled by scientific critiques of religion and by the rise of early forms of 'mass' culture. Interestingly, the ascendency of this view occurred at virtually the same time as the introduction of compulsory education in Britain, and so coincides with a debate among reformers about the virtues and problems associated with widespread literacy. After the First World War, the view of literature as a kind of secular religion enjoyed wider currency. In fact, it was one major force in establishing – through a complicated series of developments and conflicts – the recognisable paradigm of what is now often simply called 'traditional' literary study.[2]

In this paradigm, the form of 'literacy' which results from literary study often comes to mean simply being well-versed in an acknowledged canon of works, rather than having skills which make possible informed and independent choices about what we wish to read and value. It is not un-reasonable, therefore, to think of this way of teaching literature as principally a 'familiarising' process: it uses literature to encourage insights into special qualities of human expression by acquainting students with a body of what are decreed to be important cultural documents or texts.

1.1.2 *Defamiliarisation: the 'cultural literacy' argument*
In common with much recent work, on the other hand, we adopt the other main way of studying human expression through literature. This approach views studying literature not as a way of learning a culture, but as a tool for looking at one: you find out things about the world by investigating the established forms, but also the limits, of the ways in which things are represented.[3] As such, this approach is one component of a kind of education for cultural literacy which is often 'defamiliarising': analysing literary works involves suspending present forms of identification in or with a society, in order to reflect critically on what are sometimes called the 'affiliations' of texts: the connections between them and other aspects of the social world.

But why give any special emphasis to literature in this view, rather than studying all social discourses equally? One answer is that the works tradition-ally referred to as 'literature' serve to establish and maintain many of the major categories by means of which we represent to ourselves our own society and history. These major categories include ideas of ethics, identity, pleasure, politics, imagination, and so on.

1.2 *Three interlocking precedents*

So far, this all sounds like a familiar argument from recent literary theory. So let us begin by describing the differences between our academic focus and three established directions in considering language and interpretation. Firstly, we will look at two traditionally opposed approaches to studying language: the study of language in linguistics (1.2.1), and the study of language in literary criticism (1.2.2). Then we will comment on one attempt at fusion between them, stylistics (1.2.3).

1.2.1 *Linguistics: idealisation* vs *the actuality of texts*
Perhaps the contrast between theoretical linguistics and the study of literature can be shown most clearly by considering generative linguistics.

Generative linguistics describes regularities in language principally in order to move on to investigating something else: the working of the language faculty. In order to find out things about the language faculty, linguists make use of the data of introspection, or intuitions which are judgements about *possibility* within a language. To explore judgements about well-formedness, linguists employ tests such as deletion, movement, and replacement. One strength of this approach is its explicitness: tests enable you to find out when your theories don't work, and encourage you to try others. Another strength of generative linguistics is what might be called its modularity: this form of investigation does not assume that language is a unified object, for which a monolithic mode of study is appropriate and over which theoretical linguistics has a monopoly; it allows that its own clearly specified research aims may well prove of marginal relevance to people concerned with other areas of enquiry which are nevertheless still about 'language'.[4]

This simple sketch of a precisely delineated linguistic research programme draws attention to important contrasts with the study of language in literary criticism. Here, the data are still intuitions, but now they are intuitions about one particular, fixed arrangement of words or sounds. If devised and applied, tests such as replacement, movement, and deletion of course still produce changing effects, but generally in complex ways that are not amenable to clear-cut decisions. Part of the reason for this is that many factors have to be taken into account in interpreting the words or sounds of literature other than operations of the language faculty itself.

The case for keeping literary studies separate from linguistics (or at least from generative linguistics) is therefore this. Firstly, we take it as established that there are reasons, to do with education for cultural literacy, for wanting to interpret or construe representations of the human and social world. Then, since other factors than the language faculty are involved in this, it follows that interpreting representations of the social world means looking at language in context. This fact in itself does not rule out a linguistic approach. Linguistics has developed notions such as 'context of utterance' to explore the principles governing use of contextual information in language use and understanding. Nevertheless, it is only when specific meanings and assumptions are filled into any model of situation and background knowledge that interpretation takes place. We argue that it is not part of linguistics to fill in specific meanings and assumptions of this kind. What preserves the distinctiveness of literary criticism, with respect to linguistics, is the fact that it *does* have a defining concern with questions of specific context, emotional responses, and value in one already socially-established body of works and genres, and carries out on this corpus a series of case studies in ways of reading.

1.2.2 *Literary criticism: the innocence of empathy*
Literary criticism has always mediated authors and their work for an audience. Its great strength is precisely the fact that it is partisan: it shows great energy in advocating little-known, marginal and experimental works, often establishing for these works new readerships and currency. The literary critic projects himself or herself, as a kind of apostle, into the vision of a writer, and offers exegesis. As such, the importance of literary criticism lies precisely in its power of empathy, and its willingness to take up unequivocal positions on questions of what it is important or valuable in a society to say and how these things might optimally be said.

Literary criticism's scrutiny of values is often made without any accompanying systematic, or even explicit, scrutiny of its own methods or assumptions, or analytic leverage on pleasure itself, however. What makes literary criticism interesting, even so, is that there are two things left over when a linguistic analysis has accounted for all the determinants of a text: value and pleasure. But in studying a text, it is not legitimate to omit the stage of investigating determinants and move straight into pleasure and value: it is clear that study of the meanings and social significance of forms of representation needs to be reflexive with respect to its own conditions of interpretation and judgement.

Since the study of stylistics has been one major attempt to satisfy this demand, it is appropriate that we now consider stylistics directly.

1.2.3 *Stylistics*

In the 1960s, courses in stylistics appeared to offer a solid, easily-learnable linguistic basis for the kind of close reading literary criticism had long demanded: stylistics would enable us to link response with features of the text which trigger that response. In seeking to do so, it seemed to promise a solid foundation for the aspiration towards detailed analysis of much New Criticism.

Consolidation of the field, however, led to serious disputes. Two central questions in particular were exposed: (i) can there exist 'automatic' discovery procedures for studying literary texts? (ii) if such procedures exist, do they lead to 'objectivity' in interpretation? Stylistics, in effect, says texts are machines. 'Study the machine and you will understand the effect on a reader'. The problem is: sometimes you can study the machine in great detail and yet learn little that is interesting about the machine's function or significance to you. This is because so far we do not have satisfactory ways of combining together things we notice about the formal structures of a text, the various functional significances we attribute to those patterns, and the expectations or knowledge we bring to the text to begin with.

These difficulties have prompted, from within modern literary theory, a range of dismissive criticisms of the processes by which stylistics seeks out interpretations; and these have lent support to post-structuralist ideas that language will always overrun any determinate interpretation you put on it.[5] Without doubt, there is much in the post-structuralist and deconstructionist critique, according to which stylistics is simply arbitrary judgement and circularity of argument masquerading as science. But this cannot be the whole story. Acts of interpretation involving complex inferencing processes, and often accomplished with great speed, frequently lead to degrees of interpretative consensus that challenge the emerging literary-theoretical orthodoxy that language never means what you think it means. Patterns of interpretative consensus, we would suggest, indicate a need for broad, empirical studies of reception, and for research on the contribution made by the innate to interpretative acts.

Designing new courses in the linguistics of writing involves recognising theoretical difficulties inherent in the project of stylistics, and yet also acknowledging that there always exist both cognitive and social constraints on how utterances and texts are interpreted. To develop new courses on this basis, it is necessary to make two major innovations:

(i) Courses need to include a well-integrated pragmatic and cognitive dimension, relating linguistic forms to interactional and contextual factors, including background assumptions which in practice largely guide interpretation. (It is largely the variability of such background assumptions which undercuts older, textually deterministic aspirations towards dispassionate, 'objective' interpretation.)

(ii) Courses need to investigate the consensual, intersubjective nature of interpretation, by relating background ideas articulated in interpretation to socially and historically specific bodies of knowledge: to ideology and social semiotic.

In the next section, we discuss one attempt to make innovations along these lines.

2 Is there anything new about the Programme in Literary Linguistics?

We now present the instructional component of the Programme in Literary Linguistics, and in particular the thinking behind the one-year postgraduate course we offer. We cannot be sure to what extent our courses are paralleled by work in other institutions, but, in planning our curriculum, we do have a very specific debt to colleagues working in the Department of Linguistics and Modern English Language at the University of Lancaster.

Courses in the Programme in Literary Linguistics pursue four main aims:

1. they explore cross-connections between, rather than merely juxtapose, issues in language, culture and society;
2. taken together, they compare and relate literary discourse with non-literary and contemporary media discourse;
3. they develop skills in analysis and problem-solving;
4. they concern themselves explicitly with matters of curriculum development and teaching method.

We will now discuss each of these aims, trying to show how we have so far dealt with it in practice.

2.1 Connecting language, society and history

To connect the study of literature with social and historical issues, it is of course possible to incorporate within a curriculum courses on social history, ethics, or politics, alongside traditional modules such as genre, period or author studies. Many traditional courses have in fact done this. The weakness of such courses, though, is their failure to investigate the idea of 'connection' itself. Simple adjacency between units in a course misses the point that historical information becomes interesting for literary study only when it enables some specific interpretative case to be made or contested.

It is certainly possible to devise courses which study issues of causality and influence more closely than most traditional courses have done. Courses which bring together analytic skills and historical knowledge can mobilise in new ways the various elements needed to argue through a literary case that is sensitive both to the linguistic detail of a text and to the various contextual determinants of different ways of reading it.

One course we have developed along these lines is called 'Appeals to Language'. In it we try to solve the problem of interconnection by bringing together materials from different disciplines in a series of studies of exemplary or paradigmatic historical 'moments', rather than by trying to be exhaustive or comprehensive. Each topic is a debate involving conflicting views on an aspect of language and culture. Examples might be: the role of dictionaries in defining words; valuing literature as a kind of language charged with special or unusual properties; or, the different kinds of connotation and prestige of accents. Topics are then devised by choosing a historical moment where the issue is clearly at stake in a particular work or form of expression. Studying the 'Preface' to Samuel Johnson's *Dictionary*, for example, involves thinking through issues of lexicography in relation to questions of language change, language planning and national identity; studying the 'Preface' to *Lyrical Ballads* involves considering questions of poetic diction in relation both to archaism and dialect, and to notions of standard language; comparing the use of American accents and British working-class accents in British rock music involves considering a cultural form in relation to issues of social identification. Topics can be chosen from virtually any field, and need not involve any great technicality or difficulty.

In practice, three things are especially important about courses of this kind. The first is that students should see that many different kinds of perception and ideas need to be mobilised in order to throw light on problems of language and literary interpretation. This is because, as we have said above, many factors other than the language faculty affect interpretation, including historical circumstances and also the present interests, purpose and knowledge of the analyst. The second is that repercussions on the present of the debate being analysed should be explored, and possible lessons discussed. (Language planning, for example, is at this moment a crucial and volatile issue in many countries of the world.) Finally, there should be seen to be no final, correct 'answers': since we do not have real solutions for most issues about language and interpretation, students should come to value their own efforts to work through issues — to the extent that they combine material in coherent and plausible arguments — not simply as educational simulation, but as the development of views with consequences for their own long-term social identities.

2.2 *Comparing literary, non-literary and media discourse*

In common with many modern courses in stylistics and discourse analysis, we attempt to explore implications of the inadequacy of simple oppositions between literature and non-literature. The twentieth century particularly has shown the interdependence between ideas of a literary language and other forms of non-literary language. Acknowledgement of such interdependence has been brought about by two forces in particular:

(i)   the extensive use of collage and quotation from a wide range of linguistic varieties, including media forms, in much modernist writing;
(ii) the increasing influence of literary works written in native dialects of English and varieties of English used as a second language, as in India, Africa and many other parts of the world.

The break-up of a previously rather homogeneous literary discourse which these innovations indicate is often recognised in theoretical studies. But does it have implications for teaching?

If you accept fully the close interconnectedness of literary and non-literary discourse, it seems you must also be committed, as regards skills-development, not to courses teaching specific analytic techniques for literary study (so-called 'literary stylistics'), but 'stylistics' courses in a more general sense: courses in linguistic analysis providing terms, concepts and methods appropriate for commenting on *either* literary *or* non-literary texts: that is, stylistics for discourse and cultural studies. As regards coverage, since the aim is to enable students to read for themselves, the precise range of texts looked at is not particularly important, except that it should be as wide as possible in terms of history, medium, genre, and regional and class variation.

But if we combine literary and non-literary together in our teaching corpus, does the literary still have any special status at all? We think that there are four main ways of investigating this, which should be incorporated in courses in the linguistics of writing:

---

1. *'Comparison'*
Courses include tasks involving comparison between treatments of the same subject in different idioms (i.e. comparison as part of a larger study of register or discourse-type). In this kind of contrastive exercise, literature is treated as simply one among a range of 'equal' discourse varieties.

2. *'Quotation'*
Courses investigate literature's frequent allusions to, and embedding or citation of, non-literary modes of discourse (e.g. in modernist collage; as representations of conversation in literary dialogue). These comparisons make it possible for

students to explore the question of whether a separate category of 'literary' discourse exists or not. If so, what does it consist of; if not, why not?

3. *'Deviancy'*

Courses study forms of 'deviancy' in discourse, such as slips of the tongue, idiosyncratic new coinages, metaphors breaking selection restrictions, etc. Study of these ways of stretching the boundaries of language leads into assessment of the different significances which have been ascribed to such 'deviations': notions such as pathology, creativity, and pathological creativity.

4. *'Medium'*

Courses compare written texts with media texts from radio, film, television. One thing which is quickly established here is that students who learn analytic skills in conventional 'literature' courses do not have adequate resources for analysing medium-specific features of the language of media texts (such as voice quality, accent and especially intonation), knowledge of which is nevertheless indispensable for media literacy. Courses of the kind we are proposing make it possible to consider ideas such as 'creativity' or 'culture' in the context of their concrete forms of realisation: in specific forms, technologies and institutions.

What enables these four approaches to serve as investigations of the status of the literary, rather than being simply exercises in comparative discourse analysis, is the injection into them of a concern with history. As regards forms, this means considering when they start, how they develop, and how they change. As regards readers' expectations, it means investigating what we expect to find in a particular idiom, and how this affects the kind of significance we attach to things. Dealing with questions of this sort necessitates considering questions of value, and the social connotations and relative prestige of different kinds of discourse. We would claim that what distinguishes literature from non-literature is not any particular property of the texts themselves, but that they are contextualised differently.

2.3 *Developing analytic skills*

In most literature courses, what you get is two principal forms of contact: lectures (conforming to the idea of imparting knowledge and opinion), and seminars (involving more learner-centred, 'experiential' learning, through relatively unstructured discussion). Very frequently, there is little practical instruction directed towards developing interpretative skills, except by example (though courses in stylistics represent one major exception to this tendency).

But why should close reading skills be developed through open discussion in this way, rather than through more structured investigation or analysis? Historically, the answer is that, since the elements of a literary work have often been thought to be interwoven in a complex, balanced whole, the aim of a literature class should be to contemplate, describe and assess that form as it is, rather than to take it apart or experiment with it: analytic activity violates the text's integrity and effect as a totality. Most new methods for literary study, by contrast, share the aim of replacing contemplation with an arguably more effective form of learning: investigative *activity*.

This idea is hardly specific to new forms of literary study. In a prevailing educational philosophy in Western countries of 'progressivism' or 'learner-centredness', arguments have been made across the full academic spectrum for reforming modes of instruction which impart knowledge through processes of 'transmission' rather than engaging students in experiences of learning through exploration. Whatever the limitations of this 'active' approach in its strong forms, there is undoubtedly value in the general effort to develop skills of hypothesis-formation, speculation and experiment, rather than promoting book-learning and academic discipleship.

It is only recently that work of this type has begun to be done in the literary field itself. But there are two adjacent subject-areas literary study can look to for established models. Firstly, in ELT, communicative approaches have given considerable attention to activities involving groupwork, simulation, and role-play, basing these approaches substantially on research in second-language acquisition. Secondly, in linguistics, analytic techniques and testing for relevant counter-examples are routinely deployed by students to investigate all kinds of speculative theoretical claims of their own. Developed and modified in accordance with the aims described above, activities in this kind are a necessary, central component of the kinds of literature course we are developing.[6]

It is easy to devise, in the form of worksheets, a wide range of activities to enrich lectures and discussion with experimental work. Such activities can be built on a number of different principles:

1. *'Comparison' activities*
Contrast in order to focus observations and comments (e.g. compare texts about same subject in different registers; compare texts in the same genre but from different periods, etc.)

2. *'Replacement' activities*
Alter some aspect of text to monitor changing effect (e.g. substitute new words into text, like ones they replace in some respects, different in others; monitor and discuss effects produced)

3. *'Ordering' activities*
Test concepts of structure, cohesion and coherence (e.g. put sentences of a jumbled paragraph back in order; rearrange words in a scrambled sentence; reorder events or actions separately listed from the narrative of a novel, etc.)

4. *'Completion' activities: cloze procedure*
Remove elements from text to test predictive power of cues given by pattern of surrounding words which remain (e.g. delete words from text and invite participants to insert words on the basis of information gathered from context of utterance)

5. *'Prediction' activities*
Explore reading hypotheses by anticipating aspects of text during reading process (e.g. present opening of a novel or short story sentence by sentence, and collect and test out predictions about its subsequent development, etc.)

6. *'Taxonomy' activities*
Identify and catalogue features (e.g. label utterances of a dramatic text according to speech act or function, then classify the functions listed, etc.)

7. *'General problem-solving' activities*
Devise questions in which activity is guided by the knowledge that specific or determinate answers exist (e.g. identify point of transition from original author to modern author in an unfinished work later completed by someone else; identify lines of a poem previously isolated by a critic as embodying some specific property or quality, working simply from the critic's description, then check against the original selection and discuss)

8. *'Continuation' activities*
Write extension to piece of text (e.g. write four more lines to 'Kubla Khan', then analyse stylistic parameters guiding composition; finish a short story from an opening paragraph, etc.)

9. *'Composition' activities*
Rework text in another genre or idiom (e.g. write a newspaper report of an event described in a novel; draw a diagram to represent interrelationships between characters: wife/husband, victim/murderer, etc.)

Three things are important about such activities.[7] In the first place, there should be clear guidelines about what to do, since many literature students complain that they would be far more effective academically if they were clear about what exactly is expected of them. Secondly, activities should be designed around specific, achievable goals, so it is clear when they are finished. Thirdly, whilst the motivating effect of activity-work of this kind needs to be harnessed to instruction in established analytic skills and knowledge, students also need to become used to developing their own ideas, by asking their own questions.

2.4 *Teachers*

Many of the students who join our one-year course either already are, or go on to be, teachers in English Studies at tertiary level. For this reason, it would be inappropriate not to include in the course some explicit consideration of questions of syllabus design and teaching methodology.

We do two things. In the first place, we present a historical survey, comparing various approaches to English studies, in traditional literary study, in stylistics, and in linguistics. Secondly, we experiment with syllabus and teaching methods. In our present course, this means two kinds of activity: the design of a hypothetical literature programme, by working through a worksheet of choices and constraints; and the planning, implementation and discussion of a session of teaching within an undergraduate class in the department.

Such activities are especially necessary for overseas students. This is because the discipline of English Literature has been exported to many countries around the world where neither the linguistic nor the cultural context for the subject resemble that in Britain or the United States: as a result, overseas postgraduate students who go on to become teachers need to be able to improvise, as they design new courses and modify old ones to suit local educational needs. Activities simulating and exploring syllabus design and possible teaching methods are a necessary preparation for this challenge.

3. Lines of future development

The Programme in Literary Linguistics is a recently established unit, and its identity is only gradually emerging. Many of the proposals we are making are crude, in their present form; and we are only beginning to get clear, for ourselves, the unit's more longterm research aims. It seems appropriate, therefore, to end by describing very briefly each of three principal areas in which we propose to undertake further work. We understand research in each of these areas to mean both exploration of theoretical problems and the development of course materials including workbooks, problem-sets and groupwork activities. The three areas are, firstly, historical stylistics (3.1); secondly, study of the language of modern communications media (3.2); thirdly, exploration of cognitive approaches to interpretation (3.3).

3.1 *Historical stylistics*

The older a text is, the more difficult it is to understand. To deal with this difficulty, we need detailed knowledge of the history of the language, and of social, intellectual and political history. Such knowledge allows reading to engage with the temporality of forms of writing, rather than being stuck in a historical vacuum. This is an approach unlike that of New Criticism or Deconstruction.

Much of the knowledge we need already exists, in dictionaries, in histories of the language, in historical linguistics, and in the editorial work of textual criticism. Much of what remains to be done is the arrangement of this material in ways which illuminate present dilemmas of historical interpretation.

It is also the case, though, that there are many problems connected with reading old texts about which we know relatively little. An example of this would be the ostensibly erratic use of do-support in Early Modern English texts, shown in a recent article to be systematic and related to discourse prominence.[8] Problems exist especially when we consider larger patterns in discourse. Consider what happens when you think historically of the concept of register: how do the styles chosen in any piece of writing relate to the range of sociolinguistic options available to the writer at the time of composition? To use the example of *Lyrical Ballads* again, is Wordsworth's use of 'thou' a dialect form or a poetic archaism? Or again, consider the problem of coherence which arises when continuity in the text is achieved only through bridging inferences. Inferences of this kind make use of assumptions about the world; so we need to know about ideas about the world current when the text was produced if we are to reconstruct the bridging inferences which could have been brought to it then, and so reconstruct its particular, historically conditioned form of coherence.

Historical study of the sort we are describing reconstructs a moment of history. Such reconstruction then gives us a back-bearing from which to chart present-day assumptions which give the text its current forms of relevance and interest: we find out, for example, something of what it can mean to read Shakespeare now by looking at what it has meant to read Shakespeare at various moments in the past.

3.2 *The language of modern communications media*

Television, film, radio and other forms of discourse involving sound, or combinations of sound and image, are arguably the most important media or 'communicative forms' of our time. Nevertheless, we do not at present have an adequate terminology in which to describe the specialised modes of discourse these media use.

Our particular interest is in giving special attention to sounds, and the relationship between sounds and images, rather than (as in much media theory of the 1970s) to the rhetoric of images alone. In this perspective, it is clear that the distinction between 'writing' and 'speech' is too crude to capture the complex array of modes of discourse routinely used in radio, film and television. We therefore need a fresh taxonomy of discourse-types in these media. Given that these discourse-types depend on enabling conditions provided by machines, as much as on editorial choices, such a typology has to be worked out in terms of the relation between media forms and the technologies of their production. (Is speech scripted, amplified, autocued, edited? Can you play it back?) Such a typology also has to be constructed in relation to local, linguistic choices which are consistently made (allowing us instantly to identify new, specialised genres such as DJ talk, different kinds of sports commentary, documentary voice-over, etc.).

Technological conditions and linguistic choices both define forms of media discourse. But there are arguably more important questions, to do with how these discourse-types interact with larger patterns of communication and the interchange of ideas and knowledge in society. Forms are governed, at another level, by institutional policies based on ideas of interest, culture and public service. To address questions of this kind, linguistic 'communications' research needs to engage with broader social issues such as 'balance', 'censorship', and 'bias'. Together, these are instantiations of the forms of power in media, and problematise the social transition which is currently taking place in most countries from established 'literate' societies into what have been described as new cultures of 'secondary orality'.[9]

3.3 *Literature and cognitive science*

Finally, we pick up once more the question of mind and language in literary study. For modern literary criticism, the influence of psychology has been crucial, from I.A. Richards's *Principles of literary criticism* to Roman Jakobson's 'Two aspects of language and two types of aphasic disturbances'. The *Style in Language* conference itself was sponsored by a research committee on 'Linguistics and Psychology', though, looking back, it is interesting how confused the psychologist George Miller claims to be in his closing statement, compared with everyone else.[10]

As things have developed, much of the attention to mental processes in literary study has been concerned with the Unconscious rather than with routine cognitive operations; and undoubtedly, commentary on unconscious processes is important. Interpretations based on them, however, are always speculative, for two reasons. First, only psychoanalytic experience can provide them with a validating procedure; second, texts do not invite the same experimental process of dynamic interaction as patients do. Despite such difficulties, though, what remains valuable about work based in psychoanalytic concepts and procedures is that it recognises a layer of motivation in discourse and creativity which otherwise eludes both linguistics and literary criticism altogether. On the other hand, attention to psychical processes should not distract attention from other cognitive processes continuously at work in communication, such as kinds of inference.

This is a good time to renew interest in the broader domain of cognition. What seems possible is fruitful convergence between literary theories of reading and cognitive theories of communication and language-processing.

To explain how such a convergence is possible, it is necessary to return for a moment to established notions of what happens when we read literature. Jonathan Culler's idea of 'literary competence' remains perhaps the most explicit model of this activity developed in recent years.[11] But what damaged the idea of a specialised literary competence was its neglect of the socialising processes through which conventional responses to kinds of discourse are established: for literature, as Culler himself acknowledged, these are principally familiarity with literary traditions, and education in forms of conventional 'literary' interpretation. Instead of taking up the implications of this social basis for the specialised reading processes involved in reading literature, though, Culler emphasised in his work of that period static, individual possession of 'competence' – as if there was a 'literature faculty' in the brain. In this respect, Culler appeared to many people to be adopting a 'cognitive' position at the expense of being 'social'. Counterbalancing emphasis has since been given, valuably, to varied readerships and to the active process of *making* readings, especially to such notions as 'interpretative communities', or groups likely to respond to particular works or discourses in a similar way.

'Social' and 'cognitive', however, are of course complementary terms in matters of interpretation.[12] What thinking entails, and what being a bearer of ideology must also involve, is that we carry ideas in our minds, to be activated and put to work in rule-governed, though widely-varying, inferential processes. The cultural dimension of these processes is encyclopedic information about the world: in socialisation, this information is stored in memory, and continually revised and updated, as a set of propositions which form one part of the input to inferential activity. The cognitive dimension is the set of innate inferencing rules: these govern patterns of derivation from the propositions or assumptions carried in an utterance itself, when these assumptions are combined with whatever background assumptions are accessed into working-memory in order to contextualise it. To interpret something, you mobilise the cultural propositions with the utterance through the inferencing rules. The output is ideological.

If we are to avoid forcing ourselves to choose between 'cognitive' and 'social'; new accounts of inferencing urgently need to be developed. In such accounts, particular attention needs to be given to how socially-originating assumptions are stored, ranked and selected in any given situation, since only work on interpretation of this kind can show how thoughts are culturally determined even though the basic processes of thought are innate.

As a direction for research, this project is not quite as fanciful as it might seem. The development of new approaches on these lines is in prospect, following recent developments in pragmatics and cognitive psychology. New theories of interpretative processes, perhaps especially Dan Sperber's work on symbolism and the Sperber and Wilson theory of Relevance, promise to anchor reader-response criticism in a more precise, general account of inferential communication.[13] It may be some time before approaches on these lines offer direct applications to training in ways of reading. But we would like to close by suggesting that this line of further study provides a powerful stimulus to developments in the linguistics of writing into the 1990s.

Notes

1 For wide-ranging discussion of these issues, see Randolph Quirk & H.G. Widdowson (eds), *English in the World*, Cambridge, 1985.

2 Arnold's clearest statements of this view come in 'The Study of Poetry', 1880. For detailed discussion of the emergence in Britain of English Literature as an academic subject, see Francis Mulhern, *The Moment of Scrutiny*, London, 1979, especially chapter 1.

3 'Defamiliarising' approaches to literary and cultural study exist mainly in forms of critical discourse analysis, and have developed largely from structuralist cultural analyses, perhaps especially from Roland Barthes's *Mythologies* (1957), translated by Annette Lavers, New York, 1972. The term 'defamiliarisation' itself comes from Russian Formalism.

4 See, for example, the discussion of various distinct notions of language in chapters 1 and 2 of N. Chomsky, *Knowledge of Language: its Nature, Origin, and Use*, New York, 1986.

5 For various approaches to stylistics, see, Donald Freeman (ed.), *Linguistics and Literary Style*, New York, 1970, and Donald Freeman (ed.), *Essays in Modern Stylistics*, London & New York, 1981. For criticism of these approaches, see the essay by Stanley Fish in the more recent of the two collections, or Fish's full-length critique, *Is There a Text In This Class? The Authority of Interpretive Communities*, Cambridge, Massachusetts, 1980. A good deal of work in post-structuralism and deconstruction has challenged fundamental principles of much of the linguistics on which stylistics is based.

6 For a discussion of the educational benefits of problem-solving approaches in linguistics, see G.K. Pullum, 'If it's Tuesday, this must be glossematics', *Natural Language and Linguistic Theory*, vol.2 no.1, 1984, 151–6. For work seeking to integrate language approaches and literary approaches in new kinds of pedagogy, see, for example, H.G. Widdowson, *Stylistics and the Teaching of Literature*, London, 1975, or C.J. Brumfit and R.A. Carter (eds), *Literature and Language Teaching*, Oxford, 1986.

7 Published examples of activities along these lines (designed for intermediate second-language learners) can be found in John McRae and Roy Boardman, *Reading Between the Lines: Integrated Language and Literature Activities*, Cambridge, 1984. The connection between such work and modern reading comprehension resources is particularly clear in the range of activities described in Françoise Grellet, *Developing Reading Skills: A Practical Guide to Reading Comprehension Exercises*, Cambridge, 1981. What remains to be done is the publication of groupwork materials which develop linguistic, analytic skills without bypassing or obliterating the cultural and historical dimensions of literary study. For experimental examples of work of this kind, see *Strathclyde Worksheets*, twenty-five groupwork activities devised by the Programme in Literary Linguistics in association with the British Council, 1985.

8   Dieter Stein, 'Discourse Markers in Early Modern English', in R. Eaton, O. Fischer, W. Koopman & F. van der Leek (eds), *Papers from the 4th International Conference on English Historical Linguistics (Current Issues in Linguistic Theory* 41), Amsterdam & Philadelphia, 1985.

9   For background to 'secondary orality', see W. Ong, *Orality and Literacy*, London & New York, 1982. For discussion of relations between 'secondary orality' and education in language and cultural studies, see Alan Durant, 'The concept of secondary orality: observations about speech and text in modern communications media', *Dalhousie Review*, volume 64 number 2, 1984, 332–53. For analysis of one of the emerging media discourse-types, see Martin Montgomery, 'DJ talk', *Media, Culture and Society*, volume 8, 1986, 421–40.

10   I.A. Richards, *Principles of Literary Criticism*, New York and London, 1942; Roman Jakobson, 'Two aspects of language and two types of aphasic disturbances', in *Selected Writings*, 2 volumes, The Hague & Paris, 1971, pp.239–59; George A. Miller, 'From the viewpoint of psychology: closing statement', in Thomas A. Sebeok (ed.), *Style in Language*, Cambridge, Massachusetts, 1960, pp.386–95.

11   Jonathan Culler, *Structuralist Poetics*, London, 1975, or the essay, 'Literary competence', in Freeman, *Essays in Modern Stylistics*.

12   See William Downes, *Language and Society*, London, 1984, for an enlightening discussion of possibilities and problems involved in relating social facts and individual psychology with respect to language.

13   Dan Sperber and Deirdre Wilson, *Relevance: Communication and Cognition*, Oxford, 1986, and Dan Sperber, *Rethinking Symbolism*, Cambridge, 1975.

On the interpretation of poetic writing

I want to argue in this chapter that the short lyric poem represents a particularly effective exploitation of written language: indeed I shall give reasons for saying that what characterises such poems is that they realise to the full the potential inherent in the very nature of writing for the expression of meaning and are the culmination, so to speak, of graphological craft, the very apotheosis of print. A number of scholars have pointed out the kinds of cognitive benefits which can be gained from writing, how it can have the effect of altering the social constructs of reality by making provision for abstract analysis and rational control (see, for example, Goody 1977, Tannen 1982). I shall argue that writing is also particularly well suited for the exploration and exposition of the irrational as well, for the expression of apprehension beyond comprehension. I shall seek to show how writing is exploited in poems to extend awareness beyond the limits of accepted logic, how it can free the individual from the constraints of conventional thinking. In this respect the lyric poem can be seen as having an especially powerful subversive force. And herein, as I shall later claim, lies its essential educational value.

It seems odd on the face of it to say that it is characteristic of the lyric poem that it exploits the features of written language. For the lyric poem proclaims in its very name a reliance on music and an exclusive association with spoken language. Originally, its verbal features were bound, in the sense that they were dependent on the complementary counterpoint of a musical accompaniment. I know little of the history of the lyric, but it seems reasonable to surmise that as it detached itself from musical dependence and ceased to be song then the additional aural effects provided by the music had to be supplied by an increased elaboration of language which realised the possibilities of the visual medium. The writing as distinct from the composition of the lyric (John Donne or George Herbert, for example, as distinct from Sir Thomas Wyatt) can be seen as an exploitation of the linguistic sign to replace musical notation.

This modest excursion of mine into the poetics of writing has I think its own intrinsic interest. But my reason for undertaking it, the purpose which defines the discourse I am engaged in, is a pedagogic or more broadly an educational one. This (low level though it may seem to some to be) is the domain to which our discussions here (as far as I am concerned at least) are ultimately accountable. The teaching of poetry in the past has not, I think, sufficiently concerned itself with providing access to the essential character of poetry as a use of language. In consequence, the interpretation and appreciation of poems have tended to be appropriated as the privileged preserve of an élite who appoint themselves to the priestlike task of exegesis. This kind of mystical authority is antipathetic to effective pedagogy and very damaging to education. There ought to be some way of making the meaning of poems more directly negotiable by students without depending on canonical mediation. Indeed, this submission to authority runs directly counter to the point of poetry which, as I shall later argue, is precisely to reveal aspects of reality which have no authority and which can only be apprehended in the act of questioning the validity of established values. It seems to me that an understanding of how poems exploit the possibilities of written language, and how they are comparable to other kinds of discourse, provides a basis for interpretation as an activity to be undertaken on the students own initiative. This I think is particularly important since the actual process of poetic interpreting has an educational value which no other subject can adequately provide for.

The most obvious advantage of written language is that it constitutes a stable text and so resolves the immediate problem of on-line processing by allowing for continual playback. The understanding of spoken signals involves the recognition of what signification the sounds have, what types of linguistic sign they are tokens of, and at the same time the realisation of what significance they have in the context of utterance. These two aspects of understanding, the deciphering and the interpreting, set conditions of recipient design in spoken interaction. The message has to be formulated so as to allow for the limitations of the channel and of the conceptual capability for immediate processing and retention. But written language, free of these constraints, can, of course, be subjected to recurrent focusing and its messages can be constructed accordingly. Deciphering and interpretation do not have to be done simultaneously and in flight as an extempore act of mental agility. Deciphering indeed poses no problem with print. The physical characteristics of the medium can therefore be freely exploited to fashion message forms which have their own significance without obscuring the propositional message they convey. It has often been pointed out that writing is lacking in devices for expressing the nuances of meaning expressed by the variety of vocalic and non-vocalic gesture in spoken language. But writing has its own potential for the effective fashioning of secondary meanings, as the design of advertisements, and newspaper pages make clear: the size, type and spatial disposition of print all carry a signifying potential which can be realised without running the risk that propositional meaning might be lost in the processing. One might plausibly suggest that in this respect Roman Jakobson's (1960) definition of the poetic function as being an orientation to the form of the message itself is more readily realised in writing than in speech. Writing allows us time to reflect on the possible significance of form.

But the executive mode of spoken language is only in part a consequence of processing constraints: it arises also from the fact that talk is typically negotiated, achieved by reciprocal participation. Writing, on the other hand, is non-negotiable. In spoken interaction, meanings are jointly managed by addresser and addressee, each one contributing to the cumulative elaboration of the discourse, with each utterance presupposing the conclusions reached in the preceding part of the interaction. Thus each utterance fits into a scheme abstracted from preceding talk, in a process of continual reformulation. The structure is in the mind, retrospectively inferred, already processed as discourse, but not recorded as text. Writing, on the other hand, allows for analysis. Its complexity is in part a function of its non-reciprocal character, for the writer has to incorporate possible interlocutor reaction within the texture of the writing itself. It is therefore a powerful instrument for manipulation. It is also, by the same token, open to variable interpretation. Since the reader can have no say in the development of the discourse, the interpretative process takes place after the event as an act of analysis and he can draw whatever conclusions he chooses as to meaning. The interaction is not under joint control: there can be no challenge or correction in the process of discourse development but only in reaction to the textual product. Writing, by its nature, puts people at a remove from immediate social involvement: its promotes detachment. It allows for engagement without participation.

The visual *medium* of writing, then, allows for recurrent focusing. The non-reciprocal *mode* of writing leads to the independence of the message from interactive control: it exists as a completed textual product, subject to variable interpretation. In respect to both medium and mode, written language is essentially an artefact, an object for analysis. It puts the interlocutors at a remove from the realities of immediate context and allows them to create their own conditions for meaning; to use the written signs as a means for formulating their conceptions of the world without having to cope with the problems arising from the need to work towards a negotiated settlement.

When we consider a poem of the short lyrical cut that I am concerned with here, its exploitation of the possibilities inherent in the features of written language I have briefly mentioned is immediately apparent. Consider the fashioning of the medium itself: the print is assembled like a painting within a framework of white paper. The arrangement of language into parallel lines, the patterns of verse form and rhyme scheme all conspire to deny the ordinary procedures of online processing. Instead of the single dimension of temporal sequence, we have a two-dimensional spatial disposition of language. The lines in a poem, vertically arrayed, counteract linearity. These prosodic constituents do not correspond with the syntactic devices which are conventionally used for the organisation of meaning. Their separate constituents status is marked by the way they are ranged in parallel, by the customary use of the capital letter at the beginning, by the relations they contract with other constituents of rhyme scheme and verse form in the verbal pattern of the poem as a whole.

So the possibilities for spatial arrangement inherent in the visual medium of writing are exploited to devise a constituent structure which is superimposed on that provided by the conventional resources of syntax. And these visual effects of course have phonological reflexes: the reader pauses at the end of each line and inserts a silent stress before moving on to the next; lines which are seen to appear as equivalent elements of the visual pattern are assigned a corresponding metrical value, perceived not on the tympanum but on the pulses. The consequence of all this is that the continuities of syntactic sequence are disrupted by the parallel patterning of the prosodic constituents. So it is that any glance at an index of opening lines will yield plentiful instances of complete prosodic units fashioned out of incomplete syntax:

I wonder, by my troth, what thou, and I
(Did till we loved …)

That is no country for old men. The young
(In one another's arms …)

One by one they appear in
(The darkness …)

So much depends
(upon
a red wheel
barrow
glazed with rain
water
beside the white
chickens.)

Presented like this on the page, these expressions, at the same time complete and incomplete, provoke a complex response. In each case the lines end in a pause, a point of temporary closure, and this implies unity, a unit of meaning, a completion of a kind. But at the insistence of syntax, the reader's expectations are projected forward as well. The experience of closure is transient, the order implied by the prosody is elusive. There is a kind of accumulation of pressure, momentarily held back by the silent stress induced by the line ending, and then released at the onset of the next line. The reading of a poem is a succession of pulsations, so to speak, each implying a separate unit of meaning, whether or not such separation is given syntactic sanction. And whereas the syntactic units connect up by combination, the prosodic units relate to each other in paradigmatic association, reinforced by rhyme and verse form with line parallel to line, stanza to stanza, all implying significance of an alternative order co-existing with, but not corresponding to, that significance which is a function of conventional coding in syntax.

This duality of patterning is of course exploited by poets in different ways to practise deception on the reader and so to represent *in the very process of interpreting* the ephemeral and elusive nature of the reality of individual awareness that they are seeking to capture. Two examples. The first, lines from Tennyson:

The lights begin to twinkle from the rocks,
The long day wanes, the slow moon climbs, the deep

Each line here consists of the same number of syllables and at one level of prosodic patterning can be realised as metrically equivalent: iambic pentameters. But whereas in the first line there is a convergence of syntactic and prosodic pattern with the end of the line coinciding with a syntactic closure, the second line consists of two smaller convergent patterns and a third element which is complete as an iambic foot but incomplete as a syntactic structure. The two convergent patterns are both syntactically and prosodically equivalent: each consist of four single syllables, all but the first of which tend to attract separate stress, and an identically structured noun phrase and single verb: definite article, adjective, noun + verb in each case.

There are a number of observations one might make about the association between the two lines, how for example the difference of aspect is signalled by the altered rhythm as well as the choice of verb form, but the main point I want to make here has to do with the arrest at the end of the second line. The preceding convergent patterns have set up the expectation that the last two words, the last iambic foot, are the beginning of a third syntactic structure equivalent to the first two, that the last word is an adjective which will correspond with the previous two (*long-slow-deep*). And so we are prepared for a noun to appear at the beginning of the next line (*long day, slow moon, deep (sea?)*). But our expectations are denied. For instead we get:

Moans round with many voices.

The very denial of expectation (in the response of this reader at any rate) has the effect of representing this scene as an elusive experience, its ephemeral nature realised in the process of interpretation itself. A second example from Hopkins. The beginning of 'The Windhover':

I caught this morning, morning's minion, king-

Here it is the graphological device of the hyphen which is of interest. One conventional function of the hyphen is to signal the appearance of an appositional or parenthetical phrase and in this case the word *king* is taken to be lexically complete and itself in apposition to the preceding phrase, this primes the reader to expect the appearance in the next line of a further appositional expression or perhaps a parenthetical comment: *king- monarch of morning, king- royal in splendour*. But we get nothing of the kind. After the pause, and the gathering of anticipation, we are confronted with:

dom of daylight's dauphin, dapple-dawn-drawn Falcon, in his riding

Here the arrangement of the lines divides up the internal morphological structure of the word and the hyphen now converts the term into one of new coinage. And again the duality of pattern, the conventionalised encoding disrupted by prosodic realignment, forces, in the very act of interpreting, a recognition of another dimension of significance. We might propose that the units of meaning enclosed within each line represent elusive and impressionistic images, an aspect of reality and a modality of perception and involvement which cannot be caught within the conventions of established linguistic categories, and cannot be apprehended by customary procedures of interpretation. A tension, held in momentary equilibrium, is set up in the act of reading the poem, a tension between the completion and discontinuity of the line and the incompletion and continuity of the morpho-syntax, between the pattern of linear association by paradigmatic arrangement on the one hand and the pattern of linear combination by syntagmatic arrangement on the other. Thus the manner in which the language of the poem is fashioned into spatial shape represents a contradiction which is resolved in its very expression: the fragmentation and the discontinuities are fused and unified in another order of significance. The difference between these two modes of arrangement leads to a deferring of expectation and so realises in a particularly significant way the Derrida concept of *différance*. The paradigmatic pattern of the prosody, which realises absence, deconstructs the present syntagmatic pattern of the syntax and that process has the effect of reconstructing reality along a different dimension. Indeed it might be suggested that the whole deconstruction enterprise is an attempt to extend this process of poetic interpreting to all discourses and so to adopt literary appreciation as a principle of philosophical enquiry.

So far I have been considering how features of writing as a *medium* are exploited in poetry to create interpretative conditions for the extension of the signification of linguistic signs into a further significance. I want now to consider how conditions for this extension are set up also in the way poetry realises the possibilities inherent in writing as a *mode* of communication. Poetic exploitation of the written *medium* leads to a disconnection from the code and the consequent focusing on the intrinsic meanings of linguistic elements in detachment from their conventional formal environments. Poetic exploitation of the written *mode* leads to a severance of normal connection with context. Here we arrive at the autotelic nature of literary discourse referred to by Geoffrey Leech elsewhere in this volume.

What is most obvious about the written mode is, as I noted earlier, its nonreciprocal character. A text is a partial record of a covert interaction enacted by the writer whereby he anticipates the possible reaction of a putative reader, so casting himself in a dialectical dual role of both addresser and addressee in the discourse process. The writer therefore is free of the constraints which are usually imposed on interlocutors by the actuality of immediate interaction and the need to arrive at negotiated outcomes by reciprocal adjustment. So writing is detached from context in this sense and the mode of overt social activity is transposed into one of covert psychic process. Freed of its immediate administrative and managerial functions, the interaction can be devoted more to the fashioning of thought. Literature, it seems to me, and poetry in particular, takes this detachment principle even further. For here we find that writers not only recast the discourse roles for themselves, in the usual manner, but also take on a role different from that assumed by writers as individual or social persons. The roles which writers customarily enact in their covert discourse are those which are informed by social position of one sort or another. They are in this sense *responsible* roles. Writers may seek to evade responsibility by exploiting the different functions of animator, author and principal that Goffman has distinguished (Goffman 1981) but ultimately what they write is accountable to social judgements of what is acceptable. As Foucault has pointed out, the author function 'is tied to the legal and institutional systems that circumscribe, determine and articulate the realm of discourse ...'. In normal circumstances, the writer as author cannot avoid the *authority* of social role. Writing is taken to be a means of communication between people who have an identity as persons or positions (to use Bernstein's terms) within the social world.

Now what we find in literary writing, and most prominently I think in poetry, is a denial of identity, an avoidance of authority. The writer assumes an *irresponsible* role. He writes not as a person or a position but as a *persona*, a temporary transfiguration of self. The thoughts, perceptions and feelings expressed in a lyric poem are, therefore, unaccountable: they cannot be referred back to the author; they cannot be challenged because there can be no agreed criteria for their truth or justification. There is no point in making appeal to the co-operative principle informing normal communicative practice (cf. Grice 1975), whereby what is said is assumed to have factual warrant or to be relevant in respect of contextual implications based on a conventionally ordered world (cf. Sperber and Wilson 1986). If a relation to this world is to be made it cannot be done by direct reference. 'The poet affirmeth nothing and therefore never lies'. Nor can he ever be off the point. Poems do not *refer* to a conventionally sanctioned reality, they *represent* an alternative episteme of their own devising (cf. Widdowson 1984), one which carries conviction without being true, which makes a point without being relevant. And it is distinctive of this representational function that it has the perlocutionary force of persuasion without coercion.

Poetic writing, then, can be seen as extending and exploiting features of writing in general. In respect to medium the consequence is a disconnection of code and the assembly of constituents into superimposed prosodic patterning with its implication of new significance. In respect to mode the consequence is a disconnection from context, an avoidance of referential commitment, an escape from ascribed identity and authority. Exploitation of both medium and mode in this way leads to the manipulation of language for the representation of new and non-conformist realities.

The interpretation of poetic writing, then, calls for an analytic reappraisal of what linguistic elements signify within the patterns of the poem. But the analysis is done in the process of interpretation, in the act of subjective response. It is a function of engagement in the discourse, not a description of the text. Let me give a brief demonstration of what I have in mind by considering the first verse of Wallace Stevens's poem 'Anecdote of the Jar'.

I placed a jar in Tennessee,
And round it was, upon a hill.
It made the slovenly wilderness
Surround that hill.

It is not my purpose to propose an interpretation of the poem as a whole (see Keyser 1980)[1] but to show how the first verse illustrates the features of poetic writing that I have been referring to and the kind of interpretative process which they activate. The first thing to note perhaps is the way that the normal syntagmatic sequence is disrupted in the first two lines but is contained within the regularity of the paradigmatic pattern. In the first line there is a convergence of patterning, a coincidence of syntactic and prosodic closure, but this is immediately undermined by the line that follows. Both of the expressions here are disruptive. The first *And round it was* is itself irregular in structure (cf. *And it was round*) and is a sort of parenthetical intervention between the main clause in line one and its adverbial constituent *upon a hill*. And this constituent is itself misplaced in sequence since its proper place as a more particular locative expression would be before the more general locative *in Tennessee* and not after it. That is to say, the more acceptable order would be:

I placed a jar upon a hill in Tennessee.

The delayed appearance of this locative adverbial has the effect of directing attention back to the proposition contained within the first line, and revealing an oddity which the completeness expressed in the convergence of pattern initially disguises. This oddity has to do with the lexical item *place*. This would generally convey the notion of locative precision: one places things in a particular spot and this is at variance with the very general location of Tennessee. There is in the very first line, then, an association of the particular and the precise with the general and the vague, a convergence of semantic oppositions: an attempt at re-alignment of the conventional categorising of reality as encoded in normal syntax.

What then of the first expression in this second line: *And round it was*. One reading requires us to reassemble the constituents into the normal order: 'and it was round'. This would make *round* a predicate adjective. But there is an alternative. Whereas the completion of the syntax at the end of the line leads us to this interpretation by the reassembly of *structure* retrospectively, in terms of *sequence*, this expression activates the expectation, prospectively, that what we have here is not a parenthetic reference to the quality of the jar, but the onset of a co-ordinate structure with *round it* a prepositional phrase operating as an adverbial: 'round it, or around it, was ... something ...' a hill, perhaps, or a wilderness:

I placed a jar in Tennessee
And round it was a wilderness ...

But neither of these nouns, *hill* or *wilderness*, is available for such a neat completion of pattern. *Hill* is contained within a prepositional phrase which appears disruptively out of place. And *wilderness* appears later, in the third line, and within a quite different structure, and so separate on both counts: and in any case it is slovenly, so it is inappropriate that it should figure in an orderly sequence. The placing of the jar, then, as expressed in the first line, seems on first reading to be a simple and completed act, but the effect of the second line is to represent it as complex and uncertain. The placing is represented by a displacement of language and this directs attention back to what the verb *place* might signify in this created context. Previously it was assigned the most obvious meaning of 'put', but this will no longer do for the problematic process which is represented here. It would seem that we need to go back and re-interpret the term by invoking more lexical content. We might do this by realising it as the verbalisation of the cognate noun and by recategorising it as a simple monotransitive verb, making the adverbial optional:

I placed a jar. (cf. I bought a jar, I made a jar)

That is to say, I identified a jar *with* a place, or I made a place *for* a jar or I made a place *of* a jar. Interpreted in these ways, the placing of the jar can be seen as a conceptual, not a physical, act, a defining of its function in the composition of a pattern, a work of abstract art. The jar is itself both concrete and abstract, both form and function: it has a definite shape; it is round but also makes a shape of what is round it. The jar has the character of the linguistic sign itself. And the realisation of the different ways in which linguistic signs relate to each other in the process of reading the poem replicates the composition that it represents. The difference between the denoting and referring functions of the signs is thereby made complementary. And the distinction between author and reader, already blurred by the usual dialectical process of conventional writing, is here effaced completely in the immediate process of interpreting.

What I have tried to indicate in this brief demonstration is that the significance of the poem is a function of the actual experience of interpreting, the recurrent refocusing, the revised first impressions, the activation of potential meanings inherent in linguistic forms, the analytic teasing out of what the linguistic signs might signify within the dual patterning of the syntax and prosody. The syntax codifies conventional categories of reality: the prosodic patterns of association constrain the reader to deconstruct these categories and reconstruct them into a different order. Poems, then, neither *denote* established social generalities, nor *refer* to particular instances, but *represent* a convergence of these two sign functions, a temporary fusion of signifier and signified.

Conceived of in this way, the reading of poems has an important educational role to play. For the realisation of meanings which are not constrained by custom, caught, so to speak, in the act of reading, is a subversion of conformities. It releases individual awareness from the confines of what is conventionally communicable and beyond the writ of authority. This process of interpreting is an exploration of the unsanctioned world of the self, of alternative individual concepts and perceptions, which no social categories can account for but which no society can afford to disregard. This is a world that cannot of its nature be explained. It can only be experienced. And it is the business of education to create conditions for this to happen. It follows that the educational value of poetry depends on an approach to its teaching which provides for interpreting rather than one which simply provides interpretations. Such a provision will of course have the effect of promoting an understanding of the nature and use of language which is not only relevant to the interpreting of poems. It will also serve the additional educational purpose of helping to develop an informed awareness of the ways in which language is used in other socially committed discourses, *with* authority, for the exercise of power and the imposition of ideology (see Fowler 1986). The interpretation of poetic writing may seem a somewhat arcane activity – the mystic ritual of a band of white-robed scholars only, remote from the real concerns of everyday life. That it is commonly so considered is evidence of educational failure which, if it is not on our conscience at this conference, we should at least be conscious of as we indulge in the pleasures of philosophic discourse. For properly considered, and properly learnt (naturally along the lines proposed in this paper) the process of poetic interpretation is a powerful force for the protection of that perpetually endangered species the human individual.

Notes

1   I should like to acknowledge here the contribution that has been made to my understanding of this poem by two of my students: Chris Tribble and Jim Watson.

References

M. K. L. Ching, M. C. Haley & R. F. Lunsford (eds), *Linguistic Perspectives on Literature*, London, 1980.

P. Cole & J. L. Morgan (eds), *Syntax and Semantics Vol 3: Speech Acts*, New York, 1975.

R. Fowler, *Linguistic Criticism*, Oxford, 1986.

E. Goffman, *Forms of Talk*, Oxford, 1981.

J. Goody, *The Domestication of the Savage Mind*, Cambridge, Massachusetts, 1977.

P. Grice, 'Logic and conversation', in Cole & Morgan, 1985.

R. Jakobson, 'Closing statement: linguistics and poetics' in Sebeok, 1960.

S. J. Keyser, 'Wallace Stevens: form and meaning in four poems', in Ching, Haley & Lunsford, 1980.

T. A. Sebeok (ed.), *Style in Language*, Cambridge Massachusetts, 1960.

D. Sperber & D. Wilson, *Relevance, Communication and Cognition*, Oxford, 1986.

D. Tannen (ed.), *Spoken and Written Language: Exploring Orality and Literacy*, New Jersey, 1982.

H. G. Widdowson, *Explorations in Applied Linguistics* 2, Oxford, 1984.

Some questions and responses

The following is a minimally-edited record of the responses given by Jacques Derrida, in a necessarily improvisatory fashion, to a number of questions on topics concerning the main area of the Linguistics of Writing conference and the relation of his own work to it. The earlier questions were presented in written form, the later ones came from the audience. Derrida began by pointing out that he could not possibly give full answers to such questions in an hour, and that we would have to give some of his responses the forms of the ellipsis, the aphorism, the thesis without premises or demonstration. 'Serious questions', he observed, 'should not be posed, much less answered, at such speed. If I have a categorical imperative in all discussions, it is 'Decelerate'. So I apologise for the way I am going to avoid questions and answers in this session.'

Derek Attridge: Many who work in the field of linguistics and stylistics see their task as rendering explicit the codes or systems that underlie and make possible linguistic behaviour, including that of writers and critics of literary texts; the major models here, of course, are Saussure's *langue* as that which makes possible *parole*, and Chomsky's revision of this distinction as *competence* and *performance*. Do you think the endeavour to formalise such codes is a fruitful activity, even if the goal of full explicitness is never – and perhaps can never be – reached?

Derrida: Formalisation *is* a fruitful, useful activity. The mastery it provides is its first if not its only justification. So the effort towards formalisation of such codes is indispensable. One can never give up this task without running the risk of giving up rationality, scientificity itself in its most classical concept. But there is nothing fortuitous in the fact that these codifications, this formalisation of the codes, cannot be completed. And it is not only, as the question suggests,· a matter of achieving explicitness, or of the difference between 'implicitness' and 'explicitness'; I would say that it is also a scientific, rational requirement that we recognise the essential limits of codification, or the essential limits of the ideal formalisation of the code. It is also a scientific requirement that we question the authority and the limits of such Saussurean grids as the opposition between *langue* and *parole* or such Chomskyan grids as the opposition between competence and performance. You cannot, of course, reduce Saussure's work or Chomsky's work to those grids, but they must be questioned, and they have been questioned. So it is a scientific requirement that we question the presuppositions of these grids and others, those which have to do with the concept of the individual, consciousness, the unconscious, the subject, the opposition between the individual and society, and so on. And, especially, I would insist on the concept of the *event*, which is at the juncture of *langue* and *parole*, competence and performance. If I had time I would here insist on the structure of the event as at the same time unique and iterable. The event of a *mark* (which is not simply a sign – human or non-human, written or spoken, in the trivial sense of the terms) is something occurring once, but in its uniqueness it is iterable and therefore blurs the distinction, the rigorous limit, between, for instance, *langue* and *parole* or competence and performance.

What I tried to do – a long time ago – was to emphasise this impossibility of closing a code or a linguistic system in its inner, rigorous boundaries, and I did it not only in the form of theorems, theoretical demonstration, concerning for instance the possibility of grafts, parasites, undecidables, supplements, etc., but in the form of my own writings on these subjects, for instance in *Glas* or *La carte postale*.[1] From that point of view *Grammatology*[2] was at the same time a programme for a 'linguistics of writing' in the sense that Mary Louise Pratt has given to it (as a 'linguistics of contact'), the openings of the closure, and a philosophical problematisation of the impossibility – or the limited possibility – of this programme as the programme of a positive science. What occurs, what develops, under the name of 'pragmatics' today, the interest in situations in which the discursive element is not the determining element, such a pragmatics – except for some metaphysical assumptions – is coherent with what I called 'grammatology' a long time ago. When Pratt describes what she calls a 'linguistics of contact', I agree with all that she says (except perhaps with the name 'contact', about which I have some reservations), but I agree too with someone who in the name of linguistics – 'hard' linguistics – said that a linguistics of contact would not contradict the search for invariants, that is, the possibility or rather necessity of finding invariants through the opening of new contexts, graftings, etc. Science and linguistics must never give up – and here I come back to the question – the necessity, the desire, to formalise, to exhaust the analysis of codes and invariants; and of course the openings of closures, the contact situations, are a continual challenge which is not a contradiction of the search for invariants but, on the contrary, a way of provoking it and enriching it. So I would say that the relationship between the linguistics of contact and scientific linguistics, with its classical axioms, has to be articulated.

Attridge: Current analysis of language and literature is emphasising more and more their function as ideologically determined discursive practices in terms drawn from Marxist and post-Marxist accounts of the operation of ideology within capitalism and late capitalism. Do you see this approach as contradicting your own, or would you regard your work as contributing to such an analysis?

Derrida: Very briefly, I would say, no, this approach does not contradict my own, should not contradict my own, not at all. I have often insisted on that point. I have only two very small specific and punctual reservations.

First, a reservation about the function of the concept of 'ideology', which is, it seems to me, heavily loaded with metaphysical assumptions which have to be deconstructed. They have to be deconstructed because they have to do with reflection, representation, consciousness, the unconscious, imagination, the imaginary, etc., and to my knowledge no Marxist (or what the question calls 'post-Marxist' – which is an obscure notion for me) has even tried to deconstruct the concept of ideology, or submit it to deconstructive questions. So what I am doing is this – or would be this: to help Marxism to deconstruct its own metaphysical assumptions. That would be my first reservation.

Secondly, I would say almost the same about the notion of 'capitalism', especially 'late capitalism'. Each time – and it happens very often, these days – each time I fall upon this expression 'late capitalism' in texts dealing with literature and philosophy, it is clear to me that a dogmatic or stereotyped statement has replaced analytical demonstration. I am still waiting for a scientific definition of what late capitalism is; I am particularly interested in this because some British Marxists (or post-Marxists) read everything in which I and some others are interested as a symptom of late capitalism, and when they cannot reduce these (recent) texts, or the texts in which these texts are interested, to previous schemes (Marxist schemes related to capitalism in its classical form – if there is such a thing), they say, 'Well, that's late capitalism'. So with these two reservations about the concept of ideology and the concept of late capitalism I see no contradiction between what I am doing and what some 'post-Marxists' are doing. Nothing fortuitous in that, probably.

Attridge: Your work is sometimes attacked by those who speak in the name of reason, yet their attacks are often framed in terms of pragmatic rather than rational judgements. That is, they complain of the dangerous *effects* of your arguments rather than of any contradiction of the laws of reason. Do you have an explanation for this inconsistency in your critics? Do you make judgements of either kind upon your own work?

Derrida: This is a very difficult question, which is coming back strongly now. Those people who charge deconstruction with being irrationalist think each time you ask a question about reason, or about the history of reason (where does reason come from? what is the principle of reason as distinguished from reason itself? – because the principle of reason is something very specific in the history of reason), or about the ethics of rationalism (not of reason but of some sort of rationalism), that you are speaking *against* reason. So you are charged with being irrationalist and with undermining the rational, rationality, science, objectivity, and so on. And you are charged with giving up any rule and authorising yourself just to improvise, to say or write anything. But I would say that on the contrary, asking questions about reason, about the history of reason, the obscuranticism of certain forms of rationalism today in science, in ideology and so on, is a manifestation of rationalism, of a new sort of enlightenment. For instance, when Heidegger questions the principle of reason in its Leibnizian form, and when he derives the description of a whole epoch out of this principle of reason, he is not attacking reason in general; and when I read Heidegger, follow Heidegger to some extent, and then ask questions about Heidegger's questions, is that a way of attacking reason? I don't think so.

Now what these opponents in Germany or in France usually say is, schematically speaking, the following: since you don't put your questions under the authority of reason (because of course when you ask a question about reason, about the principle of reason, your question is not ruled by reason – it's not irrational either but, at the moment of the question, it's not ruled by the principle of reason but by something else, which is not simply the principle of reason in a determined form) or of truth (since the same can be said about truth – when you ask questions about truth, the origin of truth, the different kinds of truth, etc., the questions you are asking are not simply controlled by the system of truth you are questioning; which doesn't mean that your questions are wrong or false), then you may write anything, and you cannot demonstrate anything, or convince anybody of the necessity of the legitimacy of what you are saying. That's what I call obscuranticism, because when you write such new questions, when you escape the authority of the system you are questioning, you are not authorised to say just anything – you have to invent or to derive or to construct or to imply new rules. And these new rules are written or textualised or embodied in a new form of text, in new procedures of demonstration, in new forms of sociality, etc. These new forms have to be first recognised, read, discovered, and it is not always easy to do so. People say 'You're in a "pragmatic contradiction" because first you question the principle of reason or truth value, and then you want to convince your audience that what you say is rational and true.' But first you have to understand how these new questions and these new texts are written, how they are composed, what new conventions they produce – so as not to say just anything, not to say *n'importe quoi*. It is also, to some extent, a calculated negotiation with previous norms. Then you'll discover that there are some constraints and some demonstrative effects – if there were no demonstrative effects, these new texts wouldn't bother anybody. There are new ways of writing, new procedures, new kinds of demonstration, new actions, new conventions, and a new situation in which we have to learn how to read those new things.

Attridge: Do you wish to say anything about the challenge that your work seems to pose? Why is it seen as dangerous? Why do people feel threatened by it?

Derrida: It may seem dangerous − I realise, seeing the nervousness of some reactions (especially in the Academy), that some people must feel threatened ... not by my work but by all these things. I think this is probably because what these new (new and very old, older than the old) things are doing is exhibiting the hidden axioms or assumptions on which these institutions and these powers rely. When you analyse the assumptions on which these academic (but also cultural and political) powers are built, the source of authority is threatened. That's probably the explanation for the fierceness of some of the reactions. And of course in the university, when those professors (because it's always the professors, and powerful professors, who react in that way) realise that students have started reading and writing in a different way − not only having revolutionary positions in the political sense, but just having a new kind of rhetoric, writing papers differently, with (sometimes) a rich culture − then they have no available rules for evaluating them. That's why in many departments what is considered threatening is not a politically revolutionary position, if it is expressed in a coded and traditional way, rather, it is something which sometimes doesn't look political but disturbs the traditional ways of reading, understanding, discussing, writing, using rhetoric, etc. − because this undermines, or not necessarily undermines, but at least discovers, what was hidden in the institution.

Richard Rand:

Whatever Gerard Genette may say, in contradiction perhaps to what he himself thinks, the ascetic refusal on Hermogenes' part is not sterile, because we owe to this refusal the possibility of linguistic knowledge, and because no writer writes unless he has this knowledge in mind so as to fend off − even as he gives way to − all the easiness of the mimetic, and so as to arrive at an entirely different practice.

(Maurice Blanchot, *L'Ecriture du Desastre*)

Do you have any comments on this remark, in particular on the 'entirely different practice' (*toute autre pratique*) which Blanchot speaks of?

Derrida: We should spend hours and hours reading this text by Blanchot, because there are so many folds. I won't try to read the text closely but to answer the question. 'Entirely different practice' would be a practice which breaks on the one hand with the naive mimological, mimetic practice on the part of the writer (so as to participate in the scientific, linguistic movement), and on the other hand breaks with the symmetrical opposite, and opens the way to something totally different. The example – it's not the only possible example – I would give of this *toute autre pratique* would be to be vigilant about the traps of mimetic language, (the 'naturalness' of mimesis, the assumption that language is not arbitrary, etc.), but at the same time to take into account the possibility, discussed at this conference by Jonathan Culler, of re-motivating language by grafts and by writing in another way, so as not only to have a theoretical analysis of those two possibilities but to have another practice *in* writing. That's what I try to do in *Glas* in dealing expressly with this problem. If we continued to write in a traditional way on this problem, we would have ascetic, theoretical, neutral language (in some cases *about* non-neutral language) which is a sort of metalanguage. A totally different practice would be to combine, in a single text, some theorisation in some theoretical language *and* some inventive way of writing which would by its own performance open the limits which it is theoretically analysing.

Stephen Farrow: Your (anti)philosophical project has many affinities with that of Wittgenstein; but there appears to be a major conflict between your positions as regards language. For Wittgenstein the problems that philosophy has made for itself stem from the 'philosophical' desire to say what cannot be said or to understand what cannot be understood. Part of your project, however, has been to attempt such a move beyond what can be said, by a tracing of the problematic effects of the 'metaphysics of presence' in western thought. My question is both epistemological and ethical: How can we know which is the greater evil, the attempt to transgress the limits of the language, or the metaphysics of presence? Or is there some other way of representing the difference between your position and that of Wittgenstein?

Derrida: The question is difficult. Just a word. I've never said nor thought that the metaphysics of presence was an 'evil', 'the evil'. I'm inclined to think exactly the contrary, that it's good. There is no 'good' outside the metaphysics of presence, which defines 'the best'.

As to the transgression of the limits of language, it's very, very difficult. There are at least two ways of defining this transgression. If you define language in a narrow sense, that is as discursive oral speech, then when you write, and you write a certain way, you are transgressing logocentrism, the authority of logocentric language. But I think you are referring to another kind of transgression, and from that point of view I don't know if such a transgression – a transgression of what I would call the trace structure – is possible. So is this a contradiction of Wittgenstein, the later Wittgenstein? I don't know. My knowledge of Wittgenstein is not fine enough to address this problem here.

John Llewelyn: On the assumption, which I think you accept, that an analysis of a central case is advanced by an analysis of the marginal, I should like to put two inter-connected questions about formal logic, in the hope that they may shed light on the subject of literary language which is the central topic of this conference.

First: in your writings identity turns out again and again to be infected with difference. Would you say that this holds for the identity of the principle of identity itself, if *P* then *P*? Does this assert or otherwise present a self-possessed eternal validity or truth? Or, perhaps because eternal truth or validity is always omnitemporal truth or validity, is the apparent itselfness and self-identity of the principle of identity itself contaminated by difference?

Secondly, would it be valid to infer from what you write about spatial-temporised, so to speak schematised, difference, differance, that all differences are differences of degree, not differences of kind, genus, gender or genre? If we say that they are, are we not restricting the variety of differences by eliminating differences of kind, and would this not be to that extent in conflict with what I take to be one of the motives of your work, to remind your reader and perhaps yourself that there are more things in heaven and earth than are dreamt of in classical philosophy?

Derrida: Thank you for this very necessary question. I'll be very brief. The identity of the principle of identity itself is, I wouldn't say 'contaminated', but is constituted by difference – and this is not original on my part. Hegel, and Heidegger on Hegel, emphasised this point: the principle of identity implies difference. So from that point of view what I'm saying is very traditional. Then we would have to analyse the differences between the way we think difference, the way Hegel thinks difference, the way Heidegger thinks difference, and so on. That would be another development; but on your specific question – does this hold for the identity of the principle of identity itself? – my answer is yes. Difference is indispensable for the principle of identity itself; and then we have to follow the consequences.

On the second question, I will take a little longer. If I say, for instance, there is no difference of kind between difference of kind and difference of degree, what consequences will you draw out of that? You can draw two types of conclusion. First, that there are *only* differences of kind since there is no difference of kind between difference of kind and difference of degree. So there *are* differences of kind, which would contradict the hypothesis. Second, that there are *only* differences of degree, since there is no difference of kind between difference of kind and difference of degree – which reproduces the previous contradiction. This is not a game. What I call 'differance' is precisely an attempt to avoid, or to overcome, this classical opposition beween difference of kind and difference of degree. Differance is *at the same time* difference of kind and difference of degree – which means that it is neither one nor the other. Differance 'is' a difference (discontinuity, alterity, heterogeneity)

and also the possibility and the necessity of an economy (relay, delegation, signification, mediation, 'supplement', reappropriation) of the other as such:
difference and in-difference with and without dialectics. Economy of the other,
economy of the same. Let's take an example. When one says that the difference
between nature and culture is not what philosophers think it is, a difference of
kind (which implies a discontinuity) one implies that with some relays, delays,
mediations, etc., there is *some* continuity – a continuity which is not a homogeneity, since there are different structures (which doesn't mean that the structural difference is a difference in essence, in the classical metaphysical sense).
So when, for instance, one questions, and at a fundamental level, the concept
or value of essence and its correlates such as attributes or accidents or qualities,
and the concept of presence, which is implied in the concept of essence, then one
deconstructs the *opposition* of essence and non-essence (that is, degree, etc.),
and one has to reconsider the whole logic to which one refers in opposing difference of degree and difference in essence. And this is not a game, a formal game,
because it has very concrete consequences in everything we analyse – in biology,
in politics, in literature, and so on. Very briefly speaking, each time I work on
anything, the first thing I have to acknowledge is that I'm not satisfied with a
difference of kind and a difference of degree. And the logic of the supplement,
the logic of the *pharmakon*, the logic of the hymen, is each time a way of disturbing the order of this opposition. A supplement is at the same time something
you add as simply something more, another degree, *and* something which reveals
a lack in the essence, in the integrity of an entity, so what I call the logic of the
supplement is a principle of disorder at work in this very opposition. That's
what I'm doing all the time, and it's not what *I* am doing, it is the principle of
contamination or disorder which is at work everywhere; and the firm distinction
between difference of kind and difference of degree is a reaction, a terrible
reaction, in order to master this principle of disorder. If you can really separate
difference of kind and difference of degree then you can master everything.

DISCUSSION

Eden Liddelow: I would like to draw your attention to something which
affects our very presence, if we can say that, at this gathering here in Glasgow.
You have said in relation to the mystical presence of Dionysus the Aeropagite
that God is not even in his most holy places. So *il n'a pas lieu* is a statement
about event as well as place, and you have related this to the *topos* of our
colloquium. You went on to say that phatic discourse is event without
reference, but it still becomes not the thing of which one speaks but, at least
to the other to whom I address the speech, this speech will always have taken
place. Now I can't help seeing in this a kind of reverse allegory in which a
negative theology stands for the absence of the Logos from conferences on
the linguistics of writing. We've all read David Lodge's *Small World* and we
know that international conferences are the Mecca of the academic faithful
and also of academic prophets. So where is the Logos? In some kind of

mystical communion which we attempt to have with our own gods revealed
to us in the Logos which unites linguistics and literature, can we in fact enter
into the presence of that Logos in this holy place, this international conference?

Derrida: You imply that this is for you a holy place.

Liddelow: Well, of course.

Derrida: It doesn't look like my private churches ...
    As to the Logos: what do you mean by Logos in this case? 'Logos' is a very
specific Greek term used sometimes in the Gospels, but what do you mean
by it in this situation, referring to linguistics for instance?

Liddelow: To put it simply, and perhaps simplistically, all I mean really is
the presence of the word representing culture, representing expression. I see
in the relationship between what you have said about negative theology and
our presence here today a delicious irony. I thought that the recognition of
that irony might appeal to you.

Derrida: The only analogy I would find between the scene of Christian
negative theology and this one is my suffering here ...

Jonathan Culler: I imagine many people here were puzzled by your remark
a few moments ago that you had never said that the metaphysics of presence
was bad. I was wondering whether you would care to explain, first by
expanding on the remark that followed it – that there is no good outside
metaphysics of presence – and then perhaps say a word or two about what
then drives the impetus to deconstruct the metaphysics of presence.

Derrida: I start at the end because it could be a way of answering the first
part of your question. I often ask myself: why insist on deconstructing
something which is so good? And the only answer I have is something which
contradicts, in ourselves, or in myself, the desire for this good. But where does
this contradiction come from? First, I give it a name which sometimes I write
with a capital letter, that is, Necessity – and I write this word with a capital
letter just to emphasise the fact that it's a singular necessity, as a single person.
I have to deal with Necessity itself. It is something or someone, some x, which
compels me to admit that my desire, for good, for presence, my own metaphysics of presence, not only cannot be accomplished, meets its limit, but
should not be accomplished because the accomplishment or the fulfilment of
this desire for presence would be death itself; the good, the absolute good,
would be identical with death. At the same time, the one whom I call Necessity
teaches me, in a very violent way, to admit that my desire cannot be fulfilled,
that there is no presence, that presence is always divided and split and marked

by differences, by spacing, etc. So this is on the one hand a bad limit, something which *m'empêche de jouir pleinement*, but at the same time is the condition of my desire, and if such limits were erased this would be death, this *will* be death. We know all this will end very badly – *tout ça finira très mal*. Necessity is the drive, or the counterdrive; it's a drive which bars the fundamental drive towards presence, pleasure, fullness, plenitude, etc. The dream beyond Necessity (because there is a dream too – if you perceive Necessity as Necessity you have also to go beyond Necessity as a background out of which Necessity appears) is the plenitude which wouldn't be death. This combination of dream and necessity explains the indefatigable drive for deconstruction ... That's the way I live, that's my environment, and for some years I obeyed that drive ... My answer is at the same time, as you will realise, a very universal answer. I think this is valid for everybody, and at the same time a very idiomatic and limited answer.

Colin MacCabe: When you indicated very clearly some of the reasons why deconstruction bothers people within the university, I was in full agreement; but there is something that bothers *me* about deconstruction. If you look at your own work, and look at the work of people like Joyce and Artaud who have influenced that work, it seems to me that, if not related to late capitalism, which I think is a rather optimistic term – I think we're in a rather early phase myself ...

Derrida: That's also optimistic ...

MacCabe: ... is quite certainly related to what you've just referred to, and what Mary Louise Pratt referred to: the way in which the twentieth century has produced certain kinds of linguistic juxtaposition, brought certain new technologies of communication into the field, in such a way that the whole relation between speech and writing which is enshrined within the dominant literary tradition is questioned. What is very strange to me is how deconstruction, at least in an Anglo-Saxon context, has been used not to open up the literary curriculum but as a last way of going back and *saving* that literary curriculum.

Derrida: As you have formulated it, it could be, indeed, one of the 'bad effects'. I don't feel responsible for that.

MacCabe: I just wanted your comments.

Derrida: I totally agree with that. Deconstruction, if such a thing exists, should open up, and I have often insisted on that point. If in a certain phase of its elaborations it first has the 'bad effect' you are describing (but here one would have to be very careful: there are things which are to be saved in the so called 'literary curriculum'), nevertheless I think it's strategically necessary to go back to the library and read in a different way. This is necessary provided that you don't get stuck in this phase. If on the contrary you miss this phase, then you will reproduce the old thing, the old ways of reading, so you have strategically to do many things at the same time. But I totally agree with your expectation, and your hope. I did my best, especially in France, to insist on this necessity.

Just one more word – this would be an answer to a question which hasn't been cited – I don't consider deconstruction as a method, a general method, that should be applied to many fields. Deconstruction is not a method. It has some methodological effects. There are some general rules that in certain limited situations you can draw out of deconstruction and apply. I think this is the condition for teaching something as 'deconstruction', but deconstruction as a whole doesn't consist in a set of methodological rules that have to be applied to philosophy, literature, and so on. And second, deconstruction – we should say deconstructions (I don't like this word, as I have often said, but it saves time to use it) – deconstructions are not an enterprise. It's already a symptom of the situation you're describing: this change in the twentieth century in technology, in economics, in military strategies, these transformations in languages, etc. I consider deconstruction to be a symptom, but at the same time, the concept of 'symptom' has to be deconstructed, has to be analysed; it's not a symptom in the sense of a sign at the surface of what is *signified* by the sign. It's a sign which *transforms* this situation, so the concept of symptom is not pertinent enough.

Roger Sell: My question follows out of something that you've just said to Colin MacCabe. You said that if you refuse the deconstructive way of thinking, you just stay where you are, nothing happens. Would you then say that all changes in human thought in the past have been, in some sense or other, covertly, or patently even, deconstructive?

Derrida: Are you referring to changes in kind or changes in degree? Of course it would be absurd to say everything changes by way of deconstruction. But if there is change this means that there is somewhere a structural logic which makes it possible. This has to do with deconstruction. For instance, if you take a philosophical system or a social structure, it has in itself, I would say, the 'principle' of its own opening, dislocation, disintegration. If you read anything – Plato, Descartes, or a social system – you can find somewhere something inadequate which accounts for its own deconstruction. So anything which changes has to do with this possibility in a given system, the possibility of being opened up, dislocated, dissociated, has to do with the principle of internal dissociation. (Just a parenthesis on that point, apostrophising Stanley Fish, who associated mastery with closure: I would say that mastery often consists in opening, not in closing, that there is a certain amount of mastery in opening the closure, in opening the system, in leaving it open; and this is a strategic ruse of masters, not to close and to show consistently why you cannot close, the system; to show the principle of dissociation, the principle of deconstruction, *within* every set, every system, every structure.) Then we have to deal with the noun 'deconstruction'. Of course deconstruction today designates not only this principle of disintegration or dislocation in any question within a system, but a way of thematising this possibility; and to analyse the specific modernity, or post-modernity, of deconstruction as an explicit − or to some extent explicit − endeavour you would have to describe the entire western situation, the European situation, the American situation, and so on. But this has to do with the difference between the term 'deconstruction' for the explicit project (if it's a project today) and the inner possibility of deconstruction which is present everywhere.

Stanley Fish: What you've done here today is absolutely remarkable and I'm very grateful for it. You've made one mistake. But in another part of your discourse you corrected that mistake, so I am merely teasing out from your own discourse its final clarification. It seems to me that what Colin MacCabe was saying is that many hoped that the lessons of deconstruction would lead to (to use a phrase that you've used) an 'opening up', and then one can place in the position of what is to be opened up many things − like the study of literature, and things that persons would consider even more significant than the study of literature. I, however, see no *necessary* relationship (there may be a political and institutional relationship, and indeed there has been, demonstrably) between the lessons of deconstruction, if we can speak of them, and any kind of opening up whatsoever. Because it seems to me that what deconstruction gives us is an account of the operations of consciousness, an account which dislodges, or at least puts itself against, some previous accounts, but that it doesn't seem to me that one can then use a new account of consciousness − even one which is to me so persuasive as that given us by deconstruction − to *alter* consciousness. In other words, it doesn't seem to me in any sense that opening up can be a *project*. And here I found in another part of your answer this insight: you said that deconstruction is not an enterprise but in so far as we want to use the word for a moment, a symptom. Opening up, as far as I can tell, is something that's always going on; which is to acknowledge the lesson you just read to me about mastery and closure. Opening up is always what is going on, but despite the hopes that I think I detected in Colin MacCabe's question, opening up is what can never be engineered. In the last twenty years we've had two responses to the kind of discourse that Jacques Derrida has so eloquently given us. One I have called Theory Fear, and you have spoken of it today, that is the fear that if we listen to people like Derrida we will lose our hold on rationality, chaos will come again, and we will never be able to say anything because anything could be said and will therefore have no bite. That I think is wrong for the reasons which you have given. The opposite mistake is what I've called Theory Hope: the hope that we have now in effect learned that the certainties that we enjoy and the knowledge to which we would testify do not have their sources in some independent mechanism, in some Logos; and that, armed with this lesson, we can proceed to perform all kinds of new epistemological feats. I think that also is a mistake.

Derrida: Yes, I agree. As you will realise, I'm not optimistic in the way you describe, so the pathos − if there is such a thing − of deconstruction is double. For me too sometimes it's the pathos of 'opening up': we'll change things, we'll transform, reform, invent − and sometimes it happens ... There is another pathos, and this is exactly the opposite. No, nothing new, no. We'll follow deconstruction, but deconstruction is not something new; on the contrary it's a memory, it's another experience and practice of memory. So I agree with you on that point. What disturbs me is the reference to consciousness, to deconstruction as essentially a way of transforming our analysis of consciousness. On the contrary, the problem of consciousness is a very local and marginal problem for deconstruction. So why do you insist on consciousness?

Fish: I think this would get us into a long discussion of notions like intention, which always bring out the worst in everyone. And I think that if there were such a discussion I would find myself reasserting the inescapability of intention, and protesting vigorously against statements, not so much yours but some statements which have occasionally been attributed to Paul de Man, to the effect that meanings are always in excess of intention, etc. I would want to dispute that, but I think such disputes would take us far past any reasonable time limit.

Attridge: Would you like a last comment of any kind?

Derrida: I'm sorry for not having answered so many questions, both written questions and implied questions in the explicit questions. I just want to thank you for your patience.

Notes

   1   Jacques Derrida, *Glas*, Paris, 1974; *La carte postale de Socrate à Freud et au-delà*, Paris, 1980.
   2   Jacques Derrida, *De la grammatologie*, Paris, 1967.

Describing the unobserved: events grouped around an empty centre

The advent of modern science, accompanied historically by the development of scientific instruments, especially those utilising a lens as a refinement of human vision, might be said to have opened up vast and terrifying epistemological perspectives that 'no one had ever before seen'. These are the spaces in which instruments − the telescope, the microscope − allow the viewing subject to see, to witness, places where he is not, indeed, where no subject is present. He thereby directly observes an unsensed sense-data, the appearance of things in his absence, and that absence itself − his own − which scientific inference had already allowed him to conceive of and predict.

That absence, it was also simultaneously recognised, is temporal as well as spatial − the light rays that reach the lens from a distant star are not simply distant; they are also delayed. But it took the perfection, some two centuries later, of another instrument or process sometimes incorporating a lens − namely photography − to reveal places that were also times which no one had ever before seen, the appearance of things *when* no one was present. The chemical revelation and fixing of an image captured on the ground glass of a lens thus completes a process whereby something which Locke called a 'sense-idea', placed within the mind of an observer, is externalised and located within an instrument and so separated from the person of any human observer.[1] 'Any star can be photographed at any place from which it would be visible if a human eye were there.'[2]

What was accomplished first by optical instruments and the chemical processes which recorded and preserved their images was later duplicated for the other senses in dictaphones, thermometers, gramophones and tape recorders. 'Photographic plates can photograph stars that we cannot see; clinical thermometers can measure differences of temperature that we cannot feel, and so on.'[3]

What then is the epistemological status of these fragments of space-time isolated in the recorded or photographed image? The answer to this question will lead us to an area whose limits are defined by the convergence of a philosophy, a linguistics and a literature which objectivises and depersonalises the dualism of subject and object by locating it, so to speak, in an object-glass.

The literary form in which this convergence is embodied, the novel, develops during the period between the invention, at one end, of the lens and, at the other, of photography and recording instruments.

That area of convergence defines an objectivised 'linguistic subjectivity' − 'linguistic' both because the terms by which western philosophy has defined it are also grammatical − 'person', 'subject' − and because the form in which it is represented is conferred on it by language. This language, however, is not co-extensive with speech or communication, but realised only in a specific linguistic style, uniquely written and literary, the style which constitutes narrative fiction. In it certain aspects of subjectivity are foregrounded in a writing in which they are no longer the transparent vehicle for an ego-centered expression which in speech subjectivises all that can be said, including any objective propositions contained in it, but whereby the dualism only implicit in the spoken language can be incarnated in discernable syntactic features restricted to separate sentential contexts. These syntactic features form 'the evidence of narrative'; and it is they which allow the separation of subjectivity from objectivity as well as the parsing out of syntactic levels of subjectivity which, without linguistic analysis, would remain largely unanalysed and unitary.

Among the empirical distinctions thereby permitted within this novelistic language is that of a subjectivity reduced to nothing else but what the instrument can record, namely a sense-datum given to no one. The instrument is a 'sensitive' instrument, aiming to reproduce, as under laboratory conditions, only those aspects of subjectivity which crucially concern our knowledge of the external world. This makes the instrument not only 'the incarnation of a theory', as Alexandre Koyré says of Galileo's telescope, 'allow[ing] us to pass beyond the limits of the observable', by extending observation 'to reveal to our eye things invisible to the naked eye', but also the embodiment of a literary language.[4] The literary sentence incorporating the sensitive instrument's knowledge is a descriptive sentence which gives grammatical representation to the appearance of things not necessarily observered, and it is the fact that it is a written sentence which makes possible its description of the unobserved.

Such a sentence thus incorporates a theory of knowledge in which there is a place for an unobserved sense-data, the *gestalt* of the instrument. That unobserved image is composed of elements which we will call, following Russell, *sensibilia* − those objects which have the same metaphysical and physical status as sense-data, without necessarily being data to any mind' because 'there happen to be no observers to whom they are data'.[5] Distinct both from any act of sensation seizing upon them and from the putative object for which they are data, sensibilia provide a notion of sense knowledge which is private and minimally subjective in a way defined by the instrument's knowledge, without thereby existing in any mind. They thus preserve certain features of Berkeleyan ideas − those crucial to his argument − which belong, however, to no person of an observer. They conjoin the private and subjective with the impersonal.[6]

It is, once more, the instrument which presents the model for this impersonal subjectivity, 'a theoretical core in the actual experience' of sensation,[7] the 'word "physical" ... meaning "what is dealt with by physics"'.[8] 'Physical subjectivity exists equally in a photograph or gramophone record; it is present already in the events external to the percipient's body'.[9] Indeed, 'it is best exemplified by scientific instruments'.[10] The instrument then is Russell's 'complete human body with no mind inside it',[11] whereby the 'metaphysic' which is 'essentially Berkeley's: whatever is, is perceived'[12] can be read as a version of realism perhaps analogous to Wittgenstein's proposition that 'solipsism, when its implications are followed out strictly, coincides with pure realism',[13] because certain properties of the subject can be shown to exist independent of the individual subject in aspects of the physical world. As Whitehead puts it, 'it is the observer's body that we want, and not his mind. Even this body is only useful as an example of a very familiar form of apparatus. On the whole, it is better to concentrate attention on Michelson's interferometer, and to leave Michelson's body and Michelson's mind out of the picture.'[14] Frege had already figured a similar distinction in terms of the instrument: to 'the real image projected by the object glass in the interior of the telescope' there corresponds 'the retinal image of the observer'. The distinction is operated via the separability of the image from the individual observer and its externalisation in the telescopic image. The result is a reduced 'subjectivity' with certain objective properties: 'The optical image in the telescope is indeed one-sided and dependent upon the standpoint of observation; but it is still objective, inasmuch as it can be used by several observers ... [or] arranged for several to use ... simultaneously'.[15]

Each gathering of sensibilia, as on the ground glass of the telescope, represents – as in Leibniz's Monadology, Russell explains – a perspective definable independent of whether or not it is given to any observer; each perspective is one of 'an infinite number of such worlds', some of 'which are in fact unperceived';[16] each perspective is structured or organised spatially and temporally, 'toning down', as Whitehead puts it, Leibniz's 'monads into unified events in space and time'.[17] For, as Russell argues, 'Leibniz did not carry his monadism far enough, since he applied it only spatially. Not only is a man private from other people, he is also private from his past and future selves'.[18] This privacy, however, is already a property of the perspective a man, a mind, may come to occupy. Those aspects of subjectivity built into the notion of a perspective limited to a unit of space-time inhere in the very appearances of things and not in the mind or eye to whom they may appear. Such, for Whitehead and Russell, was the conclusion to be drawn from the then new doctrine of relativity, countering what Whitehead criticised as 'an extreme subjectivist interpretation' of relativity, in which 'the relativity of space and time has been construed as though it were dependent on the choice of the observer';[19] for , rather, 'the physical world itself, as known, is infected through and through with subjectivity ... as the theory of relativity suggests, the physical universe contains the diversity of points of view which we have been accustomed to regard as distinctly psychological'.[20] Built into sensibilia themselves is a dualism which preserves the trace of subject and object in their structure: 'every particular of the kind relevant to physics' – every sensible or gathering of sensibilia – 'is associated with *two* places; e.g. my sensation of the star is associated with the place where I am and with the place where the star is. This dualism has nothing to do with any 'mind' that I may be supposed to possess; it exists in exactly the same sense if I am replaced by a photographic plate.'[21] Its unity, what Russell calls 'the notion of events grouped about a centre, changing partly in accordance with the laws of perspective and partly in ways which are functions of groups with other centres',[22] must therefore be conferred on it by something other than a subject at its centre.

Thus is physical subjectivity emptied of a subject and sensibilia grouped around a potentially empty centre. What is sensed is no longer personal, is de-psychologised, but it remains nonetheless private, events in a private and impersonal space and time revealed by the sensitive instrument.

The notion of sensibilia defines a complex of language as well. The term which contemporary linguistics assigns this complex is 'deixis'. Linguistics has not explicitly recognised the link between deixis and sense knowledge, but it is implicit in the grammatical tradition which treats deixis under the heading 'demonstratives' – the Latin equivalent of the Greek *deixis*. Russell, in texts of 1940 and 1948, turns explicitly to the subject of deixis in language, calling the units comprising it 'egocentric particulars'.[23] For Russell, deixis is naturally related to the question of sense-data – the chapter 'Egocentric Particulars' in *An Inquiry into Meaning and Truth* directly precedes one entitled 'Perception and Knowledge' – the nature of this relation is already sketched in the earliest work on reference as part of the whole discussion of proper names.

This relation can be expressed with the familiar notions of linguistics and philosophy of language in terms of the special features of deictic or demonstrative referring: demonstratives constitute those elements of language which establish a relation of reference, narrowly defined as that between an utterance, an instance of language, and a sensed object or referent. The referent of a demonstrative is composed of sensibile or sensibilia. The gesture which may accompany the deictic is thus a sign that a deictic term refers to something within the range of a sense organ or sensitive instrument or calculable with respect to them as centre. 'This is a table' implies that the table referred to is perceived by the speaker at the moment of the utterance. For this reason, a statement such as 'I can't find this' is anomalous.

Such is not the case for all reference, of course. 'The Evening Star is the Morning Star', with its two referring noun phrases, in no way implies that

Venus is perceived, as 'That is Venus' does. The referent of a proper noun
or a common noun, such as *star* or *table*, when it occurs with actual reference
in an existential sentence like 'There is a table in the room', is an object posited
to exist in what Russell calls 'the public space ... of physics'.[24]

Language thus distinguishes between two forms of reference, one
designating collections of sense-data and the other putative objects in the
physical world, between, for example, 'This is a table', 'Here is the table' and
'*Voici une table*', on the one hand, and 'There is a table in the room' or *'Il
y a une table dans la chambre'*, on the other. It is this distinction that Russell
seems to be making when he points out: 'Now in English the words "there
is" are ambiguous. When I used them before, saying "There is a triangle",
I meant them in the sense of "voilà" or "da ist". Now I mean them in the
sense of "il y a" or "es gibt"'.[25] On this reading, the gulf between the world
of sense and the world of physics that Russell speaks of would be a linguistic
one as well. And, indeed, elsewhere, this is Russell's explicit position, where
it is the presence or absence of deixis which marks the boundaries between
one kind of statement and the other, for

no egocentric particulars occur in the language of physics. Physics views space-time
impartially, as God might be supposed to view it; there is not, as in perception, a region
which is specially warm and intimate and bright, surrounded in all directions by
gradually growing darkness. A physicist will not say 'I saw a table' but like Neurath
or Julius Caesar, 'Otto saw a table'; he will not say 'A meteor is visible now', but 'A
meteor was visible at 8h. 43m. GMT', and in this statement 'was' is intended to be
without tense. There is no question that the non-mental world can be fully described
without the use of egocentric words.[26]

With these examples we have imperceptibly entered the domain of the
literary, as Russell's allusion to Caesar makes clear. For the place where
this linguistic division is embodied is in the language of the novel, itself
divided between an objective Narration, recounting a public space and
time, 'impartially, as God might be supposed to view it,' in a past tense
whose pastness is not calculated with respect to a present, and a represented
subjectivity in a Now-in-the-Past, i.e., a past tense co-temporal with present
time deictics. Such is my argument in *Unspeakable Sentences* for the language
of narrative fiction, which is made up of two types of sentences with linguistic
properties not possessed by the sentences of ordinary discourse. Such is also
Maurice Blanchot's account of novelistic style in which he discovers a radical
division: 'on the one hand, there is something to tell, and that is the *objective*
reality as it is immediately present to the interested gaze, and on the other,
this reality is reduced to a constellation of individual lives, *subjectivities* ...'.[27]
That division he represents in terms of two possible uses of the pronoun *il*
within the grammar of French, one as the personal pronoun, translated by
the English *he*, 'a multiple and personalized "he", a manifest "ego" under
the veil of an apparent "he"', the other the impersonal pronoun, translated

by English *it*, of constructions like 'il pleut', of which the paradigm case for Blanchot is 'il y a',[28] the existential statement which for Russell contrasts with the deictically-anchored sentence.

The sentence of Narration, whose tense in French is the *passé simple* contains no deictics, as Benveniste pointed out.[29] 'A meteor was visible at 8h. 43m. GMT' might then be taken as equivalent to sentences of Narration such as 'Ainsi, en 1825, deux vitriers badigeonnèrent le vestibule; en 1827, une portion du toit, tombant dans la cour, faillit tuer un homme' from Flaubert and its English translation 'Thus in 1825 a couple of glaziers whitewashed the hall; in 1827 a piece of the roof fell into the courtyard and nearly killed a man'.[30]

The other sentence of narrative fiction, however, while it may contain deictic adverbs of time and place, has no direct counterpart in Russell's sentence containing deictics. For, unlike 'I saw a table' and like 'Otto saw a table', it shows a third person subject of the sensation verb instead of a first person. And unlike 'A meteor is visible now', whose *now* is contemporal with the present tense, its *now* is contemporal with the past tense. Russell's egocentric statements of the language of sense are rewritten narratively as 'A meteor was now visible' and 'Otto now saw a table'. But its third person, as Blanchot puts it, is a personalised *he*, a third person subjectivity, re-presented in a past which, in contrast to all past tenses in discourse, is simultaneously now. It is not egocentric, but it remains nonetheless subject-centred. In the various theories of the novel, this kind of sentence is treated as the representation of a third person perspective, a subjectivity occupying a past moment which is a private moment, because it occurs *here* and *now*. Thus, in the following sentences from Virginia Woolf containing a *now* cotemporal with a past tense verb, a co-occurrence which is never spoken, the point of view represented in them is ascribed to the character designated by the third person pronoun:

Now he *was* crossing the bridge over the Serpentine.[31]

The extraordinary irrationality of her remark, the folly of women's minds enraged him. He had ridden through the valley of death, been shattered and shivered, and *now* she *flew* in the face of facts.[32] [my italics]

Russell, in fact, composes such a sentence with a Now in the Past in the little 'story of adventure' he presents as a typical narrative in *Our Knowledge of the External World*:

With a cynical smile he pointed the revolver at the breast of the dauntless youth. 'At the word *three* I shall fire', he said. The words one and two had already been spoken with a cool and deliberate distinctness. The word *three* was forming on his lips. At this moment a blinding flash of lightning rent the air.[33]

The deictic adverbial 'at this moment', cotemporal with the past verb *rent*, represents a past subjective moment.

The evidence provided by the language of narrative, combined with

Russell's distinction between two kinds of referring statements, one deictic and the other existential, suggest then that the crucial difference between the two kinds of sentences is the presence or absence of a subject. If this is so, Russell's narrative sentence 'At this moment a blinding flash of lightning rent the air' or our 'A meteor was now visible' must be interpreted to mean that the flash of lightning was seen by the cynical youth or his assailant, that the meteor was visible to some observing subject.

It should be apparent that this conclusion runs counter to the thrust of Russell's theory of knowledge, which challenges the assumption that sensibilia are necessarily data to someone. The term 'egocentric particulars' Russell chooses in the texts of 1940 and 1948 for the complex of language whose referents are sensibilia is in complete conformity with grammatical tradition, which defines all deictic terms with reference to the speaking subject of the speech act. But it is not in conformity with Russell's 1914 theory of sense knowledge. For the notion of sensibilia, as we have seen, defines a spatial and temporal centre which is subjective by virtue of being so centred (in a perspective) but which contains no necessary person-subject. And that centre was defined with reference to deictic terms, but ones other than the first person pronoun. When Whitehead 'for Berkeley's *mind* ... substitutes a process of prehensive unification', that 'unity of a prehension defines itself as a *hero* and a *now*';[34] when Russell extends Leibniz's privacy to time as well as space, it refers to this spatio-temporal privacy with the special deictic terms by which language names it: 'It is not "here" alone that is private, but also "now"'. Indeed, Russell goes on to assert that, in the discussion of egocentric particulars, '"here-now" is what is fundamental to our present problem'.[35]

Of course, in an 'egocentric' model of deixis, *here* and *now* are defined as the place and the time which *I* occupy, as *my* spatio-temporal perspective: '"here" is where my body is' or '"here" is the place of whatever sensible object is occupying my attention'.[36] But the discussion of *here-now* is not dependent on its being so occupied, despite the terminology, if one has abandoned the presupposition that sense-data, if they are *given*, are necessarily given to someone. What is crucial and in no way dependent on *ego*centricity is the distinction between public and private space and time and the language which represents each. The language of private space and time is that of sense, centred in a *here* and *now*; the language of public space and time, as we saw, has no deictic centre. It may be, as Russell claims, that 'ordinary speech does not distinguish between public and private space'.[37] This is perhaps most clearly demonstrated with respect to time, because the system of tenses in speech is calculated with respect to the moment of the speech act, cotemporal with *now*, regardless of whether public or private time is designated. It is the language of written narrative, as we have seen, which distinguishes two kinds of sentences; one, the sentence of Narration containing a narrative past tense − e.g., the *passé simple* in French − which recounts 'the objective relation of before-and-after, by which events are ordered in a public time-series':

the other the sentence which represents 'a subjective relation of more-or-less remote' from the moment represented by *now*.[38] If Russell claims that 'Both private and public time have, at each moment in the life of a percipient, one peculiar point, which is, at that moment, called "now"', that is because he only has available the language of 'ordinary speech', where an objective moment designated by a date may be taken as mapped on to a subjective *now* and where there is always a percipient, the speaking subject. But in the sentence containing a narrative past tense, the moment referred to by the verb is not deictically anchored, but calculated solely in terms of before-and-after, in a chronological order which is that of the integers. In the sentence already cited from Flaubert, *badigeonnèrent* refers to an event which precedes the event referred to by *faillit tuer*, which follows the first; there is no central present moment to which both are referred. The same holds for the series of verbs in 'Puis sa mère mourut, ses soeurs se dispersèrent, un fermier la recueillit, et l'employa toute petite à garder les vaches dans la campagne.'[39] The verbs in the *passé simple* – *mourut, dispersèrent, recueillit* and *employa* – establish an order in which no moment is privileged with respect to the others. Thus, the sentence of Narration captures grammatically the features of public space and time as opposed to private space and time, as defined by Russell. For, if ' "here" and "now" depend upon perception', 'in a purely material universe there would be no "here" and "now"'. If 'perception is not impartial, but proceeds from a centre', the 'public word of physics has no such centre of illumination'.[40]

The sentence representing subjectivity in a Now in the Past retains, however, the centre of the egocentrically-organised sentence of discourse, even though it may have eliminated both the *I* and the present tense. But, returning to the problem posed by the dichotomy between Russell's 1914 theory of knowledge and his later theory of deixis, the question which can now be formulated is whether such a representation of subjectivity is necessarily organised around a subject of consciousness or Self, even if a third person subject. Implicit in the account of such sentences representing subjectivity in *Unspeakable Sentences* is the assumption that the subjective features of sentences containing deictics, as well as other embeddable subjective elements and constructions analysed as representing, minimally, non-reflective consciousness, are referred for interpretation to the sentence's unique subject of consciousness. Alternatively, this assumption takes the presence of a deictic or any other subjective element in the syntax as the sign of the presence of a subject occupying or defining the sentence's perspective or point of view. This means that a descriptive sentence presenting a specific perspective in space-time, in other words, a sentence representing sensibilia, is necessarily attributable to a particular observer, that a sentence like 'Now he threw away his cigarette'[41] or 'Quelques gouttes de pluie tombaient',[42] taken in isolation, must be understood to describe the sense-data of some observer. Another way to phrase the question is to ask whether the version of a restricted 'physical' subjectivity predicted by Russell's theory of knowledge finds any support in the evidence of language itself, thereby requiring the substitution for an *ego*centric theory of deixis one in which a sentence deictically anchored may group events around an empty centre. This question reduces to that of whether there are sentences with a deictic centre but without any explicit or implicit representation of an observer. Grammatically, such sentences would contain place and time deictics, *here* and *now* or their equivalents; they might also contain demonstratives designating sensibilia. But they would not contain those subjective elements and constructions implying the mental states of a personal subject. These would include embeddable subjective elements such as nouns or adjectives 'of quality' representing a subject's opinions, feelings or thoughts, as well as non-embeddable subjective elements such as exclamations.[43] Nor would such sentences contain any third person pronoun representing a subjectivity or be interpretable, according to its linguistic context, as the perspective of a subject.

Candidates for such sentences do indeed exist, in the form of certain novelistic sentences of description. Examples of such sentences are given below:

1. The pear tree before Mrs Littlejohn's was like drowned silver now in the moon.[44]
2. The sun had now sunk lower in the sky.[45]
3. The tree, that had burnt foxy red in spring and in midsummer bent pliant leaves to the south wind, was now black as iron, and as bare.[46]
4. Here lay knife, fork and glass, but lengthened, swollen and made portentous.[47]
5. Blue waves, green waves swept a quick fan over the beach, circling the spikes of sea-holly and leaving shallow pools of light here and there on the sand.[48]
6. Now the sun had sunk. Sea and sky were indistinguishable.[49]
7. On était au commencement d'avril ... Par les barreaux de la tonnelle et au delà tout alentour, on voyait la rivière dans la prairie, où elle dessinait sur l'herbe des sinuosités vagabondes. Le vapeur du soir passait entre les peupliers sans feuilles, estompant leurs contours d'une teinte violette, plus pâle et plus transparente qu'une gaze subtile arrêtée sur leurs branchages. Au loin, des bestiaux marchaient; on n'entendait ni leurs pas, ni leurs mugissements; et la cloche, sonnant toujours, continuait dans les airs sa lamentation pacifique.[50]

Sentences like those above whose only grammatical mark of subjectivity is a subjective past deictically anchored to a *now* are ambiguous out of context, for they in no way differ from sentences like 'Now he threw away his cigarette' or 'Quelques gouttes de pluie tombaient' cited earlier. But these two representations of sensibilia occur in contexts which provide for each an observer in the form of a fictional character, subject of a verb of sensation; they become thereby interpretable as someone's represented sense data, the perception of the character or characters (in the case of a plural subject) designated by the subject of the sensation verb. The contexts are given below:

8. Leaning out of the window side by side the two women watched the man ... Now he threw away his cigarette. They watched him. What would he do next?[51]
9. Emma mit un châle sur ses épaules, ouvrit la fenêtre et s'accouda. La nuit était noire. Quelques gouttes de pluie tombaient ...[52]

In the first example there is a progression from a statement of pure Narration – 'the two women watched the man' – to a representation of what they saw – an event occurring in a *now*, the man throwing away his cigarette – to a representation of their reflective consciousness in the form of a direct, inverted, i.e., non-embeddable question attributable to a plural third person subject: 'What would he do next?' Moreover, as was argued in *Unspeakable Sentences*, the sentence representing perception, as one form of non-reflective consciousness, can be converted into sentences of reflective consciousness by the addition of a non-embeddable subjective element or construction. Thus, 'Was he actually throwing away his cigarette now?' or 'Oui, quelques gouttes de pluie tombaient maintenant' are representations of reflections about perception and not simply representations of perceptions.

In the case of the examples from *The Waves*, however, there is no candidate for a fictional observer in any of the sentences occuring in the chapter openings from which they are taken. It is clear, in fact, from a reading of the thematic concerns of the whole novel, that Woolf means these sentences to evoke what she calls elsewhere in the novel 'the world without a self'[53] to contrast with the first person monologues of the chapters themselves which, incidentally, begin as presentations of perception: '"I see a ring," said Bernard ... "I see a slab of pale yellow," said Susan ... "I hear a sound," said Rhoda'[54] and so on. In a similar section of *To the Lighthouse* called 'Time Passes', a description of the 'empty rooms'[55] of the house consisting of sentences in which a *now* in the past occurs but, where there is no observer to attribute their point of view to appear to record a world of sensibilia, like the light waves recorded by instruments ('some random light ... from some uncovered star, or wandering ship, or the Lighthouse even'[56]) in the absence of any observer. 'Listening (had there been anyone to listen),'[57] sound waves could have been 'heard', but the verb of perception – 'listening' – remains subjectless, and the sound waves go unobserved, like the waves of the sea striking an empty shore. For 'there was scarcely anything left of body or mind by which one could say "This is he" or "This is she"',[58] no subject to which these sentences might point.

The sentences 1–7, centred in an empty *here* and *now*, become then the appropriate linguistic representation of the unobserved, *here* and *now* defining the Russellian perspective, that physical subjectivity which may remain impersonal. *Here* and *now* name a private time and place which need not be occupied by a subject represented by a first or third person pronoun or other syntactically definable subjective elements which must be referred to a subject for interpretation. The deictic system is thus internally divided between those terms which represent the (personal) subject – *I* in speech, *he, she* or a human *they* in the writing of the novel – and those which represent only a subjective centre – the deictic adverbials of time and place. Moreover, it is the personal pronouns which are defined in terms of the spatial and temporal deictics, and not vice-versa; it is *here-now* which is primary and not *I*. Around this empty centre, sensibilia, given a temporal dimension as events, group themselves. Structured by this spatio-temporal centre, which encloses the space of perception or sensation, like the photographic plate 'frames' a portion of the visible world, they provide, so to speak, its content.

That content, consisting of sensibilia, receives a name within the deictic system as well, a name which supplies the link between Russell's later explicit treatment of deictics and the earlier theory of knowledge, and in which the so-called *'egocentric'* model can be interpreted so as to eliminate the notion of *ego*-centricity as primitive, in the light of the earlier theory of proper names. For *An Inquiry Into Meaning and Truth*, despite its proclaimed egocentrism, chooses to define deixis, not in terms of *I* or even of *I-now*, which is the deictic *I*, stripped of all past, of all 'biography'; it defines it in terms of *this*. In 'On Denoting', *this* is a logically proper name when applied to a sense datum, and indeed it is the only logically proper name. As Ayer comments, 'the only function which is left for a name to fulfil is that of being purely demonstrative. Russell calls these purely demonstrative signs logically proper names'.[59] 'Since the only signs which satisfy this condition are, in his [Russell's] view, those which refer to present feelings or sense-data', comments Ayer, 'his philosophy of logic is tied at this point to his theory of knowledge'.[60] In an extended discussion of *this* in 'The philosophy of logical atomism', Russell says the following:

The only words one does use as names in the logical sense are words like 'this' and 'that'. One can use 'this' as a name to stand for a particular with which one is acquainted at the moment. We say 'This is white'. If you agree that 'This is white', meaning the 'this' that you see, you are using 'this' as a proper name. But if you try to apprehend the proposition that I am expressing when I say 'This is white', you cannot do it. If you mean this piece of chalk as a physical object, then you are not using a proper name. It is only when you use 'this' quite strictly, to stand for an actual object of sense, that it is really a proper name. And in that it has a very odd property for a proper name, namely that it seldom means the same thing to the speaker and to the hearer. It is an *ambiguous* proper name, but it is really a proper name all the same, and it is almost the only thing I can think of that is used properly and logically in the sense that I was talking of for a proper name. The importance of proper names, in the sense of which I am talking, is in the sense of logic, not of daily life.[61]

In the later treatment of 'egocentric particulars', the precise formulation of *this*, as the primitive on the basis of which the other deictics are defined, is 'the object of *this* act of attention' or 'what I-now am noticing'.[62] Thus, as is apparent, Russell defines *this* in terms of the subject, and, moreover, the subject narrowed to the speaking subject: '"this" depends upon the relation of the user of a word to the object with which the word is concerned'.[63] In other words, here the analysis of the language of sensation assumes a theory of knowledge in which all sensibilia are data to someone – 'what I-now am noticing'. It is as if Russell has available no language to describe unobserved sensibilia, unoccupied perspectives, no language with which to represent his own theory of knowledge.

He does try to construct such a language, in the form of subjectless subjective descriptions of sensibilia, by a process of elimination, in the passage quoted earlier from *An Outline of Philosophy*. Moving from 'I see a triangle' through 'A triangle is being seen' and 'There is a visual triangle', having eliminated 'A visual triangle exists' because of the 'metaphysical connotations' of *exists*, Russell arrives at 'A visual triangle is occurring' as a representation of that minimal subjectivity which is the sense awareness of instruments.[64] But he links the meaning of the sentence he wishes to construct to the reading of 'There is a triangle' in which 'there is' is translated by 'il y a' or 'es gibt' instead of 'voilà', or 'da ist', namely, the existential as opposed to the deictic reading of 'there is'. But in this case, his statement belongs to the language of physics, in which the object in the world is inferred or constructed outside of any private centre. He therefore does not succeed in finding a sentence which is at once subjective and subjectless, constituting a language of sense which is impersonal, a linguistic representation of the sensibilia recorded by the instrument. Surprisingly, he eliminates as a candidate for such a sentence one in which *this* occurs, either as a replacement for the entire noun phrase *a visual triangle* or which specifies *triangle*. For, as we have seen, *this triangle* is equivalent to *a sensible triangle*. No doubt, the avoidance of the deictic is due to the fact that for Russell *this* implies egocentricity, bringing in an observer. This assumption about the necessary egocentricity of all deictic terms, however, as we have also seen, is not justified if the language of written narrative is taken into account. Indeed, novelistic sentences of the form of those in 1−7 remain the only linguistic way to represent this impersonal subjectivity, this 'centric particularity' which is not egocentric. For speech is always occupied by the speaking subject who says 'I'; it is writing and, specifically, the writing of the novel which, by virtue of a possible absence of the first person, permits sentences which are no longer egocentric. Those speakerless sentences each have, we have argued, a different epistemological status. The speakerless sentences of Narration[65] recount a public space and time that is also centre-less − that of physics, of geometry, of history. The sentences whose past tense is cotemporal with *now* may represent a private centre which is occupied, not by a first person, the speaking subject, but by a third person subject. But other of such sentences with a *now*-in-the-past may represent an empty spatial and temporal centre, an impersonal subjectivity.

It is Russell's theory of sensibilia which lays the groundwork for such a theory of deixis as 'centred particulars' to explain the latter type of narrative sentence. In this theory of knowledge, knowledge of the external world is built upon a solipsistic basis, but an impersonal solipsism which replaces Cartesian privacy by instrumental privacy, a private *here-now* emptied of the person of any observer but in which a *this* nonetheless appears. For the *Cogito*, the sentence which names a subjectivity which is obligatorily first person and present tense, a *this is here and now being recorded* is substituted, or rather, to avoid any confusion with a sentence of speech containing a non-explicit first person, *this was now being recorded* or *this triangle was now occurring* or *The sun had now sunk lower in the sky*, or simply *this was now here*, equivalent of Barthes' photographic 'ça a été'.[66] Thus in a literary style is 'an impersonal system ... built on a foundation of essentially private sense-data', 'a reconstruction of empirical knowledge which is not egocentric', to echo without assenting to Pears's sceptical conclusion to his treatment of Russell's theory of knowledge.[67]

The sentence with *this, here* or *now*, the locus in language of a potentially impersonal subjectivity, but no subject, realised, indeed realisable, only in the writing of the novel, thus represents in language the image externalised from a subject and recorded by the instrument. The *this* pointing to, referring to, sensibilia is, like the referent it names, infected with a dualism, what Hegel calls the two *thises*: 'one this as I; and one as object'.[68] These correspond to the two places with which, in Russell, every sensible is associated , 'e.g. my sensation of the star is associated with the place where I am and with the place where the star is'.[69] 'From a real body,' writes Roland Barthes of the photograph, 'which was there, proceed radiations which ultimately touch me, who am here'.[70] The first *this* − the 'user of the word' − could, however, Russell asserts, be replaced by a machine: 'A machine could be constructed which would use the word "this" correctly: it could say "this is red", "this is blue", "this is a policeman", on suitable occasions.' His example here seems to be some kind of pinball machine − 'automatic machines that play golf'.[71] It places the emphasis misleadingly on the behaviourist notion of verbal response, whereas what is at stake is a sensibile, designated by *this*, defined independently of any observer. For that, Russell found a more appropriate machine model, one which builds in the dualism of sensibilia, of *this*, but in which 'I am replaced by a photographic plate',[72] just as in Barthes it is the light-sensitive film which stands in the place of me, who am here, to catch the emanations of the referent. The dualism of *this* is thus statable without reference to *I*, the 'user of the word', or any personal pronoun. That is why the term Barthes settles on for 'What the Photograph reproduces to infinity' is *this*:

it is the absolute Particular, the sovereign Contingency, matte and somehow stupid, the *This* (this photograph, and not Photography), in short, what Lacan calls the *Tuché*, the Occasion, the Encounter, the Real, in its indefatigable expression ... the Photograph is never anything but an antiphon of 'Look', 'See', 'Here it is'; it points a finger at certain *vis-à-vis*, and cannot escape this pure deictic language.[73]

* * *

What adjustment of literary theory is required to accommodate within the novel as a linguistic form the sentence which records, re-presents, the un-observed, what realignment of the forces distributed in the sentences of objective Narration and those representing a subject? For one is required. Like the photograph for Barthes, the sentence representing an impersonal subjectivity raises questions deriving from a '"stupid" or simple meta-physics',[74] one whose gaze is riveted to the real.

The presently dominant interpretation of the linguistic evidence of narrative fails to recognise in any explicit way the strange properties of such sentences, necessitating a theory of the novel able to accommodate this strangeness, because it comes equipped – overequipped – with a 'sophisticated' metaphysics, a 'sophisticated' theory of knowledge, which masks with the familiar face of the speaker certain simple, brute facts, subsuming all grammatical distinctions under the totalising voice of a narrator, standing in for the author. It is the novelists and novelist-theorists who have registered this adjustment, as if encountering in the very language of the novel a real and empirically determinable possibility, the disturbing presence of something impersonal, inhuman, past and, in that sense, distant, the *this was now here*. Out of this possibility of a written language proceeds an entire productive category: novelistic description, whose special properties perhaps Flaubert was the first to exploit and the first, but only the first, to thematise as the existence of the unobserved, of an infinite number of perspectives, not necessarily occupied by any human subject, enclosing each a moment and a place, sensations, events, unlike any others. This uniquely novelistic style seeks to capture, to arrest within the moment, the appearances of things independent of any observer and his or her desires, prejudices, intentions. It can be taken as the counterpart of what Deleuze, speaking of film, calls 'la conscience-caméra', the consciousness of the camera.[75] Here is that curious theme of Flaubert's writing so suggestively discussed by Genette in which 'l'irrécusable présence de l'image s'oppose à toute interprétation subjectivante' and which aspires to 'une *vue profonde, une pénétration de l'objectif*',[76] resulting in certain recognisable formal features of the novels: the suspension of narrative movement in gratuitous descriptive passages in which the 'presence of an image – a material image – prevents any subjectivising interpretation' and makes the novel, in Roland Barthes's words, 'an intelligible organism of infinite sensibility'.[77]

With Woolf, the problem of the unobserved becomes an explicit and central structuring principle of the novel's thematic form, as we have already seen. Even Proust, whose first person narration seems superficially to restrict itself to the representation of a single occupied perspective, reconstructs an impersonal and objectivised vision of the past 'upon a solipsistic basis', perhaps having discovered it in Flaubert's use of person and tense for the representation not only of third person subjects but of unsensed sensibilia, as in example 7. For it is sensation, allowed to separate itself from the subject and to incapsulate a perspective, a *here-now*, separate and existing unobserved in a past the first person no longer inhabits, which contains the ingredients a novelistic art alone can recapture, 'qui avait fait miroiter une sensation' – made a sensation shimmer or flash out like a mirrored image – 'a la fois dans le passé ... et dans le présent' ('had caused a sensation ... to be mirrored at one and the same time in the past ... and in the present', Andreas Mayor translates the passage).[78] It is significant that that sensation, preserved in a now-in-the-past, is akin for Proust to an instrument for recording sensibilia – either, here, the mirror gathering light rays or elsewhere, Russell's dictaphone or gramophone: 'a sensation from a bygone year – like those recording instruments which preserve the sound and the manner of the various artists who have sung or played into them'.[79] It is likewise significant that Proust's sentence recording the results of the final series of sensations mirrored simultaneously in present and past is a sentence whose past tense – compounded of an *imparfait* co-occurs with a deictic: 'Et *voici* que soudain l'effet de cette dure loi s'était trouvé neutralisé ...', translated by Mayor as 'And *now*, suddenly, the effect of this harsh law *had been* neutralised ...' (my italics).[80]

Finally, that mirrored moment, that past *now*, externalised from the *I* inhabiting the present *now*, partakes of the properties of unobserved moments recorded by instruments, even if it was once inhabited by a past *I*. The idea that the sensation joining past to *now* is an essentially external, unobserved moment seized in some other way than by direct observation is contained in Proust's phrase 'what normally it', *it* coreferential with 'my being' – 'never apprehends'; the sensation 'had added to the dreams of the imagination the concept of "existence" which they usually lack', making it possible 'for my being to secure, to isolate, to immobilise – for a moment brief as a flash of lightning – what normally it never apprehends: a fragment of time in the pure state.'[81] Here the *this was now here* bears witness to the existence in the real, i.e., outside any observer, of a grouping of sensible events which the *I* may have once experienced, but which he no longer inhabits as a subject.

But something more is encountered in the language of the novel than the mere possibility of unobserved sensibilia. Outside the mind and independent of human intention and desire, thereby bearing witness to the real, to the existence of something which escapes man's control, in the appearances of things themselves, endowed with a dualism, is incorporated the very gaze of the missing observer, the very sensitivity of the instrument. It is as if the novelist, like the astronomer gazing at the image in the object glass, at the photograph of things that no one has ever seen – meets there the look of things themselves, in the double sense of *look*, whereby the star, the lighthouse, Lacan's sardine can in the sea, flash back, like so many mirrors, the now disembodied look of the observer. This mindless, bodiless look is that of Deleuze's 'conscience-caméra', the 'point de vue d'un autre oeil ... la pure vision d'un oeil non-humain, d'un oeil qui serait dans les choses ... ce que Cézanne appelait le monde d'avant l'homme';[82] it is what Sartre called 'le grand regard pétrifiant des choses'[83] which he discovered as novelist in *La Nausée*. This vision, this sensation is blind, insensible, silent, unconscious – only the gathering of appearances into a 'prehensive' unity around a centre in a sensitive instrument which has no human eye, no human mind, behind it. It escapes the control of the subject, the ego, emitting its light waves, its sound waves, in the absence of man, speaker and subject, or, if it is observed, returning to look with no look of recognition, but only the impersonal stare of an eye that does not see, like the flowers in the garden of the deserted house in *To the Lighthouse*, 'standing there, looking before them, looking up, yet beholding nothing, eyeless, and so terrible.'[84] Woolf would call this unseeing and unseen look of things, mirroring the universe, variously art and death: 'the shape of loveliness itself', 'a form from which life had parted, solitary like a pool at evening, far distant, seen from a train window, vanishing so quickly that the pool, pale in the evening, is scarcely robbed of its solitude, though once seen.'[85] For Foucault it was 'la pensée du dehors', in which 'miroite un langage sans sujet assignable, une loi sans dieu, un pronoun personnel sans personnage, un visage sans expression et sans yeux'.[86] That reflecting but non-reflexive language without a subject has its purest formal realisation in the novel, Proustian telescope, the only linguistic form permitting, like the instrument, the separation of observer and observed and allowing the latter to emerge independent, unobserved, isolating, immobilising, for the space of a flash of lightning, what is normally never apprehended. It is in this sense that Barthes pronounces the novel a Death[87] – like the photograph in his analysis, whose gathering of light rays bespeak '*that* is dead and *that* is going to die'.[88]

That eyeless face, in this passage from Foucault an allusion to Maurice Blanchot's essay 'The gaze of Orpheus', to Eurydice with 'her body closed, her face sealed',[89] is the face whose unseeing eyes have seen death, like the eyes of Napoleon's youngest brother in the photograph with which Barthes begins his essay: 'I am looking at eyes that looked at the Emperor'.[90] But it is also the face of the instrument, of the photographic plate, just as the deaf voice of Blanchot's sirens, 'cette présence sourde' in Foucault's phrase, is the voice of the recording. It constitutes the very look of the world, of the object which, for Blanchot, 'chimère injustifiable si je n'étais pa là', in that deictic space of sensation, nevertheless is what creates the subject's sensible existence, 'ce regard qui continue à me voir dans mon absence', 'l'oeil que ma disparition, à mésure qu'elle devient plus incomplète, exige de plus en plus pour me perpétuer comme objet de vision.'[91] The subject, 'ce spectateur absurde',[92] is restored by a passive reflection of that *cogito* which bespeaks the look of things – 'Je suis vu'.[93] – at just that point at which his existence, his presence has been demonstrated as unnecessary:

Sans couleur, inscrit dans nulle forme pensable, n'étant non plus le produit d'un puissant cerveau, je suis la seule image renversée de toutes choses. Je lui donne, sous mon format, la vision personnelle non seulement de la mer, mais de l'écho de la colline qui retentit encore du cri du premier homme ... une unité parfaite, au prisme que je suis, restitue la dissipation infinie qui permet de tout voir sans rien voir.[94]

The subject comes to exist only in a world in which its non-existence somewhere, sometime, in some other perceptual space than that of the 'I see', is a reality, to which the sensibilia recorded by the instrument bear witness, as does the writing of the novel. And it is Blanchot who has, in addressing the specifically grammatical properties of novelistic sentences most directly confronted a 'death sentence' (the phrase is, of course, the translation of Blanchot's 'l'arrêt de mort') authored by no one − 'n'étant non plus le produit d'un puissant cerveau' − but inscribed in the very properties of language. The instrumental *cogito*, the *this was now here*, becomes not simply its reversed image, but its negation. In the writing of 'Je pense, donc je ne suis pas', Blanchot's Thomas conjures up a vision in which an optic glass unites the properties of a sense knowledge without an observing subject:

Au milieu d'une immense campagne, une loupe flamboyante recevait les rayons dispersés du soleil et, par ces feux, elle prenait conscience d'elle-même comme d'un moi monstrueux, non pas aux points où elle les recevait, mais au point où elle les projetait et les unissait en un faisceau unique.

That lens inscribes a *cogito* which is a representation of events grouped around an empty centre incorporating the dualism separated from subject and object and located within a neutral − the term is Blanchot's as much as Russell's − space and time which is neither subjective in the sense of personal nor objective in that this neutral space-time is *here-now*.

Je pense, dit-il, je réunis tout ce qui est lumière sans chaleur, rayons sans éclat, produits non raffinés, je les brasse et les conjugue et, dans une première absence de moi-même, je me découvre au sein de la plus vive intensité comme une unité parfaite. Je pense, dit-il, je suis sujet et objet d'une irradiation toute-puissante; soleil qui emploie toute son énergie aussi bien à se faire nuit qu'à se faire soleil. Je pense: là où la pensée s'ajoute à moi, moi, je puis me soustraire de l'être, sans diminution, ni changement, par une métamorphose qui me conserve à moi-même en dehors de tout repaire òu me saisir. C'est la propriété de ma pensée, non pas de m'assurer de l'existence, comme toutes choses, comme la pierre, mais de m'assurer de l'être dans le néant même et de me convier à n'être pas pour me faire sentir alors mon admirable absence.[95]

Notes

1   Roland Barthes is right to insist on the crucial importance of the chemical processes in the development of photography:

It is often said that it was the painters who invented Photography (by bequeathing it their framing, the Albertian perspective, and the optic of the *camera obscura*). I say: no, it was the chemists. For the *noeme* 'That-has-been' was possible only on the day when a scientific circumstance (the discovery that silver halogens were sensitive to light) made it possible to recover and print directly the luminous rays emitted by a variously lighted object.
(*Camera Lucida: Reflections on Photography*, translated by Richard Howard, New York, 1981, p. 80.)

These processes can be divided into two, one which develops or 'reveals' (to invoke the French technical term) a latent image captured on a light-sensitive plate or film, and another which 'fixes' that image so that it will not fade in the light, so that it will not disappear with the moment in which it occurred, unseen. In this way, the appearances of things unseen may touch the eye of an observer, as Barthes puts it, echoing Susan Sontag, 'like the delayed rays of a star' (p. 81), thereby converting all viewers of photographs into astronomers.

The process ending in the development of the photograph may thus be said to have begun when in the seventeenth century men of science gazed through 'optic glass' at what was beyond the powers of human observation. The instrument could embody that 'ideal observer' of science, guarantee of a precision and rigour in measurement beyond the capacity of the human observer, because the power of observation has been removed from the individual subject and placed safely within an impersonal instrument, not so as to place sensation beyond the reach of thought, but to make accessible to thought a more invariant and consistent data. For what was unseen by the human eye is revealed in the lens, and later, the photograph, to be much more than distant stars and invisible atoms. Perhaps it was not the painters who invented photographic space, but the lens itself, if only in the form of a mirror and 'the optic of the *camera obscura*', which revealed the structure of a perspective built into each portion of the visible, of the sensible, world, just as later the photograph would analyse the legs of running horses into sequences of movements which no painter's eye had hitherto seen.

2   Bertrand Russell, *My Philosophical Development*, New York, 1959, p. 106.

3   Bertrand Russell, *An Outline of Philosophy*, Cleveland & New York, 1960, p. 63.

4   Alexandre Koyré, *Etudes d'Histoire de la Pensée Scientifique*, Paris, 1966, p. 47.

5   Bertrand Russell, 'The relation of sense-data to physics', in *Mysticism and Logic*, Garden City, New York, 1957, p. 149.

6   Russell's sensibilia thus share with Frege's *Gedanke* this conjunction of subjectivity and impersonality which is a function of being externalisable from a mind and, for Frege, analogous, as we shall see shortly, with the image in the ground glass of the telescope. See *Translations from the Philosophical Writings of Gottlob Frege*, translated by Peter Geach & Max Black, Oxford, 1977, p. 60. Jaakko Hintikka likens this notion of Frege's to Wittgenstein's identification of 'the metaphysical subject with a totality of propositions'. 'On Wittgenstein's "solipsism"', *Mind*, 67, 1958, p. 90.

Another version of a knowledge which is externalised from a subject and thereby 'objectivised' is Popper's notion of objective knowledge, which is one not 'possessed by some knowing subject'. It 'consists of the logical content of our theories, conjectures, guesses (and, if we like, of the logical content of our genetic code)'. Karl Popper, *Objective Knowledge: An Evolutionary Approach*, Oxford, 1972, p. 73. But Popper eliminates Russellian sensibilia as candidates for objective knowledge in dismissing 'that radical form of idealism − "neutral monism" (as it was called by Mach and Russell)', p. 86. As Popper understands Russell's theory of sense knowledge, sensibilia are 'possessed by some knowing subject'.

7   Bertrand Russell, *The Analysis of Mind*, London, 1921, p. 132.

8   'The relation of sense-data to physics', p. 145.

9   Bertrand Russell, *The Analysis of Matter*, New York, 1954, p. 224.

10   *An Outline of Philosophy*, p. 62.

11   The relation of sense-data to physics', p. 145.

12   *The Analysis of Matter*, p. 213.

13   *Tractatus*, 5.64, p. 58.

14   Alfred North Whitehead, *Science and the Modern World*, Lowell Lectures, 1925, New York, 1948, p.110.

15   'Sense and reference', in *Translations from the Philosophical Writings of Gottlob Frege*, p.60.

16   Bertrand Russell, *Our Knowledge of the External World as a Field for Scientific Method in Philosophy*, London, 1922, p.94. See also *My Philosophical Development*, p.24.

17   *Science and the Modern World*, p.68.

18   For 'Leibniz', as Russell points out, 'did not carry his monadism far enough, since he applied it only spatially. Not only is a man private from other people, he is also private from his past and future selves.' *Human Knowledge: Its Scope and limits*, New York, 1948, p.90.

19   *Science and the Modern World*, p.110.

20   *The Analysis of Mind*, p.230.

21   *Ibid.*, p.130.

22   *The Analysis of Matter*, p.222.

23   See Chapter 7 of *An Inquiry into Meaning and Truth*, London, 1940, and Chapter 4 of *Human Knowledge*.

24   *Human Knowledge*, p.90.

25   *An Outline of Philosophy*, p.216.

26   *An Inquiry Into Meaning and Truth*, Harmondsworth, Middlesex, 1962, p.102.

27   Maurice Blanchot, 'The narrative voice: (the "he," the neuter)', in *The Gaze of Orpheus and Other Literary Essays*, translated by Lydia Davis, New York, 1981, p.136. See my essay *'Ecriture, narration and the grammar of French'*, in *Narrative: From Malory to Motion Pictures*, Stratford-upon-Avon Studies, edited by Jeremy Hawthorn, London, 1985, pp.1–22, for a discussion of the mistranslation of *il* in the two English translations of Blanchot's essay.

28   Blanchot, *L'Ecriture du Désastre*, Paris, 1980, p.1980.

29   Emile Benveniste, *Problèmes de Linguistique Générale*, Paris, 1966, p.239.

30   Gustave Flaubert, 'Un Coeur Simple', in *Trois Contes*, Paris, 1965, p.62, translated as 'A Simple Heart' in *Three Tales*, translated by Robert Baldick, Harmondsworth, 1961, p.41.

31   Virginia Woolf, *The Years*, London, 1972, p.267.

32   Virginia Woolf, *To the Lighthouse*, London, 1974, p.53.

33   *Our Knowledge of the External World*, p.122.

34   *Science and the Modern World*, p.68.

35   *Human Knowledge*, p.90.

36   *Ibid.*, p.91.

37   *Ibid.*, p.91.

38   *Ibid.*, p.91.

39   Gustave Flaubert, 'Un Coeur Simple' in *Oeuvres* II, Paris, Bibliothèque de la Pléiade, 1951, p.592.

40   *Human Knowledge*, p.92.

41   Virginia Woolf, *The Years*, p.103.

42   Gustave Flaubert, *Madame Bovary* in *Oeuvres*, I, Biblothàue de la Pléiade, Paris, 1951, p.374.

43   See Ann Banfield, *Unspeakable Sentences*, Boston & London, 1982, pp.196ff and, for the notion of nouns and adjectives 'of quality', Jean-Claude Milner, *De la Syntaxe à l'Interpretation*, Paris, 1978.

44   William Faulkner, *The Hamlet*, New York, 1940, p. 459.

45   Virginia Woolf, *The Waves*, London, 1972, p. 129.

46   *The Waves*, p. 148.

47   *The Waves*, p. 148.

48   *The Waves*, p. 20.

49   *The Waves*, p. 167.

50   *Madame Bovary*, p.

51   *The Years*, p. 103.

52   *Madame Bovary*, p. 374.

53   *The Waves*, p. 204. The notion is presented as a problem for art, for, in particular, a literary style: 'But how describe the world seen without a self?' The fact that Bernard at this point in the text answers 'There are no words' is first of all as an indication of the centrality of the problem of the unobserved and its representation in Woolf: the world without a self is a *seen world*. The failure of language is the failure of what Bernard here calls 'articulate words' − 'what we cannot speak about', to use Wittgenstein's formula. It is art which seeks to make manifest in language what cannot be spoken about.

54   *The Waves*, p. 6.

55   Virginia Woolf, *To the Lighthouse*, p. 206.

56   *Ibid.*, p. 144.

57   *Ibid.*, p. 153.

58   *Ibid.*, p. 144.

59   A. J. Ayer, *Bertrand Russell*, New York, 1972, p. 53.

60   *Ibid.*, p. 54.

61   Bertrand Russell, 'The philosophy of logical atomism' in *Logic and Knowledge: Essays 1901−1950*, London, 1956, p. 201.

62   *An Inquiry Into Meaning and Truth*, pp. 103−4.

63   *Ibid.*, p. 105.

64   *An Outline of Philosophy*, pp. 214−16.

65   *Unspeakable Sentences*, pp. 265ff.

66   Roland Barthes, *La Chambre Claire: Note sur la Photographie*, Paris, 1980, p. 146, translated as 'that-has-been', *Camera Lucida*, p. 94.

67   David Pears, *Bertrand Russell and the British Tradition in Philosophy*, New York, 1967, p. 269.

68   G. W. F. Hegel, *The Phenomenology of Mind*, translated by J. B. Baillie, New York, 1967, p. 150.

69   *The Analysis of Mind*, p. 130.

70   *Camera Lucida*, p. 80.

71   *An Inquiry Into Meaning and Truth*, p. 105.

72   *The Analysis of Mind*, p. 130.

73   *Camera Lucida*, pp. 4−5.

74   *Ibid.*, p. 85.

75   Gilles Deleuze, *Cinéma I: L'Image-Mouvement*, Paris, 1983, p. 117.

76   Gérard Genette, 'Silences de Flaubert' in *Figures I*, Paris, 1966, pp. 231, 228.

77   Quoted in Genette, p. 240.

78   Marcel Proust, *Le Temps Retrouvé, A la Recherche du Temps Perdu* III,

Paris, 1954, p. 872. Translated as *The Past Recaptured* by Andreas Mayor, New York, 1971, p. 133.

79   *Le Côté de Guermantes, A la Recherche du Temps Perdu* II, Paris, 1954, p. 11. Translated as *The Guermantes Way, The Remembrance of Things Past*, II, by C. K. Scott Montcrieff & Terence Kilmartin, New York, 1981, p. 5.

80   *A la Recherche du Temps Perdu* III, p. 872, and *The Past Recaptured*, p. 133.

81   *A la Recherche du Temps Perdu* III, p. 872 and *The Past Recaptured*, pp. 133–4.

82   *L'Image-Mouvement*, p. 117.

83   Cited in Genette, p. 236.

84   *To the Lighthouse*, p. 154.

85   *Ibid.*, pp. 147–8.

86   Michel Foucault, *La Pensée du Dehors*, Editions Fata Morgana, 1986, p. 48.

87   Roland Barthes, *Writing Degree Zero*, New York, 1968, p. 39.

88   *Camera Lucida*, p. 96.

89   Maurice Blanchot, 'The gaze of Orpheus' in *The Gaze of Orpheus and Other Essays*, p. 100.

90   *Camera Lucida*, p. 3.

91   Maurice Blanchot, *Thomas l'Obscur*, Paris, 1950, pp. 124–5.

92   *Ibid.*, p. 127.

93   *Ibid.*, pp. 124–5.

94   *Ibid.*, p. 126.

95   *Ibid.*, pp. 114–6.

Opening Statement: theory and practice

There is an inevitable distinction between the form of a paper given at a conference and its published form in the conference proceedings. Normally such differences are passed over in silence – to admit to them is to disrupt the objective discourse of knowledge by admitting either its temporality (it wasn't quite finished when first delivered) or, possibly worse, its mutability (it has been subjected in discussion to such cogent criticism that the argument has been completely reworked). This published paper is, however, so different from the one delivered to the conference that it is worth remarking on the differences between its spoken and its written form. The aim of the original talk was to serve as some kind of conclusion to the conference, but the title was meant to indicate that this conclusion would be not a closure, but an exhortation to future work.

The goal of the conference, in bringing together figures from very different theoretical perspectives, was not to provide some totalising moment which would reconcile these different perspectives into a definitive theoretical model for the study of the relations between language and writing. Such a suggestion, with all its finalising confidence, would be very alien to the practice of the Programme in Literary Linguistics, which sponsored the conference. In the Programme the resolution of different theoretical perspectives does not come in a master plan to be handed down in tablets of stone but in specific curricular and pedagogic suggestions produced by each individual student in relation to his or her own cultural, linguistic and educational situation.

In a conference of the kind we had organised it was impossible to undertake such work but my talk would, in some sense, stand in place of that work as an indication of what now needed to be done to turn the conference into a genuine force within a whole variety of educational systems. To that end I had produced a paper in two parts, the first of which briefly indicated the historical, social and literary determinations of the language we know as English and the second of which suggested some of the linguistic and literary implications of that account. The talk attempted to draw out some of the elements of the conference, particularly Pratt's paper and Derrida's comments on it, and to indicate some of the practical consequences for our understanding both of education and of writing.

The contradiction of the paper, which reduplicated the major contradiction of the conference, was that it was my firm belief that these practical consequences must be worked out in relation to very specific educational situations while an international conference, by definition, offers no such specificity. However, if this contradiction troubled me theoretically, it was of no pressing concern as I sat down for the general discussion session which was to precede my talk. Pressing, however, it became in the next ten minutes as howls of protest were voiced by many of the participants about a conference which had not allowed their specific situation and voices to be heard. This generalised demand for participation upset and annoyed me. Upset because I was one of the organisers of the conference and was unhappy that so many of those attending were dissatisfied; annoyed because the grounds for this dissatisfaction seemed to ignore the rationale of the conference. While an international conference inevitably involves some loss of specificity, it is also the case that one element in any specific educational situation is the international organisation of knowledge. This conference had brought together speakers from three continents to produce some kind of purchase on that international situation. The logistics and cost of such a conference meant, however, that the purchase would result from the juxtaposition and montage of differing views rather than from a detailed working out of particular positions between speaker and audience. So much had been obvious to me as an organiser and I felt that so much should have been obvious to anybody who had decided to attend the conference. My irritation was compounded by the main counterpoint in this paean of protest: many protested that Marxist positions on language had not been sufficiently represented. In fact, this complaint effectively boiled down to a complaint that language existed and could not simply be reduced into the class struggle, a fact which had dawned even on Stalin as long ago as 1952. Indeed both Pratt and Williams had offered very interesting accounts of how to understand relations between linguistic development and class struggle but they fell far short of that dissolution of language into the social which several speakers now seemed to assume.

The real gall and wormwood of this session came, however, in comments from Pratap Rughani in which he deplored the Eurocentric bias of the conference. This criticism differed from the other two in that it was both completely justified and, further, seriously undercut the aims of the conference. The initial project of the conference, as of the Programme in Literary Linguistics, was to bring together four very different elements. To a traditional stylistics revivified by discourse analysis and pragmatics was added both a concern with the social and historical development of language and an attention to the working of the signifier. However, all these are constantly informed in the Programme, as it was intended they would be in the conference, by a constant awareness of the status and significance of English both as a world language, serving as a second language for almost all international interchange, and as a world of languages as the empire strikes back linguistically across the globe. The most important development of English in this century is how a whole variety of peoples subjected to the language of the imperial master have reappropriated it for their own uses. It was this final element, crucial to us as organisers, which we had simply failed to get into the conference. Even a plea of ignorance was impossible, only incompetence could explain why there were not speakers on pidgin and creole or on the debates in the Third World about national languages, both topics of considerable importance within the programme.

It was thus a speaker in some state of confusion who stepped to the dais. On the one hand, I felt I should abandon my paper and address those who had complained about the organisation of the conference, but, at the same time, I felt that the content of the paper provided better answers than I could provide extempore, as well as addressing directly the questions raised by those who had complained of a lack of social and historical content. I was also aware that there were many in the hall who did not share the *ressentiment* so far expressed and who would themselves be annoyed if I did not deliver my paper. I managed the worst of both worlds, spending some time expressing the opinions which I have more elegantly expressed above and then, as I sensed impatience from some of my audience, hurtling into my paper. Melodrama now descended into farce as a vote was demanded from the audience as to whether I should deliver my prepared paper. Unfortunately, or fortunately, a majority voted that I should continue. However, there was now no time to deliver the paper as originally written and the whole second half had to be delivered in hurried abridgement.

I have taken the rather extraordinary context of the original delivery as *carte blanche* to completely rework this talk. The structure remains the same but I have reorganised the history of the first half to make its ideological points clearer and I have included in the second half arguments which I have only elaborated properly since the conference. In particular it is only since reading Chomsky's extraordinarily illuminating recent text *Knowledge of Language* that I have resolved many of the problems to my own satisfaction. What I have not done is to try and artificially include in the paper material which would answer Rughani's well-made criticism. I hope that the paper demonstrates its awareness of the political and social context both of the historical development of English and of the academic disciplines of literature and linguistics. There is, however, no doubt that to consider fully the role of language and literature in the relations between the first and third world we would need, at the very least, what I swore as I delivered this paper I would never again commit myself to involvement in, the organisation of another conference.

Stanley Fish has argued recently that theory can have no effect on practice.[1] This argument depends on defining theory in such a way that it becomes an impossible abstraction and to ignore the very different levels of practice and the relations between them. For me, theory can be sufficiently defined in terms of various kinds of abstraction and idealisation which enable us to discover systems of relationships which can then inform interpretation not simply at the level of individual readings but at the more basic levels of curriculum and pedagogy on which these individual readings depend. How we theoretically place writing in our linguistics will have major consequences for our practice: both educational and social. It is, of course, the case that this century has seen linguistics consolidate itself in terms of conceptions of language which ignored writing as anything but an inadequate record of speech. The reasons for this have been complex. Two important practical reasons can be briefly indicated. On the one hand this accorded with the desire of linguists cataloguing and describing the Amerindian languages to free themselves from Indo-European models.[2] More recently, sociolinguistics has so far almost entirely identified its object as the spoken language.[3] Theoretically, this consolidation of linguistics allowed Saussure to ignore the diachronic in favour of the synchronic, and Chomsky the social in favour of the individual. In fact, in both Saussure's distinction between *langue* and *parole* and Chomsky's distinction between competence and performance, we find a similar division between the abstract system of the language and the individual speaker.[4] Such theoretical choices mean that any social questions about language are considered to be *subsequent* to questions of the language's constitution.

These theories are necessarily blind to what one might call either the *sociality* or the *institutionality* of language – the different way in which they reproduce themselves, interact with other languages, grow or decline. Questions of the place of writing within linguistics are a way of focusing this blindness. In thus talking of writing I may seem to suggest, as other references at the conference have suggested, that we talk of a single and unchanging technology. But, of course, writing is not simply a technical matter of reproduction, be it stylus on wax tablet or quill pen on parchment, but a whole system of education and production which produces writers and readers and material texts. Technical and social questions are inseparable when we consider the place of writing in the production and reproduction of a language. To show how inseparable, I want briefly to reflect on the history of English. In talking of English my aim is not to produce an account which could automatically be transferred to any other language, rather it will be, briefly and emblematically, to indicate the kind of concerns we must addres if we are to understand a language's social constitution and the place that the dialectic between language and speech can play in that constitution.

English is, in its earliest recognisable manifestations, an Anglo-Latin creole.[5] It was the socially despised language of a conquered under-class. When, however, the French-speaking aristocracy lost their base in France, they gradually adopted the language of their servants and soldiers. The full social history of this development has not yet been written and, given the state of the archive, it is unlikely whether it is possible.[6] It seems probable, however, that it is this complex social history that makes early writers on

English from Caxton to Sidney so uncertain of the claims of English. It is not only when compared to the great languages of antiquity but also to rivals in Italy, France and Spain that English seems to be lacking to those who write about it before 1580. Andrew Borde need not be taken as untypical when he writes in the 1540s: 'The speche of Englande is a base speche to other noble speches, as Italion, Castylion, and Frenche'.[7]

When Caxton writes his famous preface to the *Aeneid* some fifty years earlier he is convinced of English's particular mutability and unsteadiness and he indicates with great clarity the dilemma facing the merchant class, of which he is so notable a representative. It might be hazarded as a guess that Caxton's own super-sensibility to the national and class questions are due on the one hand to his prominent membership of the London bourgeoisie and, on the other, to the fact that he himself originally spoke with a broad Kentish accent, the accent which was already defining the national standard by the fact of its exclusion as sub-standard – a language fit only for workmen and fools.[8] A national language is required for purposes of commerce and identification but these two purposes are not one.[9] Of course, everybody will need to speak the language for the purpose of commerce (and Caxton is not the only writer on the language who includes examples of members of different classes being unable to communicate for purposes of trade as evidence of the failings of the English tongue). But those who will identify the language as theirs, and will identify themselves in the language, must be limited to a ruling class. How that class will be constituted is, famously, one of the crucial political questions fought out until the Glorious Revolution of 1688 put a final seal on the settlement of the Restoration. What is never sufficiently discussed in literature courses is the extent that the literature from the 1580s onwards is a (perhaps the) privileged site where that class question is fought out linguistically. Caxton, and indeed other writers after him, had already indicated that the national language would be identified with a written language which would find its prestige in a privileged relationship to the classics, but what that written language would be from orthography to vocabulary, and even to syntax, was very definitely an open question. Before 1580 such questions had been discussed in terms of a general pessimism.[10] From thenceforth it is an aggressive optimism which seeks to define what is at stake. What is at stake is as much who is to be excluded as who is to be included. Shakespeare and Spenser make a perfect comparison here. Spenser, working within traditional pattern of patronage, linked to an aristocratic court, produces a language which is aggressively English but which requires the scholarly gloss of an E. K. to make it readable. Whether Spenser and E. K. are one and the same is beside the crucial point that this English text is only to be read by the learned and initiate circle, the language of the *Shepheardes Calendar* fitting neatly with the allegory of *The Faerie Queene* to produce an address which reproduces the allegiance to an imaginary feudal past. It is normal to regard Spenser's linguistic experiments as rather eccentric, but a different history which would have produced an early absolutist court in England might well have determined it as a dominant poetic discourse. There was, however, a very different linguistic practice which Shakespeare was employing within a commercial theatre where the audience was composed of a variety of social classes. There was still exclusion here − indeed the production of a stereotyped Kentish to mark fools and yokels as those outside the linguistic pale is part and parcel of the constitution of the national standard.[11] However, it is crucial both for Shakespeare's aesthetics and politics that one should be able to move through the various registers and dialects of English. Edgar and Prince Hal are two examples who spring immediately to mind. These alternative politics of literary language relate to the whole variety of complicated social practice but to none more importantly than education.[12] The growth of literacy in this period is very considerable and it is this growing literacy, as much as any other, which fuels the ideological battles up to and through the protectorate. Milton stands in some ways as the climax, within the high literary tradition, of an English absolutely established as a national standard but, theoretically, open to all. For Milton there is no question but that English is superior in its potential to both its contemporary continental rivals and to the languages of antiquity; the opening lines of *Paradise Lost* make this clear. At the same time Milton clearly feels that his poem is open to all those with the correct ethical stance. The paucity of the audience is determined by the lack of religious and ethically fit readers rather than by their social qualifications.

Paradise Lost, however, is written after the Restoration as a ruling class which has constituted itself politically and economically attempts to regulate the ideological sphere. This regulation takes a multitude of forms most crucially affecting religion, education, and literacy (and literacy's concomitant access to freedom of interpretation of the Bible). The language is regulated in all its forms from speech through vocabulary to syntax to text. In this regulation, Milton has a curious role to play. As the writer who has most thoroughly mastered the classical tradition, he becomes a trophy of a narrow class-based definition of English but at the same time his regicide and republican attitudes, as well as his refusal to fix meaning, means that he must be re-written.[13] Bentley sets to work. Later, Johnson, as well as producing the dictionary, will castigate Shakespeare for the varied registers he uses and long for a literary tradition which will observe the linguistic propriety which will render the literature into a language which is not spoken by the majority of the people. Many of these developments are most clearly elaborated in John Walker's *A Critical Pronouncing Dictionary* (1791) which makes absolutely clear that the aim of this regulation is the exclusion of the vast majority that do not share the 'correct pronunciation'.[14] Walker's text deliberately sets out to bring speech into line with writing and thus concludes that identification of the language with the written, and the written with a class-based education which had been at work since the beginning of the sixteenth century.

It is at this point that a fresh difficulty surfaces; the need for a literate population. This is a very different desire from the sixteenth-century wish for a population of Bible readers. The imperative now is provided directly by the developments of capital and the need for a literate workforce to participate fully in the next stage of industrial development. Throughout the nineteenth century, culminating in the provisions of 1870, universal literacy becomes a possibility and a necessity.[15] If we take 1900 as a crucial moment then we can reflect that the language any citizen will speak will bear a complicated relation to this massively reproduced standard. By a deep historical irony, it is at just this moment that linguistics is beginning to free itself from considerations of normativity and undertaking the systematic description of speech forms. It is not belittling that effort, and its necessity, to say now that, in retrospect, we can see that the study should not just have been of the spoken forms but of the relation between those forms and the officially reproduced standard. Before, however, turning to what the consequences of that might be in educational, linguistic or literary terms, I want to complicate the question a little further.

Modernism can be understood, in one of its most important aspects, as an attempt within literature to come to terms with this new educational and linguistic situation in which the vast majority of the population are now literate and the relation between speech and writing, if regulated in the educational sphere, is now deeply problematic. One has only to think of *The Wasteland* and its original Dickensian epigraph − 'he do the police in different voices'[16] − to realise how deep this crisis runs. But Eliot is concerned to find fragments to shore against his ruins, whereas much of the force of modernism − and here Joyce is for me the exemplary figure − deliberately subverts and undoes the identification of the language with the written and the written with a classically defined literary tradition. The introduction into *Ulysses* of an advertising canvasser whose call at the National Library is to search for an advertisement in a provincial paper displays ironically the new organisation of language with which Joyce concerns himself. And Joyce's radicalism is given its cutting edge by his position as colonial subject. The impossibility of merging speech and writing finds its most acute symptom in the need to find definitions for Ireland not wholly dominated by England.[17] Joyce's work, however, suffers from a constitutive contradiction, endemic to much modernism, whereby the attempt to undermine and contest the high literary tradition is enacted within commercial forms and markets which are determined by that tradition. I do not have time in this brief lecture to consider the very complex history of Ireland which condemned Joyce to exclusively written work. Emblematically, however, let us remember that Joyce opened the first cinema in Ireland.[18] And, suggestively, can we imagine a different Irish history which would have seen Yeats and Joyce participating in an Abbey multi-media centre. There the multitude of voices and gestures which crowd the pages of *Finnegans Wake* would have found a more productive cultural and political space in which to operate (it should be obvious that such an imaginary history would necessarily involve a very different national liberation than the one Ireland achieved in 1922).

But leaving aside the particular victories and defeats of Ireland in this century, this imaginary history has the advantage of immediately drawing our attention to the new media of communication: radio and cinema, followed by television and the technologies of recorded sound which have done so much to transform the linguistic space in which we move. The introduction of recorded speech as a massive part of our linguistic environment marks a change in our culture which may come to seem as momentous as printing. It also means that to understand the reproduction of any speech community we must now grasp its relation to the mass media as well as its relationship to the educational system. All this is merely obvious at some political levels (in Britain one immediately thinks of the political struggle for a Welsh language television station) but it is far from obvious at others. Any serious contemporary discussion of language must also consider this phenomenon which Walter Ong has named 'secondary orality'.[19] To continue the kind of social analysis of English into the twentieth century it would be necessary to grasp fully the importance and significance of this secondary orality.

It is in this enlarged linguistic context which I have just sketched that it becomes fully possible to envisage the linguistics called for by Mary Louise Pratt: a linguistics which understands language as constituted across the various institutional struggles and technological transformations that I have just indicated. It is important to realise that this account makes it impossible for us to think first of language, and then only secondarily the speakers that use it or the technologies that transmit it. The language is constituted in relations of power and domination, themselves inseparable from the relations which the technology enacts, which place speakers in a pragmatic situation.[20] There are not speakers and language but speakers of the language in the kind of complex relations I have indicated.

I must say, however, that I share Jacques Derrida's worries[21] about the term 'linguistics of contact'. It runs the risk of reproducing, in the notion of 'contact', many of the features of a linguistics of communication and the notion of a speech community from which Pratt was seeking to distance herself. Contact does have the advantage of immediately indicating that there is not one single community and it immediately introduces the possibility of language being used to emphasise a lack of communication as well as to facilitate communication. However, the risk is that it would seem to assume two communities meeting and that they meet on equal terms. The risk is, thus, twofold. The notion of community which Pratt so brilliantly unpicked at a primary level is now re-introduced at the secondary level. Moreover, the unevenness and multiplicity of power-relations within a language is likely to be lost because the semantic range of 'contact' would suggest one primary opposition. In searching for a more appropriate lexical item the first alternative that sprang to my mind was a 'linguistics of domination'. This term has the advantage of stressing inequality, and of alluding to the desire which is always at stake in language. However, it still suggests that there are two distinct entities: a dominating and a dominated. In addition it has the further disadvantage of suggesting that domination is always successful, of being unable to account for the play of chance and will which enables subjected sections of the linguistic community to find a voice if only in elaborate forms of mimicry or jokes. The term which I very seriously wish to suggest might perhaps best capture the situation Pratt so well described is a 'linguistics of conflict'. This final term is still misleading if it suggests that what is being described is a conflict between two different entities. There are not two groups of speakers with a different relation to the language: two speech communities instead of one. Rather the language is constituted across a whole variety of relations and struggles. Any given speaker will participate differently in those relations and struggles. It is absolutely essential to recognise that doing away with the idealised speech community also does away with an idealised speaker. There is no more necessary unity to be sought in the speaker than in the community. Just as there are a multiplicity of collectivities striving for definition and identification within a single national language (where it becomes clear that you can replace 'national', but only with some other political social or ideological entity clearly recognised by the speakers) so each speaker is him or herself a member of a multiplicity of collectivities and is, therefore, constituted as contradictory and divided in relation to the language.

This is not for a moment to deny either that there may be a single dominant conflict between collectivities (classically, in terms of class), nor that it is impossible for a speaker to identify almost completely with the dominant definition of the collectivity (the voice of the dominant and hegemonic sector). But it is important theoretically to recognise the multiplicitly, particularly as within advanced developed countries it is empirically arguable that there are at least four important collectivities in relation to speech (class, race, gender and age) and that no matter how totally there is identification with the voice of the dominant and hegemonic sector, that voice will bear traces and echoes of the conflicts it seeks to conceal.[22]

There is, however, another very important reservation to be made about the linguistics of conflict. It was made clearly by Derrida when, in agreeing with Pratt, he also signalled his agreement with a comment on that paper by someone, speaking in the name of 'hard' linguistics, who insisted that this new linguistics could not supervene or contradict the search for invariants. Derrida went on to emphasise that 'what science has to do, what linguistics has to do, is never give up the necessity, the desire to formalise, to exhaust the analysis of codes, of the invariants.'[23]

The crucial question is how we understand the relations between a 'linguistics of conflict' and a 'linguistics of invariance'. Derrida seems to assume, in the comments he made after the passage I have quoted, that the linguistics of invariance is related to the linguistics of conflict as stability to crisis.

This is, I feel, a misleading model and I would now like to outline what I think the relations between them are and the different way in which they would constitute their object and procedures.

In his most recent work *Knowledge of Language* Noam Chomsky looks back on the thirty year history of generative grammar. In the first two chapters, he attempts to rework both the methodological suppositions and the vocabulary of generative grammar to make clear how contemporary Government Binding theory is addressed to the same questions as the older transformational model. For Chomsky the only real difference is that the questions are now better understood. I am in complete sympathy with Chomsky's goals but I feel that he has, in one or two minor but important ways, misunderstood the lessons of the last thirty years' development and has opted for a new vocabulary much more misleading than the one that has become traditional within generative grammar. By following his argument I hope to produce an account which will illuminate the relations between a linguistics of invariance and a linguistics of conflict.

Chomsky's fundamental argument is that the incredibly fruitful conjunction of the study of formal languages and the study of natural languages (of which his own work is the most extraordinary example) led to a fundamental misconception. In any formal language for which one is providing a grammar the sentences of that language are completely explicit; the corpus is easily defined. This completely explicit formal language is the object of study (there couldn't be any other object). When it came to generative grammar and the study of natural languages, the mistake was made to think that once again one was studying the language extensionally, or, as Chomsky says in this text, in terms of its external features.

To define this language generative grammar used the notion of 'competence', and idealised knowledge of a speaker-hearer in a homogeneous speech community. The important point about this notion, and why Chomsky gets so impatient with those who attack it, is that it provides an absolutely automatic way of constituting the corpus. All the linguist has to do is to consult his (or her) intuitions and any sentence will immediately be judged as a well-formed member of the corpus or not. Chomsky is not interested in speakers or hearers or communities, but he is interested in finding a method of constituting his object. At the beginning generative grammar made the mistake of identifying the speaker's knowledge of the language as a method of generating a totally explicit language. There are, as we have seen in Pratt's paper, and as I have indicated here, enormous problems in thus trying to define language, speakers and communities.[24] One solution would be to re-focus on the externalised language, more adequately understood and described. Chomsky, quite rightly from the point of view of the linguistics of invariance, refuses such an option. Rather he redefines what it is that forms the object of generative grammar. So far, so good.

To do this he turns to the great Danish linguist Jespersen in order to define what he calls 'internalized language', a metaphor he quickly swops for a technical term: *I-language*. I-language is, for Chomsky, what Jespersen referred to when he held 'that there is some 'notion of structure' in the mind of the speaker 'which is definite enough to guide him in framing sentences of his own', in particular, 'free expressions' that may be new to the speaker and to others'.[25] A grammar is then defined as a theory of the I-language. Chomsky explains the historical mistake of generative grammar by arguing that generative grammar confused the I-language with the E-language and often refered to the I-language as the grammar (this is, for example, the case throughout *Aspects of the Theory of Syntax*). But, in fact, it is much easier to say that generative grammar confused its object, 'a grammar', with language. My argument is that, far from making a mistake, Chomsky was correct to call his object of study a grammar and in this technical and specific sense it forms the object of early transformational theory and later government and binding theory. This object has little to do with the dominant notions of language, but is constituted by invariant and universal features of language. Crucially we can now define the corpus of the grammar as those set of sentences within English or any other natural language which enable that grammar to be refined and made more powerful. The selection of sentences is now in terms of the questions posed by the theory.

An important problem that remains is the relation between the study of generative grammar and the study of externalised language. Chomsky is convinced that there is nothing to be gained from this externalised language. It is, at best, an 'epiphenomenon'.[26] His attitude to the commonsense attitude which would place externalised language on the agenda is blunt:

In the first place the common sense notion of language has a crucial sociopolitical dimension ... A standard remark in introductory linguistics courses is that a language is a dialect with an army and a navy (attributed to Max Weinreich). That any coherent account can be given of language in this sense is doubtful; surely, none has been offered or even seriously attempted. Rather all scientific approaches have simply abandoned these elements of what is called 'language' in common usage.[27]

This is Chomsky at his most painfully polemical for, of course, there is a long history of people who have tried to study language in this sense − Sapir and Firth to name only two of the most influential this century. And I would argue strongly that it is essential to theorise language in ways that relate closely to this dominant conception. However, Chomsky is not alone in feeling that it is impossible to theorise language at any level which corresponds to most common-sense view of languages. Richard Hudson, although extremely interested in the social variation of language, argues very powerfully that it is impossible to give any substantive sense to any unit of language above the linguistic item'.[28] All socio-linguistics can accomplish is to study particular speakers or groups of speakers in order to discover what kind of social description can be given for a linguistic item. There is no analysis that will unify these items into the languages, dialects, or varieties that both ordinary language and linguists have sought to identify. Hudson comes to similar conclusions about the notion of speech community: 'which seems to exist only to the extent that a given person has identified and can locate himself with reference to it. Since different individuals will identify different communities in this way, we have to give up any attempt to find objective and absolute criteria for defining speech communities. This leaves us on the one hand with the individual speaker and his range of linguistic items and, on the other, with communities defined without reference to language but to which we may find it helpful to relate language'.[29]

Hudson moves from the fact that linguistic items cannot be constituted into a language, to the fact that speakers define the language differently, to the conclusion that communities can be defined without relation to language. His problem constitutes our solution, however. One of the most fundamental ways in which we define our communities is in terms of shared language. The fact that linguistic inquiry demonstrates that language is never as shared as we think merely demonstrates the existence of differences within those communities while also giving material reality to notions of the free play of the signifier. The fact that individuals define the community differently merely means that there are important differences of identification. Sociolinguistic research from Labov onwards shows this to be the case, and shows further that the individual is often split him or herself as a language user, the conscious and unconscious identifications of the language frequently being very different.[30]

What all this indicates, however (and this constitutes a further stage of Pratt's argument), is not that the language or speech community does not exist but that its existence is an imaginary one. One should not confuse imaginary here with inexistent or ineffective. Psychoanalysis has taught us how effective the imaginary is at providing in its unifying images the forms of our most real identifications.[31] Socially, we have only to look at the terrible history of the twentieth century to see the devastating reality of imaginary conceptions of unity. To suppose that these conceptions cannot be studied scientifically is to resign onself intellectually to Armageddon.

To address this task sociolinguistics will have to develop real modes of social and psychological analysis. At the moment it tends to limit itself to the use of the most banal sociological or psychological categories without any recourse to concepts of class, race or gender which would bring genuine edge and understanding to what so often seems like the barren compiling of evidence (interesting as that evidence often is). It is in the development of such concepts that a 'linguistics of conflict' will have a crucial role to play in a revivifying and recasting of both the social sciences and the humanities. It should not be thought that this is simply a longer version of the tired slogan: 'what linguistics needs is Marxism and psychoanalaysis'. The problem with that slogan is that is assumes that the necessary concepts are to hand. That is, at best, only partially true. A slogan which would more accurately indicate the real state of affairs would be: 'what Marxism and psychoanalysis need is linguistics'. For it is certain that without a real attention to the sociality of language neither Marxism nor psychoanalysis is going to be able to solve its currently paralysing dilemmas. For Marxism this is constituted by the impossibility of allowing any real effectivity to political and ideological representations without sacrificing its economic analysis of class. For psychoanalysis it is its inability to provide any account of identification which regards social units larger than the family.[32] Further, it is only in the context of such a linguistics that we could develop the concepts of race crucial to the future development of the planet. The point is perhaps most simply made by saying that sociolinguistics needs to become a lot more dangerous and that it will have to accept that its formulations of problems will need to include not just linguistic description but also the imaginary identifications and real conflicts which are at stake.

What it is important to stress is that this imaginary identification of the language has real effects − it is how the language reproduces itself. In this sense the particular way in which national languages reproduce themselves − essentially through education and the media − merely reproduce a tendency within all language.[33] The arbitrary play of the signifier is such that, without such a tendency, language would simply endlessly fragment. From the speech of a mother to a child, through the influence of peer group behaviour to the dictionary and the grammar, we are dealing with different kinds of linguistic regulation, but all such regulation depends on an imaginary identification of the language − it is here that the reality of 'the linguistics of conflict' resides.

From the existence of Chomsky's language-function it does not follow that any languages would exist at all. The crucial question that Chomsky poses runs as follows:

Surely there is some property of mind P that would enable a person to acquire a language under conditions of pure and uniform experience, and surely P (characterised by Universal Grammar) is put to use under the real conditions of language acquisition. To deny these assumptions would be bizarre indeed: it would be to claim either that language can be learned only under conditions of diversity and conflicting evidence, which is absurd, or that the property P exists − there exists a capacity to learn language in the pure and uniform case − but the actual learning of language does not involve this capacity.[34]

What Chomsky rejects as absurd is to me evident: language is only learned under conditions of diversity and conflicting evidence. There is always present, however (realised at very different levels in different societies) an imaginary unity of the language. It is this imaginary unity which allows property P to function but that unity is not reducible to P. It is the speaker's conviction that there is a unity to the linguistic diversity with which it is presented that enables P to operate. P cannot provide its own definition of its object. It seems to me that this solves Chomsky's problems and also completely vindicates his own continued refusal – most notably when the folly of generative semantics was in full flight – to identify the grammar with the language.[35]

To investigate the constitution of this imaginary unity is a task of pressing educational and social importance. It may provide some of the answers to what Chomsky calls Orwell's question, the problem of how language is misused ideologically and politically.[36] We must be clear, however, that such an investigation will have the characteristics of a critical rather than a positive science. I do not claim for those adjectives any more than heuristic importance as I have no wish to get bogged down in an epistemological discussion which will, inevitably, show that it is impossible to produce any explicit criteria with which to differentiate discourses in terms of their scientificity.[37] However, there are important distinctions between sciences in which the standpoint of the observer is immediately relevant and in which the results of the research programme immediately feed back into the object, and sciences where the standpoint of the observer is not immediately relevant and in which the results of the inquiry do not immediately affect the object. This is an important difference between a linguistics of conflict and a linguistics of invariance. For a linguistics of conflict the linguistic information to be analysed will be initially specified in relation to questions of class, race and gender which are posed within contemporary political and ideological struggle. This is not, in any way, a prescription for relativism but it does acknowledge that the topics to be studied will not be determined internally by the science. In addition the findings are likely to alter the object as they feed into dictionaries, grammars and, most importantly, the educational system and the media. A concrete example will make this clear. Let us propose as an important research topic: the study of intonation in newsreaders. The study's rationale is in terms of the importance within contemporary advanced societies of the forms of direct address on television. It is very largely within this discourse that a society is given an image of itself, its imaginary identity. It is because of this importance that so much emotion is generated around the topic of bias in the media but, to date, all investigation of this bias has operated at the level of the content of declarative statements. There is no doubt in my mind that a thorough study of intonation would indicate systematic ways in which the viewer is asked to approve or disapprove of developments within society. The results of such a study would be very likely, eventually, to alter the uses of intonation that it describes. Even such a brief example can indicate the kind of controversy with which a linguistics of conflict would have to live. People would dispute the necessity of the research, its results and its consequences.

Before considering how it might be possible to encourage such research, what practical questions we must address for linguistics, literary criticism and education, I want to pose a final and inevitable theoretical question: are there any relations between the invariants and the conflicts? It may be obvious that there will be relations between the invariants and the conflicts – but I want to suggest that they are of two very different kinds. First, and most obviously, the invariants will place certain constraints on the conflicts − the imaginary unity will have very definite limits placed on it by the structures of invariance. It seems to me that the study of linguistic change and of the developments of pidgins and creoles would be the obviously privileged area for investigating this. Second, and here we reach the most speculative of regions: will the conflicts ever affect the invariants? Will our deepest syntactic and semantic categories ever be altered by the way we understand our language?

My answer is a definite but purely speculative yes.[38] It is, at this point, that I would appeal to the extraordinarily rich and suggestive chapter of Michael Halliday's which attempts to grapple with this almost unthinkable problem, unthinkable because it considers how our forms of thought alter and change. Halliday considers language as a dynamic open system: that is to say a system which persists only through change. Crucial to this system is that it constantly represents (better construes) more than one point of view about reality, while the more determinate meta-languages can only construe reality from a specific viewpoint.[39] Halliday argues that writing encodes language as determinate but that what is needed is to introduce the fundamentally rheomodal (complementary and multi-determinate) grammar of spoken language into our written forms. Much of this is persuasive and exciting but I would want to argue that Halliday underestimates the extent to which the ordinary speaker of the language has made certain fundamental identifications, sexual and social, which necessarily deny the complementarity from which they are constructed. Lurking behind this is a question even more fundamental: is it the case that to speak a language we must ignore its fundamental modes of construction? Or, to put it in psychological, rather than semiotic, terms: how far can we recognise our own identities as provisional? Although Halliday recognises the paradoxes of representation: that it is always by a process of differentiation that we produce a world of identities, he does not consider the extent to which the process of differentiation must be repressed for the identities to exist. Crucially, he does not consider the, for me, vital question: is it not the case that repressions necessary to produce a world are always anchored in a central repression, sexual or social, whereby we gain a stable identity? Halliday simply assumes (what I feel needs to be proved in both theory and practice) that language can be multiply anchored and not tied to a central semiotic division: male/female, member/outsider. Such questions would temper Halliday's optimism while still allowing us to share it. It would be in this perspective that we might consider limit cases where changes within the linguistics of conflict fed back into the invariant structures of the language. To talk in Halliday's evolutionary terms this would be one clear way to understand the inheritance of acquired characteristics.

The importance and excitement of such questions are obvious but it would be foolish to presume that we are anywhere close to articulating them in a satisfactory manner. Address them, however, we must and the current organisation of departments of linguistics and literary criticism do not, by and large, suggest that we are going to find this easy. It would be wrong to think, however, that this is a local problem limited to two disciplines. It seems to be that the whole organisation of knowledge in the universities often now functions to prevent rather than to facilitate the asking of questions. How far this is due to the micro-politics of institutions, how far to honourable fears about the loss of specific skills, and how far to the deliberate foreclosing of the crucial questions for our society is not a matter I can decide in this paper. All I can voice is an almost consuming despair that the crucial issues for our society, such as ecology or race, are only marginal at best for a western university system which harnesses potential and resources on a hitherto unimaginable scale. Despair is, however, the one unforgivable emotion – as the Catholic Church has long recognised by naming it as the sin against the Holy Ghost. In a spirit, then, of desperate optimism I want to suggest some broad lines of development within tertiary education. It would obviously be a criminal folly for linguistics to abandon the study of invariance, and such a study would be at the centre of a new organisation of the humanities and social sciences. This reorganisation would stress the need to develop the social and psychological concepts to understand the full implications of a 'linguistics of conflict' as the imaginary unity of communities and speakers gives way to a scientific understanding of their divisions and conflicts, as well as the politics, micro and macro, which forge those divisions into unities. The elaboration of these concepts will require drawing on the whole range of discipline within the humanities and social sciences in a way which is common at the highest levels of research but scandalously absent at most levels of the university system. It might be said that the great texts of modern and postmodern literature, the works of Burroughs or Joyce, would function within such a reconstituted academy as major and important experiments – the full consequences of which we have not begun to reckon in our more rational calculuses.

But if literature might function as experiment, what of literary criticism? Is it adequate to think in terms of it incorporating a greater historical awareness of the development of the language as we study the literary text? Such a local reform is, of course, necessary. I would argue, however, that the kind of considerations advanced in the first half of this paper do not simply appeal to some missing technical skill that must be provided – they indicate the extent to which literary criticism constantly represses the conditions of its own existence. If we fully comprehend the extent to which literature has always been as much an act of social exclusion as shared illumination, if we seriously accept Benjamin's terrible insight that a work of civilisation is also, always, a work of barbarism[40] then we must recognise the extent that one of the major functions of literary criticism as an institution is to preserve a cultural form, with a very specific class history, by ignoring those cultural forms based on mechanical and electronic reproduction which threaten to enlarge the audience in unacceptable ways. If the particular skills of textual criticism and the developed attention to the complexity of textual production must be preserved and reproduced, literary criticism can only develop within a genuine humanities by recognising that its object of study is the whole range of cultural productions. It is only then that we will be able to seriously investigate the cultural movements of the twentieth century and the place of writing within them in ways which seriously engage with the gains and losses of these hugely enlarged audiences, audiences which now cross class and national boundaries in fundamentally new ways. It seems to me merely obvious that this change also involves a change of name, that the chauvinist connotations of English and the class connotations of literature must be abandoned in favour of a commitment to cultural studies. Such cultural studies would find an inevitable place in the analysis of a 'linguistics of conflict'.

All this is proper material for a programmatic statement which is meant both to open and to close a conference. But this is not all vague promises for the future: promises which will run up against the rocks of inevitable resistance as those who identify their very humanity with the most limited notions of taste and standards will fight to the death any attempt to investigate that taste or those standards. The conference on the Linguistics of Writing is an attempt to start something on an international scale but, more realistically and less hubristically, it marks the achievement of something on the local scale. The Programme in Literary Linguistics at Strathclyde University is now three years old and it is one academic enterprise in which the commitment to a linguistics of conflict and a linguistics of invariance is not a matter of verbal promises but real developments. The Masters dissertations which have been produced there already provide a body of work along the lines I have outlined here, and Doctoral dissertations and books of much potential are now in preparation.[41]

The practical consequences of the linguistics of conflict are important in the context of tertiary education and the way in which the study of culture is understood, articulated and organised. However, it is possible that they are even more important in the context of primary and secondary education and the teaching of language. The draconian moulding of every child to an artificial standard is, thankfully, a thing of the past, but I would not like anybody to think that the considerations advanced here suggest that a national standard should no longer be taught. In recent years many teachers, in understandable revolt against a 150-year-old tradition of policing their pupils' language, have eagerly adopted the views of linguists that each language, or each variety of a language, is as good as any other. This position, which is true at the level of the linguistics of invariance, is dangerous nonsense at the level of the linguistics of conflict. It is just not true, for example, that Latin is as good as English as a language for science. This is not a comment about some essential feature of the structure of Latin,[42] but a comment on the fact that English has a large specialised scientific vocabulary and that the vast majority of scientific publications are in English. Similarly, no one alive to the vitality of language could pretend that Glaswegian was in anyway inferior to standard

English. However, to claim that it is adequate either internationally, or for certain crucial bureaucratic or political purposes, is to condemn speakers to their own linguistic ghetto within the national and international polity.

What, then, are the practical consequences for the teaching of English? Do we simply continue to teach the national standard while deploring its history and its assumptions? The answer is more complex than a simple yes or no. It is that we teach the national standard but we teach it as a variety. It seems to me that it is absolutely essential that teachers encourage a bi- and multi- lectalism in their pupils; that we find pedagogic means (nothing suggests this will be easy) which encourage people to learn other varieties of their own language, without devaluing their own. In some ways the development of television seems to have aided this process for, as listeners, we participate in five or six very different varieties of English a night (a full understanding of this is a necessary prerequisite of any full account of the political impact of television). To help develop such pedagogies is a pressing educational and political necessity. Richard Hudson is right to refer to 'national standards' as almost pathologically limited.[43] One of the most hopeful developments in England since the war has transformed us from a monoglot into a polyglot political entity. If we are to build on the diversity of language now spoken in Britain, it will be by developing ways of teaching a standard which does not automatically devalue and disregard other languages or other varieties. It is not too far-fetched to think that if we were to lessen the pathology of our national tongue we might lessen other associated pathological limitations as well.

Notes

1   Stanley Fish, 'Consequences', *Critical Inquiry*, vol. 11, No. 3, March 1985, pp. 433–58.
2   It is difficult to overestimate the importance of the experience of describing and analysing the Amerindian languages for twentieth century linguistics.
3   Suzanne Romaine argues in *Socio-Historical Linguistics*, Cambridge 1982, pp. 14–21 that the written language should be a necessary part of sociolinguistic study but this is still a relatively unusual position.
4   In passing it should be said that neo-Firthian linguistics has no such necessary commitment to the primacy of speech.
5   See Romaine, op. cit., pp. 56–69 for how recent research on pidgins and creoles can explicate the history of Middle English.
6   A brief and useful account can be found in Dick Leith, *A Social History of English*, London, 1983, pp. 26–31. For a chauvinist account of this period which nevertheless includes some interesting data see Basil Cottle, *The Triumph of English 1350–1400*, London, 1969.
7   Andrew Borde, *The fyrst boke of the introduction of knowledge*, ed. F.J. Furnivall, Early English Text Society new series vol. x., London, 1870, p. 122.

8   In his preface to Raoul le Fevre's *The Recuyell of the Historyes of Troye* Caxton tells he 'was born and learned my English in Kent, in the Weald, where I doubte not is spoken as brode and rude Englissh as in any place of England.' W. Crotch (ed.), *The Prologues and Epilogues of William Caxton*, London.

9   For a detailed analysis of Caxton's fascinating text see my Collins Dictionary lecture 'Righting English' published by Collins in 1984 as an occasional offprint. For a consideration of the relations between national language and capitalist economies see R. Balibar, *Le Français national* Paris, 1973.

10   R.F. Jones in *The Triumph of the English Language*, Stanford 1953, locates the change in attitude between 1575 and 1580. Jones's book is a remarkable study but he is resolutely uninterested in the class divisions that the national standard is both enacting and introducing. Nonetheless many (if not most) of his chosen quotations pick out very clearly what is at stake. Crucial to the discourse of class at this period is the metaphor of dress, a metaphor which is very evident in discussions of language.

11   Leith, op. cit., p.42.

12   See Lawrence Stone, 'The educational revolution in England 1560–1640', *Past and Present* No.28, July 1964, pp.41–80.

13   The paradoxes of Milton's position in this general development are explored in work I am currently undertaking: *John Milton: An Epic Poet in The era of Nascent Capitalism*, London, forthcoming.

14   For example, 'The vulgar pronunciation of London, though not half so erroneous as that of Scotland, Ireland, or any of the provinces, is, to a person of correct taste, a thousand times more disgusting', *Walker's Critical Pronouncing Dictionary*, corrected and enlarged by J. Fraser, Liverpool, 1852, p.17. It is only in the context sketched here that one can begin to evaluate Wordsworth's appeal to 'the real language of men', on the first page of the Preface to *Lyrical Ballads* (1800).

15   D.J. Palmer, *The Rise of English Studies*, Oxford, 1965.

16   The full quotation from *Our Mutual Friend* in the original manuscript is even more revealing of the link between the growth of mass circulation newspapers and a problematising of the status of writing: Sloppy is a foundling adopted by old Betty Higden, a poor widow. 'I do love a newspaper', she says. 'You mightn't think it but Sloppy is a beautiful reader of a newspaper. He do the Police in different voices.' T.S. Eliot, *The Wasteland: A Facsimile and Transcipt of the Original Proofs including the annotations of Ezra Pound*, ed. Valerie Eliot, London, 1974, p.2.

17   For a more detailed analysis see Colin MacCabe 'The voice of Esau: Stephen in the Library', in Colin MacCabe (ed.), *James Joyce: New Perspectives* Brighton, 1982, pp.111–28.

18   For Joyce's involvement with the cinema see Richard Ellman, *James Joyce*, New York, 1959, pp.310–14.

19   Walter J. Ong, *Orality and Literacy: The Technologising of the World*, London, 1982.

20   It should be said in passing that these considerations most heavily undercut the optimistic account of a general social pragmatics offered by Lyotard in *The PostModern Condition: A Report on Knowledge*, Manchester, 1984. Lyotard ignores throughout his text the importance of those discourses which have totally asymmetrical relations built into the relation between addresser and addressee.

21   Derrida, this volume p.253.

22   *Finnegans Wake* is the primer for considering the variety of contradictory discourses which constitute the speaking subject.

23   Derrida, op. cit., p. 253.

24   For a more detailed account of Chomsky's concept of competence and its problems, see Colin MacCabe in James Joyce Broadsheet 2, May 1980.

25   Noam Chomsky *Knowledge of Language: Its Nature, Origin and Use*, New York, 1986, p. 22.

26   *Ibid.*, p. 25.

27   *Ibid.*, p. 15.

28   R. A. Hudson, *Sociolinguistics*, Cambridge, 1980, Chapter 2.

29   *Ibid.*, p. 72.

30   See, for one example among many, Trudgill, 'Sex, covert prestige and linguistic change', *Language in Society* vol. 1, no. 2, 1972, pp. 187–8. It should be said that both Labov and LePage have recognised the importance of the imaginary in the constitution of the unity of the language but neither have sufficiently considered its conscious *and* unconscious characteristics.

31   Jacqueline Rose, 'The Imaginary', in Colin MacCabe (ed.), *The Talking Cure: Essays on Psychoanalysis and Language* London, 1981, pp. 132–61.

32   My article 'On discourse' in *Theoretical Essays: Language Linguistics, Literature*, Manchester, 1985, deals at much greater length with the relation between linguistics, Marxism and psychoanalysis.

33   Hudson argues very differently. For him the regulating qualities within a natural language are unusual and make them 'the least interesting kind of language for anyone interested in the nature of human language (as most linguists are)' op. cit. p. 34. I completely agree with Hudson that standard languages are 'pathological in their lack of diversity' (ibid.), but I feel that by considering other kinds of regulation we might enjoy the benefits of standard languages without some of their consequent pathologies. Standard languages are no more 'unnatural' than other languages, or only in so far as nations are more 'unnatural' than other forms of political and social organisation.

34   Chomsky, op. cit., p. 17.

35   The importance and significance of Chomsky's work and the entire subject that he opened up cannot be stressed enough particularly as his courageous stand on political issues has led the contemptible neo-conservatives of our time to attempt to dismiss it (see Christopher Hitchen's excellent article 'The chorus and Cassandra: what everyone knows about Noam Chomsky', *Grand Street*, vol. 5, no. 1, Autumn 1985, pp. 106–31). I think that Chomsky's determination to cling to the word *language*, even in the etiolated and technical term I-language, can be explained in part in terms of the micro-politics of the academic institution. To occupy a definite place within the academy is not simply a philosophical question; it involves access to funds, research grants and the whole infra-structure which makes research possible. This is not simply a petty point. Only those who think that institutions are irrelevant or inevitable can ignore the importance of how they reproduce and transform themselves at the micro-level. Particularly someone like Chomsky, who has had the extraordinary experience of discovering (or, as he argues, re-discovering) an important scientific object and a method to investigate it, will be particularly determined to ensure that his scientific research programme can proceed and not be abandoned or neglected. There is nothing objectionable about Chomsky determinedly defending the reality and importance of what I have termed a 'linguistics of invariance' but it is also important to find institutional space for a linguistics of conflict.

36   Chomsky admits himself that he finds little intellectual interest in what he terms 'Orwell's question', op. cit., p. xxix. This is not a merely personal problem. The deep interests of those interested in a language's fundamental structure and those interested in its imaginary functioning are very very different and seem rarely to be united in the same person. This seems, in itself, an important problem. The only attempt to theorise this that I am aware of is Jean-Claude Milner's L'Amour de la langue Paris, 1978. Ann Banfield in her forthcoming translation of the book *Amor Linguae: For the Love of Language*, London, 1988, has a long introduction which attempts to develop Milner's consideration in the setting of American linguistics.

37   Attempts within both the positivist traditon (i.e. Hempel) and the Marxist one (i.e. Althusser) have all, despite their immense sophistication, ended in failure. To go from this failure to a position of epistemological anarchy (i.e. Feyerabend) is understandably theoretically. It should not, however, lead one to think that there are no useful practical criteria for distinguishing between forms of scientific inquiry.

38   In my opinion it is only on this final point: the possibility of developments in the language actually changing the structure of the invariants, that I am in disagreement with Chomsky.

39   M. A. K. Halliday, this volume, pp. 000.

40   Walter Benjamin, *Illuminations*, Glasgow, 1973, p. 258.

41   Particularly important here will be the forthcoming work by Durant & Fabb, provisionally entitled *The Future of Literary Studies: History, Cognition, Education*.

42   I would not completely rule out such an argument. Linguists have quite rightly fought shy of comparison between languages, because the historical prestige first granted to classical languages and then European ones was then used to denigrate nonstandard or 'primitive' languages. It may be, however, that there are real ways to compare languages. What is certain is that people, particularly writers, constantly do.

43   Hudson, op. cit., p. 34 (see note 33).

Participants

Sylvia Adamson
Eleanor Anderson
C.J. Annabel
Jean Arasanayagam
Derek Attridge
Eileen Baker
Richard Bales
Ann Banfield
John Banks
Dietmar Bänsch
Peter Barry
Michael Bath
Eva Bearne
Catherine Belsey
Tony Bennett
Carson Bergstrom
Elfi Bettinger
Elizabeth Boa
J.D. Bone
Paola Bono
Steven Botterill
Margherita Bowring
Pamela Bracewell
Sara Bragg
P.J. Brew
Amanda Kate Bridges
Michael Broe
Lynda Broughton
John Brown
Rosemary Brown
Mimo Caenepeel
Nancy Campbell

Christopher Candlin
Betty Caplan
Rosalind Carroll
R.A. Carter
John Caughie
Stephen Chambers
Natalie Charkow
Cynthia Chase
Marcus Child
Donald J. Childs
Martina Cibis
Emma Clery
Anne Cluysenaar
Brian Coates
Evelyn Cobley
Andrew Cooper
John Corbett
R.M. Coulthard
David Cram
Winifred Crombie
P.M. Crompton
Jonathan Culler
Robert Cummings
Mark Currie
Pam Czerniewska
Scott Davidson
J.N. Davie
Alan Davies
Martin Davies
Robert A. Davis
Terence Dawson
Aidan Day

Perer T. Dayan
Marietta Denton
Jacques Derrida
Eddie Dick
T. Dobrzynska-Janusz
Lorraine F. Doherty
Emad Dorra
William Downes
John Drakakis
Russell Duncan
Alan Durant
Antony Easthope
Mark Eaton
Karen L. Edwards
Janet Fabb
Nigel Fabb
Jian Zhuang Fang
Stephen Farrow
Maria Aline Ferreira
Barbara Ferrin
Gail S. Fincham
Stanley Fish
Dan Fleming
Anthony Fothergill
Donald Fraser
Gordon Fulton
Brad Gadberry
Nicholas Gardiner
Christopher Garnett
Ana Lucia Gazolla
Hassan Ghazalah
Douglas Gifford
S. Glynn
G. Good
Peter Goodrich
R. Grafton-Small
Rena Grant
William S. Greaves
Michael Green
Peter Grundy
Kirsten Gutke
Suzanne Hall
Morris Halle
R. Halle

M.A.K. Halliday
R.G. Hardie
Ruqaiya Hasan
O.N. Heathcote
Vimela Herman
Lindsay Hewitt
Darrell Hinchliffe
Robert Hitchcock
John Hollander
Klaus Hofmann
A.D. Hook
Jonathan Hope
Mary Hossain
A. Howatt
Paul Hullah
L. Hunter
David Hurry
David Imrie
Paul Innes
K.R. Ireland
Mark Irvine
L.A. Jackson
David Jago
Robin Jarvis
Vanashree Joshi
Peggy Kamuf
Wendy R. Katz
Christian J. Kay
George Kearns
Ulrich Keller
Gregory P. Kelly
Sandra Kemp
Rosanne Kennedy
Paul Kiparsky
Abasi Kiyimba
John Knechtel
Bernard Knieger
Diana Knight
Susan Lynne Knutson
Gail Langley
Geoffrey Leech
Vassiliki Kolocotroni
Tom Lavelle
Ian Lebeau

Dini Lee
Michele Le Roux
Eden Liddelow
Kate Lilley
Chen Ling
S.A. Linstead
Derek Littlewood
John Llewelyn
David Lodge
Felicity Lutz
Anastasia Lygouri
Caroline Macafee
Colin McArthur
Ronald Macaulay
Colin MacCabe
Gavin James MacDonald
B.J. McGuirk
Alice McIlroy
Donald MacKenzie
Duncan McLean
Barbara MacMahon
Cleo McNelly Kearns
John McRae
Christian Mair
Merja Makinen
William Maley
Richard G. Maltby
Leo S. Marshall
Mary Mason
Olga Mattar
Susan Matthews
M.I. Millington
Sara Mills
Kosei Minamide
Martin Montgomery
T.W. Moore
Fionna Morphet
Wendy Morris
John Mountford
Jeffrey Moxham
Sakina Mrani-Alaoui
Rowena Murray
Greg Myers
V.G. Mylne

T. Nageswararao
Rafael Newman
K.M. Newton
Beta-Mban Ngoniem
Andrew Noble
C.E. Nuttall
Marc O'Day
Michael O'Toole
Margaret Omberg
Mary Orr
Charles Palliser
Marina fe Pastor
Kamal K. Paul
Geoffrey Payne
Barry Peacock
Helmut Peitsch
Graham Pechey
Margaret Philips
Seok Buay Phua
Maria O.R. Pinto
Antonia Pirrie
Roger Poole
Jenny Potts
P. Powrie
Mary Louise Pratt
Janice Price
Alan Prince
Faith Pullin
Richard Rand
D. Venkat Rao
A.E. Reiss
Michael Rogan
Andrew Rosta
Alan Roughley
Neil Roughley
Pratap Rughani
Nicholas Sagovsky
David Saunders
Stephen Scobie
A.P.M. Segal
Roger D. Sell
David R. Sewell
Joel B. Shapiro
Dan Shen

Mick Short
Sally Shuttleworth
Karl N. Simms
Nigel Simpson
G. Singh
Craig Sisman
Gillian Skirrow
John Gregor Sloss
Jeremy J. Smith
Stan Smith
Stephen David Smith
C.R. Snook
Antonella Sorace
Francis Soundararaj
Kathryn Southworth
Thelma Sowley
Michael Spiller
Corinne Squire
Stella Statman
Randall Stevenson
Deborah Stewart
Ralph Stewart
Lesley Stirling
Magda Stroinska
M.E. Stubbs
John Sturrock
Peter Swaab
Pushpinder Syal
Joe Szarka
Mary E. Tait
Douglas Tallack
Beverley Tarquini
Alison Tate
Olga Taxidou
Jane Taylor
Mary Theodoridou

Yiota Thiveou
Jenny Thomas
Rebecca Thomas
Ann Thompson
David M. Thompson
John O. Thompson
Joanna Thornborow
James P. Thorne
Glenn Timmermanns
Jane Tompkins
Christopher Tribble
Susan Triesman
Jean Ure
W. Van Peer
Eija Ventola
Torben Vestergaard
Katie Wales
Richard Walker
Chris Waters
Joan Pittock Wesson
Mike Westlake
Anita Weston-Bilardello
John Whale
Roxann Wheeler
Janet White
Jonathan White
H.G. Widdowson
Bronwen Isobel Williams
Patrick Williams
Raymond Williams
Joy Williams
Tony Wilson
David Worrall
Laura Yanne
Alan R. Young

About the speakers

Derek Attridge is Professor of English Studies at the University of Strath-clyde, and has held appointments at Oxford, Southampton, Illinois, and Rutgers Universities. He is the author of *Well-weighed Syllables* and *The Rhythms of English Poetry*, and the co-editor of *Post-structuralist Joyce* and *Post-structuralism and the Question of History*. His latest book is *Peculiar Language: Literature as Difference from the Renaissance to James Joyce*.

Ann Banfield is an associate professor in the English Department at the University of California at Berkeley, where she has been for the past ten years. She is the author of *Unspeakable Sentences: Narration and Representation in the Language of Fiction*, and has translated Milner's *L'Amour de la Langue*. Some of her articles are 'Narrative style and the grammar of direct and indirect speech'. 'Grammar and memory', 'Ecriture, narration and the grammar of French'.

Jonathan Culler is Professor of English at Cornell University, and Director of the Society for the Humanities there. He is the author of several books, including *Flaubert: The Uses of Uncertainty, Structuralist Poetics, Saussure, The Pursuit of Signs: Semiotics, Literature, Deconstruction, On Deconstruction: Theory and Criticism after Structuralism*, and *Barthes*.

Jacques Derrida is Directeur d'Études. École des Hautes Études en Sciences Sociales. Among his many works to have been translated into English are *Of Grammatology, Writing and Difference, Dissemination, Signsponge/Signeponge*. He recently set up, at the invitation of the French Government, the College International de Philosophie.

Alan Durant and *Nigel Fabb* are lecturers in the Programme in Literary Linguistics, of which Alan Durant is Director. Nigel Fabb has written papers on generative syntax and morphology, film, pedagogy, and stylistics. Alan Durant is the author of *Ezra Pound: Identity in Crisis* and *Conditions of*

Music. They are currently co-writing a textbook on the future of literary studies, to be published in 1988.

Stanley Fish is Arts and Sciences Distinguished Professor of English and Law at Duke University. His books include *Surprised by Sin: The Reader in 'Paradise Lost', Self-consuming Artifacts: The Experience of Seventeenth-Century Literature*, and *Is there a Text in this Class?: The Authority of Interpretive Communities* (which reprinted 'What is stylistics, and why are they saying such terrible things about it?' 1 and 2). His more recent work has examined such topics as professionalism, the irrelevance of theory, and legal language and interpretation.

Morris Halle is Institute Professor at the Massachusetts Institute of Technology, where he teaches in the Department of Linguistics and Philosophy. He is the author of *The Sound Pattern of Russian*, and the co-author of *Preliminaries of Speech Analysis: The Distinctive Features and their Correlates* (with R. Jakobson and G. Fant), *The Sound Pattern of English* (with N. Chomsky), *English Stress: Its Form, Its Growth and Its Role in Verse* (with S.J. Keyser), *Problem Book in Phonology* (with N. Clements), and *An Essay on Stress* (with J.-R. Vergnaud).

M.A.K. Halliday has been Professor of Linguistics at the University of Sydney since 1976. His areas of interest include how children learn language, how language creates the social order, how discourse is construed, and how text may be generated by computer. Some of his publications are *Learning How to Mean: Explorations in the Development of Language, Language as Social Semiotic: The Social Interpretation of Language and Meaning, An Introduction to Functional Grammar*.

Ruqaiya Hasan is Associate Professor in the School of English and Linguistics at Macquarie University. Her researches have been mainly in the area of semantics, sociolinguistics and discourse. She is the author of *Linguistics, Language and Verbal Art*, the editor of *Discourse on Discourse*, and the co-author with M.A.K. Halliday of *Cohesion in English* and *Language, Context and Text: a Social-semiotic Perspective*.

John Hollander is Professor of English at Yale University, and has published several volumes of poetry (for which he was awarded the Bollingen Prize in 1983). His books of literary criticism include *The Untuning of the Sky: Ideas of Music in English Poetry 1500–1700, Vision and Resonance: Two Senses of Poetic Form, Rhyme's Reason, The Figure of Echo: A Mode of Allusion in Milton and After*.

Fredric Jameson is Wm. A. Lane Professor of Comparative Literature at Duke University. He is the author of several books including *Fables of Aggression: Wyndham Lewis, the Modernist as Fascist, The Prison-House of Language, Marxism and Form,* and *The Political Unconscious.*

Paul Kiparsky is Professor of Linguistics at Stanford University. He has published papers in generative linguistics, poetics and metrics. Some of his papers on phonology are collected in *Explanation in Phonology.* He is the author of *Pāṇini as a Variationist* and *Some Theoretical Problems in Pāṇini's Grammar.*

Geoffrey Leech is Professor of Linguistics and Modern English Language at the University of Lancaster. He is one of the co-authors of *A Comprehensive Grammar of the English Language.* Other publications include *A Linguistic Guide to English Poetry, Style in Fiction* (with M. Short), *Semantics,* and *Principles of Pragmatics.* He has recently co-edited (with C. Candlin) *Computers in English Language Teaching and Research.*

David Lodge is Professor of Modern English Literature at the University of Birmingham. His critical works include *Language of Fiction, The Novelist at the Crossroads, The Modes of Modern Writing* and *Working with Structuralism,* and a new collection of occasional essays and reviews, *Write On.* David Lodge is also the author of seven novels, the most recent of which is *Small World: an academic romance.*

Colin MacCabe is Professor of English at the University of Pittsburgh. He is also Visiting Professor at the University of Strathclyde and was instrumental in setting up the Programme in Literary Linguistics. He is the author of *James Joyce and the Revolution of the Word, Godard: Images, Sounds, Politics, Theoretical Essays: Film, Linguistics, Literature,* and editor of *The Talking Cure: Essays in Pyschoanalysis and Language.*

Mary Louise Pratt is Associate Professor in the Department of Spanish and Portuguese and the Program in Comparative Literature at Stanford University. She is the author of *Toward a Speech Act Theory of Literary Discourse* and co-author (with Elizabeth Closs Traugott) of *Linguistics for Students of Literature.* She is currently studying discourse and ideology in travel writing.

H. G. Widdowson is Professor of Education at the University of London concerned with the teaching of English to Speakers of Other Languages. He was previously British Council English Language officer in Sri Lanka and Bangladesh, and has taught English literature at the University of Indonesia and Applied linguistics at the University of Edinburgh. His publications include: *Stylistics and the Teaching of Literature, Explorations in Applied*

Linguistics I and *Explorations in Applied Lingusitics II, Learning Purpose and Language Use*. His interests include the interpretation of written discourse in general and of lyric poetry in particular.

Raymond Williams is a Fellow of Jesus College Cambridge. His books include *Culture and Society, The Long Revolution, Keywords, Marxism and Literature, Problems in Materialism and Culture, Writing in Society*.

The Programme in Literary Linguistics

The Programme in Literary Linguistics was established in 1983 in the Department of English Studies at the University of Strathclyde, at that time headed by Colin MacCabe. Courses were planned by Sylvia Adamson, Alan Durant, and Colin MacCabe. Currently the Programme offers a range of instructional postgraduate courses, and supervises research in the area of literary linguistics. The Programme draws on teaching and research contributions from a large number of specialists in the University of Strathclyde and elsewhere. Core teaching staff are: Alan Durant, Nigel Fabb, Sara Mills, Martin Montgomery, and Derek Attridge.

Enquiries about the Programme are welcomed, and should be addressed to:

Margaret Philips,
Secretary to the Programme,
Department of English Studies,
University of Strathclyde,
26 Richmond Street,
Glasgow G1 1XH
UK

Index of themes

Index of names